THE SUMA ORIENTAL OF TOME PIRES

THE SUMA ORIENTAL OF TOME PIRES

AN ACCOUNT OF THE EAST, FROM THE RED SEA TO JAPAN, WRITTEN IN MALACCA AND INDIA IN 1512-1515

AND

THE BOOK OF FRANCISCO RODRIGUES

RUTTER OF A VOYAGE IN THE RED SEA, NAUTICAL RULES, ALMANACK AND MAPS, WRITTEN AND DRAWN IN THE EAST BEFORE 1515

Translated from the Portuguese MS. in the Bibliotheque de la Chambre des Deputes, Paris, and edited by

ARMANDO CORTESAO

VOLUME I

GYAN

Published by

GYAN

Gyan Publishing House
5, Ansari Road
Daryaganj, New Delhi-110002
Phone: 011-47034999, 9811692060
E-mail: books@gyanbooks.com

Distribution Network
gyanbooks.com
India, USA, Canada, UK, Australia, France

ISBN : 978-81-212-4080-2 (Set)
ISBN : 978-81-212-4659-0 (HB)
First Published, 1944

2nd Impression 2020

Printed at: Gyan Press, Delhi.

The Suma Oriental of Tome Pires Vol. I
Edited by: Armando Cortesao

WORKS ISSUED BY

The Hakluyt Society

THE SUMA ORIENTAL OF TOMÉ PIRES

AND

THE BOOK OF FRANCISCO RODRIGUES

SECOND SERIES
No. LXXXIX

ISSUED FOR 1944

COUNCIL
OF
THE HAKLUYT SOCIETY
1944

PLATE I

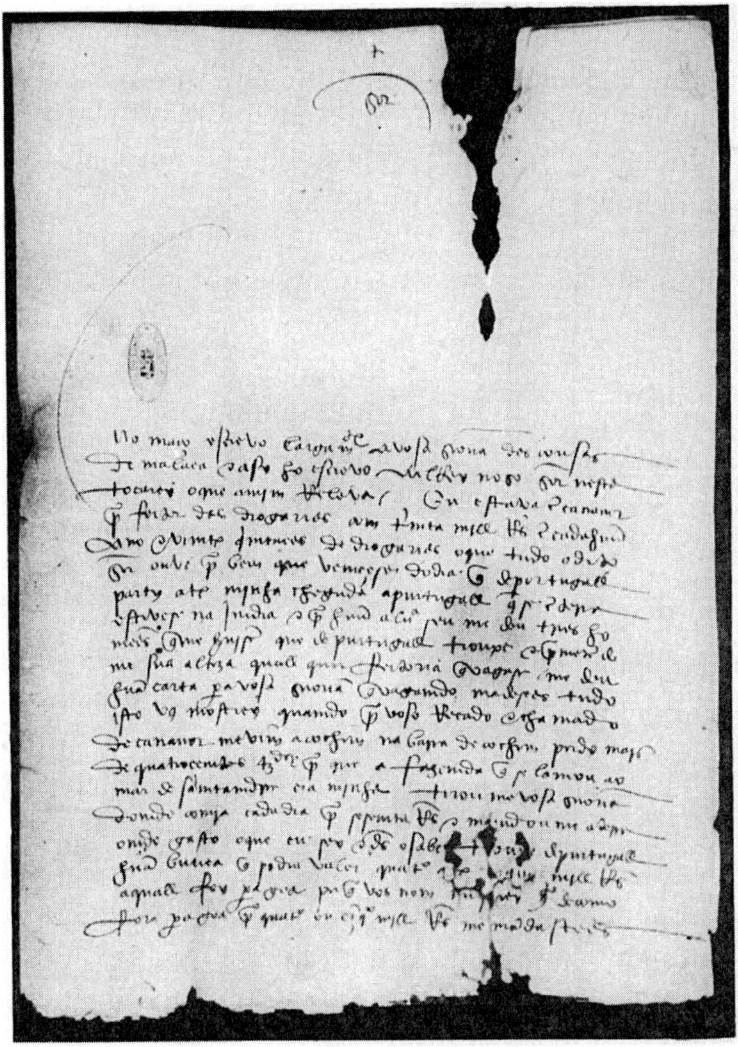

First page of Tomé Pires' original letter from Malacca, to Afonso de Albuquerque, 10th Jan., 1513

THE SUMA ORIENTAL OF TOMÉ PIRES

AN ACCOUNT OF THE EAST, FROM THE RED SEA TO JAPAN, WRITTEN IN MALACCA AND INDIA IN 1512–1515

AND

THE BOOK OF FRANCISCO RODRIGUES

RUTTER OF A VOYAGE IN THE RED SEA, NAUTICAL RULES, ALMANACK AND MAPS, WRITTEN AND DRAWN IN THE EAST BEFORE 1515

Translated from the Portuguese MS in the Bibliothèque de la Chambre des Députés, Paris, and edited by

ARMANDO CORTESÃO

VOLUME I

LONDON

PRINTED FOR THE HAKLUYT SOCIETY

1944

TO

CHARLES RALPH BOXER

A true friend, to whom the history of the Portuguese in the East owes so much

CONTENTS

VOL. I

LIST OF ILLUSTRATIONS AND MAPS

VOL. I

VOL. II

FOREWORD

WHEN I returned from Paris in 1937 and told Dr. Edward Lynam, Hon. Secretary of the Hakluyt Society, that I had just discovered the long-sought codex containing the *Suma Oriental* of Tomé Pires and the *Book* of Francisco Rodrigues, he immediately suggested that I should edit the manuscript for his Society. I gladly accepted, as no other learned Society could so appropriately publish this almost completely unknown work. Moreover the English, being the principal heirs of the great Portuguese Eastern Empire, are as much interested as the Portuguese in a document of such importance for the history of the first regular contacts between West and East.

The present study allows new light to be thrown on the first official European Embassy to China and its leader, Tomé Pires, the extraordinary man who, after being apothecary to the unfortunate Prince Afonso, son of King John II, went to India in 1511 as 'factor of the drugs', lived for two and a half years in newly-conquered Malacca, where he wrote most of the *Suma Oriental*, and then was sent as ambassador to China, where he died after some twenty years of varied and painful experiences. Till now, little was known about Pires and his Embassy, and the scanty information and scattered documents referring to both had never been brought together.

War broke out when I had nearly finished the lengthy task of typing and translating the whole manuscript. Not until 1942 could I continue my work. This is why I could not finish it as early as promised to the Hakluyt Society and to the International Congress of Geography of Amsterdam, in 1938, where I presented a brief tentative report on the codex, and announced my intention of editing it. The impossibility of working in Portuguese Archives or in Paris to clear up doubtful points, and the removal from the British Museum of much early material, caused me considerable difficulties. Furthermore, when the whole typescript was ready, war-time printing conditions forced me to reduce my editorial work by about two-fifths. All this accounts for some of the deficiencies in the present edition.

From MM. les Questeurs de la Chambre des Députés I obtained authorisation, dated 5th March 1938, for the publication of the codex; this I here acknowledge with thanks. Without the aid of many friends and correspondents I could hardly have solved several of my problems. I wish to express my gratitude to all who have assisted me. Besides Dr. Lynam, I am specially grateful to Miss P. J. Radford for her varied assistance throughout this work; to Miss M. Withers for her help in the translation up to fol. 172; to Dr. H. Thomas, Keeper of Printed Books in the British Museum, for much valuable advice, for help in the translation from fol. 173 onwards, and for reading the Introduction and Notes; to Major C. R. Boxer, now a prisoner in Japanese hands, for assistance and encouragement; to my learned friend the Viscount de Lagôa for information supplied from Lisbon; to Prof. E. Prestage for reading that part of the translation not seen by Dr. Thomas, and for valuable advice; to Prof. C. A. Moule for guidance in all matters relating to China; to Mr. G. R. Crone, Librarian of the Royal Geographical Society, for much help; to Commandant D. Gernez, of the French Navy, for help over Rodrigues' *Book*; to Dr. J. Ramsbottom, Keeper of Botany, Natural History Museum, for advice on all botanical matters; to M. C. de la Roncière, of the Bibliothèque National de Paris, Prof. W. Simon of the School of Oriental Studies, Dr. L. Giles, Mr. R. Pocock, F.R.S., Mr. J. E. Dandy of the Natural History Museum, Sir Richard Burn, Mr. C. D. Ley, J. Frazão de Vasconcelos, L. Reis Santos, Ad. Lopes Vieira, and my son Eduardo Luís, for assistance in various ways; to the Staff of the British Museum, especially Mr. J. A. Petherbridge, and of the Royal Geographical Society's Library and Map Room, especially Mr. G. Mackay, who has drawn all the illustrative maps. Last but not least, I wish to acknowledge the support received from the Society for the Protection of Science and Learning, without which it might have been impossible for me to carry on with this work.

LONDON, *August* 1944. A. Z. CORTESÃO.

INTRODUCTION

THE PARIS CODEX

IT is surprising that such an important document for the history of geography as Tomé Pires' *Suma Oriental*—surely the most important and complete account of the East produced in the first half of the sixteenth century, though it was written in 1512–15—has lain forgotten and practically unnoticed until now; the more so as incorporated with it in the same codex is the contemporary *Book* of Francisco Rodrigues with its precious maps which became world-famous in the middle of the last century.

When the Viscount de Santarém reproduced in his last *Atlas*, dated 1849, a series of twenty-six maps under the general title *Portulan dressé entre les années* 1524–1530 *par Francisco Rodrigues, pilote portugais, qui a fait le voyage aux Moluques*, he did not state where the maps were to be found. The Viscount de Santarém died in 1856, but many of the notes he left on cosmography and cartography, gathered in an almost life-long research among European archives, mainly in Portugal and France, were not published till 1919[1]. In these notes, under the heading 'Portulano de Francisco Rodrigues', we find an extensive description of Rodrigues' *Book* which ends with a very brief reference to Pires' *Suma Oriental.* The description is not altogether correct. It gives, however, a most important clue in a footnote, which says that the codex belonged at the time the description was written (1850) to the 'Library of the National Assembly', Paris. In 1933 I wrote to Paris about this codex and was told that it could not be found anywhere, though it might be in the Bibliothèque Nationale, perhaps catalogued under some unrecognizable title[2]. However, when I visited Paris later, I could not find it in the Bibliothèque Nationale, nor in any of the other public libraries where I searched. No one could trace it, and it

[1] Visconde de Santarém, *Estudos de Cartografia Antiga*, I, 148–56.

[2] This vague information misled me into asserting in my *Cartografia e Cartógrafos Portugueses dos Séculos XV e XVI* (II, 124), published in 1935, that the codex was in the Bibliothèque Nationale.

was considered lost; but I did not give up, and when in September 1937 I returned to Paris, I was glad to find in the volume *Paris, Chambre des Députés* of the *Catalogue général des Manuscrits des Bibliothèques Publiques de France*, p. 471, the following entry: '1248 (ED, 19). Journal de Francisco Roïs, pilote de la flotte portugaise, qui découvrit les Molluques. Ouvrage divisé en deux parties, la première remplie par des cartes, la deuxième contenant le texte proprement dit. Sur le plat intérieur est collé un ex-libris du chevalier de Fleurieu. XVIe siècle. Papier. 178 feuillets et 124 pages. 380 sur 265 millim. Rel. veau marbré, portant au dos le soleil de Fleurieu'. Roïs is the old or abbreviated spelling of Rodrigues. The description is not very correct, as will be seen later, but it led me to the place where the precious and long-sought codex lay in oblivion.

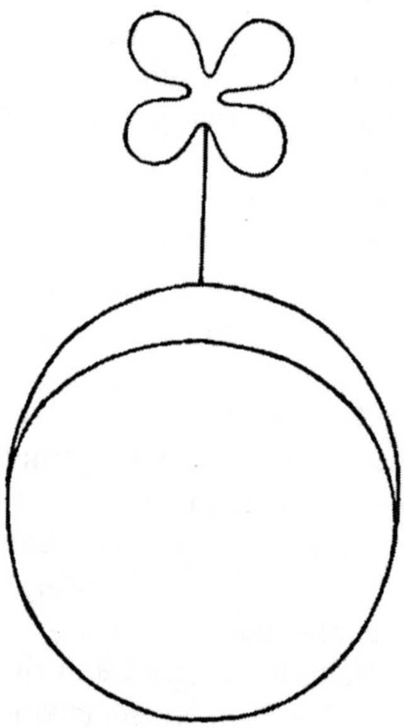

Watermark in the paper of the whole Paris Codex. (Size of original)

The volume is bound in gilt calf, and on the back is impressed the sun of the Fleurieu family; inside the cover is the ex-libris of 'Mr. le Cher. de Fleurieu', the famous French hydrographer, Comte de Fleurieu (1738–1810), a former owner of the codex. It is obvious that it was bound while in Fleurieu's possession, and unfortunately it was badly cropped in binding, part of the words in some marginal notes or additions, or in maps, and most of the original numeration of the sheets, having been cut away. The volume contains, besides 4 fly-leaves, 178 folios of thick white paper measuring 263 by 377 mm. Rodrigues' *Book*, with the drawings and maps all on the same paper, occupies the first 116 folios; Pires' *Suma* fills the other 62. The paper of the 178 folios is all the same and bears the same watermark.

On fol. 5r. is written the word *Osorio* in a later hand, probably the signature of the famous Bishop D. Jerónimo Osório, a sixteenth-century historian and book-collector, apparently an early owner of the codex[1]. Each MS has its original folio numeration, almost completely cut away when the volume was bound; but traces of it can still be seen. Another numeration was supplied, later, in Pires' *Suma*, and a completely new one, from 1 to 178, was added in a modern hand to the whole codex.

Santarém's above-mentioned footnote says also: 'It seems that this precious MS belonged to the famous Bishop Osório, a great many of whose MSS were found by the English on board a Portuguese ship, which they captured off the Azores and took to England. Later it was acquired by M. de Fleurieu'. He adds that this information was given to him by 'M. Bliller, librarian of the National Assembly'. I was unable to trace the origin of this curious information.

[1] This supposition, though very likely, is merely conjectural, because—strange though it may appear—no document bearing the signature of Bishop Osório has, so far, been found in Portuguese archives or anywhere else. D. Jerónimo Osório was born in Lisbon in 1506 and died at Tavira in 1580. He studied at the Universities of Salamanca, Paris and Bologna; in Paris he was a companion of St. Ignatius of Loyola. In 1564 he was appointed Bishop of Silves, after having been a Professor in the University of Coimbra. He was a famous and learned writer and left numerous works, mainly in Latin; one of the better known is *De rebus Emmanuelis Regis Lusitaniae invictissimi virtute et auspicio gestis libri duodecim*, Olysippone 1571. There was another Jerónimo Osório (1545–1611), nephew of the former, who was a canon of the see of Evora and also a book-collector. It has been said that when in 1596 the Earl of Essex sacked Faro he took with him Bishop Osório's books, which he later presented to the Bodleian Library. However, the bishop of Faro was then D. Fernando Martins Mascarenhas. Essex ' "quarted hymself on the bushopes howse", and two days later set fire to the town and sailed for home; but he *saved* the Bishop's library, and in 1600 made a gift of some 200 volumes to the Bodleian'. See the interesting article by Miss K. M. P[ogson], *A Grand Inquisitor, and his Library*, published together with 'A list of books presented by the Earl of Essex in 1600, still in the Bodleian', in *The Bodleian Quarterly Record*, III, 239–44. Oxford 1922. J. B. Silva Lopes says that 'among the spoil that the English took with them, was the precious library of the Bishop (Mascarenhas), composed of many books, a good part of which they say was taken to the Library of Oxford, and among them there were many of the learned D. Jerónimo Osório'. *Memorias para a Historia Ecclesiastica do Bispado do Algarve*, p. 369. Lisboa 1848. Among all the books presented by Essex there is only one in manuscript; none of them seems to bear the signature of Bishop Osório. See plate II.

When referring to Tomé Pires, Barbosa Machado says in his *Bibliotheca Lusitana* that he wrote '*Summa Oriental começando do estreito do mar roxo até a China, Dedicado a D. João III.* fol. M.S.' This was perhaps an earlier copy than the Paris MS, as will be seen later, in spite of the supposed dedication to King John III, whose reign began in 1521. Actually Pires dedicated the *Suma* to John III's father, King Manuel I. There is no doubt, however, that it was a different copy. Rodrigues' *Book* was written by himself, and Pires' *Suma* is a contemporary copy, which is evident not only from the early sixteenth-century handwriting, but also from the fact of the paper being exactly the same in both MSS. Besides, the word *Osorio* on fol. 5r. of Rodrigues' *Book* is apparently in the same hand as the notes, referring to the order of the folios, written on fols. 118v., 124v., etc., of Pires' *Suma*. It is probable that the two MSS were assembled in the same codex by Rodrigues himself, or at least in his time; they certainly were together when in Osorio's possession, before 1580. So the copy referred to by Barbosa Machado could not have been the same, otherwise he would not fail to mention Rodrigues and his *Book*, which he does not.

THE PRESENT EDITION—Though the two works are very distinct in character—one a rutter, a nautical manual and an atlas, the other a geographical, economical and historical account—they are both very valuable, were written much about the same time, have been together from an early date, and to some extent complete each other. I am glad that the Council of the Hakluyt Society agreed to publish them both together and to print the original of the very difficult and etymologically very interesting Portuguese text verbatim after the English version, which undoubtedly enhances the value of the present edition.

The present copy of Pires' *Suma* is not the original he himself wrote, and the copyist has left only too many instances of his own carelessness. Pires' style is far from clear, and this, added to the transcriber's mistakes and the most anarchic punctuation, or absolute lack of it, makes the interpretation of the text often extremely difficult; sometimes the translation has to be very free, perhaps even more of a guess than anything else. I have endeavoured, however, always to catch the real meaning of what

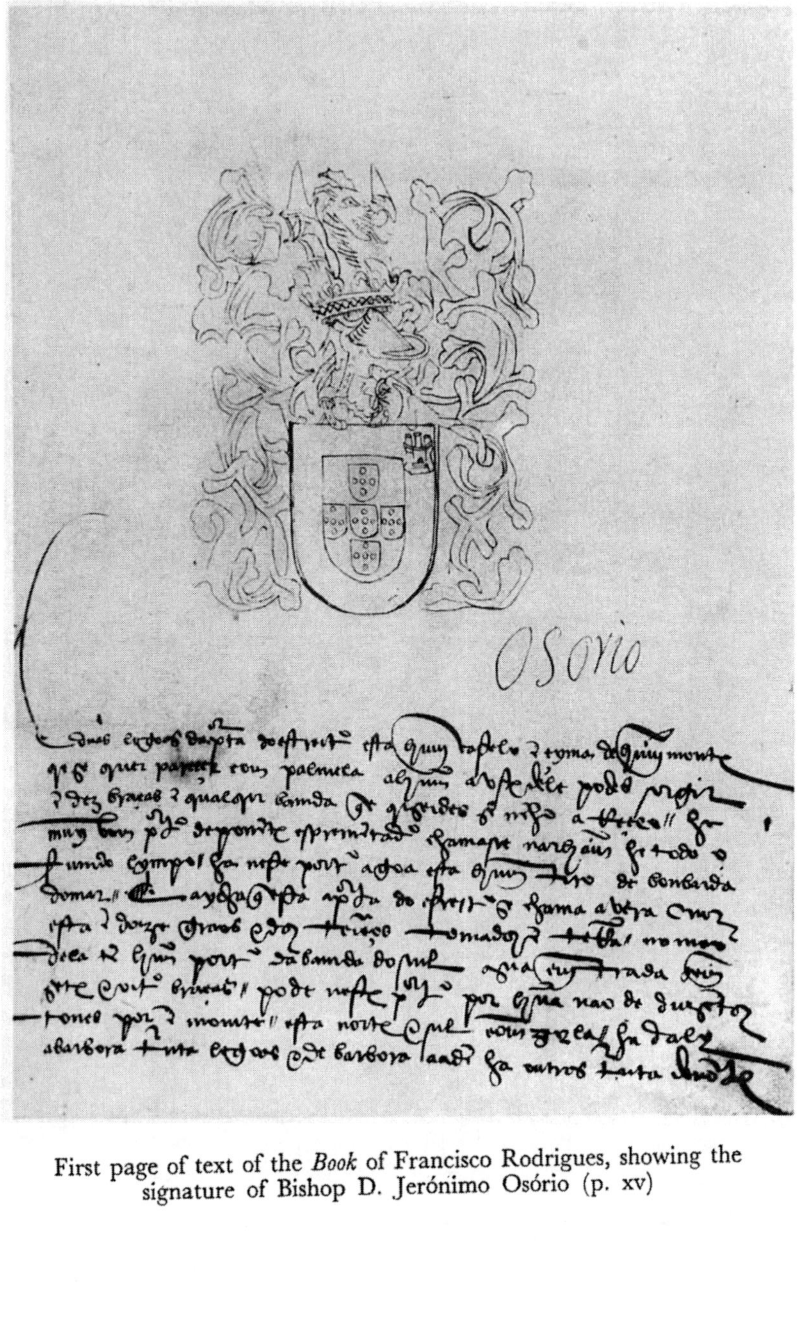

First page of text of the *Book* of Francisco Rodrigues, showing the signature of Bishop D. Jerónimo Osório (p. xv)

PLATE III

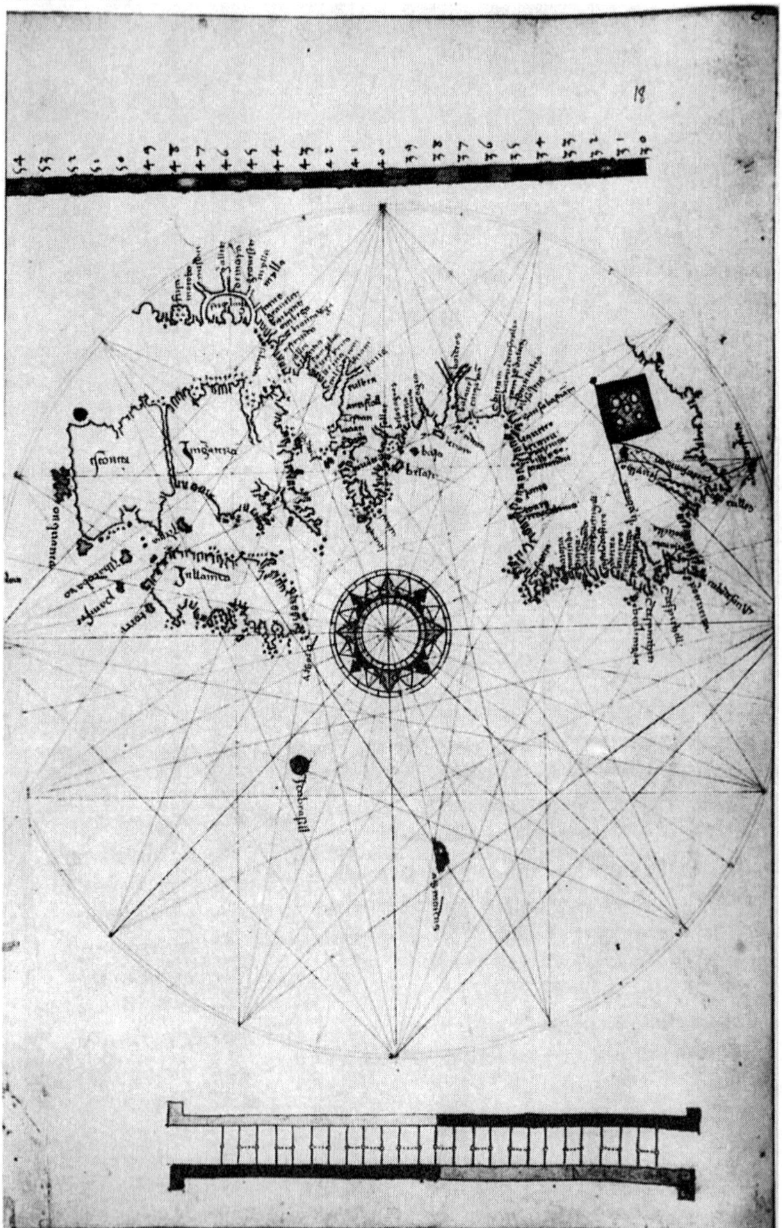

Rodrigues' map (fol. 18) of the West Coast of Europe and the British Isles (p. 519)

Pires originally wrote, not only collating the Paris MS with another copy and with Ramusio's version of part of the *Suma*, but also studying the context and other sources when available. In all the most difficult cases I sought the help and advice of such learned experts and scholars as Dr. Henry Thomas and Prof. Edgar Prestage. Even so, I am not sure that it has always been possible to reach the right interpretation; but the reader, when in doubt, has the faithfully reproduced Portuguese text for reference; from it he may attempt a better version. He will find much matter for study and discussion. Here my limited responsibility ends.

The greater importance and length of Pires' work made it advisable to print the English version before that of Rodrigues' *Book*, reversing the order in which they occur in the codex. When the two MSS were assembled together at an early date, some folios of the *Suma Oriental* were misplaced, or for some reason or other the text does not follow the order originally intended by Tomé Pires. All this has been adjusted in the English version; but in the case of the Portuguese text, its actual order and disposition in the Paris codex are faithfully kept. Both in the English version and in the Portuguese text the numeration of the folios is given as it appears in the Paris codex; this will help the reader to find without difficulty the corresponding portions in the English and the Portuguese. In annotating the text I have tried not only to elucidate every obscure point, when possible, but also to explain or emphasize the importance of certain passages for the history of geography; this will account for the length of some of the notes.

Names of Eastern persons and places, the identification of which is not always possible, are often given with such different spellings in the Portuguese text that their rendering into English becomes a complex problem. I decided, as a general rule, to print Eastern names of persons, and their official posts, as they occur in the Portuguese text, and to give explanations, and the corresponding English forms, whenever possible, in footnotes. As regards place-names, they are always given in the English form in the translation, when they can be identified and there is a corresponding English name; but the first time the name appears, and when it is repeated in a different form or much later in the text, the original Portuguese spelling follows in brackets.

Before describing the *Suma Oriental* in detail, I now give a biographical sketch of Tomé Pires; then I deal with Francisco Rodrigues and his *Book* in the same way.

BIOGRAPHICAL NOTE ON TOMÉ PIRES

Tomé Pires cuts a modest figure when compared with some of the men who shine in the history of the Portuguese in the East during the first half of the sixteenth century. Among those living there at the time, Albuquerque, the great captain and administrator, founder of an immense Empire, and Camoens, the Prince of Portuguese Poets, who sang the glory of his country and countrymen, are the greatest of all. Duarte Pacheco Pereira, D. João de Castro and António Galvão were famous as captains, administrators and navigators or writers, Garcia da Orta as a scientist, Gaspar Correia and Castanheda as chroniclers. Fernão Mendes Pinto, whose *Peregrinação* was published only thirty-one years after his death, with several alterations, was the greatest adventurer in Portuguese history, and has left us a wonderful account of his marvellous adventures. Many others won immortal fame as warriors, navigators or explorers. Even Duarte Barbosa became world-famous, but his *Book* was written just after Pires had finished the *Suma Oriental*, a much vaster work. Barbosa's *Book*, the original of which is lost, was soon translated into Spanish and Italian, and was first published by Ramusio in 1550, becoming widely known, while only a less important portion of Pires' *Suma* reached Ramusio, who published it without name of author, which he did not know.

Pires' great work was lost and has been buried in oblivion until now. The humble apothecary who arrived in India in 1511, and through his merits was chosen for the important post of first Portuguese Ambassador to China, where he died probably about 1540, has been practically forgotten, though his contribution to the early knowledge of the East is of the greatest historical importance. He is, however, a very interesting figure, and the *Suma Oriental*, besides being the earliest extensive account of the East written by a Portuguese, is also the first European description of Malasia, the detail of which was not surpassed, in many respects, for more than a century or two. Tomé Pires was above all an eager observer, a keen and inquisitive student, and a faithful, accurate and indefatigable describer; though his literary style is poor, he cannot but occupy a remarkable place among the early European writers on the East.

SOURCES—Data about Tomé Pires' life, from shortly after his arrival in India till his death, are not scarce, though they are rather incomplete; but for his life in Portugal there are only a few vague references. All we know about him is contained in the following: the present *Suma Oriental*, four letters written by him, five other documents signed by him, one letter signed by him and others, eight letters and another document by contemporaries who refer to him, and references in the chroniclers and early writers. These are summarized below.

Pires' letters: from Malacca, 7 Nov. 1512, to his brother João Fernandes, published in *Cartas de Afonso de Albuquerque*, vol. VII, pp. 58–60; from Malacca, 10 Jan. 1513[1], to Afonso de Albuquerque, *Ibid.* 4–7; from Malacca, 10 Jan. 1513, to 'Whoever is in charge of appointing officials for Malacca', *Ibid.*, 66–7; from Cochin, 27 Jan. 1516, to the King of Portugal. This last was published for the first time in the *Jornal da Sociedade Pharmaceutica Lusitana*, tomo. II, no. 1, pp. 36 *seqq.* Lisbon, 1838; then in *Gazeta de Pharmacia*, Lisbon, 1866; and again in *Obras Completas do Cardial Saraiva*, vol. VI, pp. 419–28, Lisbon, 1875. A translation of this extremely interesting document is given at the end of vol. II, Appendix II, of the present work.

Other documents signed by Pires: document dated in Malacca, 12 Nov. 1513, in which he appears as executor of the will of his brother-in-law Diogo Lopes, *Cartas*, VII, 99; receipt in Malacca, 24 Dec. 1513, *Ibid.*, 107; receipt in Malacca, 12 Jan. 1514, *Ibid.*, 112–13; receipt in Malacca, 5 May 1514, *Ibid.*, 121–2;

[1] This letter was published with the date 10 Jan. 1512. It refers, however, to some events that happened months later, such as Pires' auditing of the accounts of João Freire, factor of Abreu's fleet to the Spice Islands, who returned to Malacca in December 1512, and also the intended attack of *Pate Unus* against Malacca, which took place at the beginning of January 1513 (see note pp. 151–2). See plate I.

letter 'To the King our Lord—from the officials of Malacca', 7 Jan. 1514, signed by 'the scriveners Pero Salgado, Tomé Pires and Garcia Chaym, and the factor Pero Pessoa', *Ibid.*, III, 89–91.

Documents referring to Pires: an order of Rui de Brito, Captain of Malacca, 4 Nov. 1513, decreeing that Pires should receive what was left by his dead brother-in-law, *Ibid.*, VII, 97; letter from Afonso de Albuquerque to the King of Portugal, Cannanore, 30 Nov. 1513, *Ibid.*, I, 141–50; letter from Rui de Brito, Captain of Malacca, to the King of Portugal, Malacca, 6 Jan. 1514, *Ibid.*, III, 91–7 and in *Alguns Documentos da Torre do Tombo*, pp. 345–50; letter from Rui de Brito to Afonso de Albuquerque, Malacca, 6 Jan. 1514, *Cartas*, III, 216–31; letter from Jorge de Albuquerque, Captain of Malacca, to the King of Portugal, Malacca, 8 Jan. 1515, *Ibid.*, III, 133–9; letter from Jorge de Albuquerque, Captain of Malacca, to the King of Portugal, Malacca, 1 Jan. 1524, *Ibid.*, IV, 35–42; two letters from Cristóvão Vieira and Vasco Calvo, Canton, 1524, and 10 Nov. 1524[1]. Later copies of these two letters, extant in the Bibliothèque Nationale de Paris (Fonds Portugais, no. 65)[2], were published—introduction, original text and translation—by Donald Ferguson in the *Indian Antiquary*, Bombay, 1901–2. In the Arquivo Nacional da Tôrre do Tombo, Lisbon, there are fragments (Fragmentos, Maço 24) of the original of the first of these two letters (in Chinese ink on Chinese paper), which were published by Dr. E. A. Voretzsch in *Boletim da Sociedade Luso-Japonesa*, no. 1, Tokyo, 1929.

References in chronicles and early books: Gaspar Correia, *Lendas da India*, vol. II, pp. 473, 528–9, 678, written in the middle of the sixteenth century; Fernão Lopes de Castanheda, *Historia do Descobrimento da India pelos Portugueses*, bk. IV, chaps. iv and xxxi, bk. V, chap. lxxx, 1st ed. 1554; João de Barros, *Asia*, Decada III, bk. II, chap. 8, bk. VI, chaps. 1 and 2,

[1] Although these two letters were published as dated 1534 and 1536, this was a mistake, as will be shown farther on.

[2] The two letters of Vieira and Calvo are bound together with the MS of the *Chronica dos Reis de Bisnaga*, published by David Lopes, Lisboa, 1897. The compilation of this *Chronica* was ordered by Barros (cf. David Lopes' *Introduction*, p. lxi), and he utilized it as well as the two letters as a source of information in the writing of the *Third Decade* of his *Asia*.

and bk. VIII, chap. 5, 1st ed. 1563; António Galvão, *Tratado*, pp. 129–30, Hak. Soc. ed. (1st ed. 1563); Damião de Góis, *Chronica do Felicissimo Rei Dom Emanuel*, pt. IV, chaps. xxiiii and xxv, 1st ed. 1567; Fernão Mendes Pinto, *Peregrinação*, chaps. lxv, xci and cxvi, 1st ed. 1614; Manuel de Faria e Sousa, *Asia Portuguesa*, tom. I, pt. III, chaps. 3 and 6, and Appendice, chap. 7, 1st ed. 1666; Diogo Barbosa Machado, *Bibliotheca Lusitana*, *s.v.* Thomé Pires, 1st ed. 1752.

BEFORE ARRIVAL IN INDIA—Very little positive is known of Tomé Pires' early life. Gaspar Correia informs us that Pires was a son of the apothecary of King John II (1455–95), and Castanheda says that he had been apothecary of Prince Afonso. This was probably the unfortunate son of John II, born 18 May 1475, died 13 July 1491. There was also a Prince Afonso, seventh son of King Manuel (1469–1521), born 23 April 1509[1], but he was not yet two years old when Pires went to India, and could hardly be the Prince referred to by Castanheda.

Pires may have been in his early forties when he embarked for India. In his letter of 10 Jan. 1513 to Afonso de Albuquerque, he complains that Pero Pessoa, the new factor of Malacca appointed after the death of Rui de Araújo, probably at the beginning of January 1512, just before Pires' arrival, was so young that at first he did not want to serve as scrivener under him. He says, in the same letter, that Malacca was so important that he would like to see there 'three or four men with white beards to take care of the King of Portugal's revenue'. This shows that he was then no longer a young man. Prince Afonso married in November 1490, when he was fifteen years old. Most likely it was then that young Pires, son of the King's apothecary, was appointed as apothecary to the Prince. He could scarcely be less than 22 or 23 when the Prince died in 1491. This is confirmed by Pires himself when, at the end of his description of the Islands of Bachian, he says: 'it must be quite twenty years that I have been using the said leaves in Portugal' (fol. 158v.). That being so, Pires was born *circa* 1468, was about 43 when he went to India, and about 70 when he died perhaps a little before 1540.

[1] This Prince Afonso, who died 21 April 1540, was made a cardinal when only eight years old.

In his letter of 7 Nov. 1512 to João Fernandes, his 'brother by blood'[1], he also mentions his sister Isabel Fernandes, one Maria Godinha, perhaps his brother's wife, and one Antónia, perhaps a niece, whom he distinguishes from his brother's 'wife and children'. He also refers to 'Diogo Lopes my brother-in-law, who eats, drinks and sleeps in my house, a very good knight and a very good man'. The way in which Pires refers to '*my* brother-in-law' seems to indicate that Diogo Lopes was the brother of his wife, whom he does not mention in the letter. Perhaps Pires was a widower, and here we may possibly have the reason of his departure for the East.

The letter is addressed to 'Senhor João Fernandes, in front of the Porta da Madalena, my brother'. It is possible that Pires had lived there too. The Porta da Madalena[2] was not far from the north-east corner of the old Terreiro do Paço, corresponding more or less to the present Praça do Comércio, better known to the British as Black Horse Square, near the end of Rua Nova dos Mercadores, then the main commercial street of Lisbon, approximately the present Rua do Comércio. There were several apothecary's shops in this street[3], and it is not impossible that one of them or some other near the place belonged to Pires or to his brother, or to both. Faria e Sousa says that Tomé Pires must have been born in the Portuguese town of Leiria, because his daughter, found by Fernão Mendes Pinto in China in 1543, had the name of that town as a surname. But this is mere conjecture[4].

[1] There is nothing extraordinary in Pires' using a different surname from that used by his brother and sister. Instances of the kind are not unknown, though they are not usual.

[2] I was unable to find any other reference to the 'Porta da Madalena'. It must have corresponded to the old 'Porta do Ferro', also called 'Porta da Consolação', which was in the present Largo de Santo António da Sé, behind the former Church of Madalena.' Castilho, *Lisboa Antiga*, I, ii, 178 *seqq.*, VI, 112 *seqq.*

[3] João Brandão says in his *Tratado da majestade, grandeza e abastança da cidade da Lisboa*, p. 82, that in 1552 there were nine apothecary's shops in Rua dos Mercadores.

[4] When Pires' letter of 27 Jan. 1516 was published, D. Francisco de São Luís (Cardeal Saraiva) asserted that he was 'a native of Leiria'. This has no more foundation than Faria e Sousa's conclusion, on which it is probably based.

In the same letter Pires refers twice to 'Senhor Jorge de Vasconcelos, to whom I owe as much, on account of the favours I have received from him, as I owe you for reasons of blood'. Jorge de Vasconcelos was the director or purveyor (*provedor*) of the *Casa da Mina e India*, an establishment in which was centred the administration of Portuguese affairs beyond the seas —a forerunner of today's Ministry for the Colonies. He also says that he was enclosing a letter to Dr. Diogo Lopes, perhaps the chief royal physician, with whom Pires might have been connected after his service as apothecary to Prince Afonso. It is only natural that Pires went to India under the protection of these two important persons. In his two letters of 10 Jan. 1513, addressed to Albuquerque and to 'Whoever is in charge of appointing officials for Malacca', Pires says that in Lisbon the King—who wrote a letter to Albuquerque recommending him for the first factorship available—had dispatched him as factor of the drugs (*feitor das drogarias*), with 30,000 *reais* and 20 quintals of drugs, at his choice, every year, counting from the day of his embarkation in Lisbon, and three men to serve him, whom he took with him to India. He was also in charge of a *botica* (supply of medicines), worth 4,000 or 5,000 *reais*, which was being sent to India.

IN INDIA BEFORE GOING TO MALACCA—The fleet of six ships under the command of D. Garcia de Noronha, a nephew of Afonso de Albuquerque, sailed from Lisbon in March and April 1511. The one before this was a fleet of three ships, commanded by João Serrão, which left Lisbon in August 1510; the next afterwards left Lisbon in March 1512. One of the ships of D. Garcia de Noronha's fleet, *Belém* ('which was one of the most beautiful ships the seas have seen', according to Barros), under the command of Cristóvão de Brito, sailed from Lisbon on 20 April and arrived at Cannanore on 8 Sept. 1511[1]. D. Aires da Gama, brother of the Admiral D. Vasco da Gama, sailed at the same time on the ship *Piedade*, but later he separated from Cristóvão de Brito's ship, and after sighting Bhaktal on 7 Sept.

[1] Barros, II, vi, 10. Castanheda (III, lxxi) says that Cristóvão de Brito sailed from Lisbon on 19 April 1511 and that he went first to Goa; Correia (II, 197) says that he arrived at Cannanore in August.

went to Cannanore[1]. Pires went to India on one of these ships, which, according to Barros, were the only two of D. Garcia de Noronha's fleet to arrive in India that year of 1511. Pires' letters of 7 Nov. 1512 and 10 Jan. 1513 show that he had not been long in Cannanore when Albuquerque returned to Cochin at the beginning of February 1512, after the conquest of Malacca. In the letters to his brother and to Albuquerque, Pires says that the Governor-General had summoned him from Cannanore, where he was 'factor of the drugs', to Cochin. In his letter of 27 Jan. 1516 to the King, Pires says: 'The ships of Cristóvão de Brito and Dom Aires took to Portugal a quantity of wormwood which was bought by João Dávila when I was still in Portugal.' These ships loaded as soon as they arrived in India and were back in Portugal in August 1512. It is likely that the wormwood was not bought much before it was sent to Portugal, and if Pires was still there at that time, and by the end of 1511 was already in India, he could not have come on any other ships than those of Cristóvão de Brito and D. Aires da Gama. It can be safely concluded that Pires sailed from Lisbon on 20 April and arrived in India on 8 Sept. 1511, or a day or two later[2].

In his letter of 30 Nov. 1513 Albuquerque tells the King of disturbances and irregularities on the part of some of the men he had appointed as wardens of prizes of war (*quadrilheiros*) in Malacca. In view of this he decided, as soon as he knew of it, to send there 'Tomé Pires, apothecary of the Prince, because he seems to me a diligent man, so that he, with Rui de Araújo [whom Albuquerque had left as factor in Malacca] and the Captain should make an enquiry into all that matter'. Pires sailed from Cochin to Malacca on board the *Santo André*[3], in company with the ship *Santo Cristo*, in April or May 1512, after eight or

[1] Castanheda, III, lxxi. Correia (II, 197) says that D. Aires da Gama arrived at Cannanore three days after Cristóvão de Brito.

[2] When Pires' letter of 27 Jan. 1516 was published, D. Francisco de São Luís said: 'I believe he (Pires) went to India between 1512 and 1515.' But this is a mere and groundless supposition.

[3] A vessel of 70 tons built in Cochin by Gonçalo Eanes. *Cartas*, III, 128, 355; V, 492. This vessel formed part of the fleet that in 1513 went to Java with Pires as factor, and of the squadron that in 1516–17 took him to China. The *Santo André* was lost in October 1518 when returning to Malacca. Barros, III, ii, 8.

nine months in India. From his letter of 10 Jan. 1513 to Albuquerque it seems that the two vessels met with bad weather just off Cochin, and some cargo had to be thrown overboard, including more than 400 *cruzados* worth of goods belonging to Pires.

IN MALACCA. The *Santo Cristo* and the *Santo André* arrived in Malacca in June or July, soon after the death of the factor Rui de Araújo[1]. The letter of 7 Nov. 1512 to his brother is the first document we have about Pires' stay in Malacca. In it he says: 'I am in Malacca as scrivener and accountant (*contador*) of the factory (*feitoria*) and controller (*veador*) of the drugs.' He was enjoying good health and he was already rich, 'more than you can imagine', in spite of having more than 400 *cruzados* worth of his goods thrown overboard on the *Santo André*, and the complaints he made later, in the letter to Afonso de Albuquerque, about his salary. He asked the latter for 50,000 *reais* more for his services as scrivener, besides the 30,000 *reais* he already received as factor or controller of the drugs. He complained also that he had been most of the time in bed with fevers. 'I have been very ill, two months in bed', he says, which shows that he had fallen ill just after he had written to his brother. His brother-in-law, Diogo Lopes, was living with him in November 1512, but on 4 Nov. 1513 he had already died and Pires was the executor of his will.

On 6 Jan. 1514 Rui de Brito, Captain of Malacca, wrote to King Manuel and to Afonso de Albuquerque telling them that in March 1513 he had sent to Java a fleet of four ships to fetch spices. The fleet was under the command of João Lopes de Alvim. Three of the vessels (*navios*) were the *São Cristóvão*, the *Santo André* and a caravel, commanded respectively by Francisco de Melo, Martim Guedes and João da Silveira. 'Tomé Pires, scrivener of this factory and its accountant, went as factor of the fleet and to superintend the cargo', adds Brito. It sailed from Malacca on 14 March and returned on 22 June 1513 with

[1] In a letter written from Malacca to Albuquerque on 22 Feb. 1513, F. P. Andrade says that the *Santo André* and *Santo Cristo* arrived during the course of events that happened between the day of St. John (24 June) and the day of St. James (26 July). *Cartas*, III, 54–5.

about 1,200 quintals of cloves[1]. From his description of Java (fols. 148–55)—'as well as I have been able to examine and investigate, verifying my facts with many people'—we see that Pires visited the north coast of the island, at least from Cherimon to Grisee. When referring to Baros, a port on the north-west coast of Sumatra, he says: 'I went behind this island a matter of fifteen leagues.' This was obviously a different voyage from that to Java, but we do not know when it took place. Perhaps Pires wrote or at least intended to write another book dealing with the 'weights and measures in all the different places' of the East, as he seems to state when referring to the 'Coins and weights of Java' (fol. 150v.); but if he did, the book is now lost.

Two documents of 12 Nov. and 24 Dec. 1513 and three others of 7 Jan., 12 Jan., and 5 May 1514, show that Pires was then in Malacca; on 27 Jan. 1515, the date of *Ninachatu's* death, he was still there, as shown in the last page of the *Suma*[2]. But he must have left for Cochin soon after that date. In his letter of 8 Jan. 1515 to King Manuel, Jorge de Albuquerque, the new Captain of Malacca, mentions China and Cochin China, and the kingdoms of Siam, Borneo, *Llucoes*, and *Tamjunpura*, where is the diamond-mine, 'as Tomé Pires is bringing all these things duly explained.' This refers of course to the *Suma Oriental*. It seems that Pires sailed from Malacca at the same time as this letter, immediately after the 27 Jan. 1515, in one of the two ships that arrived in Cochin at the end of February. We know of the arrival of these two ships through two documents dated 30 (*sic*) February and 3 March 1515, in which Pero de Mascarenhas, Captain of Cochin, orders some provisions to be supplied to a boat (*atalaia*) he was sending to Goa with the news from Malacca for Afonso de Albuquerque[3].

[1] Castanheda (III, cxi) and Barros (III, v, 6) say that Alvim went to Japara to fetch some cloves salvaged from a junk shipwrecked there the year before, when returning from the first Portuguese expedition to the Spice Islands. See p. 521.

[2] Pires says: 'And if by chance I should not come before the presence of the King our Lord, or of the Governor of the Indies'; 'and that it is most important for the Governor of the Indies *to come* without delay to Malacca in force.' This seems to imply that he was still writing in Malacca. See note p. 287.

[3] *Cartas*, VI, 252–3.

RETURN TO INDIA AND EMBASSY TO CHINA. From the above quotation of Jorge de Albuquerque's letter we see that Pires left Malacca with the intention of returning to Portugal. But Pires' fate was written otherwise in the Book of Destiny. Albuquerque had sailed from Goa to Ormuz on 21 Feb. 1515 and only returned about ten months later, to die before Goa on 16 December. Meanwhile the new Governor-General of India, Lopo Soares de Albergaria, had left Lisbon with a fleet of thirteen (or fifteen) ships at the beginning of April, and arrived at Goa at the beginning of September 1515. Thence he proceeded to Cannanore and Cochin, where he arrived before the end of September. With the new Governor came Fernão Peres de Andrade, whom the King sent as Captain-Major of a fleet to go from India 'to discover China' and take a Portuguese ambassador there.

Castanheda informs us that 'the King of Portugal did not send any ambassador [from Portugal], because, thinking that the King of China was near, he ordered Fernão Peres to send there one of his captains, or whoever he might choose. And the Governor would not send anyone but this Tomé Pires, whom he sent on the advice of the noblemen and captains of India, because this Tomé Pires had been apothecary of the Prince Dom Afonso, and was discreet and eager to learn, and because he would know better than anyone else the drugs there were in China'. On the other hand Correia says that the Governor, who had gone again to Goa and returned to Cochin in February 1516, 'dispatched Fernão Peres de Andrade to China according to the orders he had brought; and he sent with him one Tomé Pires, son of the apothecary of King John, who was his great friend, and because he was very prudent, and very curious of knowing all things of India'[1]. Thus it seems that the Governor was already an old friend of Pires, a fact that must have influenced him in his choice for such an important embassy, in spite of Pires being a man of the people, as the chroniclers do not forget to emphasize. He must have chosen Pires when he met him on his first arrival

[1] It is odd that Correia seems to have forgotten that Pires was already in the East when he adds: 'therefore he embarked and came with him (Andrade) on this voyage of China, because in Portugal they talked great things about China, which Tomé Pires was anxious to learn and see, in order to write about them, as indeed he did.' II, 473.

in Cochin at the end of September. By then Pires certainly was a very rich man, and he would have liked to return to Portugal after an absence of nearly five years. But the idea of going to see for himself that great and mysterious China, of which he had heard so much in Malacca, with new and exceptional possibilities of increasing his wealth, must have attracted him powerfully. Besides, he may have had a grievance against Albuquerque, who used his abilities, but never raised him above the modest post of scrivener, in spite of justified complaints and requests. Albergaria was an enemy of Albuquerque and, according to Correia, a friend of Pires, who perhaps had been strongly recommended to him in Lisbon. By that time Pires had finished or was finishing the *Suma Oriental*, which might have impressed not only the new Governor, but also many of the 'noblemen and captains of India' mentioned by Castanheda. It must also not be forgotten that Pires, as well as his father, though men of humble origin, had been intimately connected with the court, and certainly had more education than the great majority of the Portuguese noblemen then in India. In the letter to his brother, Pires refers to the 'pampering in which I was brought up and spoiled'. Barros says: 'the ambassador . . . was called Tomé Pires, whom Lopo Soares in India had chosen for that post. And although he was not a man of very much quality, being an apothecary, and serving in India to choose the drugs which should come to this Kingdom, he was the most skilled for that mission and the best fitted for it; for besides his distinction and natural inclination to letters, according to his ability, and his liberality and tact in negotiation, he was very curious in enquiring and knowing things, and he had a lively mind for everything.' Thus, the choice of the modest but clever, industrious, experienced and well-brought-up Pires for the important post of ambassador to unknown China seems less extraordinary than it perhaps appeared to some later chroniclers[1].

[1] Osório, *De rebus Emmanuelis*, lib. XI, and Couto, *Decada* XII, v, 4, refer to the embassy and the ambassador, but do not even mention his name. We do not know whether the codex containing the *Suma Oriental*, now in Paris, was in Bishop Osório's possession when he wrote his famous book; but it seems that it was not, otherwise he might have shown more consideration for Tomé Pires' name.

Though Pires had left Malacca by the end of January 1515 with the idea of returning to Portugal, his very interesting letter of 27 Jan. 1516 'about the drugs and where they grow' shows clearly that he no longer thought of going back so soon. From this we can gather that before the Governor came again to Cochin in February 1516, Pires already knew that he was going to China.

FROM COCHIN TO CANTON. As soon as Albergaria returned to Cochin in February 1516 he despatched Fernão Peres de Andrade to China with a fleet of four ships[1], in which went the ambassador Tomé Pires. The fleet called first at the port of Pase, in Sumatra, where it would be joined by the ship of the merchant Joannes Impole (Giovanni da Empoli), a Florentine in the Portuguese service, which was there loading with pepper to take to China. But Impole's ship had caught fire and the cargo was lost, so Andrade decided that, after calling at Malacca, he would go to Bengal before going to China. However, the Captain of Malacca, Jorge de Brito, insisted that Andrade should go to China with his fleet without delay, because he was worried about Rafael Perestrelo, who had gone there the year before in a junk with other Portuguese. Reluctantly, because the monsoon was too advanced, Andrade sailed to China on 12 Aug. 1516[2] on the ship *Santa Barbara*, with António Lobo Falcão in a caravel, Manuel Falcão in another ship, and Duarte Coelho in a junk. The fleet met adverse weather off the coast of Cochin China and

[1] Góis (IV, ii) tells us that Albergaria arrived in Cochin and at once despatched Andrade to China; Barros (III, i, 2) says that Albergaria left Cochin on 8 Feb. 1516 after despatching Andrade's fleet to China; Galvão (Hak. Soc. ed. p. 129) says that the fleet to China sailed from Cochin in April. In a very interesting and still unpublished letter written from Malacca, 10 Aug. 1518, to King Manuel, Simão de Andrade says that when he arrived in Goa, coming from the entrance of the Red Sea, on 20 Jan. 1516, he found Albergaria there. Tôrre do Tombo, Gaveta 15, Maço 17, no. 27. Nor are the chroniclers very clear about the fleet's composition. Barros (II, ii, 6) says that King Manuel had ordered that it should be of four sail equipped in India; Correia (II, 473) says that Andrade sailed from Cochin in company with Simão de Alcáçova, António Lobo Falcão and Jorge de Mascarenhas. However, Castanheda (IV, iiii) and Góis (*ibid.*) mention Falcão alone, 'and the rest of the company he should gather in Malacca.'

[2] Almost all the chroniclers give this date, but Castanheda says that it was 15 August.

the ships were nearly lost. It was mid September and Andrade decided to return to Malacca. The junk went to Siam, where Duarte Coelho had been before; the other three vessels, after taking in fresh water on the coast, sailed south by way of Pulo Condore and Patani.

When Andrade arrived at Malacca he found Perestrelo back from China with great profit. He decided to postpone the expedition to Bengal, and in December went to Pase to load with pepper in order to proceed to China as soon as the monsoon permitted. In May he returned to Malacca where he found that, Jorge de Brito having died, there was a great dispute between Nuno Vaz Pereira, Brito's brother-in-law, and António Pacheco, Captain-Major of the Sea, as both wanted to succeed as captain of the fortress. After vain efforts to reconcile them, Andrade sailed from Malacca in June with a squadron of eight ships. Castanheda describes it as follows: Andrade 'commanded the *Espera*, a ship of about 200 tons, Simão de Alcáçova the *Santa Cruz*, Pero Soares the *Santo André*, Jorge de Mascarenhas the *Santiago*, Jorge Botelho a junk of a Malacca merchant called Curiaraja, Manuel de Araújo another junk of [the Malacca merchant] Pulata, and António Lobo Falcão a junk of his own; and it was a fleet of seven sail that left for China'. Barros, however, says that there was an eighth ship commanded by Martim Guedes[1].

The squadron arrived at *Tamão* or *Tumon* island[2], about the middle of the Canton River entrance, on 15 Aug. 1517, after meeting a Chinese fleet cruising off the island as a protection against the pirates. The Chinese shot at the Portuguese, without doing any harm, however, and Andrade did not return the fire, giving every demonstration of peace and friendliness. All the chroniclers describe, sometimes at great length and with much detail, what happened to Andrade and his squadron, from the arrival at *Tamão* till the ambassador Tomé Pires was landed at

[1] Correia also says seven ships, Galvão and Sousa say eight, and Góis and Osório say nine. Góis' mistake is that he says that Duarte Coelho went in a ship with Andrade; however, when Andrade arrived at *Tamão*, Coelho had been there a month, having sailed directly from Siam where he had gone the year before, when he parted from Andrade on the coast of Cochin China.

[2] Lin Tin Island. See note p. 121.

Canton[1]. As soon as he cast anchor at *Tamão*, Andrade sent a message to the captain of 'the Chinese fleet which came barking behind him', in Barros' picturesque words, 'explaining who he was and that he was bringing an Embassy of King Manuel of Portugal his Lord to the King of China.' The Chinese captain welcomed Andrade and said that 'through the Chinese who went to Malacca he also had news of the good faith and chivalry of the Portuguese', advising him to address himself to the Pei-wo (*Pio*) of Nan-t'ou, 'a man with a post like that of Admiral among us, which was the name of the office and not of the person'[2]. Andrade then sent a message to the Pei-wo—who at the same time had sent a messenger to enquire from Andrade who they were and what they wanted—to inform him 'that the principal reason of his coming was to bring an ambassador whom the King of Portugal, whose captain he was, was sending to the King of China with letters of peace and friendship, and he asked for pilots to take the fleet to the city of Canton'. The Pei-wo answered in very kind words, but stating that the permission would have to come from the officials in Canton. After many messages and delays, Andrade decided to wait no more and to go to Canton with some of his ships, using the Chinese pilots he had brought from Malacca. But as soon as the ships cleared the port they were suddenly struck by a storm, and only with great difficulty and much damage could they be saved. The Chinese ashore refused any assistance for repairing the Portuguese ships, but Andrade did as well as he could, and 'embarked on the ship of Martim Guedes, taking with him that of Jorge de Mascarenhas and the boats of the other ships, all very well prepared for peace as well as for war, and went to the port of Nan-t'ou, leaving Simão de Alcáçova as captain in charge of the other vessels. His

[1] Correia, II, 524 *seqq.*; Castanheda, IV, xxviii–xxxi; Barros, III, ii, 8; Góis, VI, xxiiii. The quotations that follow in the text are from Barros.

[2] 'The Pei-wo [an abbreviation of the title Pei-wo Tu-chih-hui, a military commander whose chief function was to guard the coast against the depredations of the Japanese pirates] at Nan-t'ou was empowered to examine all ships that came to Canton . . . *Pei-wo* is pronounced *pi-wo* in the dialect of the coastal district, and from *pi-wo* we have the form of *Pio* in Portuguese accounts and manuscripts.' T'ien-tsê Chang, *Sino Portuguese Trade from 1514 to 1644*, p. 41. On Nan-t'ou, called *Nantoo* by Pires and *Nantó* by the chroniclers, see note p. 121.

purpose was to send, from nearer the Pei-wo, his messages and requests to be allowed to proceed to Canton, and if the permission was not given, he himself would take it'. Once at Nan-t'ou he sent ashore Impole, with trumpeters and a bodyguard, pressing the Pei-wo to let him go to Canton with the ambassador. After new delays Andrade 'set sail, in view of which the Pei-wo sent him pilots, who took the Portuguese ships to the city of Canton, where they arrived near the end of September with all the pomp and festivity he could manage'. The journey up the river took three days, because Andrade did not want to travel at night.

ARRIVAL AT CANTON. About nineteen months had elapsed since Pires sailed from Cochin before he arrived in front of Canton—a voyage that, in favourable conditions, could be made in about four months. The chroniclers do not tell us of Pires' reactions to the delays, drawbacks and annoyances he suffered during all these months, but one can well imagine his desperation, impatience and anger. However, that was nothing compared with what awaited him in China, though the first contacts with the Chinese, through the Pei-wo of Nan-t'ou, must have given him a foretaste of what was in store. It may also be supposed that often Andrade sought Pires' advice, and that they acted in accord.

Displaying flags and firing a salute with all their artillery, the Portuguese ships cast anchor off the main quay, before the Huai-yüan post station[1]. The Pu-chêng-shih or Provincial Treasurer, Wu T'ing-chü[2], the highest Chinese authority then in Canton, remonstrated against what he said were breaches of the custom of the land on the part of the Portuguese, who furthermore came without official consent. Andrade replied that the firing of the artillery and the displaying of flags was due to his ignorance, and intended as a mark of respect, and as for his

[1] This information is given by a contemporaneous Chinese account of Andrade's arrival at Canton in 1517. The account, published under the Ming Dynasty in 1621 in a rather confused and sometimes inaccurate manner, was translated by W. F. Mayers, under the title *First arrival of the Portuguese in China*, in *Notes and Queries on China and Japan*, I, 129–30. Hongkong 1868.

[2] Chang, *op. cit.*, p. 42. The Pu-chêng-shih is Barros' *Puchancij* and Castanheda's *Puchãci*.

coming without consent, he explained that the Pei-wo had after all given him permission to come and sent him pilots. The Pu-chêng-shih was satisfied and, according to the Portuguese chroniclers, sent a message to the 'Governors' of the city, the *Tutam*, the *Concam* and the *Chumpim*[1], who were absent. Meanwhile Andrade ordered that no Portuguese should go ashore and no Chinese visitors should be allowed on board his ships. After a short time the three high Chinese dignitaries arrived in Canton on different days and with great ceremonial. An interview was arranged with the Portuguese. Andrade sent ashore the factor of the fleet, accompanied by a suite 'of people in gala dress, and preceded by trumpeters, in order to go with more pomp, as he saw that the Chinese were very particular in this sort of thing'. The factor told the Chinese 'Governors' how King Manuel of Portugal, 'wishing to know of and establish friendship with such a great Prince as the King of China, had sent some ships under the command of his Captain Fernão Peres de Andrade to bring an Ambassador with letters and a present; that the King of Portugal had ordered the Ambassador and the present to be delivered to the "Governors" of Canton, who could send them to the court where their King was. Andrade would return to India, and next year another Captain would go there to take back the said Ambassador, because by that time he might have accomplished his mission.' The Chinese 'Governors' 'replied with many words of satisfaction . . . and regarding the Ambassador

[1] These are the names given by Barros; Castanheda calls them *Tutão*, *Conquão* and *Compim*. The question as to what Chinese expressions are meant by these old Portuguese versions has been a matter of controversy, and it is still not quite settled. But according to Pelliot (*Un ouvrage sur les premiers temps de Macao*, p. 64) it seems that they may correspond to *Tu-t'ang*, *Tsung-kuan* and *Tsung-ping*. The meaning of these expressions, Prof. A. C. Moule tells me, is: *Tu-t'ang*—properly an officer in the first department of the Board of Censors, but also a title commonly given to a Viceroy (*Tsung-tu*) or provincial Governor (*Hsün-fu*); *Tsung-ping*—Brigadier-General, commander of the troops in a district called *Chên*; *Tsung-kuan*—commander of the troops in a department (or county) or subdepartment, *fu* or *chou*; the post was often held by the civil governor of the area concerned. Dalgado deals with these names, but his conclusions must be taken with all reserve. *Glossário Luso-Asiático*, *s.v.* Tutão, Compim, Conquão. The *Tutam* or Viceroy was 'Ch'ên Hsi-hsien, who then resided in Wu-chou in the present province of Kwang-si', Chang, p. 43.

they would immediately see that he was lodged ashore, and as soon as they received him they would write to their King asking for instructions'. Accordingly Pires was disembarked 'with a great thunder of artillery, and trumpets, and the men in gala dress, the Ambassador being accompanied by seven Portuguese, who remained with him to go on this embassy. They were taken to their lodgings, which were some of the noblest houses in the city, and the high officials soon came and visited the Ambassador.' The lodgings were the same houses where the Superintendent of the Bureau of Trading-Junks, whose name was Ying-hsiang, lived[1]. The present for the King of China, which Correia says 'should not be opened but in the presence of the King', was put in the same house under lock and key, this being entrusted to Pires. The disembarkation of the embassy must have been about the end of October 1517.

After declining several invitations to go ashore, Andrade took leave of the 'Governors', because he had received news that the Portuguese ships in *Tamão* had been attacked by the pirates, though unsuccessfully, and because some of his people in the ships in Canton were falling ill with fever and dysentry, and nine of them had died, including Impole. This time the Chinese helped fully to repair the Portuguese ships, and Andrade despatched Coelho in the junk to Malacca, where he arrived by the end of March 1518, 'with the news of how the Ambassador was received, the friendship established with the "Governors" of Canton, and how we were welcomed in those parts.' At the same time Jorge Mascarenhas was sent to discover the Liu Kiu Islands. After reaching Chang-chou and Fukien, Mascarenhas was called back by Andrade, because the latter had received news from Malacca, where the help of his squadron was needed, and because he knew from the 'Governors' of Canton that their King had told them that they could send him the Ambassador Tomé Pires. Before leaving, Andrade made proclamations 'that if anybody had been injuried by or had anything owing to him from a Portuguese, let him come to him (Andrade) to obtain all satisfaction; which was much praised by the natives, and had never before been seen amongst them'. Then Andrade set sail

[1] Chang, p. 44.

with all his squadron in September 1518[1], after nearly fourteen months in China, and arrived at Malacca 'very prosperous in honour and wealth, things rarely secured together', comments Barros.

From Malacca Andrade went directly to India, and after one year there he left in January 1520 for Lisbon, where he arrived in July. Góis ends the chapter in which he describes this visit to China by saying that Andrade went from Lisbon to Evora, where the King and Queen then were, 'who received him very well, and the King asked him very often about the things of China, and the other provinces of that region, listening to him with much pleasure, because he was curious by nature to know what happened throughout the world, in order to gather therefrom what was most convenient for the government of his estate, kingdom and dominions.' This shows the interest that the detailed news of China, brought directly by Andrade and his men, aroused in Portugal, and explains how the chroniclers had so much material for their lengthy descriptions of Canton, the arrival of Pires, and all that happened there with Andrade and his squadron.

IN CANTON. Barros says that seven Portuguese remained with Pires in Canton. In his letter, written in 1524 from Canton, Cristóvão Vieira informs us, however, that 'the people that remained in the company of Tomé Pires' were Duarte Fernandes, Francisco de Budoia[2], Cristóvão de Almeida, Pedro de Faria and Jorge Álvares, all Portuguese; 'myself, Cristóvão Vieira, a Persian from Ormuz', twelve lads and five interpreters; i.e., five Portuguese, one Lusitanized Persian and seventeen others.

In spite of the message sent by the 'Governors' of Canton to Andrade, before he left *Tamão*, that their King had told them that they could send him the Portuguese Ambassador, Pires and his suite had to wait in Canton for more than fifteen months. Further on, Barros adds that 'only after three messages from Canton to the King, and after he had sent three other messages

[1] Correia says September, Castanheda the beginning of September, Barros the end of September, and Góis says October.

[2] Further on spelt *Bedois*. I know no such name in Portuguese; it suggests a copyist's miswriting for 'Bulhões', a not unusual name in Portugal, or 'Budens', a village near Lagos, in Algarve.

to the "Governors" of the city, asking in great detail about our affairs, did he give the order for the Ambassador to go'. When Andrade left Pires with the 'Governors' of Canton, he told them that one year later another Portuguese Captain would come with a fleet to fetch the Ambassador. Andrade arrived in India about the end of 1518, and the new Governor, Diogo Lopes de Sequeira, who took charge of his office on 27 Dec. 1518, appointed António Correia, his nephew, to go with a fleet to China, obviously for the purpose of bringing back Tomé Pires' Embassy. But Simão de Andrade, a brother of Fernão Peres de Andrade, had written to the King of Portugal the abovementioned letter of 10 Aug. 1518, dated from Malacca where he was then Captain of the Sea, enumerating his services and asking to be appointed captain of one of the fortresses of Malacca, Goa or Ormuz, or to be awarded some other favour. This letter must have followed together with the news brought from China by the junk of Duarte Coelho which arrived at Malacca about the end of March 1518. The King was certainly well impressed with the successful visit of Fernão Peres de Andrade to China, and though he did not appoint Simão de Andrade to any fortress, he sent him a grant authorizing his going to China as captain of a fleet after his brother's return. Thus Simão de Andrade produced the royal grant and was sent to China instead of António Correia. In April 1519 he sailed with a ship from Cochin and was joined in Malacca by three junks, the captains of which were Jorge Botelho, Álvaro Fuzeiro and Francisco Rodrigues, all under the command of Andrade. The small fleet arrived at *Tamão* in August of the same year. Contrasting singularly with his brother, Simão de Andrade was a man of not much tact and the possessor of a temperamental and violent character, features that the chroniclers do not fail to emphasize. His substitution for António Correia, a man better qualified for that mission, was the small twist which sometimes happens in the trend of history, and which became the principal cause of the unfortunate end of Pires' Embassy, and of all the misfortunes the Portuguese suffered in China for more than thirty years.

Simão de Andrade expected, quite reasonably, that when he arrived at *Tamão* he would find that Pires was back from the embassy to the 'King of China'. Instead he ascertained that the Ambassador had not even left Canton. Pires must have been very annoyed with the unbearable Chinese delays, and naturally complained to the Portuguese Captain. Accustomed to the prestige and respect then enjoyed by the Portuguese in the East, Andrade certainly resented deeply the Chinese behaviour and took it as an affront to Portuguese pride. Not unnaturally, his indignation and irritation would be very great. It no doubt contributed to the state of mind which led to his regrettable misconduct—a point overlooked as much by past as by present-day historians, though it seems necessary for a sober judgement on this often-discussed point of history. Referring to the delays inflicted upon Pires' embassy, Barros comments: 'the majesty of this Prince (the "King of China") is such, and the affairs of this kind so slow, mainly when foreign people are involved, for all is cautions and subtleties, that much patience is needed on the part of whoever has to wait for their dilatoriness.' Patience was not Simão de Andrade's chief virtue, and he committed several acts which the Chinese authorites considered as infringements of their laws, like the building of a fort of stone and wood in *Tamão*, under the pretext of defence against the pirates, and the erection of a gallows on which a seaman was hanged. We do not know if these and other more reprehensible acts, such as the buying of kidnapped Chinese children, were practised before Pires left Canton for Peking, but no doubt they were portentous and had a most unfortunate bearing on future events.

FROM CANTON TO PEKING. Cristóvão Vieira tells us, in his letter of 1524, that Pires left Canton for Peking on 23 Jan. 1520[1]. Though Barros utilized this letter for compiling his detailed description of the embassy's adventures in China, he received information from other sources—one of them, perhaps, being Pires himself. It may be taken for granted that Pires wrote several times reporting the progress and events of his voyage after he left Cochin and at least some of his letters reached India

[1] All these dates referring to Pires' journey to Peking and back to Canton are given by Vieira and were utilized by Barros. Góis (IV, XXV) says, obviously in error, that Simão de Andrade arrived at *Tamão* in Aug. 1518, and that Pires left Canton in Oct. 1519 and arrived at Peking in Jan. 1520.

and Lisbon. Correia even says that Pires 'in the time of the Governor [D. Duarte de Menezes, who governed India from January 1522 to December 1524] sent him [the Governor] a book in which he gave an account of the riches and greatness of the King of China, which appeared to be hardly credible' (II, 678). Unfortunately there is no trace of anything written by Pires from China.

The embassy sailed up the river in three Chinese galleys, with silken awnings and displaying Portuguese flags. At the foot of the mountain range north of Kwang-tung they left the boats and proceeded through the Mei-ling pass in litters, on horseback and afoot. Duarte Fernandes, one of Pires' suite, died in these mountains. From there Pires wrote to Simão de Andrade reporting on the progress of his journey. Thence they proceeded northward to Nanking, where they arrived in May 1520. The Emperor was in that city, but he would not receive the Portuguese ambassador there, and sent him word to proceed to Peking and wait there for his arrival. Through Vieira we know that on the 2nd August letters were sent to Canton, which were delivered to Jorge Botelho and Diogo Calvo in *Tamão.* Vasco Calvo says that the letters were addressed to D. Aleixo de Menezes, and that Jorge Álvares was asked to take them[1]. We do not know the date of Pires' arrival in Peking, but he was already there when the Emperor entered the city in February 1521[2]. While the Emperor was in Nanking, there arrived an ambassador sent by the ex-king of Malacca to complain to his suzerain against the Portuguese 'sea-robbers' who had taken his kingdom, and asking for help as he was the Emperor's vassal. He had brought one letter from his king, and at the same time the Emperor received another letter from two mandarins of Peking, and yet another from the mandarins of Canton piling up complaints against the Portuguese, mainly on account of the

[1] Fol. 130v. Though Calvo wrote *Dom Estevão,* this is a mistake for *Dom Aleixo,* as will be seen below. Jorge Álvares could not have taken the letter because he died in Tamão in 1521. He was the first Portuguese who went to China, in 1513, and there he was buried in 1521, as I have shown elsewhere. *Expansão Portuguesa através do Pacífico,* p. 164. See notes pp. 120, 283.

[2] Góis (IV, XXV) says that Pires 'spent four months in the way' from Canton to Peking, but he is obviously referring to the time spent in actual travel.

misdeeds of Simão de Andrade in *Tamão*. Furthermore, Pires had brought with him three letters for the Emperor from King Manuel, Fernão Peres de Andrade and the 'Governors' of Canton. Andrade's letter had been mistranslated into Chinese by the interpreters; they wrote according to the custom of the country, saying among other things that the King of Portugal wanted to be a vassal of the Emperor of China. The letter of the Canton 'Governors' had been written and handed to Pires while they were still under the good impression left by Fernão Peres de Andrade. When the sealed letter of King Manuel was opened and translated in the imperial palace, it was found that its spirit was (of course) quite different from that of the letter written by the interpreters in the name of Andrade[1]. The interpreters accepted responsibility for Andrade's letter, but an inquiry was opened and all the members of the Embassy were ordered not to approach the imperial palace. Though, according to Vieira, the Emperor magnanimously said 'these people do not know our customs; gradually they will get to know them', more charges, some of them quite fantastic, were being brought against the Portuguese. After telling us that one of the charges was that 'we bought kidnapped children of important people and ate them roasted', Barros comments: 'They believe this to be true, as being about people of whom they had never heard; and we were the terror and fear of all that East, so it was not too much to believe that we did such things, just as we too think of them and other far-flung countries, about which we have but little knowledge.' Some early Chinese historians go even so far as to give vivid details of the price paid for the children and how they were roasted[2].

Meanwhile the Emperor Wu-tsung died three months after his arrival in Peking, and was succeeded by Shih-tsung, a youth of fourteen. The embassy was then ordered to withdraw from the capital and return to Canton with the presents brought for the Emperor, which were refused. Some high officials in the court declared that the embassy was not genuine, and wanted strong action taken against the Portuguese, maintaining that

[1] Vieira gives many details about all these letters. *Op. cit.*, fol. 104.

[2] Chang, p. 48.

they should die as spies; but their diplomatic status saved them for the time being. However, according to Vieira, of the five interpreters, one died of sickness and 'the other four were beheaded in Peking for having left the country and brought the Portuguese to China', and their servants were given as slaves to the mandarins as having belonged to traitors.

Back in Canton. Finally Pires and his companions left Peking on 22 May and arrived in Canton on 22 Sept. 1521. Francisco de Budoia died during the journey. From Peking instructions were sent to Canton that the ambassador and his suite should be kept in custody, and that only after the Portuguese had evacuated Malacca and returned it to its king, a vassal of the Emperor of China, would the members of the embassy be liberated.

In the meantime, after the departure of Simão de Andrade, the ship *Madalena*, which belonged to D. Nuno Manuel, coming from Lisbon under the command of Diogo Calvo, arrived at *Tamão* with some other vessels from Malacca, among them the junk of Jorge Álvares, which the year before could not sail with Simão de Andrade's fleet, because she had sprung a leak. When the instructions issued from Peking against the Portuguese arrived in Canton, together with the news of the death of the Emperor, the Chinese seized Vasco Calvo, a brother of Diogo Calvo, and other Portuguese who were in Canton trading ashore. On 27 June 1521 Duarte Coelho arrived with two junks at *Tamão*. Besides capturing some of the Portuguese vessels, the Chinese blockaded Diogo Calvo's ship and four other Portuguese vessels in *Tamão* with a large fleet of armed junks. A few weeks later Ambrósio do Rego arrived with two other ships. As many of the Portuguese crews had been killed in the fighting, slaughtered afterwards or taken prisoners, by this time there were not enough Portuguese for all the vessels, and thus Calvo, Coelho and Rego resolved to abandon the junks in order the better to man the three ships. They set sail on 7 September and were attacked by the Chinese fleet, managing however to escape, thanks to a providential gale which scattered the enemy junks, and arrived at Malacca in October 1521. Vieira mentions other junks which arrived in China with Portuguese aboard; all were attacked, and the entire crews were killed fighting or were taken prisoners and slaughtered later. From Diogo Calvo's ship there remained, besides Vasco Calvo, seven other Portuguese and four servants, who escaped the slaughter because they said that they belonged to Pires' embassy. But many others died in prison, some of hunger, many strangled, 'after carrying boards stating that they should die as sea-robbers', one struck on the head with a mallet, and others beaten to death.

Pires and his companions arrived at Canton a fortnight after the three Portuguese ships had escaped from *Tamão*, and they found themselves in a most difficult position. They were immediately summoned to the presence of the *Pochanci*[1], and Pires was told to write to the Portuguese in Malacca telling them to return the country to its ex-king. Let Vieira describe for us what then happened: 'Tomé Pires replied that he had not come for that purpose, nor was it meet for him to discuss such a matter; that it would be evident from the letter he had brought that he had no knowledge of anything else. . . . With these questions he kept us on our knees for four hours; and when he had tired himself out, he sent each one back to the prison in which he was kept. On 14 August 1522 the *Pochanci* put fetters on the hands of Tomé Pires, and on those of the company he put fetters, and irons on their feet, the fetters soldered on their wrists; and they took from us all the property that we had. Thus, with chains on our necks, and through the city, they took us to the house of the *Anchaci*[2]. There they knocked off our fetters and put on us stronger chains; on our legs fetters were soldered, and chains on our necks; and from there they sent us to this prison. At the entrance to this prison António de Almeida died from the heavy fetters that we bore; our arms were swollen, and our legs cut by the tight chains. This, with a decision that two days afterwards they would kill us. Before it was night, they put fetters once more on Tomé Pires and conducted him alone, barefoot and without a cap, amid the hootings of boys, to the prison of Kuang-chou-fu (*Cancheufu*), in order to see the goods that they had taken from us, which had to be described; and the mandarin

[1] Pu-chêng-shih or Provincial Treasurer. Cf. Ferguson, p. 51.

[2] An-ch'a-shih or Provincial Judge. Cf. Chang, p. 56.

clerks who were present wrote down ten and stole three hundred . . . The goods that they took from us were twenty quintals of rhubarb, one thousand five hundred or six hundred rich pieces of silk, a matter of four thousand silk handkerchiefs which the Chinese call sheu-pa (*xopas*) of Nanking, and many fans, and also three *arrobas* of musk in powder, one thousand three hundred pods of musk, four thousand odd taels of silver and seventy or eighty taels of gold and other pieces of silver, and all the cloths, pieces of value, both Portuguese and Chinese, the pachak of Jorge Botelho, incense, liquid storax, tortoise-shells, also pepper and other trifles[1]. These were delivered into the factory of Kuang-chou-fu as the property of robbers. The present of our Lord the King which he sent to the King of China is in the factory of the Pochanci' (fols. 106–7). Ferguson sums up thus: 'After a farcical show of respect for the members of the embassy, extending over ten months, these were all imprisoned, and the whole of their property and the presents from the king of Portugal to the emperor were confiscated, the lion's share, as might be expected, falling to the mandarins'[2]. Fernão Mendes Pinto tells us that in 1541 he saw the mandarin of *Nouday* 'mounted on a good horse, with certain cuirasses of red velvet with gilt studs of ancient date, which we afterwards learnt belonged to one Tomé Pires, whom the King Dom Manuel of glorious memory sent as ambassador to China, in the ship of Fernão Peres de Andrade, when Lopo Soares de Albergaria was governing the State of India'[3].

Meanwhile from India, where the news of this state of affairs had not yet arrived, another fleet of four ships under the command of Martim Afonso de Melo Coutinho sailed for China in April 1522. Coutinho had left Lisbon just one year before, commissioned by Dom Manuel with a message of good-will to the

[1] This is according to the Lisbon original fragments of Vieira's letter. Barros (III, vi, 2), following the Paris MS (ff. 106–7), gives a slightly different list (see p. xlvi below) of the goods confiscated. But instead of saying, like Vieira, that the goods were taken from *them*, he says that they were taken from *him* (Pires). This alteration was perhaps the reason for Sousa's unfair comment (I, iii, 6). There would be nothing extraordinary in all those goods belonging to Pires, who had already amassed a considerable fortune even before going to China; and after all the goods did not belong exclusively to him.

[2] *Op. cit.*, pp. 18–19.

[3] *Peregrinação*, LXV.

Emperor of China, for which purpose he carried another ambassador with him. He arrived at Malacca in July and there he learned of the misfortunes that had happened to the Portuguese in China. Nevertheless he determined to continue his journey, accompanied by another ship and a junk with Ambrósio do Rego and Duarte Coelho, who reluctantly and only under pressure from Jorge de Albuquerque, then Captain of Malacca, consented to go back to China, where the year before they had had a narrow escape, as seen above. Coutinho's fleet of six sail left Malacca on 10 July and arrived at *Tamão* in August 1522. They were soon attacked by the Chinese fleet. The Portuguese had many men killed and taken prisoners, two ships and the junk were lost, and after vain efforts to re-establish relations with the Cantonese authorities, Coutinho returned with the other ships to Malacca, where he arrived in the middle of October 1522. Though some chroniclers put the blame on the Chinese, Chang quotes Chinese sources which assert that the Portuguese should be held responsible for the outbreak of hostilities[1].

According to Vieira the mandarins again ordered that Pires should write a letter to the King of Portugal, which the ambassador of the ex-king of Malacca should take to Malacca, in order that his country and people might be returned to their former master; if a satisfactory reply did not come, the Portuguese ambassador would not return. A draft letter in Chinese was sent to the imprisoned Portuguese, from which they wrote three letters, for King Manuel, the Governor of India and the Captain of Malacca. These letters were delivered to the Cantonese authorities on 1 Oct. 1522. The Malay ambassador was not anxious to be the courier, nor was it easy to find another. At last a junk with fifteen Malays and fifteen Chinese sailed from Canton on 31 May 1523 and reached Patani. In his letter of 1 Jan. 1524 to King Manuel, Jorge de Albuquerque, Captain of Malacca, says that D. Sancho Henriques, Captain-major of the Sea at Malacca, had gone to blockade Bintang at the beginning of July 1523, and thence went to Patani with Ambrósio do Rego and another ship to wait for a Portuguese junk that was in Siam,

[1] *Op. cit.*, p. 59.

'and to learn news from China from the Chinese that come there.' Ambrósio do Rego returned first to Malacca with news, which he learned from 'an interpreter who acted between the Chinese and Portuguese when they were at peace. He told him that there were living [in Canton] from eight to thirteen Portuguese, and it was not certain how many, because one said eight and another thirteen; and that they said that the ambassador Tomé Pires was still living. A message came to the king of Bintang from his ambassador [in Canton], and the man who brought it soon returned. The report which the king of Bintang was spreading in the country is that the Chinese intended to come against Malacca. This is not very certain, though there are things that may happen. If they come, they will do great harm, unless the Captain-major [of India] shall come in time, as I am writing to him. However, in my opinion they will not do so, as they also say in China that they desire peace with us'[1]. This document sheds some light on the matter. It is obvious that the three letters brought in the junk from Canton never reached their destination, being very probably retained by agents of the ex-king of Malacca, a master intriguer who had plenty of reasons for hating the Portuguese, and perhaps even Pires in particular. The man who brought a message to the king of Bintang 'soon returned', says Jorge de Albuquerque. Vieira tells us that the junk 'returned with a message from the king of Malacca, and reached Canton on the 5th September' (fol. 110v.). We do not know what the message was, but we may well guess, for, as Vieira states, 'On the day of St. Nicholas [6 Dec.] in the year 1522 they put boards on them [the Portuguese prisoners] with the sentence that they should die and be exposed in pillories as robbers. The sentences said: "Petty sea robbers sent by the great robber falsely; they come to spy out our country; let them die in pillories as robbers." A report was sent to the king according to the information of the mandarins, and the king confirmed the sentence. On 23 Sept. 1523 these twenty-three persons were each one cut in pieces, to wit, heads, legs, arms, and their private members placed in their mouths, the trunk of the body being divided into two pieces round the belly. In the streets of Canton,

[1] *Cartas*, IV, 41–2.

outside the walls, in the suburbs, through the principal streets they were put to death, at distances of one crossbow shot from one another, that all might see them, both those of Canton and those of the environs, in order to give them to understand that they thought nothing of the Portuguese, so that the people might not talk about Portuguese. Thus our ships were captured through two captains not agreeing, and so all in the ships were taken, they were all killed, and their heads and private members were carried on the backs of the Portuguese in front of the mandarins of Canton with the playing of musical instruments and rejoicing, were exhibited suspended in the streets, and were then thrown into the dunghills. And from henceforward it was resolved not to allow any more Portuguese into the country nor other strangers' (fol. 109).

Vieira's letter, probably finished in November 1524, says that of all the Portuguese only he and Vasco Calvo were still alive, and that 'Tomé Pires died here of sickness in the year 1524 in May'. This date, however, cannot be accepted without much reserve, as we shall see.

VIEIRA'S AND CALVO'S LETTERS. The copies of the two letters from Cristóvão Vieira and Vasco Calvo extant in the Bibliothèque Nationale in Paris were probably made in the second half of the sixteenth century. Though the letters in these copies are dated 1534 and 10 Nov. 1536, it is not difficult to show that they were both written in 1524, Vieira's being finished just a little before Calvo finished his on the 10th November. The two letters, besides being very important for the study of Pires' biography, are outstanding documents in the history of the first European relations with China; the date at which they were written is therefore important, and it is time that this point was cleared up.

In the first place neither of the letters refers to any event later than 1524; it is extremely unlikely that during the ten or twelve years between 1524 and the supposed dates of the letters nothing worth mentioning had happened. There are two points in the letters suggesting that they were written after 1524, but they are copyist's mistakes. In Vieira's letter it is stated: 'In the year 1524 they equipped a fleet of salt junks which they took by force; and until the year 1528 they prepared fleets' (fol. 118v.). 1528 is a copyist's mistake for 1523. Further on Vieira asks for a Portuguese fleet to be sent to China, and adds: 'The first thing will be to destroy the [Chinese] fleet if they should have one, which I believe they have not' (fol. 122v.). Similar mistakes are frequent in the letter. For instance, the heading of Vieira's letter says that Fernão Peres de Andrade reached China in 1520, though he arrived in 1517. On fol. 108v. it is stated that Martim Afonso de Melo Coutinho went from Malacca to China in 1521, but in fol. 121 it is correctly said that he arrived in 1522. In the Paris copy it is said that among the goods taken from the Portuguese by the Chinese were 'three thousand and odd pods of musk, four thousand five hundred taels of silver' (fol. 107), but in the Lisbon original fragments it reads 'one thousand three hundred pods of musk, four thousand and odd' [taels of silver]. The Paris copy states that 'sixty died in the ship' (fol. 108v.), while the Lisbon fragments say correctly that 'seven died in the ship'. Where the Paris copy says 'On the 23rd of September 1523 these twenty-four persons' (fol. 109), the Lisbon fragments say 'On the 24th September 1523 these 24 persons'. Where the Paris copy says 'thirty leagues' (fol. 112v.) the Lisbon fragments say 'forty leagues'. Where the Paris copy says 'some eight to ten leagues' (fol. 113), the Lisbon fragments say 'twenty to thirty leagues'.

The other point is in Calvo's letter: 'Let these letters, Sir, be shown to the captains-major; let them not be kept secret, Sir; for if Jorge Álvares had shown the letters that he took to Dom Estêvão and they had known about us, I am confident that we should not have remained here in this prison either dead or alive. Within two years either the governor would have sènt, or from Malacca something would have been ordered by means of which we should have been rescued from here' (fol. 130v). Ferguson[1] thought that this 'Dom Estêvão' was Dom Estêvão da Gama, the son of Dom Vasco da Gama, who in 1534 was captain of Malacca and in 1540–2 was Governor General of India. But there is another mistake here: the copyist wrote 'Dom Estêvão' where the original must have had 'Dom Aleixo'. Dom Aleixo de Menezes, nephew of the Governor-General Lopo Soares de Albergaria, went with a fleet to Malacca in 1518 and in 1520 he

[1] *Op. cit.*, pp. 29 and 157.

was acting Governor-General of India while the Governor-General Diogo de Sequeira went to the Red Sea[1]. In 1521 Dom Aleixo was in Cochin where he despatched several ships for Malacca and China, among which probably was the ship of Diogo Calvo that arrived at *Tamão* in 1521. There was not then any 'Dom Estêvão' in India to whom letters could have been sent. The letters in question may be those written 2 Aug. 1520 from Nanking, or Peking, mentioned above, and perhaps some more written by Vasco Calvo from Canton. The reference to Jorge Álvares, who died 8 July 1521 in *Tamão* (a fact unknown to Calvo), as taking the letters to 'Dom Estêvão' (da Gama) who arrived for the first time in India 11 Sept. 1524, is an insuperable anachronism. Many similar mistakes were committed by the copyist. For instance, in the heading of Vieira's letter he wrote that it is from Critóvão Vieira and Vasco Calvo, and in the heading of Calvo's letter he wrote that it is from Cristóvão Vieira. A collation of the Paris copy with the Lisbon original fragments of Vieira's letter reveals many such mistakes.

In the above quoted passage Calvo shows his surprise because within two years nothing had been done to rescue him and his fellow prisoners. It is obvious that he referred to letters written after he had been made a prisoner, which he reckoned were received in 1522; thus he was writing in 1524. There is evidence in his letter that he wrote at the same time as Vieira: 'where Cristóvão Vieira writes' (fol. 132v.), he says; 'as Cristóvão Vieira relates in these letters' (fol. 133); 'proposals after the tenor of those set forth in the letters of Cristovão Vieira' (fol. 134v.); 'Cristóvão Vieira has written with one of our pens' (fol. 135v.). Other points in the letter might be interpreted as confirming the dates of 1534 and 1536; their careful examination, however, shows that they do not contradict the date 1524. Above all there is Barros' testimony. There is no doubt that the

[1] Barros, III, iii, 10. In a letter written from Cochin, 2 Nov. 1520, to King Manuel, the Auditor of India, Pedro Gomes Teixeira, says that during Sequeira's absence the government was divided between 'Dom Aleixo, in charge of the finance and administration of the sea, and Captain Rui de Melo, in charge of the people ashore'. This important and lengthy document was published for the first time by A. Cortesão and H. Thomas, *Carta das Novas*, pp. 127–38.

chronicler utilized the two letters in the composition of the chapters in which he describes these events. It is Barros himself who says: 'And according to the two letters that we received two or three years later (after the return of Pires to Canton and his imprisonment) from these two men, Vasco Calvo and Cristóvão Vieira, who were in prison in Canton.' This is quite positive, and coupled with the evidence contained in the letters themselves, leaves no doubt about their date: they were both written in 1524 and perhaps both finished in November; the dates 1534 and 1536 are the copyist's mistake.

It is surprising that Ferguson, after translating and editing the two letters so carefully, did not notice that their dates could not be 1534 and 1536, though he expresses amazement at some of the anachronisms and incongruities above mentioned, which he tried in vain to explain or could not understand at all. Neither have those who consulted and quoted Ferguson's work noticed or mentioned them.

AFTER 1524. Though Vieira says that 'Pero de Freitas in this prison and Tomé Pires died of sickness in the year 1524 in May' (fol. 112), he asks further on for a Portuguese fleet of ten or fifteen ships to be sent to China, and that its captain should write to the Chinese authorities demanding the release of Tomé Pires —'Let the ambassador be sent to me before I arrive in Canton' (fol. 123). This, however, might have meant that the Portuguese captain was to pretend that he did not know of Pires' death. It may also be that the sentence was badly written or badly copied, as in many other instances, and that its true meaning was— 'Pero de Freitas was in this prison with Tomé Pires, and he (Pero de Freitas) died here of sickness. . . .' But the more likely meaning is—'Pero de Freitas died in this prison, and Tomé Pires died of sickness [somewhere else] in May 1524.' As a matter of fact Vieira shows in other parts of the letter that he seemed convinced that Pires was dead.

Only Vieira refers, and not very clearly, to Pires' death in 1524. Barros says that after Coutinho's ship escaped from *Tamão*, the Chinese 'made many of our people prisoners', and that 'they finally killed Tomé Pires, and also those taken prisoner with him, and total war then existed between us and them. And according to what some of our people afterwards wrote, more died of hunger in prison and the bad treatment they received there, than by condemnation.' The executions took place only after the confirmation from the Emperor had arrived at Canton in September 1523. Though Barros is obviously referring to Vieira's letter, he does not mention the date of Pires' death. Castanheda, who at the time was in India, says that the King of China 'ordered the arrest of our ambassador and those who were with him, and ordered that they should be kept separated from one another, and that all their goods should be confiscated; and some say that the ambassador fell ill with grief and died; and others say that he died by poison. And because I was not able to learn the particulars of these [events], I relate it briefly in this manner.' However, Correia, who for almost all those years was also in India, says quite positively—'It was the King (of China)'s pleasure to order the arrest of our ambassador, and that he should be taken to another town, where he lived for a long time (*e leuar a outra terra em que esteue muyto tempo*), till it should be the King's pleasure to speak to him; but he never more let him come back, and there he died.'

Now Fernão Mendes Pinto says in the *Peregrinação* (XCI) that when in 1543 he passed through the town of *Sampitay*, on his way from Nanking to Peking, he met a Christian woman who, after showing a cross tattooed on her arm and inviting him and his companions to her house, told them 'that her name was Inês de Leiria, and that her father was called Tomé Pires, who went from this kingdom [i.e. Portugal] as ambassador to the King of China, but because of a disturbance that a captain of ours made in Canton the Chinese regarded him as a spy and not as an ambassador as he said, and seized him with twelve other men he had with him, and after they had sentenced them and subjected them to many floggings and tortures, of which five soon died, they banished the others, separated from one another, to divers places, where they died devoured by lice; only one of them was living, who was called Vasco Calvo, a native of a place in our country named Alcochete, for so she had many times heard from her father, shedding many tears when he spoke of this. And that it chanced to her father to be banished to that district where he married her mother, because she had some property of her own, and made her a Christian; and during the whole twenty-seven years that he abode there married to her they both lived very catholically, converting many heathen to the faith of Christ[1].' When living in Almada, opposite Lisbon, on the other side of the Tagus, Pinto was visited in October 1582 by the Jesuits G. Maffei, J. Rebelo and G. Gonçalves, who went to gather from him some information about China and Japan. Maffei left a note recording the conversation they had with Pinto, in which, among other things, we read—'He says that there are some other traces of Christianity in China, which are relics of Tomé Pires, the first ambassador to go there and who died in China, and of his companions. He says that a daughter of [one of] these [men][2] in memory of her father's Christianity had a cross tattooed on her arm near her hand, and when she met some Portuguese she tucked up her sleeve and showed the cross, saying in Portuguese the only part she knew of the Paternoster, which produced amazement and tears on either side. She was rich and sheltered them in her house. Of the same company there was also in the city of Kwang-si (*Cansi*), before it was destroyed by the Tartars, a certain Portuguese married to a Chinese woman with four children.' Pinto describes also how in 1544 he encountered in the town of *Quansi*, not far from Peking, an old man who, after some incidents, told him: 'I am, my brother, a poor Portuguese Christian, by name Vasco Calvo, brother of Diogo Calvo who was captain of the ship of D. Nuno Manuel, a native of Alcochete; and it is now twenty-seven years since I was made a captive with Tomé Pires, whom Lopo Soares sent as ambassador to this Chinese King, and who afterwards came to a disastrous end due to a disturbance of a Portuguese captain' . . . Then 'he began again telling me about all his life,

[1] *Peregrinação*, CXVI.

[2] The Portuguese rendering is not very clear. Though it is not expressly stated here that the father was Pires, the *Peregrinação* is quite positive on the subject. This note was found by the learned Orientalist Rev. G. Schurhammer, S.J., among Maffei's papers in an archive of the Society of Jesus. Schurhammer published it for the first time under the title *Um documento inedito sobre Fernão Mendes Pinto* in *Revista de Historia*, XIII, 81–8, Lisboa 1924, and then translated it into German in his work *Fernão Mendez Pinto und seine 'Peregrinaçam'*, pp. 35–42, Leipzig 1927.

and all the rest of his adventures, since he left this kingdom until then, and also about the death of the ambassador Tomé Pires and of the others whom Fernão Peres de Andrade left with him in Canton to go to the King of China, which, according to what he told me, does not very well agree with what our chroniclers write'[1].

Faria e Sousa was the first chronicler to use Pinto's information in a full chapter rectifying what he, following Barros, had written before about the supposed death of Pires in Canton[2]. Then Abel-Rémusat[3], in 1829, gives an account of Pires' adventures in China in part based also on Pinto's information. R. H. Major, in his excellent Introduction (p. xxxvii) to Mendoza's *History of China*, quotes Rémusat's account in order to complete Mendoza's description of Pires' embassy, which is more or less based on Barros, and defends Pinto against William Congreve's lines in his *Love for Love* (1695) 'Ferdinand Mendes Pinto was but a type of thee, thou liar of the first magnitude'[4]. Commenting on Major's defence of Pinto, Ferguson writes: 'I am astonished that such an able scholar as Mr. Major, in his Introduction to the Hakluyt Society's edition of Mendoza, should, after referring to Mendez Pinto's alleged adventures in China, conclude: "Upon the whole, his remarks leave no doubt, we think, of the truth of his having been an eye-witness of what he records" ' (p. 36n). For Ferguson all that Pinto says about Pires is 'fabrication', 'unblushing falsehood', 'mendacity'. No less surprising is a similar attitude assumed by another outstanding scholar, Henri Cordier. After transcribing part of Rémusat's account of the encounters of Pinto with Inês de Leiria and Vasco Calvo, Cordier, without giving any reason

[1] *Peregrinação*, CXVI.

[2] When, at the end of the preliminaries to his *Asia Portuguesa*, vol. I, Sousa mentions the books he utilized, he says: 'Many doubt the veracity of Fernão Mendes Pinto's Historia Indica; but as many, who travelled through those parts, say that he could have told things still more difficult to believe. I hold him to be very truthful, for many compelling reasons; but if he is not, it is in things which are outside my province.'

[3] *Nouveaux Mélanges Asiatiques*, II, 203–6.

[4] It must be said that Congreve puts the taunt at Pinto in the mouth of Foresight, the fool in the play, 'an illiterate old fellow, peevish and positive, superstitious, and pretending to understand Astrology, Palmistry, Physiognomy, Omens, Dreams, etc.'

whatever, dismisses the whole question in six words: 'Pinto mentait et Rémusat se trompait[1].'

Can this matter be dismissed so summarily? As pointed out above, Barros does not mention any special date for Pires' death, though he was following Vieira's letter which states that Pires died in May 1524; and the copy of Vieira's letter, published by Ferguson, is full of mistakes of every kind. Castanheda, who in 1528 went to India where he lived for about ten years, shows that he does not know anything positive about Pires' death and still less its date; but he asserts that the order for the arrest of Pires and his companions determined that 'they should be kept separated from one another'. Correia, who in 1512 went to India and lived there for many years (in India, where he died, he wrote the *Lendas*), occupying such posts as that of Afonso de Albuquerque's secretary, says, quite positively, that after Pires' arrest in Canton he was taken to another town where he lived for a long time. Furthermore, Ferguson himself quotes the contemporary Chinese source, mentioned by Mayers in *Notes and Queries*, in which it is stated that 'the interpreter was subjected to capital punishment and his men were sent back in custody to Canton, and expelled beyond the frontiers of the province'. Mayers says in a footnote that by the interpreter in question Tomé Pires himself was meant. Ferguson, basing his statement on Vieira's letter, declares that this is an error: 'it was the native interpreters who were beheaded.' Cordier (p. 521), however, agrees with Mayers' interpretation. What seems more probable is that the confusing reference means that the interpreters were beheaded, and the Portuguese who escaped death were expelled from Canton province. As has already been shown, it seems from what Vieira says that Pires was in another prison, and it is not clear that he meant that the ambassador had died also. Besides, it is rather strange that Vieira should give so much detailed information about the death of his other companions and be so brief about the death of the most important of the Portuguese in Canton—the ambassador himself. He does not even say the day on which the death occurred, or what happened to the body. Pires was in another prison, and obviously Vieira obtained

[1] *L'Arrivée des Portugais en Chine*, p. 520.

his information second-hand. That Vieira and Calvo were not very well informed is shown, among other things, by their ignorance of the death of Jorge Álvares in 1521 in *Tamão*. It is quite possible that the Chinese purposely deceived Vieira, telling him that Pires had died, when in fact he was sent out of Canton according to the instructions from Peking. Against Vieira's doubtful statement there is some fairly positive evidence to show that it is unjustifiable to label Pinto's information as 'unblushing falsehood'.

An important point overlooked by Ferguson in Vieira's letter was this—'The women of the interpreters as also those of Tomé Pires that were left in this city in the present year were sold as the property of traitors' (fol. 112). If Pires had 'women' before 1524, and was about fifty when he arrived at Canton in 1517, there is nothing so extraordinary in the fact of Pinto meeting in 1543 a woman who told him she was a daughter of the unfortunate Portuguese ambassador and a Chinese woman. As regards Pinto's meeting with Calvo, Ferguson based his assertion of 'mendacity' mainly on the supposition of Calvo's letter having been written in 1536. After what has been said above it is more reasonable to assume that Pinto was truthful than to say, as Ferguson did—'We may take it as absolutely certain that Vasco Calvo died in prison in Canton within a year or two of writing the letter of 1536'.[1] There is, however, an obvious incongruity in Pinto's statement that Inês de Leiria told him that Pires had been married to her mother for twenty-seven years, which is repeated when he reports that Calvo told him that twenty-seven years had elapsed since he and Pires were made captives; as

[1] *Op. cit.*, p. 38. Ferguson does not give the reason for his 'absolute certainty'. In the introduction to his edition of the *Peregrinação* (Lisboa 1908) J. I. de Brito Rebelo had already remarked (p. xxiv) that Ferguson had overlooked the reference in Vieira's letter to 'the women of the interpreters and also those of Tomé Pires' and the groundless though peremptory assertion about Vasco Calvo. Ferguson's bias against Pinto is only too evident. On Pinto's references to the terrible massacre of the Portuguese by the Chinese in Liampo and Chang-chou (*Chincheo*) in 1545 and 1549, Ferguson comments: 'I consider both these stories to be pure fiction, without any basis in fact; and I even feel very doubtful whether such an island as "Lampacau" ever existed except in the brain of the writer' (p. 39). Pires was right, however, as has been recognized by Cordier himself (*op. cit.*, p. 523) among others.

their arrest happened in 1522, only twenty-two years had elapsed, not twenty-seven. This inaccuracy seems more strange because Pinto shows that he read what the chroniclers had written on the matter, and he could easily have checked his reckoning[1]. On the other hand, if Pinto really wanted to invent a whole story about Pires, for the purpose of deceiving his readers, he could easily have made it more true to life by adjusting his description to the Chroniclers' accounts and mentioning Vieira, about whom he says nothing. That he did not do so is one more proof of Pinto's good faith. Pinto returned from the East to Portugal in 1558, and only began writing the *Peregrinação* eleven or so years later; after so many adventures it is not likely that he had been able to keep a book of notes, at least of that early period[2]. He was writing from memory—and a wonderful memory it was. It is not surprising that due to a *lapsus memoriae* or even a simple *lapsus calami* he wrote twenty-seven instead of twenty-two years.

Inês de Leiria's account, as Pinto has transmitted it to us, needs also some sort of adjustment in one or two minor points. As regards the inaccuracies it must be borne in mind that she spoke to Pinto in Chinese, because she knew only a few words of Portuguese, and after more than twenty-six years Pinto can be excused for committing a few not very serious mistakes when writing from memory. He could not even remember the year of Pires' death, which Inês de Leiria and Calvo must have told him; if he really wanted to deceive he could invent one date more. Inês' mother may have been one of the women of Tomé Pires, referred to by Vieira as having been 'sold as the property of traitors' in 1524. When in 1520 Pires went from Nanking to Peking by the Grand Canal, and also on his return some months later, he passed by the city of *Sampitay*, as Pinto did twenty-

[1] Pinto did not begin to write the *Peregrinação* before 1569; both *Livro* v of Castanheda's *Historia* and Barros' *Decada* III were published for the first time in 1554 and 1563 respectively. Brito Rebelo, still convinced that Pires really died in Canton in 1524, thinks that when the MS of the *Peregrinação* was 'corrected', before its publication, 'the correctors transferred to the father the period of time which really referred to the daughter.' *Loc. cit.*

[2] Pinto however refers in chapters cv, cvi and cvii to 'a small book called *Aquesẽdo* dealing with the greatness of Peking, which I brought to this kingdom'.

three years later. It is likely that on one of those occasions Pires met the mother of the future Inês. We do not know where he went when banished from Canton in 1524, but it would not be difficult for him to find his way to *Sampitay*, where Inês' mother 'had some property of her own'. Though Pinto does not tell us the year of Pires' death, it seems from his account that Pires had died a few years before Pinto met Inês de Leiria, perhaps not long before 1540. Pires certainly tried to communicate with Malacca but, it seems, unsuccessfully, for during twenty years or so after 1524 the Portuguese unfortunately were not allowed into China, and communications with the outside world became much more difficult; though it may not have been impossible for Pires to send some letter or other message out of China, it was by no means an easy thing.

SAMPITAY. As regards *Sampitay* it is possible to deduce from Pinto's account that it corresponds to the present town of P'ei chou or Hsin-p'ei-chou, a place near the northern limit of Kiangsu province. The frequency with which Chinese place-names change through the centuries, makes the identification of those mentioned in early accounts sometimes extremely difficult. Perplexities such as we find in Pinto's account of his journey from Nanking to Peking occur in more or less every early account. Pinto's journey, as described in chaps. LXXXVII-C of the *Peregrinação*, can be summarized as follows: With his eight Portuguese companions and thirty or forty other captives, Pinto embarked on a *lantea* (a swift rowing boat) and left Nanking early one morning. At sunset they moored at the village of *Ninhacutem*, which was the native place of the guardian or man in charge of them, the *Chifu*, as he was called, where they remained for three days. He refers to the 'impetuous current' of the river (Yangtze Kiang) the name of which was *Batampina*, meaning 'fish flower', perhaps on account of the 'infinite quantity' of fish there is in it. On the fourth day of their journey they reached *Pocasser*, a good town twice as large as Canton, where there was a great pagoda. They left the next day and arrived at another large town called *Xilingau*. Following up the river, next day they saw large fields with plenty of cattle and other stock, for the space of ten to twelve leagues, and they reached the small town of *Junquileu*.

Here they found the mausoleum of the ambassador *Trannocem Mudeliar*, uncle of the king of Malacca, who had come to China forty years ago to ask for help against the Portuguese[1]. The river was then narrower than at Nanking. The banks up the river are full of 'cities, towns, villages, hamlets, fortresses and castles'. Eleven days later they reached the town of *Sampitay*, where they stayed for five days. After passing many other towns and other places, and towns entirely formed by boats, they arrived in Peking on 9 Oct. 1543.

Now let us examine this part of Pinto's itinerary. He says that on the fourth day of his journey, and after stopping three days at *Ninhacutem*, he reached *Pocasser*, which seems to correspond to Chinkiang[2]. *Ninhacutem* must have lain not far from Chinkiang, for only one day was actually spent on the voyage from Nanking, which, thanks to the 'impetuous current', was long enough to cover the 43 miles of river separating the two cities. From there

[1] This town is referred to in *Comentários* (III, xxx) as *Janquileu*, and the Malay ambassador is called *Tuão Nacem Mudaliar*. The mausoleum had an inscription which the *Comentários* and Pinto give practically in the same words; but they give quite different descriptions of the monument itself, so that Pinto could hardly have taken the story from the *Comentários* (the first edition of which dates from 1557, while the *Peregrinação* was begun some twelve years later). It seems to me more likely that some of Pinto's companions, or even Pinto indirectly, had supplied the information used by the author of the *Comentários*. It is obvious that Pinto wrote something like *Tuan nacem*, which the editor of the *Peregrinação* misread as *Trannocem*, as he certainly did with many other exotic names. It is not easy to make this name —*Tuam Nacem Mudeliar*, or Tuan Hasan Mudeliar—fit into that complicated period of confused early Malayan history. Pires refers to a *Tuam Açem* or Tuan Hasan; but it seems that he was a first cousin, not an uncle, of king Mahmud of Malacca, who ordered him to be killed with others of his family in 1510. See pp. 252–4. Malacca was taken by the Portuguese in 1511, so the voyage of the ambassador to China had been made about thirty, not forty, years before.

[2] In chap. lxxii Pinto refers to the 'custom house of Pocasser', and in chap. ccxxii he mentions the liberation of 'five Portuguese who had been prisoners in the city of Pocasser for more than twenty years'. In both cases *Pocasser* may correspond to Chinkiang. It could hardly be a misprint. However, I cannot find any explanation for the name. Prof. Moule tells me: 'In the sixteenth century Chinkiang was not called anything like *Pocasser*. The only loop-hole is that some towns occasionally had popular names which have not been recorded in the official histories.' This may be the case here. As, according to what Pinto says, the *Chifu* was a native of *Ninhacutem*, a village near *Pocasser*, it is only natural that he may have learned that name, like other names along his course, from his native guardian.

he went to *Xilingau*, which may correspond to Yangchow[1], the most important town at the beginning of the Grand Canal north of the Yangtze, 45 li (15 miles) from Chinkiang. Pinto says that one day after passing another place 5 leagues beyond *Xilingau* he saw large fields for the space of 10 to 12 leagues (32 to 38 miles) before *Junquileu*. The place 5 leagues beyond *Xilingau* must be Shaopo, the next important town, which lies 50 li, 16 miles or 5·6 leagues, from Yangchow; *Junquileu* may correspond to a small town, which Gandar calls *Wei-kiué-leou*—Wei-ch'üeh-lou in English—between Fanshui and Paoying, about 160 li, 56 miles or 17·5 leagues, from Shaopo today[2]. Eleven days after *Junquileu* Pinto reached *Sampitay*, the town where Pires had probably died a few years before. This town must be Hsin P'ei chou, P'i chou or P'ei chou (lat. 34° 25′, long. 118° 6′), which today lies six miles north-east of the nearest point on the Grand Canal, in the neighbourhood of a small lake or morass, in a maze of canals. P'ei chou is Marco Polo's *Pingiu* or *Piju*, which he calls 'a great, rich, and noble city, with large trade and manufactures, and a great production of silk. This city stands at the entrance of the great province of Manzi, and there reside at it a great number of merchants who despatch carts from this place loaded with great quantities of goods to the different towns of Manzi'[3]. It is also mentioned in an Itinerary of 1276, translated and edited by A. C. Moule. Yen Kuang-ta, the author of the Itinerary, says that, travelling by boat, he 'stopped for the night outside the walls of P'i chou . . . All the officials went into the city of P'i to see the sights. The city wall and the walls of the houses were broken down, and the people were living in

[1] J. B. du Halde, in his description of the Grand Canal, going from north to south, says: ' . . . la ville de Yang tcheou, l'un des plus célèbres ports de l'Empire. Peu après il (the Canal) entre dans le grand fleuve Yang tse Kiang, à une journée de Nanking.' *Description de l'Empire de Chine*, III, 156.

[2] For these distances I follow Gandar's important work *Le Grand Canal*, pp. 66–75, which gives the complete itinerary of the Canal from Hangtcheou (Hangchow) to Peking. F. J. Mayers, however, gives an itinerary or table of distances for this part of the Canal, between Chinkiang and Chunghing, the total of which amounts to 511 li. *Record of a Trip in North-East Kiangsu, October 1920*, p. 29, Shanghai 1921. Gandar's distances for the same amount to 485 li, with individual differences as large as 20 li (7 miles). One li is equal to 576 metres; one mile is equal to 2·8 li.

[3] II, lxiii. Yule, *Marco Polo*, II, 141. See A. C. Moule, *Hangchou to Shang-tu.*

the ruins. From this point all the towns we passed were in this condition. We spent the night on the open bank'[1]. It seems that either this happened after Polo's description or, more probably, that the city had recovered before he left China in 1292.

P'i chou, P'ei chou or Peichow are the names usually found in modern books and maps. But, for instance, on a 1928 map 'Compiled by Messrs. The Asiatic Petroleum Co. (N.C.), Ltd., Shanghai' it appears as Sinpichow, and in the *China Postal Atlas* published in 1919 at Peking, the Chinese characters indicating this town mean the same. In this edition of the *Postal Atlas* the correct reading of the three characters is Hsin P'ei chou; beside these there are two other characters in brackets which read P'ei hsien. *Hsien* means district. In a more recent edition of the *Postal Atlas* (Nanking 1933) the place, besides the two Chinese characters, has only the corresponding word Pihsien, in accord with the modern official Chinese nomenclature, *chou* having been changed to *hsien* by the Republic. *Hsin*, which means 'new', is often spelt *sin*, or in the case of places in the south *sun*. For example, a Cantonese would read as *sun* the same character that in the north is read as *hsin* or *sin*. Under the heading Hsia P'ei, i.e., Lower P'ei, a modern Chinese Geographical Dictionary[2] says that the old wall of Hsia P'ei (or old P'ei chou) still exists east of the present P'ei—three li east of P'ei chou, according to Playfair[3]. From the above-mentioned Itinerary of 1276 we see that the city of P'ei was then in ruins, perhaps as a consequence of the Mongol conquest or of the terrible floods that in the thirteenth century forced the Yellow

[1] *Loc. cit.*, p. 397.

[2] *Chung kuo ku chin ti ming ta tz'u tien* [General Dictionary of the ancient and modern Place-names of China], Shanghai, Commercial Press, 1931. According to this Dictionary, in the Later Han (A.D. 25–220) the Seat of the Government of the Hsia P'ei Kingdom was at the 'Old Wall of Hsia P'ei'. 'The Old Wall is east of P'ei Hsien in the modern Chiang-su' (Kiangsu). Though the chronology in such cases is not always very clear and sometimes even contradictory, we gather from the four articles referring to P'ei in the Dictionary (pp. 48 and 537) that the name and status of the city changed several times through the centuries; it seems also that it changed place more than once. None of the four articles refers to either the 'old' or the 'present' cities as *Hsin*, 'New', but at least the two modern maps mentioned above are quite explicit.

[3] *The Cities and Towns of China*, 2549.

River to change its course and thus flow through the region where P'ei was situated, or as a consequence of both. It is evident that in Pires' and Pinto's time a new town had long been built on the bank of the Canal, westward of the ruined one, and perhaps it was called Hsin (or Sun) P'ei, i.e., New P'ei. *T'ai* means 'terrace' and *t'i* (or *t'ai* in Cantonese) means 'embankment' or 'a dyke', 'a bank'[1]. I venture to suggest that in Pinto's time the place was called Hsin (or Sun) P'ei t'ai, i.e., *Sampitay*, or that at least that was the usual name among the boatmen and therefore that was what they called it in speaking to Pinto. This part of Kiangsu province, crossed by the old course of the Yellow River, has been through the centuries the scene of such terrible floods, with consequent changes in the hydrography of the region and probably in the course of the Canal[2], that it is quite possible that after Pinto's time the Canal moved westward. This point of the Canal is 480 li, or 170 miles, from Wei-ch'üeh-lou or *Junquileu*, which means an average of 15·5 miles a day for the eleven days Pinto took to cover the distance, with several locks or sluices to pass through[3] and the water running strongly north-south.

It is not surprising that Pinto in writing *Sampitay* gives a better version of this place-name than in many other cases. Not only did he stay there longer than in any other place during his journey, but the meeting with Inês de Leiria and the story she told about Tomé Pires must have impressed him more than anything else and so was firmly fixed in his memory. It is easy to find many inaccuracies in Pinto's account, but in several points his good faith cannot be doubted. We must, however, allow for some inexactitudes, owing to the fact that he was writing from memory many years later, which made him mix up many of the very exotic oriental names, to the fact that we do not possess the MS of his book and that, no doubt, the editor of the *Peregrinação* (first published thirty-one years after Pinto's death) could not understand most of the names of places and persons

[1] H. A. Giles, *A Chinese-English Dictionary*, 10,577, 10,914, 10,917.

[2] See Gandar, *op. cit.*, pp. 29 *seqq.* On a map published in Yule's *Marco Polo* (II, 144) Peichau is placed on the east bank of the Canal and only a few miles north of the old course of the Yellow River 'from *circa* A.D. 1200 to 1853'.

[3] Gandar, *op. cit.*, p. 26. W. J. Garnett, *Report of a Journey through the Provinces of Shantung and Kiangsu*, p. 19, London 1907.

written by Pinto and probably corrupted many of them, as in the case of *Tuam Nacem* mentioned above. In the case of Tomé Pires, as in many others, the thorough study of the problem has shown how inconsistent and unfair can be the accusations showered on Fernão Mendes Pinto by his detractors[1]. There are still many points in the *Peregrinação* waiting to be explained, perhaps waiting in vain, as has happened in many early accounts. Even in Marco Polo's *Book*, in spite of the exhaustive studies to which it has been subjected, there are points that cannot be understood. In almost every chronicle or early account of travels, place-names that cannot be identified, erroneous and contradictory statements or dates are found, as can be seen over and over again in the course of the notes which accompany the present edition of Pires' *Suma*. However, nobody dreams of saying that Correia, Galvão, Castanheda, Barros, Couto or some other early writer lied, or wrote unblushing falsehoods or mendacities when what they say does not correspond to the proved and established truth.

Pinto's adventures and travels undoubtedly form one of the most wonderful chapters in the history of voyages, and the beautifully written book which he bequeathed to posterity is indeed a jewel in this fascinating kind of literature. The great traveller and writer certainly deserves a fairer treatment, and his memory ought to be referred to with more respect. It is indeed time to pay Fernão Mendes Pinto the reparation to which he is entitled[2].

[1] George Phillips writes: 'I have in my possession a copy of Marsden's edition of *Marco Polo*, owned by Dr. Morrison in 1826, which offers a curious illustration of this, for I find at the end of the book written in pencil the following estimate of the character of the great traveller: "With all deference to the learned Venetian, I come to the conclusion that he is an arrant liar." ' *The Seaports of India and Ceylon*, p. 215. Fernão Mendes Pinto has yet to find his Sir Henry Yule.

[2] One of the many extraordinary adventures of Pinto, during the twenty-one years he spent in the East, was his entry in 1554 as a novice in the Society of Jesus and his abandonment of it in 1556—a serious and unpardonable offence, it seems. Cristóvão Aires, one of his biographers, writes: 'The animadversion of the Jesuits against Pinto, to the point of ordering his name to be stricken out in all their records, contributed much to the systematic discredit of the *Peregrinação*.' *Fernão Mendes Pinto e o Japão*, p. 3. Pinto wrote two letters to the Society, while in its service, one from Malacca in 1554, and

SUMMING UP. Too many queries, alas, are strewn through this attempt to reconstruct Tomé Pires' life. But, maintaining all reserves where evidence is merely circumstantial, the biography of the first European ambassador to China may be sketched as follows: Tomé Pires was born about 1468, perhaps in Lisbon,

another from Macao in 1555; the Jesuits published the first of these letters but not the second, and later the author's name was erased or altered in both of them. See the very interesting and valuable work of Jordão de Freitas, *Fernão Mendes Pinto*, pp. 57–60. Several Jesuit historians utilized the manuscript of the *Peregrinação* before its publication; the first of them was G. Pietro Maffei in his *Historia Indica* (1589), but the mention of Pinto's name was carefully avoided. In his *Historia da Igreja no Japão* the Jesuit João Rodrigues, called Tçuzzu (1561–1634), refers to Pinto only in order to label the *Peregrinação* as a 'book of counterfeits'. A. Cortesão, *Cartografia*, I, 165–6; *A Expansão Portuguesa através do Pacífico*, pp. 170–2. The *Peregrinação* was published for the first time in Lisbon, 1614, after being *corrected* by the chronicler Francisco de Andrada. Francisco de Herrera Maldonado, whose translation of the *Peregrinação* into Spanish was published in Madrid, 1627, says in his introduction: 'Francisco de Andrada, Chief Chronicler of that Kingdom of Portugal, received this original script of Fernão Mendes Pinto, that he might order, correct and arrange it before being printed . . . but he left this book so imperfect that instead of correcting he damaged it further, so that the wrong arrangement he gave it was the reason for its truth breeding doubts and opinions among narrowminded men . . .' fol. lv. This may explain why the *Peregrinação*, after being *corrected*, does not make the slightest reference to such an important event in Pinto's life as the three years he passed in the Society of Jesus, a period during which the Governor-General of India sent him as official ambassador to Japan (1554–6). It has been said that Pinto was expelled from the Society of Jesus 'because he was a *marrano*, i.e., of Jewish blood', and this quite groundless stretch of the imagination has even found its way into the *Encyclopaedia Britannica* (*s.v.* Pinto, Fernão Mendes). Elsewhere I have already shown that Pinto was not expelled, and proved that he was not of Jewish extraction. *Fernão Mendes Pinto não era de origem judaica*, in *Seara Nova*, No. 842, 2 Oct. 1943, Lisbon. If many Jesuits in the past, and some in the present, have attacked Pinto, exceptions can be mentioned. In 1710 Padre Francisco de Sousa, S.J., wrote in his *Oriente Conquistado*: '. . . Pinto well known for the book of his peregrinations, as true in the judgement of the learned as doubtful in the opinion of the vulgar' (p. 106); in 1925 the Rev. L. Besse, S.J., and the Rev. H. Hosten, S.J., wrote: 'The chief witness is Fernão Mendes Pinto, whose veracity on the events of Burma between 1545 and 1552 can hardly be doubted.' *Father Manoel da Fonseca, S.J., in Ava* (*Burma*) (*1613–1652*), p. 45. In *Journal of the Asiatic Society of Bengal*, vol. XXI, 1925. Though many early as well as modern authors have verified and proclaimed the honesty of the author of the *Peregrinação*, the anathema has been pronounced, and the slander has never disappeared. In the last edition of *Roget's Thesaurus of English Words and Phrases*, 'Fernão Mendes Pinto' is still given as synonymous of 'deceiver, liar, story-teller, ass in lion's skin', etc.

where he may have lived in the Porta da Madalena, near the north-east corner of the present Praça do Comércio. His father was the apothecary of King John II, and Tomé Pires himself was the apothecary of Prince Afonso. On 20 Apr. 1511, perhaps then a widower, Pires embarked in Lisbon for India, where he arrived on 7 Sept. or a few days later. In Lisbon he had been appointed 'factor of the drugs' in India, but after eight or nine months in Cannanore and Cochin, Afonso de Albuquerque despatched him to Malacca to make an inquiry about some irregularities, and also as controller of the drugs, scrivener, and accountant of the factory. Pires sailed from Cochin in April or May and arrived in Malacca in June or July 1512. From March to July 1513 he went to Java as factor of a fleet. He left Malacca about the end of January 1515 and arrived in Cochin at the end of February. The greatest part of the *Suma Oriental* was written in Malacca but finished in India. Pires intended to return to Portugal, but the new Governor-General, Lopo Soares de Albergaria, his old personal friend, chose him, on the advice of other Portuguese captains and noblemen in India, to go as ambassador to China. He sailed from Cochin about the end of February 1516, called at Pase and went to Malacca whence he sailed to China on 12 August. Adverse weather caused the fleet which accompanied Pires to return to Malacca; he sailed again from Malacca in June 1517 and arrived at *Tamão* on 15 August, and at Canton near the end of September, disembarking about a month later. After more exasperating delays Pires and his suite left Canton on 23 Jan. 1520, arrived at Nanking in May, and before February 1521 he was in Peking, having travelled by the Grand Canal. After a very bad reception by the court officials he left Peking on 22 May, without seeing the Emperor, and arrived back in Canton on 22 Sept. 1521. Pires and his companions were immediately imprisoned, and on 14 Aug. 1522 he was put in fetters. By the end of 1523 or beginning of 1524 he was banished from Canton and went to *Sampitay*, a town on the banks of the Grand Canal, where two years before, when travelling between Nanking and Peking, he had met a Chinese woman of some wealth by whom he had a daughter called Inês de Leiria. Pires must have died in *Sampitay* not very long before 1540, when he was about seventy years old. *Sampitay* corresponds to the present small town of Hsin-P'ei-chou, Sinpichou or Pihsien, near the northern limit of Kiangsu province.

Tomé Pires can hardly have imagined what the future had in store for him when he agreed to lead the ill-fated embassy to China. When he was on the point of returning to Portugal, happy and rich, what seemed to be a golden opportunity came to him of rising in social status and enormously increasing his wealth in knowledge and money. But he lost all he had, and after terrible sufferings, anxieties, humiliations and miseries, he died unknown, forgotten and hopeless in some town of far-distant China. After reading the *Suma Oriental* and knowing how it was written, in the spare time of a very busy life, we can be sure that, from the time he left Cochin in 1516 until his death some twenty odd years later in China, Pires continued to write. We know, through Correia, as mentioned above, that before 1524 Pires sent the Governor of India 'a book in which he gave an account of the riches and greatness of China'. But no trace of this precious book exists today, no more than of the book dealing with 'weights and measures in all the different places' of the East which Pires himself announces in the *Suma*. The *Suma Oriental* and the letter of 27 Jan. 1516 'about the drugs and where they grow' may give us some sort of idea of what Pires must have written about that China which he knew so thoroughly and intimately. A small reference in Cristóvão Vieira's letter gives some idea of the pains taken by Pires in his study of China—'Tomé Pires said that Nanking lies in 28 or 29 degrees, Peking in 38 or 39 degrees[1].' The correct latitude of Peking is 39° 54′ and the latitude of Nanking is 32° 5′. Nanking is obviously Vieira's mistake; perhaps he meant Nan-chang (lat. 28° 30′ N), through which Pires probably passed on his journey between Canton and Nanking.

It was a great loss to the history of science and of geography that Pires' writings on China disappeared, both those which he sent before 1524 as well as those he never managed to smuggle out of China.

[1] Voretzsch, *op. cit.*, p. 62. Pires' name, which appears in the Lisbon fragments of Vieira's original letter, has been omitted in the Paris copy (fol. 112v.)

THE 'SUMA ORIENTAL' OF TOMÉ PIRES

THE LISBON MANUSCRIPT. Besides the Paris MS there is another in the Biblioteca Nacional of Lisbon, without name of author and containing a portion only of the *Suma Oriental.* This forms part of a codex, MS 299, which begins with a *Chronica geral dos reinos de Guzerate,* fols. 1–41v., and is completed with the *Soma horientall que trata do mar Roxo ate os chims,* fols. 41v.–98v. Fols. 42–47 are missing. According to the index in the codex, it formerly contained also a *Chronica troiana,* which is now in MS 298.

The whole codex is in the same clear hand of about the middle of the first half of the sixteenth century. The beginning is identical with fol. 118v. of the Paris MS, but the text from 'nacimento do njllo' until about the third quarter of fol. 121 r. is lacking, as it occurred on the six missing folios; then follows the description of Arabia, Ormuz, Persia, *Noutaques, Risbutos,* Cambay, Kanara, Narsinga, Malabar, Bengal, Arakan, Pegu, Siam, Cambodia, Champa, Cochin-China, and China[1]. All the rest—Ceylon, Choromandel, Indian Archipelago, Lequios, Japan and the history of Malacca are not dealt with at all. Not only the headings and order of the chapters or items are different in the two MSS, but also the text differs in many points and is much more reduced in the Lisbon MS, mainly in the descriptions of Siam and China. A few variations between the two texts have been pointed out in the notes to the English version, when necessary, but many more exist.

The Lisbon MS must be a copy of some now lost original, which was not that from which the Paris MS was copied. Though the reductions in the text as far as Bengal might be explained as a mere desire to simplify on the part of the copyist or whoever ordered the copy to be made, the same simple explanation could not be applied to the very reduced text after the description of Bengal. On the other hand, the Lisbon MS, at

[1] The folios in the Lisbon and Paris MSS correspond as follows: 41v. = 118v; 48r. to 59v. = 121r. to 125r.; 59v. to 63v. = 130r. to 131v.; 64 = 130r.; 65r. to 70r. = 132r. to 134r.; 70r. to 84v. = 125v. to 129v.; 84v. to 98r. = 134r. to 139v.; 98r. to 98v. = 161r. to 162v.

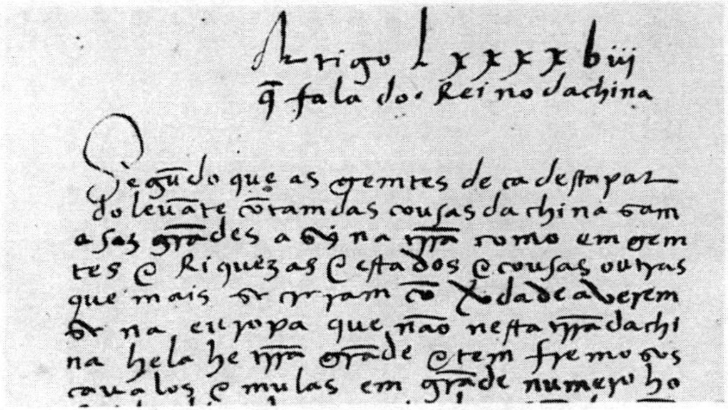

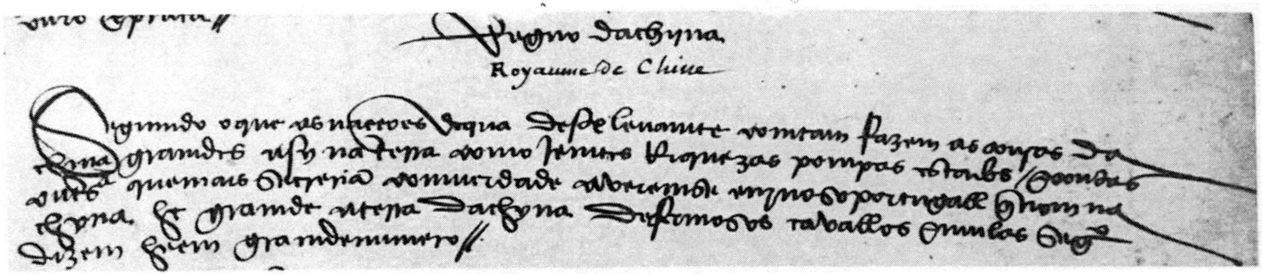

The first lines referring to China in Tomé Pires' *Suma Oriental*. Above—Lisbon MS; below—Paris MS (pp. lxiv-lxx)

PLATE V

Rodrigues' panoramic drawing (fol. 43) of Alor (pp. 202, 526)

least in the passage referring to Malik 'Aiyaz, adds some information to that given in the Paris MS[1]; the date 1522 shows that it was added much after the actual writing of the original and not by Pires himself. Not only are there words and passages which are wrong in the Paris MS and correct in the Lisbon MS, but vice versa, words like *agenb* and *çamarcante* in the former appear wrongly written in the latter. It is possible that the Lisbon MS is the copy of some preliminary report sent by Pires not long after his arrival in Malacca. He must have received instructions, before he left Lisbon, to send reports similar to the *Suma Oriental*, mainly of an economic character though with a historic background. Pires may be referring to this preliminary report, or some other written shortly after it, when in the letter from Malacca 7 Nov. 1512 he says to his brother: 'To the King our Lord I write extensively about the things of Malacca', and then adds that this is sent together with other letters to 'Senhor Jorge de Vasconcelos', the director of the Casa da Mina e India, an early Ministry for the Colonies. Through his stay in Malacca Pires was able to gather much more information about the Far East, the Indian Archipelago, and Malacca itself with the neighbouring countries, which he may later on have included in the *Suma Oriental*. On the other hand there is no doubt that the *Suma Oriental* was officially kept secret, and it is quite possible that only the part of it referring to matters already in the public domain was allowed by the Portuguese authorities to be transcribed and to leave the carefully closed State Archives; the Lisbon MS may be a copy of that transcription.

RAMUSIO'S TRANSLATION. In his *Primo Volume delle Navigationi et Viaggi*, printed in Venice 1550 for the first time, Ramusio publishes, after the *Libro di Odoardo Barbosa*, the *Sommario di tutti li regni, citta, & populi orientali, con li traffichi & mercantie, che iui si trovano, cominciando dal mar Rosso fino alli populi della China. Tradotto dalla lingua Portoghese nella Italiana*. The translation was made from an original similar to the Lisbon MS[2], and

[1] See note p. 35.

[2] As the *Encyclopaedia Britannica* says, the original of this *Summary of all the Kingdoms, Cities, and Nations from the Red Sea to China* has never been printed or noted elsewhere. Article: *Ramusio, Gian Battista.*

it has the part corresponding to the six folios missing in the latter. The translation of this part shows many differences from the Paris MS; for instance the whole section from the reference to the lack of rain in Egypt to the description of Mecca, in fol. 119v. of the Paris MS, is missing in Ramusio. But there are also differences between the Lisbon MS and Ramusio's translation; besides many minor ones, there is a large omission in the description of the Persian Gulf. After five lines under the heading *Del golfo Persico*, Ramusio follows with the Nodhakis (*Naitaques*), whom he calls *Motages*, leaving out all that is contained in fols. 54r.–57r. of the Lisbon MS about the rivers Euphrates and Tigris, and about the Sophy. When referring to Malik 'Aiyaz, Ramusio's translation has the same reference to the year 1522 as in the Lisbon MS. This shows that the copy he used was not made from Pires' original but from a copy similar to the Lisbon MS.

Ramusio did not know who was the author of the account he translated. In the 'Discorso di M. Gio. Battista Ramusio sopra il Libro di Odoardo Barbosa, & sopra il Sommario delle Indie Orientale' which precedes the translation of both, he says: 'In the same way the summary, according to what I have been able to gather, that too was composed by a Portuguese gentleman, who sailed over all the East, and having read Barbosa's *Book*, wished to describe almost the same things in his own way and according to the information which he had received, and specially about that part where are the Moluccas, which have to the north a long coast of mainland, which some Portuguese pilots think, from information received about it in Malacca, runs towards the east; and according to what I have been told, he tried to describe it more in detail than was possible for him, that being one of the most singular and notable parts which is described on the globe, and completely inhabited and full of cities and white people, endowed with good intellect and courteous, and there being there, besides that one, many islands well populated and abounding in all things necessary for human sustenance. Nevertheless when he returned home, if he wanted his book to be seen, he was forced to take away all that part which towards the end deals with the Moluccas and the spices.

And I at that time having ordered with great trouble and difficulty the book to be transcribed in Lisbon itself, I was only able to get one copy, and that imperfect; and I did the same for Barbosa's *Book* in Seville. So much can the interests of the Prince effect. I could well have wished that as I did not fail to take every care to obtain these books, a happier fortune would have brought them into my hands more complete and more correct, and I would much more gladly and quickly have printed and published them; not for any other end or purpose than to please students who take pleasure in such reading. . . .'[1]

Though he wrongly assumed that the author of the *Sommario* had read Barbosa's *Book*, which actually was written a couple of years later, Ramusio's report is very interesting. We see that he had got information about the *Suma Oriental*, complete as we know it through the Paris MS, but he was unable to obtain a full copy in spite of all his strenuous efforts. Whoever supplied him with his incomplete copy had to tell him that the author had been forced to leave out all the matter concerning the Moluccas and the spices—a specious story to cover his inability to do better. What was most important and interesting for Ramusio had been left out, i.e., just the information about the precious spices, the Moluccas and the other islands of the Indian Archipelago, of which nothing more was known than vague references in early writers, the fanciful description of Varthema, who never went beyond India, the very incomplete and second-hand account of Barbosa, and the exciting but brief description of Pigafetta, dealing almost entirely with the relatively small part he saw. It is easy to understand Ramusio's obvious disappointment. In accordance with the policy of secrecy in the matter of discoveries, followed by the Portuguese Crown since the first half of the fifteenth century, the important information about the Spice Islands and the East Indies could not be given forth. Though Spain had officially desisted from her pretensions to the Moluccas by the Treaty of Saragossa (22 April 1529), the

[1] This translation follows the 1613 edition (I, 287v.). The words 'almost' (*quasi*) and 'and the spices' (*& delle spetierie*), and the sentence 'So much can the interests of the Prince effect' (*Tanto possono gl'interessi del principe*), are not in the 1550 edition (I, 310v.).

Spaniards never gave up, and their spies never ceased trying to obtain all the information they could until 1580, when that unfortunate period of Portuguese history began, during which Portugal was under Spanish domination for sixty years[1]. Thus the part of Pires' *Suma* that was allowed to leak out, or that some foreign agent was able to obtain—that in the Lisbon MS and in Ramusio's translation—contained nothing more than unimportant open secrets. The *Sommario* which reached Ramusio had been shorn of everything that might be deemed State secrets. 'Tanto possono gl'interessi del principe', as the famous Venetian sadly says.

THE PARIS MANUSCRIPT. We have seen already that the sixty-two folios containing the *Suma Oriental* form the second part of the codex in which the *Book* of Francisco Rodrigues occupies the first part. The handwriting is so similar to that of Pires' letters, extant in Lisbon, that one is led at first to believe that the present copy of the *Suma* is in the author's own hand[2]. However, a careful examination shows definitely that it is not in Pires' hand. Apart from paleographic reasons, there are many indications in the manuscript indicating that it is a mere copy, and that it could not have been written by Pires himself. In the description of Persia the transcriber of the Paris MS (fol. 122v.) wrote *Ydamca* instead of India, which appears correctly in the Lisbon MS, and consequently in Ramusio's translation (see note p. 21). When referring to the merchants of Persia the Paris MS (fol. 124r.) has *cauo* for Cairo, which is correct in the Lisbon MS and in Ramusio (note p. 29). At the beginning of the description of the 'Kingdom of Cambay' there is a word missing in the Paris MS (fol. 125r.), but in the Lisbon MS and in Ramusio the sentence is complete (note p. 33). A little further

[1] See my essay *O Descobrimento da Australásia e a 'Questão das Molucas,'* pp. 148 *seqq.* I have even reason to believe that the Portuguese had discovered Australia in 1522, and that the secret was jealously kept, as I have shown in another essay—*A Expansão Portuguesa através do Pacífico*, pp. 155–9.

[2] The late Commander Fontoura da Costa, to whom I had sent photostats of the *Suma Oriental* so that he might collate the handwriting with that of Pires' letters in the Tôrre do Tombo, wrote me saying that he had consulted several experts, and the first impression was that the handwriting of the *Suma* 'seems really that of T. Pires'. But later investigations have left no doubt in my mind that it is not from Pires' hand.

on, the Paris MS has, wrongly, *Dalmãs*, which is correctly given as *gemte darmas* in the Lisbon MS and so in Ramusio (note p. 34). In the description of the 'Kingdom of Narsinga' the Paris MS (fol. 126r.) has *que*, which the Lisbon MS correctly gives as *porque*, and so too does Ramusio; the same with *arte* in the one, and *corte* in the others (notes p. 64). When referring to the 'Nayars of Malabar', the Paris MS (fol. 127v.) wrongly has *pequeno Douro*, while the Lisbon MS has correctly *pedaço douro* (note p. 71). When describing the 'Kingdom of Kranganur' the copyist of the Paris MS (fol. 128v.) left out the words *cõ a vimda dos portugueses he*, which are in the Lisbon MS (note p. 79). At the beginning of the 'Kingdom of Comorin' the Paris MS (fol. 129r.) left out the words *O Reino de Comorim cõfina*, which are in the Lisbon MS and likewise in Ramusio; under the same heading it seems that the copyist of the Paris MS missed a whole line—*assy como nos chamamos a duques marquezes comdes & outros* (notes p. 82). In the description of the 'Kingdom of Cochin-China' the Paris MS (fol. 138v.) has *q̃oat[o] Juncos*, which is a mistake for *q̃oarent[a]*, as it appears in the Lisbon MS and similarly in Ramusio (note p. 114). These and other divergences of the same kind, some of them mentioned in the notes, point to the same conclusion, i.e., that the Paris MS is a copy and could not possibly come from Pires' hand.

It is possible that the copy mentioned by Barbosa Machado was the original. Unfortunately he does not say where it was, but he might have seen it in the precious royal library of the Paço da Ribeira, or in the still more precious archives of the Casa da India, which was on the ground floor of the same building, both destroyed by the fire that broke out when Lisbon was devastated by the great earthquake of 1755. Barbosa Machado published vol. III of his *Bibliotheca Lusitana*, where he refers to Pires, in 1752. We do not know where the present copy of the *Suma Oriental* was made, or how it came to be bound together with the *Book* of Francisco Rodrigues. However, when Rodrigues returned from the first voyage to the Moluccas, in 1512, Pires was already in Malacca. They might have had tastes in common, and perhaps became friends. They might have met in India before Pires left for China, and it is quite possible that

Rodrigues obtained a copy of the *Suma Oriental*; perhaps he had a copy especially made for him. But even if they did not meet in India, they certainly met in Canton. Rodrigues was one of the captains of the fleet of Simão de Andrade which arrived at *Tamão* in August 1519, and Pires did not leave for Peking till January 1520. It is likely that Pires sent the original of the *Suma Oriental* to Lisbon before he left Cochin for China, but he certainly kept a second copy or the original draft with him. When the two men met again, Pires probably showed Rodrigues the *Suma Oriental*, which he might have seen before in India or in Malacca, while it was still being written, or Pires may even have handed it to Rodrigues, in view of the difficulties and uncertainties he was anticipating. And if Rodrigues had not a copy already, either one was made while Pires was still in Canton or not much later. The fact that Rodrigues' *Book* is from his own hand and the present copy of the *Suma Oriental* is written on the same kind of paper, strongly suggests that it was made under Rodrigues' order and was first in his possession.

Pires introduces confusion into the division of his work. After saying in the 'Third Prologue' that the *Suma* will be divided up on the lines of the five principal rivers—Nile, Tigris, Euphrates, Indus, and Ganges—he goes on to assert that the five books in which it will be divided will treat: the first from Arabia to Cambay, the second to Bhatkal, the third to Bengal, the fourth to China, and the fifth will be all the islands. These two divisions cannot, of course, be fitted into each other. Then follows, under the heading 'Division of the present *Suma*', a new division which does not fit either of the previous ones. It is also in five books: first—the beginning of Asia, from Africa to the First India; second—to the end of Middle India; third—High India till Ayuthia; fourth—China, Liu Kiu, Japan, Borneo, *Luções*, and Macassars; fifth—all the islands in detail, i.e., the Indian Archipelago. It seems that Pires followed approximately this order, but the copyist of the Paris MS, after beginning the description of the 'Kingdom of Cambay' (fol. 125r.), follows with 'Kingdoms in the land of Kanara' (fol. 125v.), which belongs to bk. II and must come after the 'Kingdom of Goa'; the rest of the description of Cambay (fols. 130r.–131v.) comes after the description of the Malabar. This may be the transcriber's fault, as he wrote at the head of fol. 125v.—'Here you will leave this and look for Cambay which follows after,' and also at the head of fol. 130r.—'It is before the kingdoms in the land of Kanara.' It seems less probable that the mistake originated with Pires himself; besides, in the Lisbon MS and in Ramusio's translation the text follows in the proper order. Under the heading 'Pattars of Cambay' (fol. 131r.) we read: 'You shall find what manner of men they are back in the description of Malabar.' But the Lisbon MS (fol. 62r.) says: 'como adiamte direy no malabar' (as I will say further on in the Malabar). This variance in the Paris MS may be due to the transcriber's substituting *atras* (back) for *adiamte* (further on) in order to adjust the word to the arrangement of his copy. The same hand that wrote 'Osorio' on fol. 5r., also wrote at the bottom of fol. 131v.: 'Here ends the first book; and the second, about the Kanarese and Bhatkal, begins further back.' To complicate things still further, when the Paris MS was assembled, fols. 161r.–163v. (pp. 89–94 of a previous numeration, perhaps when the codex was in Osório's possession), containing the rest of bk. IV, which begins on fol. 139r. with the 'Kingdom of China', were placed after the end of bk. V and the 'Account of the island of Ceylon', which ends on fol. 160v.

It happens also that after he finished bk. V with the 'Account of all the islands', Pires wrote about Ceylon (fol. 160), which he does not mention in any of the divisions of the *Suma*. At the beginning of the 'Account of Ceylon' he explains, however: 'As I followed the coast of the mainland, I had no mind to deal with the island of Ceylon, and afterwards I almost forgot about it; and it did not seem right to fail to speak of it even in a place inserted out of the proper order; but the scarcity of paper made me do this, and so as not to put in a leaf and break the original order.' This shows that he tried to keep to his original plan, and thus the confused disposition of the text in the Paris MS could hardly be his fault. In view of this the 'Account of Ceylon' is placed at the end of bk. II, in the present version, after the 'Kingdom of Comorin', the southernmost of Malabar and India. The last fifteen folios of the Paris MS (164r.–178v.) contain the lengthy historical, geographical and economic description of

Malacca, which could hardly be fitted into the scheme drawn up by Pires, even in bk. III, though after Pegu and before Siam he inserted a note, far from clear, which might suggest that Malacca was dealt with elsewhere. So this is, appropriately enough, given as bk. VI in the present version. The order of the whole text has been accordingly adjusted in the English version, but the Portuguese text is printed exactly in the order of the Paris MS; as stated above, the numeration of the folios, which is kept in the original and in the version, will help readers to find the corresponding portions in the two languages.

Summing up, the present version of the *Suma Oriental* is geographically divided, in general lines, as follows:

Preface;
Bk. I—From Egypt to Cambay, with the Red Sea, Arabia, Ormuz and Persia;
Bk. II—From Cambay to Ceylon, with the Deccan, Goa, Kanara, Narsinga and Malabar;
Bk. III—From Bengal to Indo-China, with Burma and Siam;
Bk. IV—China to Borneo, with Liu Kiu, Japan and Philippines;
Bk. V—Indian Archipelago;
Bk. VI—Malacca.

WHERE AND WHEN THE *SUMA ORIENTAL* WAS WRITTEN. Though the greater part of the *Suma Oriental* was written in Malacca, it is probable that it was begun and finished in India. During the two years and seven months he lived in Malacca, Pires was extremely busy with his official duties, as he himself says at the end of the Preface: 'most of my time was taken up with my duties in connexion with Your Highness' revenue, and the time I devoted to the present work was my leisure.' It is improbable that he was so busy when in India, before embarking for Malacca, and during the twelve months between his return to India and departure for China. During the seven months after his arrival in India he must have collected much information and begun to write the *Suma*; and that he finished it in India is clear from the end of the Preface. There are other passages leading to the same conclusion. In the description of Malacca Pires refers several times to what will be said in the description of China, Sumatra, Java, Bengal, etc., which shows that he wrote it before most of what he says about Malacca; but referring to the 'Ports of Siam' (fol. 137r.) he writes: 'as we have already said in the kingdom and district of Malacca.' Then, when dealing with the weights and measures of Malacca (fol. 176r.), he says: 'Now I will tell how it (Malacca) was taken, and what happened up to the time of my departure for Cochin.' This shows that later, probably when in Cochin, he added to what he had already written in Malacca. Though part of what he wrote on China, Bengal and the Indian Archipelago may have been written in India, he certainly wrote most of it when still in Malacca. For instance, when describing the 'Land of Surabaya' (fol. 154r.) Pires says: 'He (*Pate Bubat*) has already written to this fortress (of Malacca), and they have written him twice.'

The way Afonso de Albuquerque is mentioned in the Preface—which must have been one of the last things written—shows that Pires had finished the *Suma* before the death of the great Governor (16 Dec. 1515). We can conclude that the greater part of the *Suma Oriental* was written in Malacca, and the rest in Cochin, during the years 1512–15.

THE VALUE OF TOMÉ PIRES' WORK. The *Suma Oriental* was a report sent to King Manuel, perhaps in discharge of a commission taken by Tomé Pires before he left Lisbon. His style is far from clear, and no doubt it often becomes more confused owing to the transcriber's mistakes, which sometimes produced words without any meaning, mainly when dealing with local names or expressions. Some passages, as for instance at the end of the description of Java, are almost impossible to translate, for their meaning can hardly be guessed. Similar mistakes, committed by careless or unscrupulous transcribers, appear in other contemporary manuscripts which are known only through second-hand copies, as in the cases of the *Book* of Duarte Barbosa and the *Livro de Marinharia*. But the translation of Barbosa's famous work is a less complicated task, for besides Ramusio's translation, made from a copy seen by Barbosa himself in Seville, there exists a Portuguese copy of the manuscript printed in 1821, and made more understandable through punctuation and revision.

The character of the *Suma Oriental*, devoted mostly to economics, does not afford many opportunities for literary brilliance. But, in spite of the general poverty of style, Pires shows a culture well above what might have been expected from a man of his class, and there are occasional flashes from his pen. This is especially noticeable in the Preface, where he tried his best, although remarking modestly: 'I am a Lusitanian and a man of the people, whose custom it is to belittle their glories and to make too much of the bad things; and the work of composing treatises or summaries is more for foreigners than for natives, because they know how to adorn their compositions'. But then he adds: 'For instance, we see them tell wonders of the Mediterranean Sea, which is a fifteen days' voyage, always within sight of land; so what would they do if they saw the famous eastern conquest of all the ocean, in the course of which there were things as deserving of remembrance and honour among men as they were accounted worthy before God.' There are other passages in the *Suma* where Pires rises above dry description: when, for example, he refers to 'cool Ormuz . . . with all the elegance of beautiful white women' (fol. 122r.); or when he remarks of the burning alive of widows in Blambangan that 'thus they lose their bodies in this life and their souls burn in the next' (fol. 154v.). Nor is he lacking in a sense of humour, as when he ends an interesting reference to the importance of Malacca with the hint that there 'you find what you want, and sometimes more than you are looking for'. He never ceases to praise Malacca, 'end of monsoons and beginning of others'; 'no trading port as large as Malacca is known, nor any where they deal in such fine and highly prized merchandise. Goods from all over the East are found here; goods from all over the West are sold here' (fol. 160r.). Under the heading 'Reason for the greatness of Malacca', together with his enthusiasm he discloses, perhaps better than anywhere else, his vision, spirited criticism and common sense, ending with these picturesque and revealing sentences: 'And true it is that this part of the world is rich and more prized than the world of the Indies, because the smallest merchandise here is gold, which is least prized, and in Malacca they consider it as merchandise. Whoever is lord of Malacca has his hand on the throat of Venice. . . . Who understands this will favour Malacca; let it not be forgotten, for in Malacca they prize garlic and onions more than musk, benzoin, and other precious things' (fol. 178r.). Though he says that 'a captain is sufficient to rule and govern, with governors according to the nations of the merchants', he could not help adding, about the many nationalities of the merchants living there, that 'a Solomon was needed to govern Malacca, and it deserves one'.

The prevailing note throughout the whole *Suma* is that of honesty, which, no doubt, greatly enhances its value. Just as Duarte Pacheco had said before him, 'experience, which is the mother of knowledge, removes all doubt and misapprehension'[1], so too Pires says in the Preface: 'We here have been through everything, and experienced it and seen it.' He does not fail to emphasize his endeavours to find the truth: 'The great island of Java [i.e. his account of it] is finished; as well as I have been able to examine and investigate it, verifying my facts with many people; and whatever they seemed to me to agree about thoroughly, that have I written down, and they certainly do not depart from the truth' (fol. 154v.). In the description of the 'Islands of Timor where the white sandalwood comes from', Pires asserts once more: 'and I asked and enquired very diligently whether they had this merchandise anywhere else, and everyone said not' (fol. 155v.). When he could not verify by himself, he often says that he writes 'according to the information I obtained'. Referring to the Amboina and Banda islands and the navigation about them, he is careful enough to state: 'If in what I say of these islands, together with Banda, I disagree with the pilots, it is not my fault, because in this I am relying on people who have been there; I have learnt this from Moors, from their charts, which I have seen many times, and if their charts are not to be trusted, let it be clear that this should be for reading

[1] *Esmeraldo de Situ Orbis*, G. H. T. Kimble's Hakluyt Society edition, p. 12. Pacheco's famous book was written in 1505–8 and published for the first time in Lisbon 1892.

and not for navigation' (fol. 156v.). After mentioning the imaginary 'breath-snakes', he adds: 'I have never met a man who has seen one' (fol. 128r.). About the story of the kings of Cambay being 'brought up on poison', he remarks: 'But I do not believe this, although they say it is so' (fol. 130v.). About the women of Nias island who 'are made pregnant by the wind', he comments: 'The people believe in this, as others believe in the Amazons and the Sybil of Rome' (fol. 146r.). Of the Papuan 'men with big ears who cover themselves with them', he says: 'I never saw anyone who saw anyone else who had seen them. This story should be given no more importance than it deserves' (fol. 159r.).

The first two books of the *Suma Oriental* have only a limited interest, though they bring a valuable contribution to the study of the countries covered by them; but the other four books describe the until then almost unknown world beyond India, by one who lived for two and a half years in the centre of the Far Eastern countries, and visited some of them. Leaving aside the accounts of medieval European travellers, Pires' *Suma* contains the first trustworthy information on the countries and islands lying from Bengal to Japan. The information given about the lands visited by himself is, of course, more valuable and vivid than that which he obtained second-hand; but even the latter is exceptionally interesting for the time, owing to the place where he collected it and his official position, which brought him in direct touch with the cosmopolitan world of oriental travellers, ship's captains, pilots and merchants who frequented Malacca, to say nothing of the reports of many Portuguese. No need to emphasize the especial value of the great wealth of first-hand historical, geographical, ethnographical and commercial information about each and all of the countries and peoples with whom he dealt—it will be easily gathered from the text of the *Suma* and, in many cases, from the accompanying notes. As an instance, among many other important items, three may be mentioned: we find here, for the first time, the name Japan, which appears under the form *Jampon*; Pires' description of Sumatra was not surpassed in detail and accuracy for a couple of centuries; the information about Java, derived from his visit to its north coast, is the most remarkable; the historical account of

Malacca is not only the earliest known, but contains much information not found elsewhere.

The Portuguese discoveries, from the first quarter of the fifteenth century to the first quarter of the sixteenth, and the invention of printing about 1450, were the two main factors in that cosmopolitan enlightenment of the Renaissance, the foundation of Western Civilization. The period of the discoveries coincides with the golden century of Portuguese history. The adventurous spirit of the Portuguese people led them to the science of navigation, which enabled their ships to unveil the mysteries of the great oceans and search out far distant lands, many of them quite unknown to the world, or of which there were only vague references in Europe. With the navigators went the warriors, the missionaries, the merchants, and the men of science and investigators, like Duarte Pacheco, D. João de Castro, Garcia da Orta, Duarte Barbosa, Tomé Pires and many others. Their writings are imperishable monuments[1]. The now happily rediscovered *Suma Oriental*, the value of which was probably surpassed by the later, now unfortunately lost, accounts Pires no doubt wrote in China, is enough to win for him an important place among those Portuguese who, extending and developing their world discoveries, made a great contribution to human knowledge and progress[2]. Above all, Tomé Pires was the

[1] The Hakluyt Society alone has published some twenty-five volumes with early Portuguese books of voyages and other geographical records, and many more dealing in part with Portuguese discoveries and voyages.

[2] Marsden wrote more than two and a half centuries after Pires: 'The Portuguese being better warriors than philosophers, and more eager to conquer nations than to explore their manners and antiquities, it is not surprising that they should have been unable to furnish the world with any particular and just description of a country [Sumatra] which they must have regarded with an evil eye.' *The History of Sumatra*, Preface. Marsden did not know, of course, of Pires' *Suma*, neither did he know the *Livro de Duarte Barbosa*; he hardly even mentions the description made by Pinto of his visits to Sumatra in 1539 (*Peregrinação*, xiii–xxxii). Marsden makes, however, this curious and honest remark, hesitating between the bad reputation of Pinto and his accuracy and proved reliability: 'Many transactions of the reign of this prince (about the years 1539 and 1541) are mentioned by Ferdinand Mendez Pinto; but his writings are too apocryphal to allow of the facts being recorded upon his authority. Yet there is the strongest internal evidence of his having been more intimately acquainted with the countries of which we are now speaking, the character of the inhabitants, and the political trans-

earliest sixteenth-century European to write a large, conscientious and reliable description of the East as a result of his personal observation. As with so many of his countrymen, and many from other countries, he paid a high price for the privilege of serving his fatherland and humanity.

THE PILOT AND CARTOGRAPHER FRANCISCO RODRIGUES

So little is known about Francisco Rodrigues that it is impossible even to attempt a biographical sketch. Besides the information we can gather from Rodrigues' *Book* itself, he is mentioned in two letters of Afonso de Albuquerque to King Manuel, written from Cochin, 1 April and 20 August 1512; in the *Comentários*, III, xxxvii; by Castanheda, III, lxxv; by Barros, II, vi, 7, and III, vi, 1; by Góis, IV, xxv. But all these simply mention Rodrigues in connexion with some event in which he took part, saying nothing about his origin and the rest of his life.

The first known reference to Rodrigues appears in Albuquerque's letter of 1 April 1512, in which he writes of a 'piece of map' he is sending to the King. It was taken from 'a large map of a Javanese pilot, containing the Cape of Good Hope, Portugal and the land of Brazil, the Red Sea and the Sea of Persia, the Clove Islands, the navigation of the Chinese and the *Gores*, with their rhumbs and direct routes followed by the ships, and the hinterland, and how the kingdoms border on each other. It seems to me, Sir, that this was the best thing I have ever seen, and Your Highness will be very pleased to see it; it had the names in Javanese writing, but I had with me a Javanese who could read and write. I send this piece to Your Highness, which Francisco Rodrigues traced from the other, in which Your Highness can truly see where the Chinese and *Gores* come from, and the course your ships must take to the Clove Islands, and where the gold mines lie, and the islands of Java and Banda, of

actions of the period, than any of his contemporaries; and it appears highly probable, that what he has related is substantially true: but there is also reason to believe that he composed his work from recollection, after his return to Europe, and he may not have been scrupulous in supplying from a fertile imagination the unavoidable failures of a memory, however richly stored.' *Ibid.*, 428–9.

nutmeg and maces, and the land of the king of Siam, and also the end of the navigation of the Chinese, the direction it takes, and how they do not navigate farther. The main map was lost in *Frol de la Mar*. With the pilot and Pero de Alpoim I discussed the meaning of this map, in order that they could explain it to Your Highness; you can take this piece of map as a very accurate and ascertained thing, because it is the real navigation, whence they come and whither they return. The archipelago of the islands called *Celates*, which lie between Java and Malacca, is missing'[1]. In the other letter, of 20 Aug. 1512, Albuquerque informs the King that he had sent a fleet to the Moluccas, under the command of António de Abreu, one of the pilots of which was 'Francisco Rodrigues, a young man who has been here, with very good knowledge and able to make maps'. The *Comentários* also mentions this voyage, as pilot of Abreu's fleet, of 'Francisco Rodrigues, a young man who has always been in India as a pilot, and he knew very well how to make a map if necessary, and this is why he (Albuquerque) sent him there'.

Part of the maps and all the sketches contained in his *Book* were drawn during, or as a result of, his voyage to Banda. Rodrigues must have drawn many maps, but unfortunately none has reached us, apart from those in the Paris codex, as far as is known.

THE VOYAGE OF DISCOVERY TO THE SPICE ISLANDS. After seizing Malacca in the middle of August 1511, and before sailing back to India in December of the same year, Afonso de Albuquerque sent ships with ambassadors to Pegu and Siam, and a fleet of three vessels to discover the Spice Islands. The fleet was commanded by António de Abreu, in the ship *Santa Catarina*, with Luís Botim as pilot; the second in command was Francisco Serrão, in the ship *Sabaia*, with Gonçalo de Oliveira as pilot; the third vessel, a caravel, was commanded by Simão Afonso Bisagudo, with Francisco Rodrigues as pilot. In this armada went 120 Portuguese, 60 slaves 'to work the pumps' and two native pilots[2]. Though the chroniclers mention Rodrigues in the

[1] I have dealt at length with this map, and about Rodrigues as a cartographer in my *Cartografia*, II, 122–30.

[2] Albuquerque himself, the *Comentários*, and Correia (II, 265) mention two native pilots, but Barros (III, v, 6), says that 'besides the Portuguese pilots, Abreu took some Malay and Javanese who were used to that navigation'.

third place among the pilots, and Correia says that Gonçalo de Oliveira was the pilot-major of the fleet[1], Rodrigues styles himself on the cover of his *Book*, 'Pilot-major of the armada that discovered Banda and the Moluccas.' As the *Sabaia*, on which Gonçalo de Oliveira was pilot, was shipwrecked shortly after passing Java, and the junk in which Serrão was returning, probably with Oliveira as pilot, was also shipwrecked shortly after leaving Banda, it is possible that Oliveira—who after all seems to have been either inefficient or unlucky—did not come back with Abreu, and that Rodrigues was, in fact, the pilot-major in the voyage from Banda to Malacca.

The small fleet sailed from Malacca perhaps in November 1511[2]. All the chroniclers refer, with more or less detail, to this voyage, but only Galvão and Barros, mainly the former, give information which enables us to trace the itinerary of the fleet. Barros says that from Malacca Abreu went to Grisee (*Agacim*), Amboina, Banda, and back to Malacca. But Galvão writes: 'At the end of this year 1511, Afonso de Albuquerque sent three ships to the islands of Banda and the Moluccas (*Maluco*). And there went António de Abreu as their captain-major, and one Francisco Serrão; there were 120 persons in the ships—no more vessels nor men went to discover New Spain with Christopher Columbus, nor with Vasco da Gama to India, because the Moluccas are no less wealthy than these, nor ought they to be held in less esteem. They went through the strait of *Sabam* along the island of Sumatra and in sight of many others—leaving them on the left hand towards the east—which are called Selayat (*Salites*), past the islands of Palembang (*Palimbão*) and Lucipara (*Lusuparam*); from there they sailed by the noble island of

[1] When Albuquerque refers to the three Portuguese pilots, he mentions Gonçalo de Oliveira first and Rodrigues last, though the latter is the only one he distinguishes with the special reference of being 'a young man of very good knowledge and able to make maps'.

[2] Albuquerque says that Abreu's fleet 'sailed in the month of November, two and a half months before I left' (letter of 20 Aug. 1512). Though Correia asserts that Albuquerque left Malacca for India on 1 Dec. 1511 (II, 268), Galvão and Castanheda (III, lxxv) say that he left in January. The *Comentários* and Correia confirm that Abreu sailed in November; Castanheda says at the end of December; Fernão Peres de Andrade and Jorge Botelho (*Cartas*, IV, 151 and 156), say December.

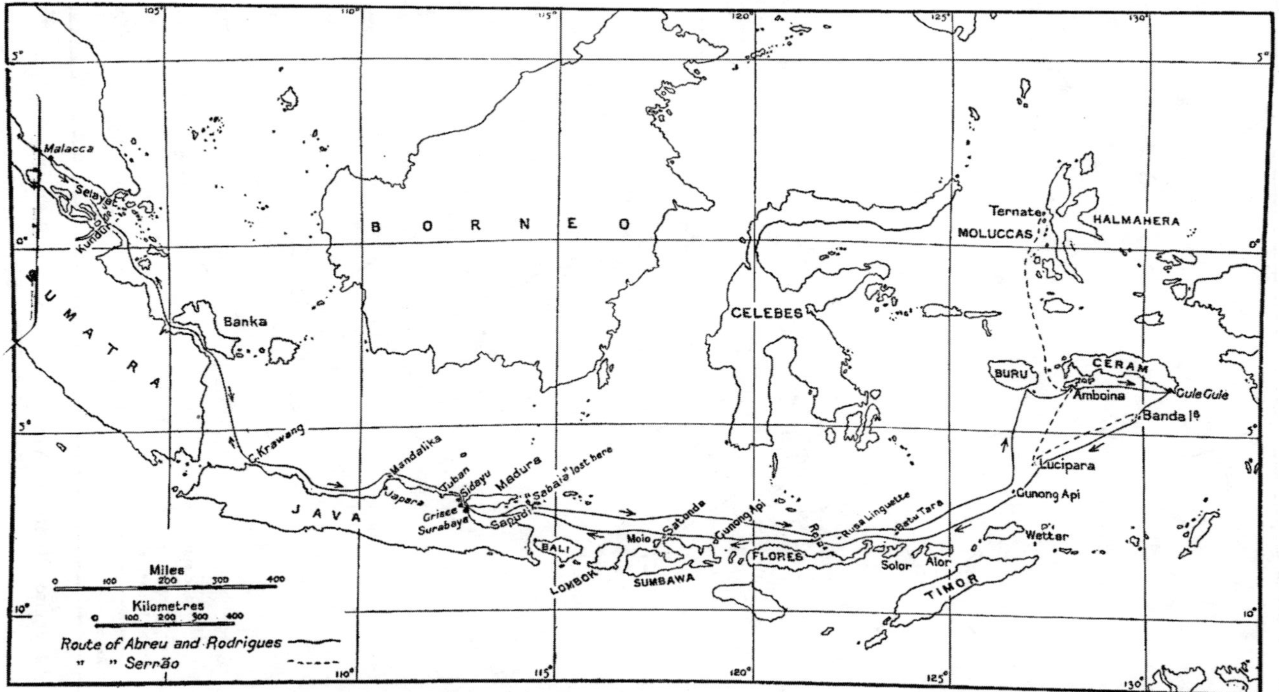

Francisco Rodrigues' Voyage of Discovery to the Spice Islands in 1512 (pp. lxxix-lxxxiv)

PLATE VII

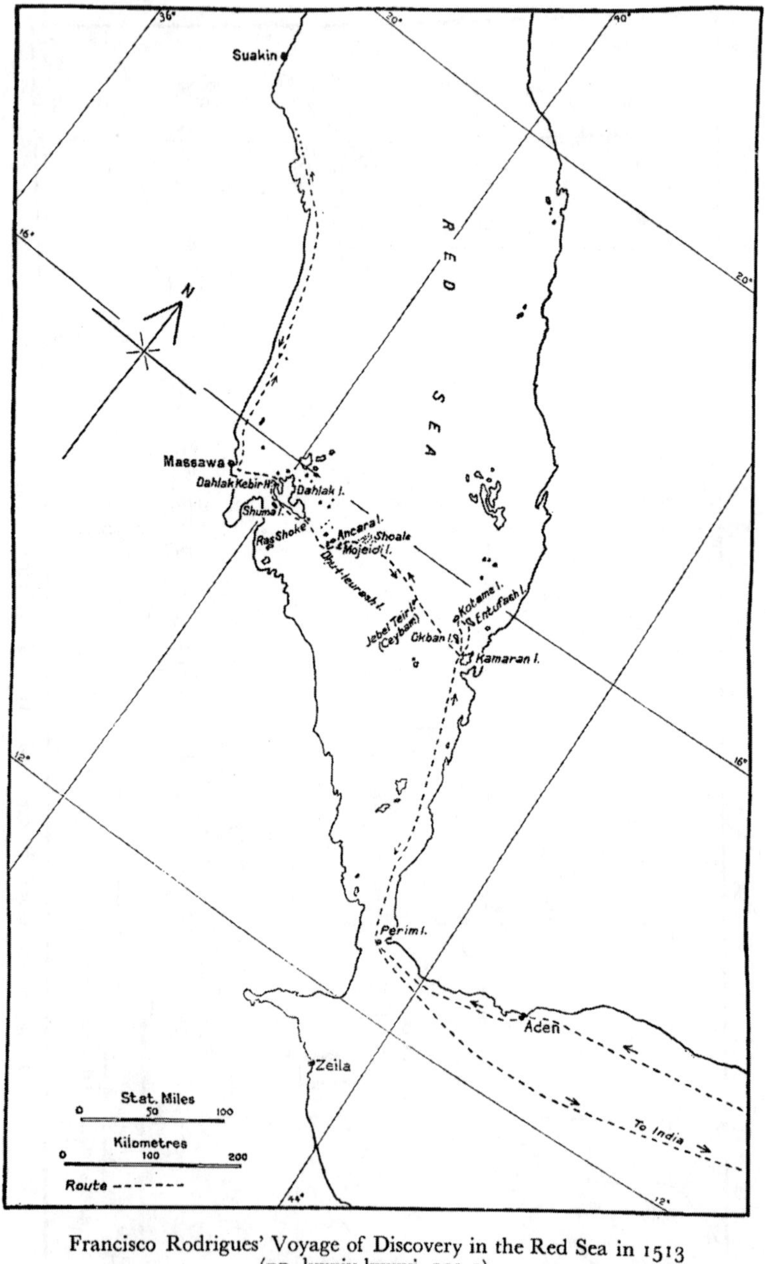

Francisco Rodrigues' Voyage of Discovery in the Red Sea in 1513
(pp. lxxxiv-lxxxvi, 291-5)

Java, and they set their course east, sailing between it and the island of Madura (*Madeira*).' Then Galvão describes the people of Java and continues: 'Beyond the island of Java they sail along another called Bali (*Balle*), and another close to it called Lombok (*Anjano*), Sumbawa (*Simbaba*), Flores and Solor (*Solor*), Adunare and Kawula (*o Galao*), Malua or Alor (*Mauluoa*), Wettar (*Vitara*), Rozengain (*Rosolanguim*) and Aru (*Arus*)—whence are brought the dried birds which are much valued for plumes—and others lying in the same parallel on the south side in seven or eight degrees of latitude, and so near to each other that it seems like a single land. The course along these islands must be above five hundred leagues; the cosmographers called them the *Jaoas*, though now they have different names as you see here. They say that beyond these islands there are others inhabited by white people . . .' After this digression Galvão returns to Abreu's voyage from Madura onwards: 'António de Abreu and those that went with him set their course toward the north of a small island called Gunong Api (*Gumuapè*), because from its highest point streams of fire run continuously to the sea, which is a wonderful thing to behold. From there they went to the islands of Buru (*Burro*) and Amboina (*Damboino*), coasted along that [island] called Ceram (*Muar Damboino*), and anchored in a haven called Guli Guli . . . where they burnt the ship in which Francisco Serrão was, for she was already old, and they went to Banda, which is in eight degrees on the south side, where they loaded cloves, nutmeg and mace in a junk that Francisco Serrão bought there . . . In the year 1512 they sailed from Banda towards Malacca, and in the shoals of Lucipara and Turtle Islands (*Lusopino*) Francisco Serrão was shipwrecked with his junk; from there he went back as far as the island of Mindanao (?) (*Mĩdanao*) with nine or ten Portuguese who were with him, and the king of the Moluccas sent for them. These were the first Portuguese (*Espanhoes*) that came to the Clove Islands, which lie from the equinoctial towards the north one degree, where they stayed seven or eight years. António de Abreu made his way to Malacca, having discovered all the sea and land [above] named[1].'

[1] *Tratado*, ff. 35–6.

Besides the data supplied by Barros and Galvão, some information can be gathered from other documents, mainly some of the maps and drawings of Rodrigues himself. On the map on fol. 36 we find the inscription *pude homde sse perdeo a ssabaia* (*Pude*, where the *Sabaia* was lost) corresponding to Sapudi island which lies near the easternmost point of Madura. Two of the drawings (fols. 94 and 95) show Sapudi island with the inscription *aqui se perdeo a sabaia// & esta Jlha se chama pude* (here the *Sabaia* was lost, and this island is called *Pude*) at the south-eastern point of the island, which is recognizable by the small island Raas (*Jlha de Raz*) complete with the three islets near its eastern point[1]. Diogo Brandão says, in the evidence he gave in the 'Process of the Moluccas', that after the loss of Serrão's ship, the other ship and the caravel went 'near Banda but could not reach it on account of adverse weather, and they had to winter in a haven 25 leagues from Banda, called Gule Gule (*Gullygully*); and, the weather becoming favourable, three months later they went to Banda'[2]. Rui de Brito Patalim states in the same 'Process of the Moluccas' that, after Serrão's ship was lost, 'the two [remaining] vessels went to Banda because the weather was not favourable for going to the Moluccas[3].' Some other information, though indirect, may be gathered from a rutter from Malacca to Java and Banda, dating from the first half of the sixteenth century, contained in *Livro de Marinharia.* It says that when a ship arrives off Cape Flores she must sail towards Batu Tara or Komba, a small island twenty-five miles to the north of Lomblen, then go north-eastwards, and after passing Lucipara (*Gilimão*) she must follow the course north-north-east which will take her to Buru, from where she will sail south-eastwards and reach Banda (p. 267). Pires himself wrote: 'From it (Batu Tara) the route is straight ahead for Banda and Amboina; . . . the other islands along by Solor are not much good for trade because they are out of reach' (fol. 155v.). No doubt this was the route followed by Abreu, and so Rodrigues recorded

[1] These statements of Rodrigues cannot be contradicted, because he was there, and what he says is confirmed by the evidence of Diogo Brandão, of Jorge de Albuquerque and of Andrade, although, besides Galvão's information, Barros says that Serrão's ship was lost between Amboina and Banda.

[2] *Cartas*, IV, 170.

[3] *Ibid.*, p. 167.

it on his map (fol. 37). This map—which covers the Flores Sea, the Banda Sea and the Moluccas—has only thirteen names and inscriptions, seven of which refer to the said route: Cape Flores—Batu Tara—Buru—Amboina—Ceram—Gule Gule—Banda.

With these elements the itinerary of Abreu's expedition from Malacca to Banda can be traced as follows: passing through the channel between Kundur island and Sumatra, and through Banka strait, they reached Grisee, in north-east Java, where they landed for the first time; sailing eastwards Serrão's ship was lost at the south-eastern point of Sapudi island; they sighted Batu Tara and then Gunong Api, landed at Buru and Amboina, sailed along the south coast of Ceram, anchored at Gule Gule, where the two remaining vessels were delayed by bad weather, and finally sailed to Banda[1].

A junk was bought there for Serrão, and the three ships, after loading, set out on the return voyage. Shortly after they left Banda they ran into a storm and Serrão's junk parted from the

[1] In his essay *L'œuvre géographique des Reinel et la découverte des Moluques*, Hamy dealt with António de Abreu's voyage, analysing Rodrigues' map and Galvão's description. According to Hamy, instead of sailing directly to Batu Tara and Gunong Api, and then going north, straight to Buru—as he really did—after Java, Abreu would have carried on along the chain of islands, which lie to the east, as far as Aru (530 miles east of the meridian Gunong Api—Buru), from where he would have returned west, discovered Banda, gone to Buru (more than 200 miles west-north-west), returned again eastwards, going to Gule Gule, and from there returned directly to Malacca. This strange interpretation is due mainly to a mistranslation of a word in Galvão's description. After describing the people of Java, Galvão writes: 'Beyond the island of Java they sail (or go = *vam* or "*vão*") along another called Bali', etc., meaning the people of Java (*a gente desta ylha*), whom he refers to in the previous sentence, not Abreu and his companions. When Galvão refers to the latter (*Antonio Dabreu & os que com elle hiam*), he always uses the past tense 'they went' (*foram*), 'they took their course' (*tomaram sua derrota*), and so forth. The same mistake was committed by Hakluyt, when he translated *vam* into 'they sailed', a mistake which Bethune overlooked in his Hakluyt Society's edition of Galvão's *Tratado* (p. 116). Hamy had to adapt all his interpretation to the mistranslation of the word *vam*, which led him to other mistakes (see note p. 204, and my article *O Itinerário de António de Abreu*, in *Seara Nova*, No. 796, 14 Nov. 1942, Lisbon).

Abreu arrived at Malacca in December 1512 and left with F. P. Andrade for India in January 1513 (Castanheda, III, cii), and then sailed for Portugal. He died in the Azores before reaching the mother country, according to the evidence of Sequeira in the 'Process of the Moluccas', and Barros, III, v, 6.

other vessels and was shipwrecked on the Lucipara islets and shoals. Eventually Serrão and nine Portuguese who were with him reached the Moluccas, where he continued living till his death, which occurred probably at the beginning of 1521. Abreu's ship and the caravel proceeded on their course until they sighted an island which Rodrigues represents in the first of his panoramic drawings, with an inscription saying that 'This was the first land we sighted when we came from Banda to Malacca'. Though another inscription on the same drawing says that it is the 'Beginning of the island of Solor', it must correspond to Alor island (see note on Solor, p. 202). They followed westwards along the north coast of the chain of islands, Rodrigues' panoramic views being drawn as seen from the sea. The last seventeen of the sixty-eight drawings correspond to Java, and the last of them, which must have been drawn off Cape Krawang, north-east of modern Batavia, has an inscription saying: 'And as far as this we discovered the island of Java.' Then they sailed north-westwards and reached Malacca in December 1512, one year after they had started on their voyage. Of the 120 Portuguese who had left for the discovery of the Spice Islands, only 80 returned to Malacca; 10 remained there and 30 died during the voyage. See plate VI.

THE EXPEDITION TO THE RED SEA. The next news of Francisco Rodrigues is given by himself in his *Book*, when he describes the 'Voyage that I made with João Gomes, captain of the caravel, to Dahlak' (fol. 5r.). This voyage took place in June–July 1513, when a Portuguese fleet under the command of Afonso de Albuquerque entered the Red Sea for the first time. We do not know exactly what happened to Rodrigues when he returned to Malacca in December 1512, but he did not stay there long, and he probably sailed to India with Fernão Peres de Andrade and António de Abreu in January 1513. By that time Albuquerque was in Goa assembling the fleet of twenty sail in which he went with 1700 Portuguese and about a thousand natives[1] to the Red Sea. In his letter of 4 Dec. 1513, written

[1] All chroniclers agree that there were 1700 Portuguese, but they differ regarding the number of Malabars and Kanarese; they also agree as to the number of sail, except Correia, who says 24, and Castanheda 19.

from Cannanore to King Manuel, describing at great length the expedition to the Red Sea, Albuquerque does not give the date he set sail from Goa, and the chroniclers are at great variance. Correia says Jan. 28, the *Comentários* Feb. 8, Barros and Góis Feb. 18, Castanheda only says 'March 1513'. The fact that in Dec. 1512 Rodrigues was in Malacca, which he left perhaps at the beginning of Jan. 1513, and that he reached Goa in time to sail with Albuquerque's fleet, shows that the date indicated by Barros and Góis, or even that given by Castanheda more vaguely, must be nearer the truth.

The armada set sail to Cape Guardafui, went to Sokotra, and then proceeded to Aden. After an unsuccessful attempt to seize the town (March 27), Albuquerque sailed towards the Red Sea, which he entered in April. His idea was to go to Suez and destroy the fleet which, according to intelligence he had gathered, the Sultan of Egypt was mustering in order to attack the Portuguese in India; but the monsoon was already nearing its end. The fleet passed beyond the island of Kamaran till it reached the islands Okban, Kotame and Entufash, where it lay at anchor for several days, waiting for favourable winds which would allow it to proceed; but as the winds did not blow, and drinking water was lacking, Albuquerque returned to Kamaran at the beginning of June. It was then that he decided to send João Gomes' caravel, mentioned by Rodrigues, to explore as far as Dahlak and Massawa. Albuquerque in his letter of 4 Dec. to King Manuel reported as follows: 'Returning to Kamaran for the second time, and having decided to make ready to sail in August, I determined to send the caravel out to sea to try to get a *jelba*[1], in order to obtain some news of the land, for throughout the whole year the strait is navigated by these small rowing or sailing *jelbas*. I ordered her to try to reach the island of Dahlak (*Dalaca*) and Massuwa (*Meçuá*), and I gave her a pilot from the same land. And with this I did not mean more than to send João Gomes in the caravel to spend some days discovering land throughout this strait wherever he could. He managed so well that he reached the island of Dahlak and some islands near it, where there are pearl fisheries; he could not get a [*jelba*], because they are light

[1] A small native boat used on the shores of the Red Sea.

and swift craft, which led him through those shoals and sandbanks in such a way that he did not follow the true navigation route. He arrived at Dahlak and moored off some shoals in the harbour. The caravel's skiff went ashore; the people did not care to ask who they were, for throughout the whole strait our entry had been known for some days and the place warned, in such a manner that I certify Your Highness that no more boats or *almadias*[1] came out, nor did birds light on the sea, so stupefied was the Red Sea with our arrival, and so deserted. They only asked them what they wanted. João Gomes told them that I had ordered him to go there, and if they wanted merchandise he would sell it. They answered that there were no merchants in the land, only fighting men. And so they took leave of them, and went around the island and explored it thoroughly. As he had no certain instructions from me, he did not draw near to the main land of Prester John, called Harkiko (*Arquico*), which could be seen as clearly as Ribatejo from Lisbon. Massawa lies farther, in a bay along the coast, one day's voyage[2]. After he had seen everything and discovered all those islands around there, he returned by the main deep-sea route, through which the merchant ships sail. And he did no more than I have said, because he had no other directions or instructions from me, but to discover the way, with the idea of our going there, should some wind arise that would enable us to sail; for if I had entirely mistrusted the weather, I should have provided better in this case, and men I had ready with instructions and letters to send to Prester John. These men they would have set on the main land in charge of his captains, who would have taken them [with them]. I believe he would have done all this, trustworthy man that he is. And he brought me Dahlak painted (on a map), and the islands and sea, the best he could. I am sending this map to Your Highness'.[3] Barros also says that João Gomes brought 'the

[1] A small native boat.

[2] This part of Albuquerque's letter does not agree entirely with Rodrigues when he says 'we ran along the coast of Abyssinia for nine or ten days without seeing . . . any manner of port nor a place where we could disembark' (fol. 6v.). In fact the island of Massawa lies four or five miles north-north-east of Harkiko.

[3] *Cartas*, I, 220–1.

islands mapped as they lay, without anything else'[1]. The pilot of Gomes' caravel was one Domingos Fernandes[2], so Rodrigues was probably sent by Albuquerque with the special task of surveying that part of the Red Sea. Though from the reference of Albuquerque and Barros, mainly the former, it might seem that Gomes himself had made the map sent to King Manuel, we may now safely assume that Rodrigues was its author[3]. It is, however, somewhat strange that Rodrigues does not mention such a map, or that it was not included in his *Book*. See plate VII.

By the end of August Albuquerque was back in India.

After the expedition to the Red Sea, no more is known of Rodrigues until 1519, when he went to China with Simão Peres de Andrade, as we have seen before. Barros says that Andrade's ship was joined in Malacca by three junks, one of which was commanded by Rodrigues, but Góis mentions three ships (*naos*) instead of junks. The squadron arrived in the Canton River in August 1519. In the biographical note on Tomé Pires I have already dealt at length with this disastrous expedition of Andrade. There Rodrigues again met Pires, whom he had known at least in Malacca, when in December 1512 he returned from the expedition to the Spice Islands.

This is all that is known about Francisco Rodrigues. Viscount de Santarém says that he was a pilot born in the Azores, who in 1553 was serving with the English when Thomas Windham (called Tomas de Gidom, or Gidne, in contemporary Portuguese documents) attacked Madeira[4]. The name is a common one, and elsewhere it has been shown to be highly improbable that the two pilots are one and the same person[5]. Many other name-

[1] *Decada* II, viii, 2. [2] *Comentários*, IV, ix.

[3] João Gomes, who, as Barros (II, vii, 5) says, was 'nicknamed *Cheiradinheiro*' (Scent-money), is frequently mentioned by the chroniclers but never as a mapmaker. He was killed in 1519 in the Maldives, where he had gone with an expedition to build a fortress in the island of *Mafacalou* (possibly a contraction of Male and Farukalu), and by the depredations and robberies he practised there he certainly justified the nickname. Góis, IV, xxxii; Correia, II, 568–70.

[4] *Quadro Diplomático*, II, pp. lxxv *seqq.*; J. Blake, *Europeans in West Africa, 1450–1560*, p. 321.

[5] Viterbo, *Trabalhos Nauticos dos Portuguezes*, II, 252–5; A. Cortesão, *Cartografia*, II, 129–30.

sakes of Francisco Rodrigues appear in the chronicles and documents referring to the first half of the sixteenth century, but they have nothing in common with the pilot, cartographer and captain, who left his valuable *Book* to posterity.

THE BOOK OF FRANCISCO RODRIGUES

The *Book* of Francisco Rodrigues occupies the first part of the Paris codex. The original numeration was cut away in binding, and the present numeration, added probably when the codex was bound, begins on the second fly-leaf and goes up to 116. The numbers given in the original table of contents do not correspond with the present numeration, which causes much confusion. For instance, fols. 12 and 14 in the original table of contents correspond with present fols. 9 and 10, and fols. 20 and 22 with 14 and 15, which might indicate that what Rodrigues calls folios (*folhas*) were actually pages and that some folios are missing. But, besides the anomaly of some even numbers corresponding with rectos of folios, it happens that fol. 17 of the original table corresponds with 11 of the present numeration, 22 with 15, 26 to 34 with 18 to 26, and 36 to 38 with 27 to 29. The next 87 folios are not included in the table of contents. Fols. 2v., 3v., 4v., 7v., 8r., 9v., 14v., 15v. and 16v., the versos of fols. 17 to 36, 38 to 85, and 87 to 112, 113r., and the versos of fols. 114 to 116, of the present numeration, are blank. All the writing, in text, maps and drawings, seems to be in Rodrigues' hand. The highly ornamented word *Emmanuel*, at the head of the first page, shows that Rodrigues dedicated his *Book* to King Manuel. See plate XXVIII.

The somewhat mixed contents of Rodrigues' *Book* can be grouped under four distinct headings: nautical rules, rutters, maps, and panoramic drawings. After these have been described it will be possible to study the problem of the date of the *Book's* composition.

NAUTICAL RULES. Fols. 7v.–16r. and 86 contain nautical rules (*Regimentos*). The first rules, signed twice *Framcisquo Rooiz* or *Roiz*, are for ascertaining the latitude at noon, the position of the observer to the Sun in relation to the equator being known; these

PLATE VIII

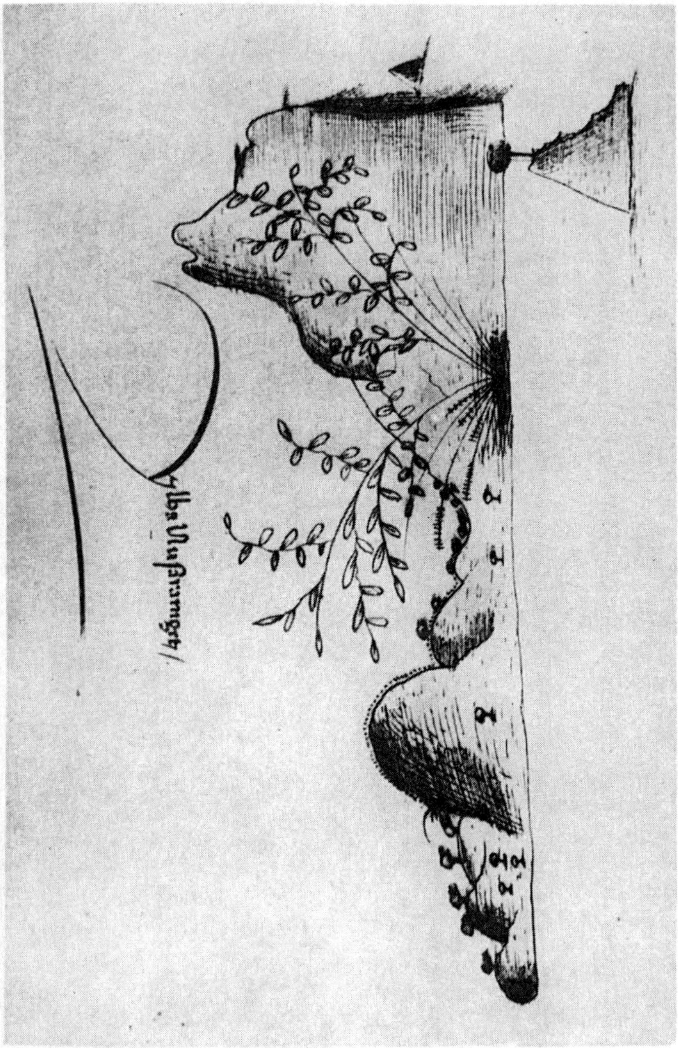

Rodrigues' panoramic drawing (fol. 58) of Sukur Island or Rusa Linguette, seen from the south. It agrees in every detail with a modern description (pp. xci-xcii)

PLATE IX

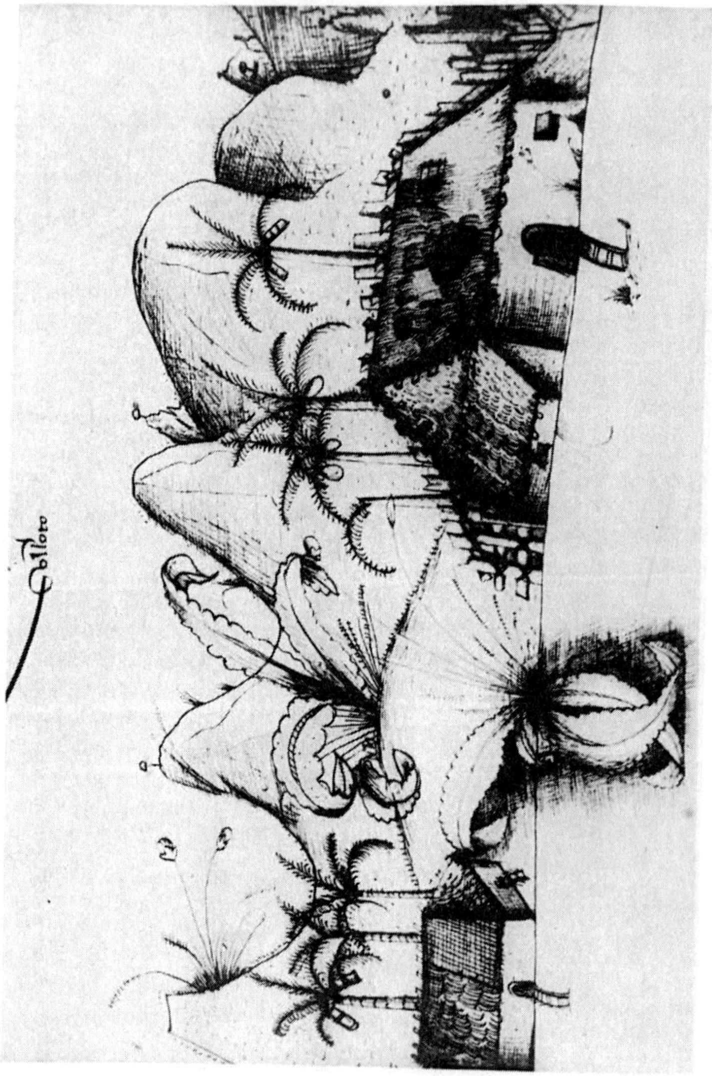

Rodrigues' panoramic drawing (fol. 54) of part of an island, perhaps Adunare (p. 526)

rules are illustrated by a curious figure, in colours, for the graphic determination of the Sun's declination (plate XXXI). They are followed by a table of the Sun's declination for a leap year only. Next comes a 'Canon of leagues', much used by the Portuguese, for ascertaining the distance sailed along any point of the compass, for each degree of latitude, reckoned at 17½ leagues in one case and at 16⅔ in the other. The first case is illustrated with a figure in colours showing a compass rose for measuring a degree in leagues (plate XXXIII). Finally, Rodrigues gives a *regimento* for ascertaining the Sun's declination, with some confused examples, and goes on to discuss the matter in a 'Chapter to explain how you should navigate by shadows'.

These nautical rules must be copied from manuscript *regimentos* which, after the end of the fifteenth century, passed from hand to hand among the Portuguese pilots. Some of these rules or instructions are found in the famous so-called *Regimento de Munich*, the earliest known edition of which dates from 1509 (?) though it must have been printed before, perhaps in 1495 (?). Such is the case with the first figure for determining the Sun's declination and the table of the Sun's declination for a leap year. The whole matter is duly dealt with, at some length, in the notes to the text[1].

RUTTERS. The description of Rodrigues' voyage of exploration and survey to Dahlak, which carried him on in sight of the coast of Abyssinia, is the first rutter in the *Book*. This voyage has been dealt with above and in the notes to the text. The other rutter, rather schematic, is called 'Route to China', i.e., sailing from Malacca to the Canton River, and is discussed in a note to the text (pp. 302–3). They will be referred to again later in this Introduction.

MAPS. There are twenty-six maps or charts in the *Book*, each occupying the recto of one folio. There are also four folios intended for maps which were never drawn; one has only a

[1] These notes were sketched in 1937 by the late Commander Prof. A. Fontoura da Costa, an authority on early Portuguese navigation. They were to some extent developed by Commander D. Gernez, of the French Navy, now in London. The former had undertaken to write a more detailed study of Rodrigues' nautical rules, intended to form a special section of this Introduction, but unfortunately he died 7 Dec. 1940 (b. 9 Dec. 1869).

system of wind roses, two have a central wind rose and a scale of leagues, and the other shows a scale of leagues only.

The Viscount de Santarém had facsimiles made of the twenty-six maps and reproduced them in his *Atlas* of 1849[1]. These facsimiles, especially when in colours, are beautifully done, but of those of the maps with scales of latitudes and of leagues, only no. 4, corresponding to fol. 18, is complete; the others lack the scale of latitudes (except no. 16, corresponding to fol. 30, which has part of it), and some also the scale of leagues. This omission of non-essential parts of the maps was made, obviously, in order to save space. But there were slips too on the part of the copyist; for example, the wind rose on no. 7, corresponding to fol. 21, is incomplete, and on no. 20, corresponding to fol. 37, the word *ambom* (Amboina) is missing. The order of the reproductions in Santarém's *Atlas*, numbered 1 to 26, corresponds with the following order of the MS folios: 116, 115, 114, 18 to 35, 37, 36, 38 to 42. In *Estudos de Cartographia Antiga* (II, 148–56) we find a description of the maps by Santarém, sometimes very detailed, but with too many inaccuracies[2].

[1] Though this *Atlas* is dated 1849, it comprises the maps published in the two previous editions, of 1841 and 1842, plus the maps engraved, or distributed, between 1845 and 1855. I have written elsewhere, at length, on the Viscount de Santarém and his monumental work. *Cartografia*, II, 365–404. Besides the note (the precise date of which we do not know) published in *Estudos de Cartografia Antiga*, the first reference made by Santarém to Rodrigues' *Book* and its maps is found in a letter he addressed from Paris, 12 Oct. 1850, to the Ministry of Foreign Affairs in Lisbon, which financed the publication of the *Atlases*, stating that he 'had just discovered the portolano of the Portuguese pilot Francisco Rodrigues, of 1529'. In another letter of 15 Feb. 1851 he reported on the state of his work. On Nov. 1851 he wrote that four of the maps had already been engraved, and on 28 Jan. 1853 he reported the engraving of the other twenty-two maps of Rodrigues. These documents were published in 1909 by Jordão de Freitas, *o 2° Visconde de Santarem e os seus Atlas Geographicos*, pp. 114–23. On 5 June 1854 Santarém sent to the Ministry a list of fifty-seven copies of the *Atlas* he had presented before 9 April 1851 (new sheets were sent, or were supposed to be sent, loose later, as they were being engraved) to several learned institutions and personalities in various countries.

[2] For example, the map (fol. 22), with the outline of the Brazilian coast, is given as 'West coast of South Africa'. Many mistakes, like this particular one, are probably due to the difficulty of interpreting Santarém's writing; but others were undoubtedly made by him. Two instances: When describing the sketch with the Gulf of Tong-King (fol. 38), he writes—'On the wind rhumb is written the word *Varia*, which seems to indicate the compass

The maps, following the order in which they occur in the *Book*, can be divided in five groups: (*a*) The first nine maps, from Europe to East Africa, are drawn on the approximate scale 1 : 13,000,000 and are more or less copied from existing Portuguese prototypes; (*b*) the three from North-east Africa to Malacca are drawn on the same scale and contain a quantity of new information; (*c*) the six from Sumatra to the Moluccas are drawn on various scales from 1 : 4,500,000 to nearly 1 : 8,000,000 and are entirely new; (*d*) the five maps from Malacca to north China, which are entirely new, though simple sketches; (*e*) the three maps with the Mediterranean and Black Sea are drawn on the approximate scale 1 : 6,000,000 and follow existing prototypes. All the maps but the last three have the word *norte*, in small writing, near the end of the rhumb line from the central wind rose which points northwards. These maps, which are reproduced from photographs for the first time in the present work, are described in *Appendix II*.

PANORAMIC DRAWINGS. These occupy the rectos of 69 folios—43 to 85 and 87 to 112. Only the first drawing is in colours; the last twenty-four drawings show only the outline of beaches and mountains, but the first forty-five show also plants, native houses and the natives themselves.

All these drawings were made when Rodrigues was returning from Banda to Malacca, as he saw the land from the sea, sailing along the north coast of the chain of islands from Alor to western Java. The outlines of mountains and sea coasts are continuous through almost all the drawings, as if separate drawings were cut from a general one; this forms a remarkably accurate view of these islands as seen from the sea. Most of the mountains, bays, and villages shown can easily be identified if we compare the drawings with, for instance, the *Eastern Archipelago Pilot*, vol. II. For example, the *Pilot* says: 'Sukur island or Rusa Lin-

variation in these regions.' '*Varia*' is simply a misreading of the word *norte*, which is written on twenty-three of the twenty-six maps, indicating the north. On the description of the sketch with the Canton River (fol. 40) Santarém wrote: 'At the head we read, in Chinese characters, the name of a city, and next—Cidade da China.' The 'Chinese characters' are simply a flourished letter *A*. But these were only notes, published posthumously, without any editing, and rather carelessly; Santarém was too careful and scrupulous to publish them without previous checking.

guette has a conspicuous summit, 865 feet ($263^{m}7$) high, on its north-eastern side, probably the remains of an old crater; the western side of this peak descends very steeply to a fresh-water lake. . . . In the south-western part the island is low and flat. The entire island is wooded, but uninhabited. There is a sandy beach along the west coast, and the east coast is rocky; the north and south coasts are alternately sandy and rocky. A rock, with a single tree on it, lies on the coastal reef extending about two cables from the south-east point of the island.' This description corresponds exactly with the drawing of the *Jlha Nusaramgeti* (fol. 58), even to the 'rock with a single tree on it'. See plate VIII.

The note of realism given to many of the first forty-five drawings, with the representation of volcanoes in activity, houses, plants and natives, is sometimes particularly vivid, as in fol. 60. This no doubt represents the village of Mausambi, in Flores, which appears in the drawing just east of Raja Island, and shows a native palace or temple surrounded by a palisade of stakes, houses, plants and several natives, one of them climbing a coconut palm, the other on top of a hill shooting with a bow at a strange bird (perhaps a *nore*, a variety of parrot which Rodrigues saw in Amboina, Ceram or Banda) perched on a lofty mountain (probably Olo Muku, 3006 ft.) only the summit of which is visible. The drawings are described in *Appendix II*.

One of the curious features of these drawings is the rather artistically drawn plants which decorate many of them. It appears that Rodrigues wanted to give some idea of the local flora, but if that is the case he made a very imperfect attempt, and his drawings are of little use for identifying the plants. The coconut palm (*Cocus nucifera* Linn.) is the only species which can be identified with certainty; it appears in several of the drawings, near the shore. A grass which figures on nearly all the drawings is probably *Imperata cylindrica* Beauv., a species with silvery spikes which is common in the Malayan islands and would probably attract the attention of any one sketching the flora. This grass comes up in large quantities wherever the ground is cleared, and soon becomes a pest. It is known to the Malays as *alang-alang*. The grass-drawings are not all uniform, but it seems that this species must be intended. Another species whose identity is almost certain is *Gynandropsis gynandra* Briq., a widespread tropical weed; this appears in drawing fol. 63. A plant with broad heart-shaped leaves, which appears in some of the drawings, looks like *Alocasia macrorrhiza* Schott, an Aroid much cultivated in Malaya. Apart from the above it is not possible to make any suggestion with confidence[1].

THE DATE OF RODRIGUES' *BOOK*. Rodrigues' *Book*, composed of several distinct parts, was written and drawn over a period of years. When the Viscount de Santarém reproduced Rodrigues' maps in the *Atlas* of 1849 and described them in the note in *Estudos de Cartografia Antiga*, he said that they were drawn between 1524 and 1530; but he did not give the reason for his assertion. The first nine maps, of the western European, Brazilian and African coasts, and the last three, of the Mediterranean and Black seas, are copied from prototypes now more or less known and their interest is limited; but the fourteen maps from Suez to China, mainly those of the Far East, which are entirely new, are of exceptional importance and their dating has particular interest for the history of the cartography of those regions; they therefore deserve special attention. The dating of these maps of the East Indies has been studied by C. H. Coote, E. T. Hamy, G. Collingridge, J. Denucé and E. C. Abendanon. After discussing the problem in my *Cartografia*, I came to the conclusion 'that it cannot be said, as some of the above authors have done, that the date of the Atlas (i.e., Rodrigues' maps of the Eastern Archipelago) is 1511–13 or ±1512, because it was made a little after 1512, though it does not seem an easy task to determine its precise date—unless some document can be found which will supply us with elements so far unknown' (II, 129).

Rodrigues drew or at least completed his maps at different dates, as can be seen at once from the part which comprises the nautical rules and the maps as far as Malacca, mentioned

[1] Mr. J. E. Dandy, of the British Museum (Natural History), to whom I owe the above information on the botanical aspect of the drawings, tells me that Mr. I. H. Burkill, a botanist with first-hand knowledge of the Malayan flora, 'thinks that the author of the drawings, judged by his pen-work, was a bit of an artist, and that he was just playing with the forms he saw—designing in fact.'

in the original table of contents, and all the other matter—rutters, the last fourteen maps, and the panoramic drawings—not mentioned in the table of contents. No doubt the map which shows the eastern part of the Red Sea (fol. 27) was drawn before Rodrigues' expedition to Dahlak and the coast of Abyssinia in 1513, otherwise he would have represented on the map the islands he saw, which he does not. On the other hand, the inscription *agoada de Joham lopez dalluim/ elle descobriu daqui ate Japara* (Watering place of João Lopes de Alvim. He discovered from here to Japara), on the map with north-western Java (fol. 30), refers to a voyage made in March 1513 (see p. 521). This shows that the map was drawn after that date. It might be argued that this inscription was added some time after the map had been drawn, but its names and inscriptions seem to have been written at one and the same time. It is not easy to find on the other maps any indication which might lead to an exact determination of their date. The only conclusion we can reach is that some of the maps, as those with the Red Sea and India (fols. 27, 28) or at least the former, were made before April 1513, when Albuquerque entered the Red Sea. But they must have been made at the beginning of 1511 or not much before, because it is not very likely that Rodrigues, the 'young man' referred to by Albuquerque, had much time to draw them before the seizure of Malacca in August and his sailing for the discovery of the Spice Islands in December of that year. The other twelve eastern maps (between fols. 29 and 42) were drawn in 1513 or shortly afterwards, probably with the help of sketches and notes gathered during the voyage of 1512 and information obtained from oriental pilots.

Rodrigues certainly drew these maps before his voyage to the Canton River in 1519. We can even infer that they were not drawn after or much after 1513. The rutter from Malacca to the Canton River, written on the verso of fol. 37, facing the first of the maps connected with the route to China, indicates that it was added after they had been drawn. This rutter was obviously based on information gathered from some oriental pilot, possibly Chinese, before Rodrigues had direct news from the first Portuguese who went to China in 1513 and returned to Malacca about

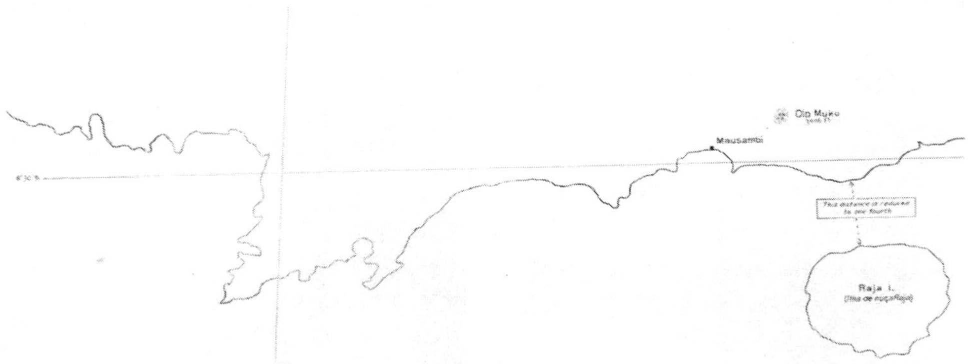
Mausambi
Raja I.

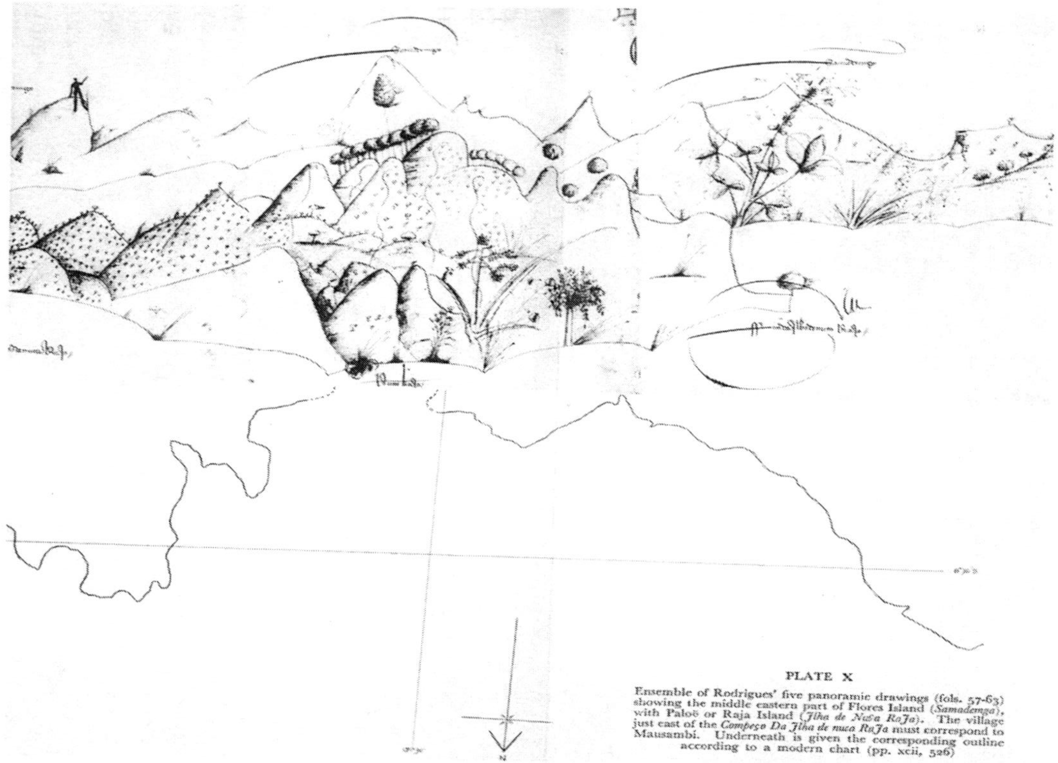

PLATE X

Ensemble of Rodrigues' five panoramic drawings (fols. 57-63) showing the middle eastern part of Flores Island (*Samadenga*), with Paloë or Raja Island (*Jlha de Nuša RaJa*). The village just east of the *Compeço Da Jlha de nuca RaJa* must correspond to Mausambi. Underneath is given the corresponding outline according to a modern chart (pp. xcii, 526)

the middle of 1514 (see note p. 120), otherwise it would not be so schematic, and probably the distances would have been given in leagues, not in native *jaos* (note pp. 302–3). Rodrigues was in India by the end of August 1513, back from the Red Sea. We do not know whether he remained there or went again to Malacca, but we may assume that he received the information reporting the voyage of Alvim to Java in March 1513, just before or when he was drawing the maps of the Eastern Archipelago and the Far East which are contained in his *Book.*

In the rule to ascertain the Sun's declination by the shadows (fol. 86r.), Rodrigues gives an example for the year 1520, related to a Perpetual Almanach of 1508, which might suggest that this part of the *Book* was written in 1520, after Rodrigues had gone to China in 1519. But if this was so, we can hardly explain why the *Book* does not contain a better rutter and better maps recording the voyage from Malacca to the Canton River. The year 1520 referred to was, in all probability, a mere example without any bearing on the actual year of the writing.

It seems from all this that Rodrigues' *Book* was abruptly sent to Lisbon, perhaps on some urgent official demand, shortly after he drew the maps of the Eastern Archipelago and China, i.e., about 1514. In fact he had no time to complete some maps for which folios were prepared but never used, nor could he finish the panoramic drawings of Java, left in outline, but which he probably intended to decorate like the others. Though positive evidence is scant and much of the deduction has to be circumstantial, we come to the conclusion that Rodrigues' *Book* was finished not later than 1514, and that the maps of the Eastern Archipelago and the Far East, the most important of all, can be dated *circa* 1513.

VALUE OF FRANCISCO RODRIGUES' WORK. Rodrigues' *Book* is an important document for the history of geography. Some of its components, for instance, the nautical rules and part of the maps, may be regarded simply as contributions towards the study of a subject already well documented in contemporary and earlier sources; students, however, may find in them abundant matter for speculation and discussion. As regards the rutters of the voyage to Dahlak and the route from Malacca to China, the twelve maps of the Eastern Archipelago and coasts from the Bay of Bengal to China, and the panoramic drawings of the southern islands of the Eastern Archipelago, these are entirely new, and their value and importance are paramount.

Both the rutters have the particular interest of being the first known, at least in a modern European language, for any specific voyage in the Red Sea and in the Far East. It is much to be regretted that the rutters of Rodrigues' voyages to the Spice Islands in 1512 and to China in 1519, which he probably wrote, have not come down to us. We can hardly understand why he did not include in his *Book* a rutter of the voyage to Banda. Perhaps he was unable to finish it in time, before the *Book* was suddenly sent to Lisbon. As regards a map of the Red Sea made during or after the expedition of 1513, it may be assumed that he drew such a map and that it was sent by Albuquerque to King Manuel, as stated above. With his taste for writing about his voyages and observations, and the skill shown in his cartographical work, there is no doubt that Rodrigues wrote much more and drew many more maps, all now unfortunately lost.

The six maps representing the Eastern Archipelago constitute the most important part of the *Book*, because they are the first of that part of the world ever drawn by an European as the result of his direct observation. The sequence of panoramic drawings, though comparatively less important, is apparently unmatched and full of interest, their accuracy being remarkable.

Francisco Rodrigues' *Book* and the *Suma Oriental* of Tomé Pires, written about the same time, complement each other to some extent. Their inclusion in the same codex was as natural as is their publication together in the present edition.

THE SUMA ORIENTAL OF TOMÉ PIRES

PREFACE

Fol. 117r.

To the most serene prince, the most high and most powerful King the King our Lord, here begins the preface to the *Suma Oriental* (Account of the East).

IT is natural for men to desire knowledge, as the master of philosophy testifies; and as this desire is active and fervent in each one according to what befits him, it is not without merit that it is stronger in your Royal Majesty than in any other prince in the world, for your dominions are the greatest. Who does not know that they stretch from the beginning of Africa to China, including the whole of Africa and Asia and part of Europe along the sea coast, with an infinity of islands, [and that they are] very great, rich and very populous within their boundaries, in which dominions there are many provinces, and a large number of kingdoms and a multitude of regions over which your Royal Highness is lord, with beautiful and [un]conquerable fortresses, with many men and arms and exercises of war, subjugating kingdoms in the heart of the Moorish dominions? Who can doubt that your armadas are the largest in the world, as there are always plenty for some to go to Arabia, others to the First India, others to the Second and the Third, in such a way that no one has power to navigate anywhere in your dominions without your permission, and the Moors in the farthest corners are as much intimidated as those in the centre? It is certainly a thing deserving of great glory that such great kings and lords as those of these parts, that is the Sultan of Cairo, the king of Aden, the king of Ormuz, the Sheikh Ismail (*Xequesmaell*) or Sophy—a man famous throughout the world—the Nodhakis (*Naitaques*),

Rajputs (*Resputes*), Cambay on this side [of India], India from Malabar to the province of Choromandel, and Klings (*Quelijs*), the kingdoms of Orissa (*Orixa*), of Bengal (*Bengala*), Arakan (*Racan*), Pegu, Siam (*Siãoo*), Kedah (*Queda*), Malacca, Pahang (*Pahaoo*), Trengganu (*Talimganor*), Patani, Trang (*Terrãoo*), *Odia*, Cambodia, Cochin-China (*Cauchi China*), China with all the islands, powerful peoples both on sea and on land—upon all these Your Highness wages war, carrying your banners into their lands in the name of our Lord Jesus Christ. Of all these, those that are vassals live peaceably and those that are rebels live in fire and torment and are more occupied in protecting themselves than in fighting with your armadas. All this is caused by Your Highness' great power here, which is exercised and extended in war by the most magnificent and exalted knight Afonso de Albuquerque, your Captain-General, who is brave, astute and provident in war and most wise in the other human arts, and who never ceases his labours, fighting continuously now in High India, now in Arabia, and in the midst of it all he never ceases fighting against the name of Mohammed (*Mafamede*). It is clear that God's omnipotence is favouring these efforts because He wills to make Christianity take root throughout your kingdoms, and that these things are accomplished by an immense expenditure of money such as no Christian King has ever made before, because they are never ceasing; yet it must all be considered as money well spent because it is a thing which so exalts, increases and augments our holy Catholic faith, bringing such humiliation, loss and damage to the false diabolic opinion of the abominable, ignominious, false Mohammed, the head of all the vain Moorish religion, that Your Highness has gained great fame and honour among princes in this world and infinite merit before the Most High God, who has so magnificently begun, carried on and almost finished these things.

First foreword. For which reasons—that happen fortunately—occupied as I am with duties which brought me to India and with others entailing a great deal of work that were allotted to me here, I wished that I had some spare time in which I could write something true, so that time could be profitably spent in reading it; and I decided to undertake this *Suma Oriental*, and to begin with the Red or

Arabian Sea and go as far as China including all the islands and to leave out the African part as that is better known. I am not undertaking this account with bold presumption, because that would not be modest, but I ask that where I may be found lacking, it be excused, because my efforts were in good faith, for I have seen such great things that, without offence to some people who have written, their works needed to be corrected. It seemed to me an honourable thing to put some part of all this glory into writing, as if I were so bold as to have the mind of a Greek, the tongue of a Roman and Betic vivacity | to speak of *Fol. 117v.*
such simple, and yet such fortunate things as these of the East; but as I am a Lusitanian and a man of the people, whose custom it is to belittle their glories and to make too much of the bad things; and as the work of composing treatises or summaries is more for foreigners than for natives, because they know how to soften their compositions; for instance, we see them tell wonders of the Mediterranean Sea, which is a fifteen days' voyage, always within sight of land; so what would they do if they saw the famous eastern conquest of all the ocean, in the course of which there were things as deserving of remembrance and honour among men as they were accounted worthy before God. If this account is not so impressive as it should be, put it down (?) to my being versed in another art, which I have learnt in the course of time and in which I could give a better account of myself, because necessity was there a stronger incentive to me than in this book reason.

Second foreword

If I were as speedy as the troglodites and the people who killed the Viceroy[1], in going to see for myself, as I was diligent in research into that which I did not see, it would not be surprising if this brief account were more copious (instead of being limited to the land measured along the sea coast). Anyone who likes may laugh at me for going out of my province and out of my proper sphere; but having seen how men speak about things of which they know nothing, without being reproved, it seemed to me that I was less at fault in speaking of these matters,

[1] D. Francisco de Almeida, first Viceroy of India. He was killed with sixty-four other Portuguese, of whom twelve were captains, by the natives in Table Bay, Cape of Good Hope, on 1 March 1510.

because the things I want to speak of are for Your Highness' service and I am your subject and I have a reason for writing if I get the help that is befitting. If I cannot speak with fitting distinction, then the fault is mine, because I have no knowledge of my own. And in this *Suma* I shall speak not only of the division of the parts, provinces, kingdoms and regions and their boundaries, but also of the dealings and trade that they have with one another, which trading in merchandise is so necessary that without it the world could not go on. It is this that ennobles kingdoms and makes their people great, that ennobles cities, that brings war and peace. In this world it is customary for merchandise to be clean—I do not speak of the dealings in it, which are held in esteem—for what can be better than that which is based on truth. Pope Paul II was originally a merchant and he was not ashamed of the time he spent in trade, and the scholars of Athens used to praise trade as a wonderful thing, and nowadays it is carried on throughout the world, and particularly in these parts it is held in such high esteem that the great lords here do not do anything else but trade. It is pleasant, necessary and convenient, although it brings reverses, which make it more esteemed.

Third foreword concerning the arrangement [of this Suma].

I begin in accordance with the everyday procedure in every kind of work, things being first marked out and then cut. The present *Suma* will be divided up by the lines of the five principal rivers in this part of Asia: the Nile, the Tigris, the Euphrates, the Indus and the Ganges.

The Nile divides Africa from Asia and Persia of the Arabians as far as the Tigris; from the Tigris to the Euphrates is the province of the Nodhakis Persians; from the Euphrates to the Indus
Fol. 118 r. are the Rajputs | and Cambay on this side of Goa; from the Indus to the Ganges is Malabar with India and the province of the Klings which contains the kingdom of Orissa. The Ganges has two mouths, one in Cambodia and the other in Bengal, which contains many kingdoms as we shall see later, and from Cambodia to China the rising of each river will be dealt with. And the present *Suma* will be divided into five books: the first will treat of Arabia, Egypt and Persia as far as Cambay; the second will be from Cambay to Bhatkal (*Baticalla*); the third

will be from Bhatkal to Bengal; the fourth will be from Bengal to China; the fifth will be all the islands and that will be the end of the *Suma*.

Division of the present Suma.

It seemed to me convenient in this work to follow the same mechanical way as any craftsman uses in his work, to mark out and then cut it. The *Suma Oriental* is divided into four parts or books[1]; the first will deal with the beginning of Asia, starting from Africa to the First India; the second will be from the First India to the end of Middle India[2]; the third will be the High India on the other side of the Ganges, ending at Ayuthia (*Odia*); the fourth will be about the kingdom of China and all the provinces subject to it, with the noble island of Liu Kiu (*Lequeos*), Japan (*Janpon*), Borneo, the *Luções* and the Macassars (*Macaceres*); the fifth will be about all the islands in detail. And I will divide Asia according to the principal rivers, giving the beginning and the end of each, and if there appears to be anything added or left out in this division, thus differing from the cosmography of Friar Anselm[3] and Ptolemy and others, it must not be looked upon as an invention, because their knowledge was based on second-hand information rather than experience, and we here have been through everything, and experienced it and seen it. And if this reason be not acceptable it must be remembered that a tailor often makes mistakes in cutting in a small area, so it is very much more difficult over such a great distance. I will not try to excuse myself for any carelessness in not speak-

[1] 'Four' is an obvious mistake for five. There is throughout great confusion in the division of the *Suma*, and the three plans proposed by Pires do not coincide. Moreover he added, out of place, new matter which does not fit properly in any of the five books. To complicate matters still further, the transcriber does not seem to have followed the order in which Pires wrote, and when the MS was bound some folios were misplaced. I have rearranged the English text, as explained in the *Introduction*, p. lxxii.

[2] Farther on (p. 65) Pires identifies Second India with Middle India.

[3] *Fradansellmo* or 'Frade Anselmo', i.e. Friar Anselm, a Franciscan friar who visited the Holy Land in 1507–8, and in 1509 published a pamphlet—*Descriptio Terræ Sanctæ*. It is included in Joannes de Stobnicza—*Introductio in Ptolomei cosmographiam, etc.*, ff 33–44, Cracoviæ, and in Henricus Canisius—*Thesaurus Monumentorum, etc.*, Tom. IV, pp. 776-794, Antuerpiæ, 1725. Friar Anselm's nationality is unknown, but possibly he was a Pole. Pires may have known of, or had a copy of, the 1509 pamphlet, but it seems that he used it in this citation only.

ing as clearly as I should, because most of my time was taken up with my duties in connexion with Your Highness' revenue, and the time I devoted to the present work was my leisure, as may be seen from the register of the accounts I kept in Malacca and of my duties in the factory there, all at the command of the Captain-General, who ordered it in Your Highness' service[1]; of which I made lengthier reports.

[1] It should be made clear that the duties performed at the command of the Captain-General were his official tasks, and not the work of his leisure.

SUMA ORIENTAL

WHICH GOES FROM THE RED SEA TO CHINA

Fol. 118v.

COMPILED BY TOMÉ PIRES

FIRST BOOK

[EGYPT TO CAMBAY]

[Egypt to Ormuz—Ormuz—Persia—Nodhakis—Rajputs—Cambay]

[EGYPT TO ORMUZ]

Division of Asia from Africa.

ASIA is separated from Africa on the Mediterranean side by Alexandria, and on the eastern side by the River Nile and from ocean by the south, according to this division, it is separated from the Abyssinian Ethiopia by it and Arabia Felix[1].

Birth of the Nile.

The Nile, the first and most important river, rises near the Cape of Good Hope and flows through Abyssinia in small streams; at the end of Abyssinia, near Arabia Felix, it becomes navigable; it takes an easy course to Egypt and flows into the Mediterranean Sea through several mouths, the chief of which is Damietta (*Damjata*), which passes within about half a league of the city of Cairo. In July and August it is in flood and waters the land, and the people who live on the banks of the river take their flocks and belongings and go up to the hills; and when the water goes down and begins to dry, they sow, from September onwards. The people of Egypt say that this miracle proceeds from the Abyssinians, a Christian people, and for this reason the Abyssinians can go freely and untaxed throughout the Sultan's

[1] This confused sentence is written exactly the same in the Lisbon MS. but it was rearranged in Ramusio's translation.

land, and are held in esteem. The river flows violently and from Abyssinia it is not good to navigate in that direction.

Abyssinia. Abyssinia is bounded on the Red Sea side by Arabia Felix; on the African side by the deserts and by part of Ethiopia; on the ocean side from Guardafui to Sofala it is sixty leagues away from the sea. They are Christians. They have much land and they have both warriors and merchants. They have foodstuffs in their land and gold. They have no seaports and come to trade in Zeila and Berbera and in the Arabian ports along the strait. These people are renowned among the Ethiopians. They all have woolly hair, and instead of being baptized they are branded on the forehead. They have priests, patriarchs and other monks. They go on pilgrimages to Jerusalem and Mount Sinai every year. They are considered in these parts to be loyal, true and faithful knights, and often from being slaves they rise to be kings, chiefly in Bengal.

People come from Aden, from Sheher (*Xãri*)[1], from Fartak, from Dahlak and Suakin to trade with these Abyssinians. The things most prized in Abyssinia are rosewater, dried roses, glass beads, coarse cloth from Cambay and some silks, all kinds of beads, crystal, white cloths, bales of dates, opium.

Abyssinian merchandise—gold, ivory, horses, slaves, foodstuffs, etc.

Fol. 119r. It is convenient that we should continue our account from here to China. In the Asiatic part along the side of the sea every-

The Red Sea. thing is measured and described. This sea has three names: Red Sea, Arabian Sea and Strait of Mecca—Red Sea because of the red barriers which are at the end near Suez, Arabian Sea because it is surrounded by the Arabs, and Strait of Mecca because Mecca, a place of pilgrimage for the Moors, whose Mohammed was born there, is within it; but the proper name is the Arabian Sea.

Size of this sea. From the entrance to this strait up to Suez this sea is bordered by four provinces: on the eastern side lies Arabia Petrea, on the Abyssinian side Arabia Felix. This reaches as far as the Dahlak islands, and Arabia Petrea extends almost to Mecca. Arabia

[1] *Xãri*, more often called *Xaer* or *Xael* by the sixteenth-century Portuguese. The present town of Sheher or Esh-Shihr on the coast of Hadhramaut.

Deserta begins at Mecca and extends to Tor and goes along towards the Mediterranean Sea and divides the province of Egypt from the land of Judea. From Tor and Dahlak is the province of Egypt, that is, it occupies the point or almost the third part of the strait surrounding it.

The strait is entirely surrounded by the above-mentioned lands which are almost all desert and uninhabited and bare without fruit anywhere. There are some islands in the strait with a few inhabitants, like Kamaran, Dahlak, and Suakin, which are there. In this strait there are many rocky banks and they are difficult to navigate. Men do not navigate except by day; they can always anchor. The best sailing is from the entrance to the strait as far as Kamaran. It is worse from Kamaran to Jidda and much worse from Jidda to Tor. From Tor to Suez is a route for small boats [only] even by day, because it is all dirty and bad. This strait has hot winds, so that anything that die, either man or beast, is not allowed to putrefy, but is dried, and from these animals mummy is brought from there to our part of the world. This is not really the mummy, it is the moisture which flows from the dead bodies, after they have been embalmed with Socotrine aloes[1] and myrrh, so that the liquid which flows from our bodies and from these substances is called mummy[2].

The land of Egypt begins at the Mediterranean Sea and includes part of the strait of Mecca. It is bounded on one side by Africa and on the other by Arabia Deserta of Judea. It is all land that is sown at the flooding of the Nile and this sowing is done more between Cairo and our Mediterranean Sea, because between Cairo and the strait it is uncultivated land, but is easier to travel over than the desert. In this province is the city of Thebes where Theban opium is made, which is known here as *afiam*, a thing which is much used here for eating, and in our

Fol. 119v.

Province of Egypt.

[1] Watt says that 'Indian aloes seem first to have been mentioned by Garcia da Orta (1563, Coll. II) as prepared particularly in Cambay and Bengal'. *The Commercial Products of India*, p. 59. Though, when dealing with the Cambay trade, Pires does not mention aloes among the products exported or imported, he refers to the aloes of Cambay in his letter of 27 Jan. 1516 (Appendix I).

[2] In the same letter of 27 Jan. 1516, Pires refers at length to this disgusting stuff, which was formerly supposed to have magical and medicinal properties; but he was cautious enough to state his disbelief.

country it kills. In this country of Egypt it does not rain except for a day or less once a year or once in two years. And the rain which falls is warm, and is of no use. In order to make use of the land, when the Nile is in flood they dam the water, so that they can afterwards water the gardens. All this province is lacking in water.

Where the Sultan is. The chief city of all this land is Cairo. The Sultan is always there. He has many slaves to guard him, Mamelukes, which in the language of the country means people bought with money. There must be as many as five thousand of these and they guard his person. Most of them are renegades who were Christians. He has a large number of wives. He never goes out, nor is he ever seen by the people of the city. He has ministers of Justice—who rarely administer it. When they are annoyed with the Sultan these Mamelukes choose someone else and kill the other. He must be a renegade and they say that this is done because the Christians apostatize in order to attain this dignity—which may be true. Neither son nor relative inherits, but successors are chosen in the said way. He must be a renegade Christian and the more times he has been sold the greater his consequence in the kingdom. The Sultans of Cairo are very poor and even more so now. Those of this kingdom are called *Maçarijs*[1] in these parts. In all his province he has no king, only captains. The Moorish Sophy of Persia, who is known as Sheikh Ismail here, is at war with him, as we shall see later in the description of Ormuz, and he is losing part of it; but as their sons do not succeed, they do not work for the liberty of their country.

He has dominion over Judea and some part of Syria, the principal city of which is Damascus, as well as over Chaldea, Palestine and *Aydumea*[2]. He is not very well obeyed in any of these parts. The greatest revenue he had, on which he maintained himself, was from the pilgrimage to the Holy Sepulchre and the duties on spice passing through Cairo. He is now already getting very little from the spices, and please God that he will get still

[1] From the kingdom of *Maçaram*, probably Mekran according to Danvers, *The Portuguese in India*, I, 314.

[2] Perhaps Aidin, a petty Turkish sultanate near Smyrna in the fifteenth century. Today it is a vilayet.

less from the Holy Sepulchre. The other neighbouring regions are every day joining the Sheikh Ismail against him.

City of Jidda (Judaa). The city of Jidda is on a river, half a league from the sea. It is almost as large a city as Aden but not so strong. It has not such walls and is said to be a weak thing. It must have about five thousand inhabitants and it belongs to the Sultan of Cairo. | Every *Fol. 120r.* year one of the Sultan's slaves is made captain with revenues. The city has no natural products or fruits except dates. Much meat, fish, wheat, rice, barley and millet are brought from Zeila and Berbera and from the islands of Suakin. It has many merchants and is a great trading city. Ships anchor half a league away and that half league to the city is a fathom deep at low tide and three fathoms at high tide. There are men for the garrison, horsemen. The port has water in abundance. All the merchandise of India is unloaded at Jidda. It is about ten days' journey from Aden.

The House of Mecca. A day's journey on land from Jidda is Mecca where Mohammed was born and his descendants. The house of Mecca is large and well built. It has about a thousand people, many of them merchants. The Captain of the city is called *Xecbarqate*[1]. He is one of the Sultan of Cairo's men. This place has no water. It comes in a cart from a place called Arafat (*Arefet*) a league from Mecca[2]. The foodstuffs come from Jidda.

Medina (Almedina). Medina is four leagues journey from Mecca, on the road to Cairo, some way into the desert of Arabia Deserta. It has about a hundred inhabitants. Mohammed with his daughter, son-in-law and companions, lies in a tower in this place. It is a great place of pilgrimage. It has good dates and little water. It is forty days' journey from Cairo to Medina, four from Medina to Mecca, one from Mecca to Jidda and ten from Jidda to Aden with [a favourable] wind.

Where the Sultan's armada is being made. Suez is three days' journey from Cairo. It is the end of the straits and is not a port, nor is it an inhabited place. They say that an armada is being prepared there against us. There are no

[1] Barakat II, who was sherif of Mecca from 1497 to 1525, being a vassal of the Egyptian Sultan.

[2] There is a place called Kahwat Arafat, with a spring conspicuously marked, on the 1 : 253,440 War Office map of S.W. Arabia, some 30 miles (9 leagues) due east of Mecca. This spring still supplies Mecca by means of a covered water conduit.

fortresses nor inhabited places along this three days' journey, only the sea, which is full of rocks and shallows. The wood, at least, that they need has to come from outside his kingdoms, because in all his land and all round the straits there is nothing but sea rushes which grow on beautiful rocks.

The people of this province are warlike. They have many caparisoned horses and they have guns. They are dextrous with the lance on horseback, holding the bridle in one hand, and they wear spurs like the Arabian warriors. They have camels with two humps. These people have many mercenaries who fight so that the others may live by their efforts, and some of them go about pillaging the country. There is little justice because of the fighting people, for they do not live in harmony together.

Christians of the Cimtura.[1]

In this province and also among the Arabs there are many Christians—some of them circumcized and some of them not. The circumcized are called Jacobites and the others Melchites. They have two Lents, one at Christmas and the other the same as ours. They do not marry one another [i.e. Jacobites do not marry Melchites] and many of them are hermits and men of holy life, and some of them are men of property and they are numerous. They are found in Jidda, in Tor and in Mecca. They are considered by these people to be good men.

Fol. 120v.

Their trade in India.

The merchandise which these people take to India comes from Venice in Italy. It comes to Alexandria, and from the Alexandria warehouses it comes by river to the factors in Cairo, and from Cairo it comes in caravans with many armed people. It comes to Tor, but this is not often, because on account of the nomad robbers they need many armed people to guard the merchandise. But at the time of the Jubilee (*Jubileu*)[2], which is

[1] *Cimtura* or *cintura*—Besides meaning waist, *cintura, scintura* or *escintura* (from the Portuguese verb *cindir, scindir* or *escindir*, in Latin *scindere*) formerly also signified a cut or a slash. Thus in this case it may mean 'circumcision'.

[2] This is certainly not the jubilee-year at the beginning of which the liberation of all Israelitish slaves and the restoration of ancestral possessions took place. Pires means perhaps the Islamic Haggi, or great pilgrimage to Mecca which is fixed for certain days in the first half of the month Dulheggia. But as the Hejira has not a corresponding fixed date in the Gregorian calendar, for it depends on the lunar months beginning with the approximate new moon, the Haggi runs in time through the whole year. 1481 was the nearest

held every year in Mecca on the first day of February, when many people come, [the merchandise] is sent to Mecca with them. And from there it comes to Jidda and from Jidda it comes to the warehouses they have in Aden and from Aden it is distributed to Cambay, Goa, Malabar, Bengal, Pegu and Siam.

Merchandise they take to India. They take different kinds of coloured woollen cloths, hats, glass of all kinds and colours, *azernefe*[1], vermilion, quicksilver, copper, steel, arms, silver, gold coinage, opium, mastic, all sorts of glass beads, liquid storax[2], rosewater, camlet (*chamalotes*) of many colours, both fine and other kinds, many fine and costly tapestries and carpets of good workmanship, both large and small, many mirrors.

Arabia Felix. Arabia Felix lies between (?) the Red Sea and Abyssinia. Some say that it reaches Mogadishu (*Magadoxoo*) and goes as far as the Dahlak islands, and they say that it is all a land of white people where there is none of the woolly hair which is proper to this Arabia. Others say that it only goes as far as Cape Guardafui; it is called Felix because it is not so barren as the [other] two, if it extends as far as Mogadishu; its ports are already known, if

year in which the beginning of the Hejira fell on the 1st February; in 1513 it fell on the 7th February, and in 1514 on the 28th January. It may be that the pronunciation of the word Dulheggia sounded to Pires like *Jubileu* ('Joobeelio').

[1] All this portion is missing in the Lisbon MS. The word *azernefe* is repeated further on under the heading 'Merchandise from Malacca for Siam', but it was left out in the Lisbon MS, as if the transcriber did not understand or did not know the word. Ramusio translated it in both places as *orpimẽto*, which means orpiment, yellow arsenic or trisulphide of arsenic. The word *azernefe* is not found in Portuguese dictionaries, but in a letter to Afonso de Albuquerque, written from Malacca in 1510 by Portuguese captives, *azernefe* is mentioned as one of the commodities which it would be profitable to bring there. *Cartas*, III, 12. Watt says that orpiment is a product of India and that it has also always been imported from Burma and China, which agrees with Pires' statement. It seems as though the word *azernefe* (perhaps a simple corruption of the word *arsenico*), meaning orpiment, had vanished from the Portuguese language, as did the word *fruseleira*, also used by Pires, as will be seen later, note pp. 96–7.

[2] Liquid Storax, taken by the Arabs to India, is the fragrant balsam yielded by *Liquidambar orientalis* Mill., of Asia Minor. It is a different product from the 'true storax', styrax benzoin or gum benjamin of commerce, yielded by the benzoin tree, *Styrax benzoin* Dryand., of the Malay Peninsula and Archipelago. In the letter of 1516 (Appendix I) Pires refers at length to liquid storax, which, in his opinion, did not exist.

it extends from the cape to Dahlak; then before you sail through the mouth of the strait it has Zeila and Berbera, and when you are in the straits it has Dahlak and El Qoseir (*Laçari*). From this El Qoseir, which is a port with few inhabitants, they can get to the Nile in three days and in ten you can embark at Cairo; but this not often, as the nomads waylay travellers on this road.

The people of this Arabia are clean and noble. They have fortresses and horsemen. They are at war with Abyssinia, which borders on this Arabia, and they make raids on horseback, in the course of which they capture large numbers of Abyssinians whom they sell to the people of Asia. This land has wheat and good water. People come to trade in these ports from many places, from Cambay, from the whole of Arabia, but chiefly from the city of Aden. They bring coarse cloths of many kinds, glass beads, and other beads from Cambay; from Aden they bring raisins, from Ormuz dates, and they take back gold, ivory and slaves and trade with them in the said ports of Zeila and Berbera. They trade with other places too. Goods are brought from Kilwa, Malindi, Brava, Mogadishu and Mombassa in exchange for the good horses in this Arabia. They have no cities and no king. They live in bands (*cabilas*)[1]. They are a plundering people and very wild. These two ports are an outlet for the whole of Abyssinia, because very little goes to Cairo.

Arabia Petrea.

Arabia Petrea is divided from Persia by the Strait of Ormuz, and from the river that goes to Mecca[2] it is divided from Arabia Deserta by the port of Jidda and along the land it is a populous region and forms part of Palestine[3]. It was called Arabia Petrea because it is bare, sterile and mountainous, all stony and having little water. This province has some cities along the sea coast. It has Jidda, Aden, Fartak (*Fartaque*), the Masirah or Mosera (*a Maseira*) of the cape of Ras el Hadd (*Roscallhate*), and farther

[1] *Cabildas* in the Lisbon MS. Both forms come from the Arabic *ḳabā'il*, plur. ḳabīla, 'tribe', which some Arab writers use as a synonym of Berbers and which were formerly used by the Portuguese to designate Moorish tribes in North Africa. Then they were by extension applied in the East to any band of Moors, either belonging to one or more families or simply living together.

[2] Wadi Fatima.

[3] Pires mixes up Arabia Petrea with Arabia Deserta. These names are properly placed on the large map in the pocket at the end of this volume.

up along the shores of the Strait of Ormuz it has Kalhat (*Calahate*), Muscat (*Mascate*), Quryat (*Curiate*) and other places. Going inland over the mountains, it has good cities with many inhabitants and beautiful land with many people living in it. Of all these cities and places | Aden is the noblest, and a very strong place. The inland cities are called Zabid (*Zebit*), Taizz (*Taees*), Beit el Fakih (*Beitall Faquj*), *Camaran*[1], Sana (*Cana*), *Çinam*[2]. *Fol. 121r.*

The people of this Arabia are warlike. They fight on horseback in the same way as we do, with spurs, and holding the reins in one hand and a lance in the other, and they have a great number of men. The horses in this Arabia are better than all the others in any of these parts. They have a large number of camels and oxen which they use, and other animals. They are hunters, very hard-working men, haughty and presumptuous. This province has a king who is obeyed by all and who is said to be a vassal of the Sultan [of Egypt]. This [king] is always inland as there is always war in his country, because many [of his people] are nomads and the land is rocky, and they will not live in peace and they have no alternative but to steal.

And because Aden is the only populous town in this Arabia, and is the key not only of Arabia but of all the strait, both for those entering and for those leaving, I would say that the rest is all subordinated either to Aden or to Ormuz, and some live independently. Jidda and Mecca and the hinterland are under the Sultan's rule. Aden is the key to the seaports, not to mention the mountains on the mainland (?).

Aden lies at the foot of a mountain, almost flat on the plain, a little town, but very strong, both in walls, towers and ramparts, as well as in all the paraphernalia of gun towers, loopholes, much ordnance and many warriors—for there are always many people of the country paid to fight, apart from the fact that at any alarm a large number [of the people] from inland rush to help. Inside the city there is a beautiful fortress, with a captain in it always prepared as he should be, because for the last ten years they [*Aden*]

[1] This *Camaram* cannot be the Island of Kamaran, because Pires is referring to 'inland cities'. It may have been miscopied, and may stand for the two places Khramr and Amram, north of Sana, or for the city of Al-Makrana, which Varthema called *Almacarana*.

[2] *Çinam* may correspond to Jizam, which Varthema called *Gezan*.

have always been afraid of our armadas, and all the Moors help this city so that it shall not be taken. They fear that if it were taken the end would soon come, because it is all they have left. And this city has already had a great battle, and would have been stormed if the ladders had not disastrously broken with the weight of the people scaling the walls[1]. And the battle was a famous thing because [to capture] such towns the camp has to be taken first, and this town was all but lost by the Moors. This was a famous exploit, although the city was not taken; and it was not very happy afterwards, and its Kashises[2] feel that its destruction will soon come.

With whom they trade. This town has a great trade with the people of Cairo as well as with those of all India, and the people of India trade with it. There are many important merchants in the city with great riches, and many from other countries live there also. This city is a meeting place for merchants. It is one of the four great trading cities in the world, and it has dealings inside the straits with Jidda, to which it trades most of the spices and drugs in exchange for the said (merchandise?). It trades cloth to Dahlak and receives seed pearls in exchange; it trades coarse cloths and various trifling things to Zeila and Berbera in exchange for gold, horses, slaves and ivory; it trades with Sokotra, sending cloth, straw of Mecca, Socotrine aloes, and dragon's-blood; it trades with Ormuz, whence it brings horses; and out of the goods from Cairo it trades gold, foodstuffs, wheat, and rice if there is any, spices, seed pearls, musk, silk and any other drugs; it trades with Cambay, taking there the merchandise from Cairo and opium, and returning large quantities of cloth, with which it trades in Arabia and the Islands, and seeds, glass beads[3], beads from Cambay, many carnelians of all colours, and chiefly spices and drugs from Malacca, cloves, nutmeg, mace, sandalwood, cubeb, seed pearls and things of that sort.

[1] Assault of Afonso de Albuquerque on Aden, in March 1513.

[2] *Caciz* or Kashis among Arabs and Persians means a Christian priest. However, Pires, as well as other sixteenth-century Portuguese writers, used the word to designate any priest, especially a Muslim.

[3] *Matamingos*, or *Matamũgos* as in the Lisbon MS. An ancient word meaning glass beads. The lexicographer António de Moraes e Silva records the two forms. *Diccionario da Lingua Portuguesa*, 1st ed. 1789.

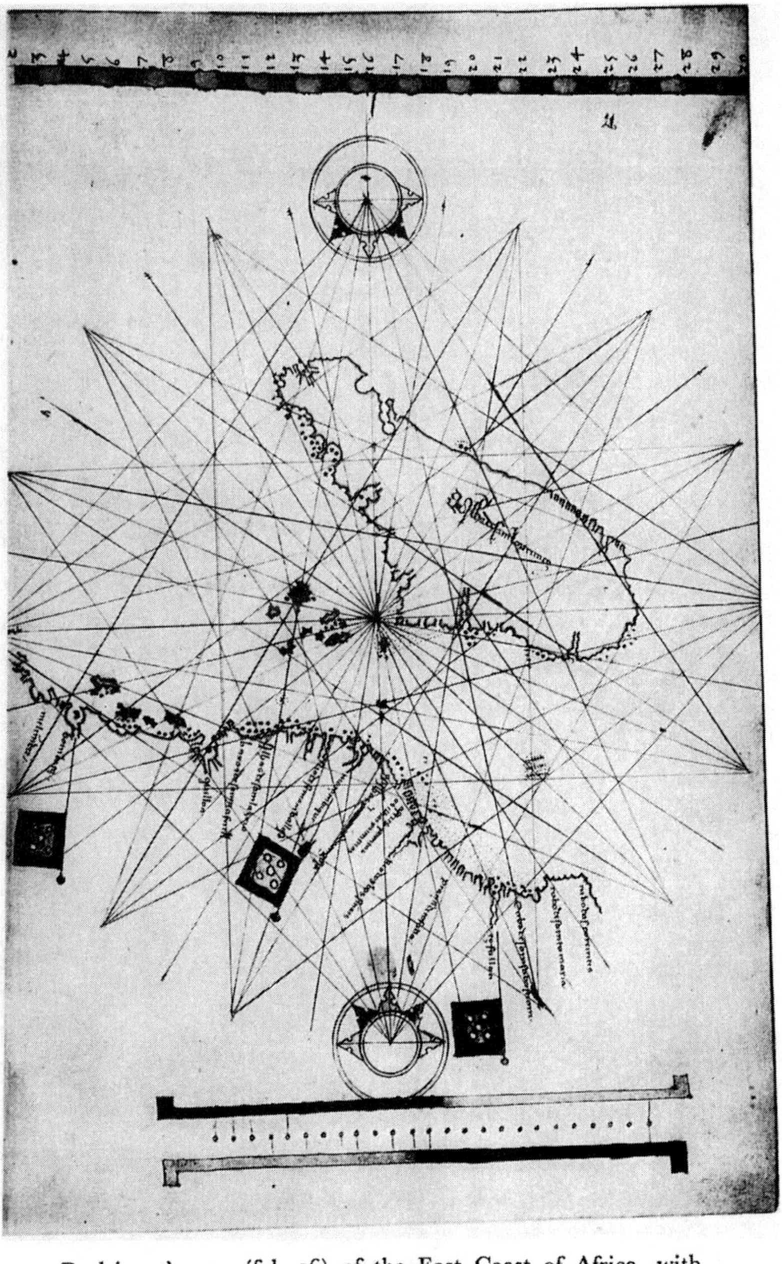

Rodrigues' map (fol. 26) of the East Coast of Africa, with Madagascar (p. 520)

PLATE XII

Rodrigues' map (fol. 27) of the North-east Coast of Africa, part of the Red Sea and of Arabia (p. 520)

It takes a great quantity of madder and raisins to Cambay, and also to Ormuz; it trades with the kingdom of Goa, and takes there all sorts of merchandise and horses both from [Aden] itself and from Cairo, and receives in return rice, iron, sugar, *beatilhas*[1] and quantities of gold; it trades with Malabar in India, where the main market was Calicut, whence it took pepper and ginger; and it traded merchandise from Malacca with Bengal in return for many kinds of white cloths, and it traded the merchandise from Malacca also with Pegu in exchange for lac, benzoin, musk and precious stones, rice also from Bengal, rice from Siam, and merchandise from China which comes through Ayuthia. And in this way it has become great, prosperous and rich, and the king receives all his revenues from Aden alone, for all the rest is nothing. There is no doubt that the madder alone brings the king 100,000 *cruzados*.

Fol. 121v.

Trade.

The merchandise of Aden.

The merchandise of Aden consists of horses, madder, rose-water, dried roses, raisins, opium, and, with the goods coming from Cairo, these make up a large amount (?). People come to the port of Aden from all the above-mentioned places, and they [the merchants of Aden] go everywhere. It is a thing worth seeing, famous and rich, although its drinking water has to be brought in a cart. All the merchandise is gathered there and they keep as much of it as is necessary for the town's trade and for consumption there. The merchants there keep the spices by them, and send them to Cairo in this way: they go from Aden to Kamaran, from Kamaran to Dahlak, from Dahlak to the islands of Suakin, whence they can go all along the straits of this Suakin, to a port called El Qoseir on the Arabia Felix side, and from there it is three days' journey to the Nile and ten days to Cairo; only they do not go this way because of the thieves, but after they have reached the Island of Suakin[2] they go to Jidda, sailing by day, and many are lost because the straits are stormy on account of the land winds; and those who are going to Jidda

[1] *Beatilha* is an old Portuguese word for fine muslin, or a sort of very thin cloth made of cotton or linen.

[2] Pires refers indiscriminately to 'islands' or 'island' of Suakin, perhaps according to the source of his information. Though the town of Suakin occupied the main island, 'there lie in this bay three other islands' as D. João de Castro had already written in his *Roteiro do Mar Roxo*, p. 99.

unload, when they reach Jidda. At the time of the Jubilee, great caravans come to Mecca, and the merchants join them, since they satisfy the leaders. It is a seventy days' journey to Cairo, and sometimes they go from Jidda to Tor by sea; but not often because it is not a main road to Cairo and they are always robbed. The king of Aden always lives in the City of Sana, which is inland, where he has seven or eight large cities with many inhabitants, and most of the Arabs there are Rafadis[1], followers of the Law [of Mohammed], and the king dare not kill them for fear of the Sheikh Ismail, king of Persia and follower of Ali. There is much rosewater in this land of Sana, and dried roses, which are much prized in Abyssinia, and in this city there are finer carnelians than those from Cambay, and there are not so many of them.

Travellers who want to go from Aden to Cairo go to Jidda, and from Jidda to Tor and from Tor to Suez, and they get to Cairo in three days—or rather in five days—if the horse goes well, for it is desert.

Suez, Tor, Jidda.

I shall not talk about Tor or about Suez, because they are not ports nor towns. Suez has been talked of for the last three or four years, because they say that it is a place where an armada is being made. There are no houses there nor within a radius of twenty leagues of it. It is an exposed and solitary place, with bare ground and no grass. It is not possible to go from Suez to Tor except by day and in small light craft, as the water is all shallow and full of rocks. Tor has not more than twenty houses. These belong to Christians of the type I have described above. The inhabited places are very much in the midst of the nomad robbers. The road from Tor to Jidda is almost as wretched as the other. The whole of that land is accursed and there is no profit in it. Jidda is the port of Mecca, small and shallow. In the whole of the straits there is no other place but Jidda. It is on bare ground. They say now that it is being fortified as the people are afraid. It has a garrison. The way from Jidda to Aden is dangerous, but not so much so.

[1] *Rafadi, Rafazi* or *Rafizi* means heretic. It is the name that the Mohammedan Sunnis (orthodox and traditionists) contemptuously give to the Shi'ites (separatists), a rival sect which considers Ali and his descendants as the legitimate successors to the Caliphate.

After Aden comes Fartak, the islands of Kuria Muria and Masirah. The people here are all nomads, merchants and good warriors. Many go from Fartak to Sokotra, Zeila and Berbera as garrison captains. These people also live by trade, but it is not much. From Cape Ras el Hadd (*Roshallhate*) inland the land is under the dominion of Ormuz. The people of Fartak have beautiful swords and all other kind of arms. They are daring men.

This land of Arabia Deserta in the straits of Mecca begins at Jidda and extends as far as Tor and goes to the Mediterranean *Fol. 122r.*
Sea and divides the land of Egypt from Judea. Some affirm that *Arabia*
Mecca is in this country and not in Arabia Petrea. There is *Deserta.*
nothing to be said about this country. It has nomad robbers. It has no trees nor fruit, nor is there water except in a few places known to the nomads. They are robbers and have no other mode of life. They are beyond reason, malicious and go about in bands (*cabilas*) seizing whatever they can find.

ORMUZ

Next in order the civilized island of Ormuz is represented for us with all its kingdom and with the many islands in the straits there. This kingdom, besides being rich and noble, is the key to Persia. It borders on Arabia Petrea on the [*word missing*][1] side, where it has cities under its sway, and on the Cambay side [it is bounded by] the Nodhakis, and on the mainland [it is bounded by] the great Persian province. The islands of Bahrein belong to the kingdom of Ormuz, and also all those in the Strait of Ormuz, and also the Moorish king with the red cap, who is a follower of the sect of Ali, newly converted. The people of Ormuz are warlike and have good arms and horses; they are civilized and domestic men. This kingdom stretches from Cape Ras el Hadd inwards along the straits. It has many people with houses of good workmanship.

The city of Ormuz is in an island which is almost joined on to Persia, about a league away. It has walls, houses with terraces, towers, and ramparts in it. It is very cool, and is one of the four

[1] In this case, as in many others, the transcriber of the Lisbon MS simply omitted the obscure passage.

[great cities] on this side of Asia, with all the elegance of beautiful white women. Its neighbours have no advantage over it in trade. If things to eat are in question neither the Flemings nor the French come up to its citizens; and it has fruits like ours in abundance. The city has people in it from many parts, big merchants. Only this island lacks water; the city contains many cisterns and wells, but now the water that is constantly drunk comes in jars from the mainland in almadias, and is sometimes dear, according to the weather. If however the water from the mainland is not forthcoming, there is water in the city—neither very good nor for so many people. It has islands near it which also have beautiful water. This city was founded on account of the port.

Ships from outside are constantly coming there with merchandise and Ormuz trades with them all. Wherefore the king of Ormuz is immensely rich from the Ormuz dues. Ormuz is ancient both in arms and in trade, and is held in esteem in these parts. Its trade is very necessary in these parts, and it is a very populous, rich and honoured city.

The Straits of Ormuz.

Between Arabia Petrea and the land of Persia there is an arm of the sea with some beautiful towns on either shore, and this is called the Strait of Ormuz. It is not all navigable and for the most part any one who is in the middle can [only] see the land on one side and towards the end [he can see] both. It is navigable farther in. Four or five days' sail with favourable wind from Ormuz there are many islands, the chief of which are called Bahrein, where there is the best pearl fishing in these parts, and these pearls are an important item in the trade of Ormuz, and they are plentiful, and they are generally whiter and rounder than those from anywhere else.

The trade of Ormuz.

Ormuz trades with Aden and Cambay and with the kingdom of the Deccan and Goa and with the ports of the kingdom of Narsinga and in Malabar. The chief things the Ormuz merchants take are Arabian and Persian horses, seed pearls, saltpetre, sulphur, silk, tutty, alum—which is called *alexandrina* in our part of the world—copperas, vitriol, quantities of salt, white silk, many tangas—which are silver coins worth about (?) sixty-five *reis*—[1]

[1] 'The Goa tanga was worth 60 *reis*, that of Ormus $62\frac{34}{43}$ to $69\frac{33}{43}$ reis', which agrees with Pires. *Hobson-Jobson*, *s.v.* See note p. 142.

and musk, sometimes amber, and a great deal of dried fruit, wheat, barley and foodstuffs of that kind.

They bring back pepper, cloves, cinnamon, ginger and all sorts of other spices and drugs, which are greatly in demand in the land of Persia and Arabia, and some of which go to Aden when there is a great deal; but as they are already costly at Ormuz I do not think much goes from there to Cairo for despatch to Italy. They also bring back as much rice as they can, [also] *beatilha*, white cloth, and iron, although their great idea is to bring back pepper, rice and gold with them. Horses are worth a high price in the kingdoms of Goa, of the Deccan and of Narsinga, | so the Ormuz [merchants] go to these kingdoms *Fol. 122v.* with them every year. A horse may be worth as much as seven hundred xerafins—coins worth 320 *reis* each[1]—when it is good. The best are the Arabians, next are the Persians and third are those from Cambay. These latter are worth little, as we shall see later.

PERSIA

Because Ormuz lies near Persia and because Persia is the mainland from which our account starts, it did not seem to me right to leave that country undescribed ; and if I give myself rein in speaking of Persia, it deserves it if only because it is opposed to Mohammed.

The great province of Persia has only the kingdom of Ormuz on the ocean side. Its boundary on the Cambay side is formed by the Nodhakis; on the side of Arabia, by the Strait of Ormuz; inland by the mountain ranges of Delhi (*Delj*); and on the side of Armenia [it goes] nearly to Babylon; and through Media it comes to India[2]. This province is divided into more than forty kingdoms and regions of this land, some of it inhabited and very good, and some of it is mountainous and uninhabited. In their

[1] According to Nunes (*Lyvro dos Pesos da Ymdia*, p. 32), in 1554, the *Xerafin* of Aden was worth 360 reis, that of Ormuz 300 reis. Each xerafin was worth five silver tangas. Further on, when dealing with the Malacca coinage, Pires refers to '*xarafins* from Cambay and from Ormuz', which were worth three *cruzados* (p. 275)..

[2] Although it is written *Ydamca* in the Paris MS, it should read 'India', as in the Lisbon MS and in Ramusio's translation.

language the whole of this province taken thus together is called *Agenb*, and we in our language call it Persia. All the people of *Agenb*[1] are called Parsees (*parses*), which we call *persas* or *persyanos*—Persians.

Provinces and cities of Persia. The best provinces or kingdoms of this Persia are four: Khorasan (*Coraçoni*), Guilan (*Guilani*), Tabriz (*Taurini*) and Shiraz (*Xitaçy*); and in these four provinces there are four chief cities: Tabriz (*Tauris*), Shiraz (*Xiras*), Samarkand (*Çamarcante*) and Khorasan. The people called *Rumes*[2] are in the Khorasan region, and those of Guilaṇ are Turkomans, warlike men and fighters who are highly esteemed in these parts, and who are said to be of Christian birth. The people of Tabriz and Shiraz are like [those of] Paris in France; they are domestic, handsome men and courtiers, but above all the women of Shiraz are praised for their beauty, their fairness of skin, their discretion and the neatness of their dress; so that the Moors say that Mohammed would never go to the province of Shiraz lest he should like it so much that he would never go to Paradise when he died. To these four is also added the province of Media, which they call *Mjdonj*[3] here, which also has a principal city

[1] *Agenb* corresponds to *Al-'Adjam*, an Arabic expression, referring to the whole of the people of Persia. *Agenb* appears as *agens* in the Lisbon MS, and as *Azemini* in Ramusio.

[2] Barros (IV, iv, 16) writes that 'the Moors of India, not understanding the divisions of the Provinces of Europe, called the whole of Thrace, Greece, Sclavonia, and the adjacent islands of the Mediterranean, *Rum*, and the men thereof *Rumi*, a name which properly belonged to that part of Thrace in which lies Constantinople; from the name of New Rome belonging to the latter, Thrace took that of *Romania*. And thus *Rumes* and Turks were different nations; because the latter had their origin in the Province of Turkistan, and the *Rumes* in Greece and Thrace, in view of which they considered themselves more important than the Turks'. After the seizure of Constantinople the term *Rúm* was applied by the Arabs and other peoples of the East mostly to the Turks of the Ottoman Empire. This was the position when the Portuguese arrived in India, as described by Tomé Pires and later by Orta, Barros and Couto, though not very clearly. Orta goes so far as to say that only the Turks of Constantinople were called *Rumes*, and not those of Anatolia, though this was the home of the Rúm empire. Even today the Greeks living in Ottoman territory are still called Rúmi. The various uses of the term throughout the centuries made it rather indefinite and have led to a considerable amount of confusion which, even in recent times, has not been explained satisfactorily enough. No wonder Pires is not very clear.

[3] The Lisbon MS has *mũdini*. Omitted in Ramusio.

called Shúshan (*Ssusan*), and which also belongs to Persia. Now in [the book of] Esther, about Ahasuerus and his wife Vashti, it tells clearly of this city[1]. All these provinces are ruled by the Sheikh Ismail, who is known there in the regions behind the wind as the Equaliser (*Jguoalador*) or Sophy. And as we said in the description of Ormuz that the king has the red cap which is the sign of this Sheikh, it is fitting that we should say where he and his law had their beginning. And the whole of Europe is known here as the people behind the wind. The Persians are horsemen, with arms of every kind beautifully adorned, and with swords of good workmanship. They are men of our colour, form and feature. There is no doubt that those who wear the red cap are more like the Portuguese than like people from anywhere else. The caps are high with twelve pleats and narrowing from the head to the top, and with a coif coming round. The Sheikh Ismail spends most of his time in Tabriz, which is fifty days' journey on camels from Ormuz. The land of Persia has all kinds of domestic animals, such as we have in our own country; and the land of Persia has many ounces, lions, and tigers.

The Persians are very fond of pleasure, very orderly in their dress, and use many perfumes. They anoint themselves with aloes and with costly scented unguents. They have many wives. They are served by eunuchs, and the eunuchs who have charge of the women rise to be great lords. The Moors in general are all jealous men, and thus for all their good looks most of them are sodomites, including the Persians and the people of Ormuz. And they do not consider this to be unsuitable to their condition, nor are they punished for it, and there are even public places where they practise this for money. And those who suffer this are beardless and go about dressed like women, and the Moors laugh at us when we point out to them the turpitude of this sin.

This land of Persia is the most ancient and the most noble of *Fol. 123r.*
all Asia. It has always had monarchs [who are] great lords. This country has many famous provinces. It is they who obtained this Empire of Nabucodonosor and his son Cyrus and Darius and Ahasuerus and Xerxes and others. It was in this land that

[1] In the Lisbon MS this passage was altered; Ramusio suppressed it.

the great Alexander made his widespread conquests. It is not sterile and mountainous as some writers say, but abounding in all delights, with domestic men, full of courtesy, well dressed, magnanimous and valiant in feats of arms, with beautiful horses. They are hunters of wild beasts and of all sorts of birds. And the land of Shiraz is the choicest of Persia, a land abounding in wheat, wine, meat, fruits and—like our own country—not lacking in nuts, chestnuts and dried figs.

Origin of the sect of the Sophy[1].

In the time of Mohammed, a Moorish Arab, he [Mohammed] had Ali for a son-in-law, Ali who was his nephew and married to his daughter Fatima. There were four companions in Mohammed's company; one was called Othman, another Abu Bakr, another Omar and another *Hacabar*[2]. These were helpers in the Koran. After Mohammed's death Abu Bakr was elected captain because he was the oldest. Ali did not suffer this willingly, and showed that the said choice should have fallen upon him as nephew and as son-in-law[3]. He refused to obey Abu Bakr, and when Abu Bakr died Othman became the chief, and thus all of them and then Ali. They say that all these four were Christians and they are all buried in Medina, a place in Arabia which is three days' journey across the desert from Mecca.

From these four who came after Mohammed, there come to be four kinds of Moors, called Shafi'i (*xafij*), Malike (*malaqj*), Hanafi (*anafij*), and Hanbali (*hambarj*)[4]. Each one of them

[1] Sofi or Sophy was the name given for a long time by the Europeans to the Shah of Persia. This '*Sofi*' was Safi-ud-Din (which means 'Purity of Religion') a great supporter of the mystical doctrine of Islam—Sufism, dating from the second century of the Hejira—the principle of which is that through meditation, ecstasy and rigorous observance of discipline, man can raise himself almost to divinity and be identified with it. From the name of the doctrine the name Sufi, or Sophy, was given to this ancestor, and that of Safavi to the dynasty which began with Ismail in 1499 and lasted till 1736.

[2] In the Lisbon MS the four names are given as *Tamão, Bulbacar, Hamaar,* and *Acamar*. The whole of this chapter on the Sophy is omitted in Ramusio. The first four Caliphs who succeeded Mohammed were Abu Bakr, Omar, Othman, and Ali, who died respectively in 634, 644, 656 and 661, all of them disciples and companions of the Prophet. It seems as if this *Hacabar* or *Acamar* is some mistake of the transcriber. I cannot find any name which might properly suggest *Hacabar*.

[3] Ali was cousin and son-in-law of Mohammed, not nephew.

[4] *Xafij, malaqi, anafij* and *hambarj*, appear as *xafim, malaquĵ, anafy* and *ambari* in the Lisbon MS. These four schools of law of the Sunnis date from

departed from Mohammed's own intentions at his death, and each wished to endow himself with a spirit of false prophecy, like Mohammed, whence there are still these four kinds of Moors in those parts today, far removed from one another in the manner of their beliefs.

When it came to his turn to govern, Ali also began to make himself out a prophet, and greater than the others had been, and he wrote a book in which he said evil things about his father-in-law and the companions, thus affirming that he had a better spirit of prophecy than the others, and pointing out things to their discredit[1]. And he commanded that from thenceforward they should name Ali in their prayers and not Mohammed, saying that he had won much land at the point of his lance, that the twelve signs of the heavens were with him and that they had come together at his birth to make him a knight and a great prophet, and that he did not want any Moor to believe what his father-in-law had said about putting the sun in his sleeve, and [he also did] other things to undermine the authority of Mohammed, as the Moors know. And the immediate result of this were the followers of Ali, who are called Shi'ites (*Zeidis*)[2] and Rafadis and are Moors who believe in Ali; and the Sheikh Ismail is a Rafadi.

As Ali had been severe in his rule, after his death some of his followers went over to the beliefs of Mohammed and others still held those of Ali. The followers of Mohammed and others increased so greatly in numbers that they published a law to the effect that all followers of Ali must die, saying that he had not been a prophet nor a saint, but that he had been a good knight

the ninth century. Islam is divided into three principal sects whose differences are mainly about the office of the Caliph—Sunnis, Shi'ites and Khawarij. The Sunnis, who hold that the Caliphate must be filled by election, and that the Caliph is not infallible, are the most numerous of the Muslims—at present about 150 millions out of a total of 235 millions.

[1] *Sentences of Ali*, translated by W. Yule, Edinburgh 1832, contains collections of proverbs and verses which bear the name of Ali.

[2] *Zeidis*, appears as *Zeylldes* in the Lisbon MS. The Shi'ites, from Shi'a—'the party of Ali', are second in importance to the Sunnis. They hold that Ali and his descendants are the rightful Caliphs, and that the Caliphate is not an office of election but given by God, the Caliph being infallible. There are about twelve million Shi'ites today, mainly in Persia.

in his time; wherefore it has come about from that day to this that many Moorish followers of Ali have been executed as heretics in the Moorish countries, so that the followers of Ali have been considered to be outside the law, and they do not go to Mecca, and yet however much they were punished for Ali, he always had many secret followers among the Moors until the time of this Sheikh Ismail.

Birth of the Sheikh Ismail or the Sophy. Sheikh Ismail is a Persian, native of the region of Shiraz, a nobleman by birth, and belonging to the great Shi'as, who are men who despise the world and live in solitude so that they may remain in poverty. The father of this Sheikh was one who was held by the Moors to be a good man, and he descended from the family of Ali, and had three sons. The Sheikh Ismail is the middle one[1], and they are all still alive. Sheikh Ismail's father used often to talk to the king of Shiraz and they were friends. They often conversed together, talking in such a way that the king of Shiraz became offended with the Sheikh and killed him. Some say that the Sheikh kept admonishing the king of Shiraz to learn about Ali's teaching and to accept his opinion. Others say that they had a quarrel and that the king of Shiraz favoured Mohammed while the Sheikh was in favour of Ali, so that the Sheikh was killed there. And they say that the dead Sheikh had these sons by a Christian woman, an Armenian of good parentage, and that he had converted her to the beliefs of Ali. And for five years after the death of his father, the Sheikh Ismail stayed with his mother and with one of his uncles, an Armenian Christian.

Fol. 123v. When the father died, there is no doubt that the son stayed in his mother's house from the time he was ten years old, which was when they killed his father, until he was fifteen. When he was a boy of fifteen he lived in the company of his Christian relations, with whom he stayed for six years. The Christians fed him and taught him, and he took from them what seemed to him good, and he was always obedient to them, so that he grew up in goodness and discretion; and on the advice of his Christian relatives he sent a letter to the king of Shiraz asking the king to

[1] Ismail was the youngest of the three brothers, not the middle one, as asserted by Pires.

give him food as he had killed his father. He was answered with a staff and a rosary, by way of mockery, that these were his because he was a Sheikh [but] a poor man. The indignant boy, instructed in our faith by his relatives, went to a king near Shiraz and asked for help against him, since the king was his enemy, and for the loan of some money, with the help of which —added to some which his relatives gave him—he sought to kill the king of Shiraz. He received help, and by his own industry got together two thousand men and raided the land. After having robbed it he decided one Friday, against the will of those he had with him, to enter the city by day. He entered and they say that he killed sixty thousand men and had the city in his hands and pillaged it[1], and that he raised his forces to the strength of thirty thousand warriors, with whom he waged war for seven or eight years, so that he has the whole province of Persia with all its kingdoms on his side. Of the two thousand men collected together by the Sheikh Ismail three hundred were horsemen, two hundred of these being Armenian Christians related to his mother and the remaining hundred being relatives of his father. The men on foot belonged to the latter. The money he had was for maintenance, and he had no more people [than this] at the beginning of his undertaking, and now his people are beyond numbers. When he entered the city of Shiraz he had eight thousand fighting men, including six thousand horsemen.

All these things he does by the advice of these Christians. They say that he never destroys any Christian dwelling nor kills any Christian. They say that he must have with him ten thousand men—Armenian Christians, and some of other nations, with whom he carries out the great enterprises, and all the kings yield themselves to him and obey him. He reforms our churches, destroys the houses of all Moors who follow Mohammed and never spares the life of any Jew. He makes war on the Sultan wherever he finds him, and on the people of Turkey. He is growing in power. He sends the red cap to the kings. If

[1] 'Ismail attacked Tabriz, which surrendered, and was proclaimed Shah.' Sykes, *A History of Persia*, II, 159. Pires is not very clear; it looks as if he sometimes mistakes Shiraz for Tabriz.

they take it they are friends and if not they become mortal enemies[1].

This Sheikh must be a man of from thirty to thirty-two years old. He lives most of the time in Tabriz. He is small of body, with powerful limbs, and wears the cap[2] himself. In older times the Moors belonging to this sect used not to wear the cap; but this Sheikh commands that it be worn. Some say that the twelve folds secretly represent the twelve apostles[3]; but the most certain thing he often publishes [is] that he praises Ali as the greatest prophet of all, that the heavenly signs served him, and for this reason he wears the twelve folds [in his cap], which has to be red as a sign that whoever will not accept it will have to have a red cap made with his own blood. They say that he is a gracious, liberal man, and he orders the death of every Mohammedan who is known to drink wine, but allows it those who wear the red cap, so that there is now no man in all Persia who does not belong to his sect. The citizens of note wear the cap, and if the poor people have not the wherewithal to buy they do not wear it; however, they are all followers of Ali. They say that he is noble in his person. He already has sons. He has many wives. In the lands of the Moors, that is, in that of the Sultan [of Egypt] and in that of the king of Aden, many people are joining this sect, and they do not dare to kill them, and every day many Mohammedans are coming over to Ali's side. Many of the Syrian Arabs have already been converted to the sect of Ali, which the Moors consider a bad sign. The Sheikh is a circum-

[1] When Pires wrote this, the great defeat inflicted by Selim the Terrible, Sultan of Turkey, in 1514, upon the Sheikh Ismail, from which he escaped with difficulty, after being badly wounded and nearly taken prisoner, had not yet occurred.

[2] Mestre Afonso, who came from India to Portugal through Persia, in 1565–6, refers to this headgear as follows: 'All the rest of the Moors . . . with the exception of the relatives of Mohammed who wear the hair in long plats under their turbans, wear hats, which are made of red cloth like large round caps, quilted with cotton-wool, and from the centre there rises a straight horn of the same cloth, which they call hat (*carapução*), two spans long and as thick as an arm, divided vertically in twelve folds, in memory and veneration of the twelve sons of Ali, whose sect they follow.' *Ytinerario de Mestre Affonso*, p. 192.

[3] These twelve *Apostles* were the twelve Imams, descended from Ali, origin of the important sect of the Shi'ites—the Twelvers.

cized Moor and a follower of Ali, although many Moors say that he is a Christian. He sends learned Moorish subjects of his to the kings to argue for the sect of Ali against Mohammed's doctrine. And the ambassadors sent by this Sheikh are attended by many mounted men, well dressed people of good appearance, very sumptuous, with vessels of gold and silver, which show forth the greatness of the Sheikh. To all the Moorish kings he sends gifts and presents, and learned men so that they may follow his law. He says that he will not rest until he sees all the Moors made followers of Ali in his time, and after that will come that which he knows ought to come. The Moorish people are for this new Sheikh and are so much the more angry at Your Highness' power[1].

There are a large number of merchants in this land of Persia, *Fol. 124r.* and the land in itself does a great deal of trade covering the country from Cairo[2] as far as the land of the Armenians, where there are many rich and noble provinces. And a great deal of trade comes to Persia from Turkey through Syria. The land of Shiraz (*Xiria*)[3] and [other lands in this country] have a great deal of silk from which rich cloths are made, and many kinds of camlet in fine colours and very good. They have great quantities of tutty, a great deal of alum, copperas and antimony, which the Moors use. They have many horses and many foodstuffs. They have many turquoises which are found in the land of Shiraz (*Xiras*). They have much wax, honey, butter. All these things are natural products of the country. From the Delhi side beyond the mountain range there seem to come by way of Siam, from kingdom to kingdom, musk, rhubarb, agallochum or apothecary's lignaloes, camphor. All these things and many others come to Ormuz: great carpets and tapestries, woollen cloth of many kinds and colours, hats and

[1] In the Lisbon MS this paragraph ends quite differently: 'And afterwards he says that that will happen which he knows [will happen], and they think that it will be his becoming a Christian, as they say he is in secret.'

[2] In the Paris MS it is distinctly written *cauo*, which may mean 'cape' or 'end'; but in the Lisbon MS we read *cayro*, and *Cairo* in Ramusio, though in the latter the arrangement of the paragraph was slightly altered.

[3] In the Lisbon MS *Xiria* has been mistranscribed as *Riq*^{a} (*Riqueza*, wealth).

caps such as they wear, much beautifully ornamented armour. They return a large quantity of spices and drugs, chiefly pepper —for they are still greater eaters of soups (*potagees*) than the Germans—in which they trade greatly, distributing it among their countrymen. They buy seed-pearls, rice, white cloth, *beatilha*, benzoin and things of that sort.

This land of Persia with all its regions lies between two rivers, the Tigris and the Euphrates, and some people affirm that these two rivers do not run into the ocean, but that they end in Persia and that they go into the Persian Gulf into a large navigable sea or salt-water lake which there is in Persia and which is entirely surrounded by land, with beautiful dwelling-places, in the province of Guilan, and that boats sail [there] and that it is about twenty leagues across, that there are storms there and much fish which is salted and sent wherever it can go in Persia, and some is dried. Others say that this sea is larger, but I verified my information with many people who told me that this is the measure, which seems to me to be large. This is far from Ormuz —more than two months' journey on camels. Others say that the Tigris flows through Syria and comes to an end almost in the sea in the Strait of Ormuz, a matter of twelve leagues, and that it has already become small because it divides into branches. It flows rapidly, it is narrow and not navigable; in some places it can be crossed on foot, and in others with rafts or boats as you will. An arrow is called in Parsi *tir*, and on account of the swiftness of the river it is called Tigris[1].

The Euphrates rises in Armenia and they say that it flows into the ocean and that it divides the Nodhakis from the Rajputs; and the people of Cambay call this river *Frataa*, and [they say] that it comes from the farthest confines of Persia, and little use is made of the land through which this [river] flows. It is a large river and does not flow so swiftly as the Tigris and it is navigable inland with light boats, sailed by the people of these parts through which it flows. Leaving Persia and going towards India by sea we come to the land of the Nodhakis.

[1] On the Persian word *tir*, 'an arrow', and its connexion with the name of the river Tigris, see *Hobson-Jobson*, *s.v.* Tiger, note.

NODHAKIS

The Nodhakis (*Naitaques*)[1] have the Persians as neighbours on the one side and the Rajputs on the Cambay side, and inland they have the mountainous land of the province of Delhi, and on the other they have the sea. These Nodhakis are heathens; there are no Moors among them. It is a large country with many inhabitants who are spread over the country inland. They have no king and live in bands (*cabilas*). None of these ever recognized the name of Mohammed. They have a language of their own. They have no cities. They have villages in the mountain ranges, and this river[2] makes them very powerful, because it waters the whole of the plain. The land itself produces a great many foodstuffs: wheat, barley and fruits. Most of them are pirates and go in light boats. They are archers, and as many as two hundred put to sea and rob, when they have an opportunity, and sometimes they get as far as Ormuz and enter the Straits in their marauding, and that is what they live on. These men carry bows, swords and lances, and they are not very domestic. Often they come and anchor at the mouth of this river on account of the weather, and it is a road with shallows and rocks. Sometimes the Nodhakis seize any ship that goes there, and at other times they go to the kingdom of Cambay to the ports there, and if they find anything they steal where they can. They fear no one, nor have they any rivers in their lands where they can take refuge, and there are many in these parts. They are known to be men of this kind.

Those who sow and work in the land have many horses and *Fol. 124v.* many mares on which they go about like the nomads, and steal whatever they can find. These people live in peace and friend-

[1] *Noutaques* in the Lisbon MS; *Motages* in Ramusio's translation. Barbosa does not refer to this people, but Dames says in a note on the Sheikh Ismail that the *Nautaques* referred to by several sixteenth-century writers, are the Nodhaki tribe of Baloches, in which he agrees with Barros. This region corresponds approximately to a part of the Persian province of Kamir and to Baluchistan.

[2] Pires does not say which river this is, but he must refer to the *Rio dos Noutaques* which appears in several Portuguese sixteenth-century maps. It is possible that this river corresponds better to the present Dasht River, as seems more clearly indicated by *R dos noutaces* on L. Homem's map of 1554.

ship with the Rajputs, and they do not forgive the Moors anything, and [they forgive] any other people. The Nodhakis have great affinity with the Rajputs, and although they have lived for so long in lands surrounded by Moors, they could never have been subjugated. They are bold highwaymen. The land of the Nodhakis is more extensive and more populated than that of the Rajputs, but the Rajputs are a better people as I shall explain later in the proper place.

RAJPUTS

The Rajputs (*Resputes*)[1] have the Nodhakis for neighbours on the Persian side, and on the Cambay side their land is bounded by Cambay itself. Inland there is the land of Delhi and on the other side is the ocean. These Rajputs are heathens with no Moors among them. They have no king; they have an overlord whom they obey. Their land has powerful fortresses and strongholds. They are brave men and riders. They have many horses, and most of them have mares, on which they fight. Their land is rich and very good. Its foodstuffs are many and it is cultivated and vigorous in itself. And there is not much land because it has been taken from them. These people are better fighters than their neighbours and they are constantly at war with the king of Cambay. They often harm him and put him to confusion because they are cunning and learned and with small forces they are able not only to hold their own but also constantly to harry the people of Cambay. They are not powerful enough to be able to fight against Cambay in the field in squadrons, but their idea is to make sudden attacks on horseback. They seize booty and capture one another. These Rajputs are skilful in war, vigorous and great archers.

They also have an outlet to the sea, where they keep rowing boats and seize booty wherever they can find it, like the Nodhakis; but all their power is on land. Some people affirm it was some of these Rajputs and Nodhakis who had access to the Amazons whose country inland is bounded by theirs and by

[1] *Risbutos* in the Lisbon MS; *Rebutes* in Ramusio's translation.

Cambay, as I shall explain in my description of Cambay[1]. On the Delhi side their country stretches inland in great ranges of mountains. This region has already had a king, but a while ago they killed him and no other was made afterwards. This kingdom has the beautiful cities of Herat (*Ara*), *Crodi*, *Vamistra* and *Argengij*[2]. The chief captain of all this kingdom is called *Pimpall Varaa*[3], and one of his sisters who is called *Bibi Rane*[4] is married to the king of Cambay, to whom her father gave her in the interest [of the state] before he died, and they say she is beautiful.

[CAMBAY]

The noble kingdom of Cambay is bordered on one side in the direction of Persia by the region of the Rajputs, and on the side of the Second India by the great kingdom of the Deccan (*Daquem*), and inland by the kingdom of Delhi and on the [*word missing*, other?] side by the ocean[5]. This kingdom separates from that of the Deccan between Mahim (*Maymi*) and Chaul. The kingdom itself is large, abundant in all kinds of wheat, barley, millet, vegetables, fruits, and having many horses, elephants, game-birds and many others in cages, of different kinds and highly prized. The land is thickly populated and has beautiful cities both on the coast and inland, as well as large villages. It has horsemen and much artillery and every warlike device,

Fol. 125r.

Kingdom of Cambay.

[1] In the Lisbon MS this sentence reads: 'Some assert that these *Rjsbutos* were those who had relations with the Amazons who on one part of the hinterland border on Cambay.'

[2] ARA is Herat, the city in western Afghanistan. It appears also as *Hara, Harah, Eri, Heri* or *Heriunitis* in old reports of Asiatic travels. Cf. *Cathay and the Way Thither*, I, 190, 293; III, 22.

CRODI—*Crode* in the Lisbon MS, *Crodi* in Ramusio. Perhaps Kotri, a town in the District of Karachi.

VAMISTRA—*Vamiste* in the Lisbon MS, *Vamista* in Ramusio. Vamansthali, ancient city and capital, near Girnar and modern Bilkha, in Kathiawar, Bombay? *Imp. Gaz. of India, s.v.* Girnar.

ARGENGIJ—*Argemgij* in the Lisbon MS, *Argengo* in Ramusio. The city of *Arguda*, of Ptolemy's *Geography*, or Argandi, south-west of Kabul? Cunningham, *The Ancient Geography of India*, p. 38.

[3] *Vara* only in the Lisbon MS and Ramusio.

[4] *Bibi* means lady in Persian, and *Rane* or *Rani* is either the consort of a Hindu rajah, or *rana*, a queen. It appears as *Biberade* in the Lisbon MS and in Ramusio.

[5] According to the Lisbon MS.

also many caparisoned horses, much armour of great beauty, both plate-armour and coat-of-mail, lances with beautiful heads, long swords, daggers—all beautifully ornamented. All is great. The people have many men at arms[1] and warriors. From outside they have *Maçaris*, Arabs, Turkomans, *Rumes*, Persians, that is from Guilan and from Khorasan, and Abyssinians, all untainted races, with whose assistance they are constantly fighting with the neighbouring kingdoms with whom they are at war. Among these nations there are many who are renegade Christians.

Cities on the coast and inland.

The principal cities on the coast are Surat (*Çurrate*), Rander (*Ranei*), Diu. Cambay has other ports with many inhabitants: they are Mahim (*Maymj*), Daman (*Damanã*), *Patan*, Gogha (*Guogua*)[2], Diu. Gogha and Mahim are governed by *Melequiaz*[3], a Persian Moor of the Guilan race. Daman, Surat and Rander are under the jurisdiction of *Dasturcan*[4], a Moorish lord born in Cambay. Patan is governed by the son of the king of Cambay,

[1] Although it is written *Dalmãs* (of souls) in the MS, it should be '*de armas*' (at arms), as in the Lisbon MS and in Ramusio.

[2] RANEI—*Reneri* further on, *Rjnell* in the Lisbon MS, and *Reiner* and *Reinari* in Ramusio. It is found as *Reynel*, *Reinel* or *Reiner* in Barbosa and the Portuguese chroniclers. Ribeiro's maps of 1527 and 1529 show *Reinel*, as in Barbosa. This is explained by the fact that Ribeiro and Centurione when in Seville, where the maps were drawn, translated into Italian the *Livro de Duarte Barbosa*. It corresponds to the modern Rander, on the other side of the Tapti River, almost opposite Surat.

MAYMJ, *Maymi* or *Maỹ*—This appears as *Mejmym* or *Majm* in the Lisbon MS. It corresponds to Mahim or Kelve Mahim, at the present day a small port about half-way between Dahanu and Agashi. This must not be confused with the *Maimbij* which corresponds to the Mahim or Mahikavati on Bombay island. See note on p. 39.

PATAN—*Patão* in the Lisbon MS, *Patam* in Ramusio. It appears as *Patan*, *Patane* and *Pate* in many sixteenth-century Portuguese maps and chronicles. It must correspond to the modern Veraval.

GUOGUA or *Guogarj*, appears as *Goga* and *Gogary* in the Lisbon MS, and as *Goga* and *Gogari* in Ramusio. It is recorded as *Porto de goga* in Rodrigues' map of the western part of India. It is Gogha, a port in the District of Ahmadabad on the west coast of the Gulf of Cambay.

[3] All the Portuguese chroniclers, including Albuquerque in his *Cartas*, and other sixteenth-century writers, refer at length to *Melique Az*, or Malik'Aiyaz, and his relations with the Portuguese. *Melique*, from the Arab *Malik*, king, meant also prince, governor and chief in the East.

[4] Dastur Khan.

who is called Sultan *Xaquendar*[1]. The city of Cambay is made the jurisdiction of *Sey Debiaa*, a person of importance in the country, a noble Moor of repute among them. The principal inland cities are Champaner (*Champanell*) and Ahmadabad (*Medadaue*), Baroda (*Varodrra*) and Bharoch (*Baruez*)[2]. These cities have Grand Viziers or Captains, men by whom the whole kingdom is governed. This *Melique Az* was a foot soldier, an archer, and was given governorship on the Diu side, because it was the least important part of Cambay[3] and almost all wild jungle before our discovery of India; and because the ports of the Deccan were always kept under restraint, Diu became great through our friendship, and now it is an important place where there is more respect for justice than anywhere else in the kingdom. There are three hundred horses in its stables, which are kept up out of the revenues of the land.

Distance from the coastal towns to Champaner.

From Diu to Champaner is eight days' journey; from Cambay to Champaner is two days' journey; from Surat and Rander to Champaner is five days, all over land.

Chief cities.

The best city of the interior is Champaner. It is not large, but it is civilized and well built; and the city with the most trade is that of Cambay. It is on the gulf [and this] is full of shallows, between one and four fathoms deep. This town has the best merchandise, and almost all its trade is in the hands of heathens. The other towns have good ports with fortresses in them. The kingdom of Cambay does not extend far inland.

[1] Sikandar Khan, the eldest son of Muzaffar II, who did not become sultan till 1525.

[2] CHAMPANER—*Champanell* in the Lisbon MS, *Campanel* in Ramusio. 'The proper form of the name is Champānēr.' Dames, I, 123. A ruined city twenty-five miles north of Baroda, at the north-east foot of Pavagarh, a fortified hill of great strength. *The Imp. Gaz. of India, s.v.*

MEDADAUE—*Madadane* in the Lisbon MS, *Medadune* in Ramusio, *Andava* in Barbosa. This is Ahmadabad.

VARODRRA—*Barodria* in the Lisbon MS, *Zarodria* in Ramusio, that is Baroda.

BARUEZ—The same in the Lisbon MS, *Banues* and *Barmez* in Ramusio. It corresponds to Bharoch or Broach, the most important port between Cambay and Surat.

[3] The transcriber of the Lisbon MS added some further information: 'This is *Meliquias*, who died in the year 1522. He was an archer, and before that a captain [*sic for* captive], and many times sold. He was made governor of Dio because it was the least important port in Cambay.'

Coinage. The smallest coin in this country is a copper one thicker than the *ceitil*. They have silver coins called *mastamudes*, worth three *vintens* apiece. They also have another silver coin called *madaforxas*[1]. Gold is also current in the same denomination and in bars by their standards and values.

Fol. 130r. *Concerning the kingdom of Cambay.* The king of Cambay is called Sultan *Madaforxa*[2], and his father was called Sultan *Mafamud*[3]. This king is at war with the king of Mandu (*Mandao*) and with the king of Indo and with the Rajputs and to some extent with Delhi, and I will therefore speak of these a little.

This king of Delhi stays inland. His land was formerly the greatest in these parts. He had dominion over the Rajputs, Cambay and part of the kingdom of the Deccan, the king of Mandu and the king of Indo. This king's land encompasses the whole province of Narsinga, and he is constantly at war with the Bengalees and with the kings of the hinterland whose lands border on Orissa, and with Orissa. He was a heathen. The kings of Delhi have been Mohammedans for a hundred and fifty years. They had captains in all these kingdoms. Each of them rose up and made himself king, as the one in Cambay did. High mountains[4] intervene between Delhi and Cambay, so that the king of Delhi could not attack Cambay. There is only a small pass into the land, which is held by a Gujarat Jogee who does not allow the people of Delhi to enter Cambay; and when this king writes to the king of Cambay he calls him 'my vizir' or 'captain'. This king of Delhi has a large and very mountainous country. The mountain ranges which pass through his

[1] CEITIL—An old Portuguese coin worth only one-sixth of a *real*.

MASTAMUDES—Pires' *mastamude* corresponds to the old Persian silver coin *mahmudi*, called *mamude* by the Portuguese chroniclers and in the Lisbon MS, which had currency in Cambay and the Gujarat.

VINTEM—A Portuguese coin equal to 20 reis, or 1d. at par.

MADAFORXAS—*madrafaxaos* in the Lisbon MS, an old silver or gold coin which had currency in Cambay and the Gujarat, called by the Portuguese chroniclers *madrafaxos*, *madrafaxas*, *madrafaxaos* or *madrafaxões*.

[2] Mudhaffar or Muzaffar Shah II, called *Soltão Madrafaxa* in the Lisbon MS and *Soltam Moordafaa* by Barbosa.

[3] Mahmud Shah I, called *Soltão Mafamede* in the Lisbon MS and *Soltam Mahamude* by Barbosa.

[4] The Malwa Plateau, bounded on the south by the Vindhya Range and on the north-west by the Aravalli Range.

country are the Caucasian mountains of which cosmographers tell us. His land has countless kinds of food, people, horses, elephants. There are innumerable heathen in his kingdoms. His country extends a long way inland. This king is called the King of the Indies, and he continuously lives inland.

King of Mandu (Mandao)[1].

On the skirts of this mountain range[2], bordering on the land of Cambay, is the king of Mandu. This is the kingdom where the women whom we call Amazons used to fight in olden times. Now they no longer take part in warfare, but they still hunt on horseback with buskins and spurs after their guise. They say that this king still has about two thousand women who ride with him[3]. This king has many subjects, and his land is rocky and strong. Mandu also borders on the Rajput country. This king of Mandu is subject to the king of Delhi. This king has only been a Mohammedan for a short time.

Kingdom of Indo[4].

The kingdom of *Indo* has already been converted to [the faith of] Cambay. They are already all Mohammedans. It is a small and mountainous country. They say that indigo comes from here and a small quantity of lac is also produced here; and a great deal of the Cambay merchandise comes from the Rajputs, Mandu and Delhi, and [Cambay] distributes their goods for them, because the other provinces, that is Delhi, Mandu, *Indo* and others, are inland, while Cambay has a sea-coast.

This kingdom of *Indo* used to be very famous. It is inland. And from this kingdom there runs a river which flows into the

[1] *Mãdou* in the Lisbon MS, *Mandou* or *Mandó* in the Portuguese chroniclers, corresponds to Mandu or Mandogarh, now a ruined city in the Dhar State of Central India, 'on the summit of a flat-topped hill in the Vindhyan range.' *Imp. Gaz. of India, s.v.*

[2] Vindhya Range.

[3] In his letter of 26 Jan. 1516, Pires refers again to these Amazons of Mandu, 'warlike women who now fight on horseback'. Appendix I.

[4] The origin of the names Indus, India, Hindus and others of the same etymologic group is the Sanskrit *Sindhu*, 'the sea'. In many Asiatic languages the word *Sindh* actually indicates the sea or an important river, whence the River Sindh. Pliny had referred to 'the Indus, called by the inhabitants Sindus'. McCrindle, *Ancient India as described by Megasthenês and Arrian*, p. 143. The earlier Mohammedans distinguished *Sind* and *Hind* as different parts of the whole region which we call India, the latter name being applied to the country beyond the Indus. It seems that Pires' Kingdom of *Indo*, which he says is a 'small thing', lay in the present Rajputana, somewhere between the Punjab and Cambay. *Hobson-Jobson, s.v.* India and Sind.

sea; it is called *Çindy* by some, others call it the *Indy*; and the people of the kingdom are called *Indios*. This river divides the Rajputs from Cambay. This kingdom used to be at the head of Cambay. This is where India begins, and it is on account of this kingdom that the king of Cambay was called the king of the First India. It is a large river. There is a large town where it flows into the sea, with many ships and merchants both heathen and Mohammedan. The governor is an *Indo* heathen.

Ports of Cambay up to the Deccan.

Imdi, Kharepatan (*Carapatani*), Patan, Diu, Manar (*Manna*), Telaja (*Tata telaya*), Gandhar (*Guendarj*), Gogha (*Guogari*), Cambay, Bharoch (*Baruez*), Surat (*Çurrate*), Render (*Reneri*), Dahanu (*Dionj*), Agashi (*Agagy*), Bassein (*Baxa*), Mahim (*Maimbij*)[1].

[1] In the Lisbon MS these names read as follows: 'Imde/ barapatão/ patão/ dio/ manuaa/ tatelaya/ guãdari/ gogary/ cambaia/ baruez/ Rejnell/ çurrate/ diuny/ agazy/ baxaa/ maimby/'.

IMDI—On P. Reinel's maps of *c.* 1517 and *c.* 1518—the closest in date to Pires' writing—we read *daulcinde* near a river which seems to correspond to the modern Porali River, but it must be the westernmost mouth of the Indus. The map of *c.* 1540 has *diull* and *diu(l)çimde*. This river of Reinel's maps appears in later ones, of the middle sixteenth century, as *R. dos guzarates* and *R. simde*, some of them showing *diul* or *diuli* (L. Homem, 1554) on the right-hand bank, near the mouth. This is the *Diul* or *Diulsinde* of Barbosa and other early Portuguese writers and cartographers. Barros refers to 'Diul situated on the first mouth of the Indus, on the side of the west', I, ix, I. *Diul* is the Portuguese form for Dewal or Daibul, which according to Yule was 'a once celebrated city and seaport of Sind, mentioned by all the Arabian geographers, and believed to have stood at or near the site of modern *Karāchī*'. *Hobson-Jobson*, *s.v.* Diul-Sind. Diul-Sind may also be the port Sonmiani, at the mouth of the Porali River, an important place before the rise of Karachi, through which much of the trade of Central Asia was carried via Kalat. *Imp. Gaz. of India*, *s.v.* Sonmiani. Although it is not easy to explain why Pires wrote *Indi* for 'Diul-Sind', it seems that he meant the latter, as there was no other important port before Kharepatan.

CARAPATANI—Kharepatan. *The Imp. Gaz. of India* (II, 33, 1908 ed.) refers to 'Khārēpātan plates bearing the record of the Śilāhāra prince Raṭṭarāja of A.D. 1008'. At the mouth of the Hab River there was a port called Kharak, with a considerable commerce. The entrance to Kharak harbour became blocked with sand, and its inhabitants migrated to a place called Kalachi Kun, on the other side of the river, near Karachi, a recent foundation. Cf. *Imp. Gaz. of India*, *s.v.* Karāchi City. *Pattan* means 'a port' in Hindi, which combined with *Kharak* seems to have given Kharepatan or Pires' *Carapatani*.

MANNA—Must be Manar, at the Manali River, between Telaja and Gogha.

TATA TELAYA—Telaja.

GUENDARJ—The old town of Gandhar, at the mouth of the Dhadar River, in the Gulf of Cambay, which appears as *gandar* or *r. de gandar* in several

It is about three hundred years since the kingdom of Cambay was taken from the heathen; but there are still a great many of them in Cambay, almost the third part of the kingdom, mostly men whose faith forbids them to kill any living thing or to eat anything that has had blood in it. There are an infinite number of these. The heathen of Cambay are called Banians. Some among them are priests with beautiful temples. Most of them | are Brahmans and men given to religion; others are Pattars (*Patamares*)[1], the more honoured Brahmans; others are merchants, as we shall see later. The heathen of Cambay are great idolaters and soft, weak people. Some of them are men who in their religion lead good lives, they are chaste, true men and very abstemious. They believe in Our Lady[2] and in the Trinity, and there is no doubt that they were once Christians and that they gradually lost the faith because of the Mohammedans. These heathens have upright writing like ours. When they die their wives burn themselves [alive], if they are honoured women, or

Heathens of Cambay.

Fol. 130v

sixteenth-century Portuguese maps. It is the *Guindarim* of Barbosa.

DIONJ—This stands for modern Dahanu, which lies thirty-two miles south-south-west of Daman. *Dinuy* in Barbosa, *Danu* in the Portuguese chronicles and several maps. In *Livro de Marinharia* (p. 223), *Danu* is situated eight leagues from Daman. There is still an old Portuguese chapel in Dahanu.

AGAGY—*Agacim* or *Agaçaim* in the Portuguese chronicles, stands for Agashi, which gives its name to the present Agashi Bay, twenty-eight miles from Dahanu, into which the Waitarna River empties.

BAXA—Stands for the modern Bassein. *Baxay* in Barbosa, *Baçaim* and south-west *Basaim* in the Portuguese chronicles and maps.

MAIMBIJ—*Majmby* in the Lisbon MS; also called *Mayambu* or *Mombaym* by the Portuguese. This is Mahim or Mahikavati, the first town built on Bombay island, perhaps at the end of the thirteenth century. The name still survives in 'Mahim Bay', on the extreme north of the island. Castro refers to the 'Island of *Bombai* or *Mayam*, which are the same'. *Roteiro de Goa a Dio* (1538–9), p. 81.

[1] Though Pires wrote *patamares* he means the Pattars, a class of Brahmans. Further on, when dealing with the Brahmans of Malabar, he spells the word as *patadares* (p. 68). Referring to the Pattars of Cambay, Pires says that 'these are the ones who carry the letters, if they come as couriers, because they are safe from thieves' (p. 42). There is here, possibly, a curious confusion through an association of ideas. According to Dalgado (*s.v.*), *Patadar* or *Patamar* is a Luso-Indian word from the Konkani *pattemar* (a courier), meaning a foot runner, a courier, or a swift light boat.

[2] This belief that the Hindus were once Christians and worshipped Our Lady seems to have been current among the Portuguese in India at that time. Barbosa (I, 115) also mentions it. On the Trinity see note p. 66.

if they prize their honour. There are still great lords among these heathens of Cambay, men who rule in the kingdom. Among them is a certain Brahman called *Milagobim*[1], a person who is greatly esteemed for his qualities and richer than all the men in the East, and a man of great credit and renown. These heathen all have long hair. Some of them have long beards which they cannot shave; others have long hair. They belong to various sects and beliefs; they are subject to the Moors.

King and Kingdom of Cambay.

The kingdom of Cambay must have seventy or eighty leagues of coast, and inland it is not large but noble, and rich and civilized, with large, strong cities with good walls and towers. The Moorish lords live honourably. They have a great many horses—there is one lord in Cambay who has from five to six hundred horses and the rest are mares—large well-constructed houses and palaces. The king is not much obeyed, because of the foreigners. Most of the people of Cambay are poor and the great ones among them are rich. The king must be a man of about forty. He is called Sultan *Madaforxa*. They say and affirm that these kings are brought up on poison, because they are very tainted, so much so that if a fly touches them it dies; and that their women are brought up on the same food, and if they spit, it is poison; and that if anyone else puts on their clothes, they say he dies suddenly[2]. But I do not believe this, although they say it is so. This king is given to all manner of vice in eating and lechery. They say that otherwise he is judicious. Most of the time he is among his women, stupefied with opium.

There are about thirty thousand horsemen in the kingdom of Cambay, and three hundred elephants, about a hundred of which

[1] Also referred to later as *mjlaguobim* and *mjligobim*. When describing Surat, Barbosa (I, 149) says that 'Hitherto a Heathen named Milocoxim held sway and governed here, whom the king of Cambay ordered to be slain on account of evil reports about him. This man was a great friend of the Portuguese'.

[2] Barbosa refers in great detail to Mudhaffar Shah being brought up on poison. Varthema mentions the same thing. It seems that the story was current at the beginning of the sixteenth century. Cf. Dames, I, 121–2. In Garcia de Resende's *Miscellanea*, published for the first time in 1554, there is the following stanza about Sumatra: 'There are kings who are accustomed,/ taught so from childhood,/ always to take poison/ in very small quantities/ until they are used to it./ And if they give it them in their food/ it cannot do them any harm./ And if anyone drinks their wine,/ or if a fly feeds on their spittle,/ he dies without hope of life.' (St. 91.)

are fighting elephants. The best town on the coast from the point of view of buildings and of garrison is Diu; and the town in the interior with the most foreigners is Champaner, which is always the seat of the kings of Cambay. Champaner contains beautiful palaces, and many people of good breeding. The chief lords after the king are: *Milagobim* the heathen, then *Chamalc Malec*, and then *Asturmalec*, and the fourth is *Codaudam*[1]. These four, with the king, govern everything. Each of these has a great many mounted followers when he goes to the palace, and they all have a great retinue. They are lords who are natives of the kingdom and they are responsible for the administration of justice, and the government of the kingdom, and the king's revenue; and they are the electors of the kingdom when the king dies. They are all lords by title. The king has up to a thousand wives and concubines. This king is called the king of principal India, and because this kingdom is noble only on account of its trade, I thought it necessary to speak of it.

Trade of Cambay.

I now come to the trade of Cambay. These [people] are [like] Italians in their knowledge of and dealings in merchandise.[2] All the trade in Cambay is in the hands of the heathen. Their general designation is Gujaratees, and then they are divided into various races—Banians, Brahmans and Pattars. There is no doubt that these people have the cream of the trade. They are men who understand merchandise; they are so properly steeped in the sound and harmony of it, that the Gujaratees say that any offence connected with merchandise is pardonable. There are Gujaratees settled everywhere. They work some for some and others for others. They are diligent, quick men in trade. They do their accounts with figures like ours and with our very writing. They are men who do not give away anything that belongs to them, nor do they want anything that belongs to anyone else; wherefore they have been esteemed in Cambay up to the present, practising their idolatry, because they enrich the kingdom greatly with the said trade.| There are also some Cairo merchants *Fol. 131r.*

[1] These names are given in the Lisbon MS as 'milagolỹ, camlemalle, asturmallee, cadãodão'.

[2] In the Lisbon MS it reads: 'They seem to me better than Italians in the knowledge of all merchandise.' Ramusio omitted the reference to the Italians.

settled in Cambay, and many Khorasans and Guilans from Aden and Ormuz, all of whom do a great trade in the seaport towns of Cambay; but none of these count in comparison with the heathens, especially in knowledge. Those of our people who want to be clerks and factors ought to go there and learn, because the business of trade is a science in itself which does not hinder any other noble exercise, but helps a great deal.

Pattars (Patamares) *of Cambay.*

The Pattars of Cambay are the most honoured Brahmans. They are originally descended from the kings of Cambay, because in older times the kings were Brahmans, as they are in Malabar today. These [Pattars] take the merchandise through the country, and the merchants are greatly esteemed. Even when going through robber-infested country, the merchants are not molested if they are accompanied by a Pattar; and they have this distinction in these parts. And if they rob them, they kill themselves, or wound themselves with daggers, and the other Brahmans anoint the images with their blood and drag them along, until justice is done, and they do it and give them back what is theirs. The Brahmans are held in great esteem among the heathen; and these are the most honoured because they do not eat anything that has been living. These are the ones who carry the letters, if they come as couriers[1], because they are safe from the thieves. You shall find what manner of men they are back[2] in the description of Malabar.

And so both the Gujaratis and the merchants who have settled in Cambay—the chief city of *Miligobim*—sail many ships to all parts, to Aden, Ormuz, the kingdom of the Deccan, Goa, Bhatkal, all over Malabar, Ceylon, Bengal, Pegu, Siam, Pedir, Pase (*Paeçe*) and Malacca, where they take quantities of merchandise, bringing other kinds back, thus making Cambay rich and important. Cambay chiefly stretches out two arms, with her right arm she reaches out towards Aden and with the other towards Malacca, as the most important places to sail to, and the other places are held to be of less importance.

[1] See note p. 39.

[2] The transcriber may have substituted *atras* (back) for *adiante* (further on), as written in the Lisbon MS, in order to adjust the word to the arrangement of his copy. See *Introduction*, p. lxxi.

The merchants from Cairo bring the merchandise which comes from Italy and Greece and Damascus to Aden, such as gold, silver, quicksilver, vermilion, copper, rosewater, camlets, scarlet-in-grain, coloured woollen cloth, glass beads, weapons and things of that kind. *How they trade in general: Cairo.*

[The merchants of] Aden bring the above mentioned goods with the addition of madder, raisins, opium, rosewater, quantities of gold and silver and horses that Aden gets from Zeila and Berbera and the islands of Suakin, in the Strait, and from Arabia, and they come to do business in Cambay. They take back with them all the products of Malacca: cloves, nutmeg, mace, sandalwood, brazil wood, silks, seed pearls, musk, porcelain, and other things which may be found in the [list of] merchandise from Malacca, as well as the following from the country itself: rice, wheat, soap, indigo, butter [and lard?][1], oils, carnelians, coarse pottery[2] like that from Seville, and all kinds of cloth, for trading in Zeila, Berbera, Sokotra, Kilwa, Malindi, Mogadishu, and other places in Arabia. And this trade is carried out by ships from Aden and ships from Cambay, many of one and many of the other. *With Aden.*

And it [Cambay] trades with all the other places I have mentioned, bartering one kind of merchandise for another, as none of them can maintain itself without trading with the others. Anyone who wants more detailed knowledge of the merchandise of each country will know what the merchants take back from there, and I do not put it down here because the merchandise of each country can be seen in the account of it.

It has all the silks there are in these parts, all the different kinds of cotton material, of which there must be twenty, all of great value; it has carnelians, indigo and a little lac which the land produces, pachak, catechu[3], a great deal of good opium, *Merchandise of Cambay.*

[1] Pires uses the word *manteigas*, 'butters', which may mean simply butter, or butter and lard. In Portuguese *manteiga de vaca* is the ordinary butter, and *manteiga de porco*, hog's lard.

[2] *Malegua*, as it appears in the MS, is a Portuguese word which was formerly also spelt *malega* (as in the Lisbon MS). Today it is spelt *malga* and means usually a bowl or soup-dish. In this case its meaning is 'pottery'.

[3] The two words *pucho* and *cacho* used by Pires, correspond to pachak and catechu. Sometimes transcribers put the two words together, as for example

wormwood[1], tincal, cotton, soap in large quantities, dressed hides, leather, honey, wax; the following foodstuffs: wheat, barley, millet[2], sesame-oil, rice, butter, meat, and things of that sort, coarse pottery of different kinds, all natural products of Cambay, or brought thither from the countries of the neighbouring kings.

Fol. 131v. The people of Ormuz bring horses to Cambay, and silver, gold, silk, alum, vitriol[3], copperas, and seed pearls. They bring back the products of the country and those brought there from Malacca, because they come to Cambay for all the Malacca merchandise. The people of Ormuz take back rice and food-

Trade with Ormuz.

in the Portuguese edition of the *Livro de Duarte Barbosa* (p. 289), where these two drugs appear in a single word *cachopucho*. This led Dames to believe, after discussing the matter at length (I, 155; II, 173, 234), that it was *cajeput*, 'a fragrant essential oil produced especially in Celebes and the neighbouring island of Bouro' (*Hobson-Jobson, s.v.*). The name *cajeput* is taken from the Malay *kayu-puteh*, which means 'white wood'; the product comes chiefly from *Melaleuca leucadendron* Linn., 'a large bush or a tree, very variable, found from Tenasserim to the Moluccas', also called Paper-bark-tree, the wood of which is much in demand in Malaysia. Cf. Burkill, *A Dictionary of the Economic Products of the Malay Peninsula*, pp. 1431–3. No reference is found to *cajeput* in any early Portuguese writing. *Cachopucho* is referred to by Barbosa as a product taken from Cambay to Malacca and China, and further on he says: '*cacho* and *pucho* (which are Cambay drugs).' Watt does not mention *cajeput*. Orta deals at length with *pucho* (XVII) and with *cacho* (XXXI). Pachak is costus, the root of *Saussurea lappa* C. B. Clarke. Catechu or cutch is a pale yellow gum from *Acacia catechu* Wild.

[1] There are several species of wormwood, or Pires' *erva lombrigueira*. The one found in Portugal is *Artemisia variabilis* Ten. Coutinho, *A Flora de Portugal*, p. 636. Dames (I, 154), as well as several Portuguese-English dictionaries, identify the *erva lombrigueira* with the southernwood or *Artemisia abrotanum*. He says, however, that the southernwood alluded to was 'probably the *Artemisia indica* or Indian wormwood'. Watt (pp. 93–4) refers to several species of the genus *Artemisia* as found in India, but neither to *A. variabilis* nor to *A. indica*.

[2] The word *milho* used by Pires corresponds in Portugal today to maize or Indian-corn, *Zea Mays* Linn. But he certainly does not mean this one, since maize came to India from America, possibly brought thence direct by the Portuguese. Cf. Watt, p. 1132. There are also in Portugal the '*milho zaburro*' —*Andropogum Sorghum* Linn., '*milho meudo*'—*Panicum miliaceum* Linn., and '*milho painço*'—*Setaria italica* Linn. Coutinho, pp. 65, 67. Pires meant by *milho* the *Sorghum*—great millet, *jowaur* or *juar*, and *Pennisetum typhoideum* Rich.—Bulrush, cumboo or spiked millet, which are extensively grown at Cambay and in other parts of India.

[3] The *aziche* (vitriol) of the Paris MS appears as *azinhaure* (aloes) in the Lisbon MS.

stuffs for the most part, and spice. They bring bales of soft dates from Ormuz, and also some in jars and dried dates of three or four kinds.

With the Deccan and Goa, with Malabar and other places.

They trade with the kingdom of the Deccan and Goa and with Malabar, and they have factors everywhere, who live and set up business—as the Genoese do in our part [of the world]—in places like Bengal, Pegu, Siam, Pedir, Pase, Kedah, taking back to their own country the kind of merchandise which is valued there. And there is no trading place where you do not see Gujarat merchants. Gujarat ships come to these kingdoms every year, one ship straight to each place. The Gujaratees used to have large factories in Calicut.

Trade with Malacca.

The Cambay merchants make Malacca their chief trading centre. There used to be a thousand Gujarat merchants in Malacca, besides four or five thousand Gujarat seamen, who came and went. Malacca cannot live without Cambay, nor Cambay without Malacca, if they are to be very rich and very prosperous. All the clothes and things from Gujarat have trading value in Malacca and in the kingdoms which trade with Malacca; for the products of Malacca are esteemed not only in this [part of the?] world, but in others, where no doubt they are wanted. A more detailed description of its merchandise will be found in the account of Malacca. If Cambay were cut off from trading with Malacca, it could not live, for it would have no outlet for its merchandise.

Trade with Java.

The Gujaratees were better seamen and did more navigating than the other people of these parts, and so they have larger ships and more men to man them. They have great pilots and do a great deal of navigation. The heathen of Cambay—and in older times the Gujaratees—held that they must never kill anyone, nor must they have an armed man in their company. If they were captured and [their captors] wanted to kill them all, they did not resist. This is the Gujarat law among the heathen. Now they have many men-at-arms to defend their ships. Before the channel of Malacca was discovered they used to trade with Java round the south of the island of Sumatra. They used to go in between Sunda and the point of Sumatra island and sail to Grisee (*Agraci*) whence they took the products of the Moluccas,

Timor and Banda[1], and came back very rich men. It is not a hundred years since they gave up this route. There are keels, anchors and other parts of Gujarat ships in Grisee, which they show, saying that they are left from the time of the Gujaratees.

The merchants who come and start companies here for Malacca

As the kingdom of Cambay had this trade with Malacca, merchants of the following nations used to accompany the Gujaratees there in their ships, and some of them used to settle in the place, sending off the merchandise, while others took it in person, to wit, *Maçaris* and people from Cairo, many Arabs, chiefly from Aden, and with these came Abyssinians, and people from Ormuz, Kilwa, Malindi, Mogadishu and Mombassa, Persians, to wit, *Rumes*, Turkomans, Armenians, Guilans, Khorasans and men of Shiraz. There are many of these in Malacca; and many people from the kingdom of the Deccan used to take up their companies in Cambay. The trade of Cambay is extensive and comprises cloths of many kinds and of a fair quality (?)[2], rough clothing, seeds such as nigella, cumin, *ameos*, fenugreek, roots like rampion, which they call pachak, and earth like lac which they call catechu[3], liquid storax and other things of the kind.

[1] In the Paris MS it is written *do ouro*, but the Lisbon MS has *bamda*, and Ramusio *Bandam*.

[2] After *he boos* (of a fair quality) the Paris MS has the words *em cããos*, the meaning of which I cannot find. The two words have been omitted in the Lisbon MS and in Ramusio.

[3] NIGELLA—The word *alipiuri* used by Pires is the old Portuguese name *alipivri* for the seeds of Nigella, small fennel or black cumin—*Nigella sativa* Linn. Watt (p. 811) says that this plant 'a native of Southern Europe', used by the natives as medicine or a condiment, is 'extensively cultivated in India for its seeds'. Burkill (p. 1556), however, comments: 'Watt states that the cultivation is extensive in some parts of India, but this is scarcely correct, and it is rare to find it away from the extreme north-western parts of the country'. This fully covers Cambay.

CUMIN—Pires' *cominhos* is the true cumin—*Cuminum Cyminum* Linn., a plant more or less cultivated in most provinces of India.

AMEOS—Orta (XI) refers to the *ameos* (*âmios* or *amis* in modern Portuguese) calling them 'wild cumins' (*cominhos rusticus*). This must correspond to the bishop's weed, the umbelliferous *Ammi majus*, which like the cumin belongs to the tribe *Amminea*. Ficalho (*Coloquios*, I, 148) suggests that Orta 'might have given this name (*ameos*) to some *Umbelliferae* of aromatic seeds, which are frequent in India'. The word has been omitted in the Lisbon MS and in Ramusio.

FENUGREEK or fenugraec, Pires' *allforua* or *alforva*, is the *Trigonella foenum graecum* Linn. 'A robust annual herb, wild in Kashmir, the Panjáb and the Upper Gangetic Plain; cultivated in many parts, particularly in the

They return loaded up with all the rich merchandise of the Moluccas, Banda and China, and they used to bring a great deal of gold. It was upon the Gujaratis that it weighed most heavily when Malacca came into Your Highness' possession, and it was they who were responsible for the betrayal of Diogo Lopes de Sequeira[1]; and today they sing in the market-places of Malacca of how the town has had to pay for what the Malayans did on the advice of the Gujaratis.

higher regions.' Watt, p. 1081. Orta, XIII. It is also a native plant in Portugal.

RAMPION, Pires' *Rvy pomtiz* or *ruipontiz* (which is also called *ruiponto, rapuncio, raponcio* or *raponço* in Portuguese), is *Campanula Rapunculus* Linn., a plant with a tuberous esculent root. '*Ruipònto*—Pharmacology. "*Raiz do ponto*", which looks like rhubarb, comes from Asia', says Morais, *Diccionario da Lingua Portugueza, s.v.* (Lisbon, 1789). This explains why Pires says that pachak (*pucho*, which the transcriber spelt *puçha* here) is 'roots like rampion'.

CATECHU—There was a time when the *cacho* or catechu was supposed to be a natural earth, and as it reached Europe by way of Japan, in the seventeenth century it even received the name of *Terra Japonica*. See note on catechu, pp. 43–4.

The transcriber of the Lisbon MS perhaps was unable to understand this piece of Pires' writing, and simply suppressed what he did not understand.

[1] See note pp. 235–6.

[*SECOND BOOK*]

[CAMBAY TO CEYLON]

[Deccan—Goa—Kanara—Narsinga—Malabar—Ceylon]

[DECCAN]

Fol. 132r.

Kingdom of the Deccan (Daquem).

WE will describe the great and warlike kingdom of the Deccan. It is separated from the kingdom of Cambay along by *Maymi* or *Maÿ*[1], and from the kingdom of Goa by Kharepatan (*Cara patanam*), and from the country inland where the king of Narsinga is, and from the kingdom of Orissa by a narrow inlet, and on the side of Cambay upwards by the mountains which are between India and Delhi. This kingdom produces plenty of foodstuffs, and the land is well cultivated. It is a larger kingdom than that of Cambay and the people of the country are better warriors, gallant by nature [like] the people of the land of Kanara, and the peons are very hard working. This kingdom contains many white people. It must be two hundred and fifty years since this kingdom was won from the heathen by the *Rumes* and Turks and Persians. Like the kingdom of Cambay it has many inland cities and many seaports.

Seaports.

If you sail from Mahim to the kingdom of Goa the ports in the kingdom of the Deccan are as follows: Chaul, Dande (*Danda*), *Mataleni*, Dabhol (*Dabull*), Sangameshwar (*Sangizara*), Kharepatan (*Carapatanam*)[2].

[1] Kelve Mahim.

[2] In the Lisbon MS these names read as follows: 'chaull dãda mataline/ dabull/ samgisarra/ carepatão/'.

CHAULL—Chaul or Cheul is a place of great antiquity, formerly one of the most important seaports in Western India; still called Port Chaul on the Admiralty Charts. As Pires says further on, the port of Chaul was already declining in his time. It is situated on the north side of the wide harbour formed by the estuary of the Kondulika River or Roha Creek. Recorded on Rodrigues' map as *chaull*.

DANDA—There is a place called Dande on the north side of Rajpuri Creek, in the eastern part of Janjira harbour, which must correspond to Pires' Danda. On the map published by J. S. King in his *History of the Bahmani Dynasty* (*The Indian Antiquary*, vol. 28, Bombay, 1899) the place appears as Danda, but situated on the south side of the creek. Further north on the

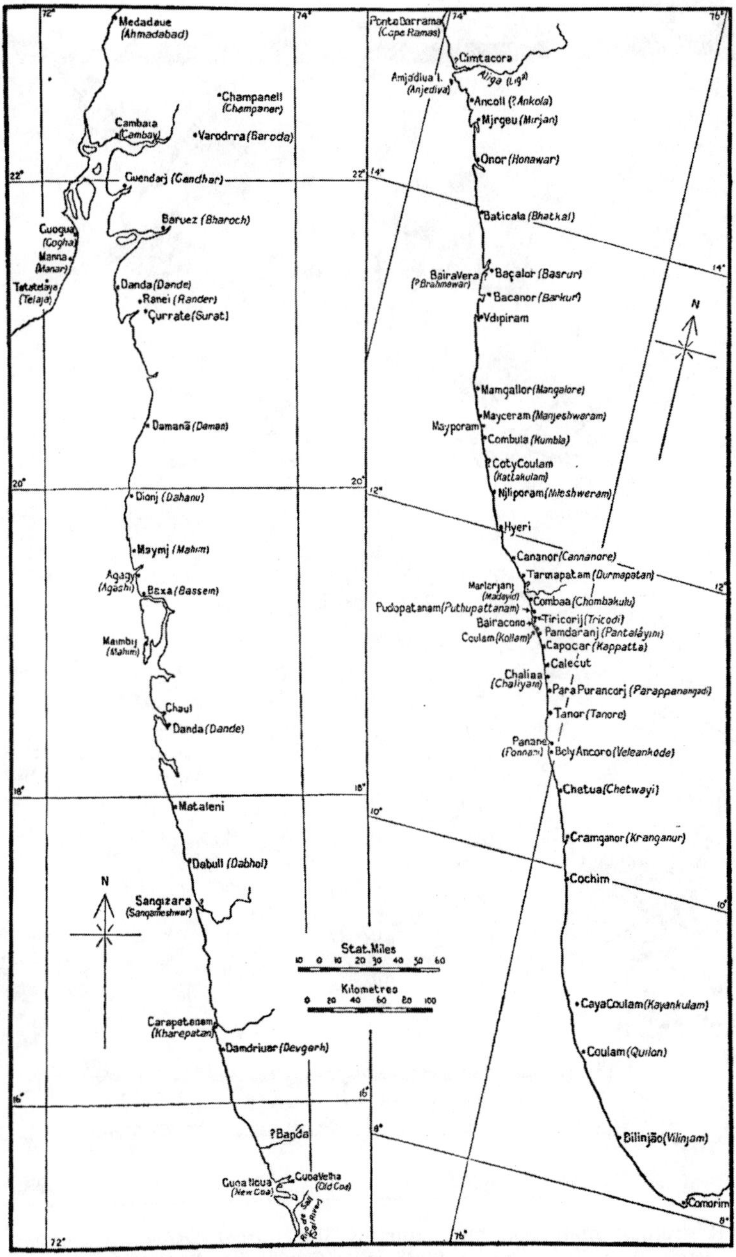

The West Coast of India according to Tomé Pires (pp. 33-84)

PLATE XIV

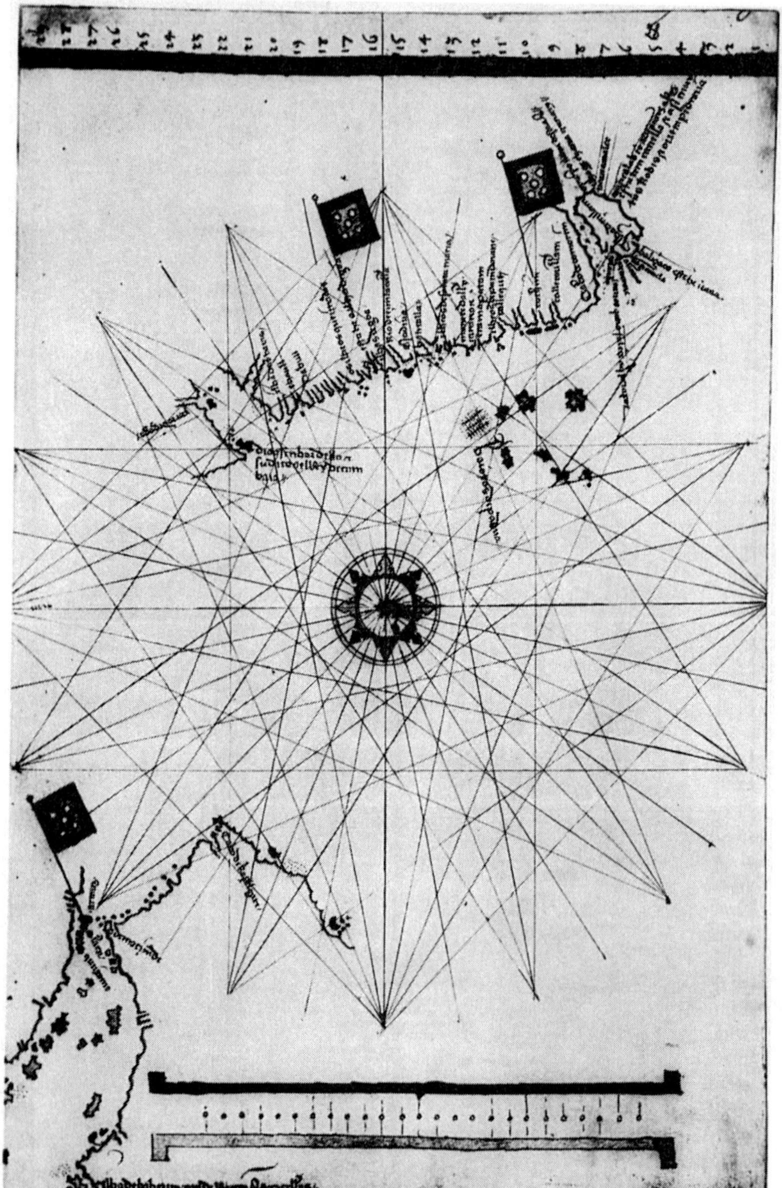

Rodrigues' map (fol. 28) depicting the East Coast of Arabia, eastern part of the Persian Gulf, West Coast of India, Ceylon and the Laccadive Islands (p. 520)

There are twenty towns in the kingdom of the Deccan, the ones with the most inhabitants being Bidar (*Bider*), Bijapur (*Visapor*), *Cidador*, Sholapur (*Solapor*), Raichur (*Rachull*), Sagar (*Çagar*), Kulbarga (*Quellberga*), Koyer (*Queher*), *Bayn*[1]. *Principal inland towns.*

coast, between Roha Creek and Rajpuri Creek there is another place called Dande. The name survives also in the village Revadanda, where the fort built by the Portuguese still exists. Chaul and Revadanda have now spread so much towards each other that they are more often called Upper Chaul and Lower Chaul. Castro says that *Danda* is 'one of the greatest and most famous rivers of this coast, being four leagues from Chaul'. *Roteiro de Goa a Dio*, p. 48. On the Reinel maps of *c.* 1517 and *c.* 1518 *Danda* appears to the south of Dabhol, but on all the other early maps it is placed immediately south of Chaul. *Cifardam* on L. Homem's map of 1554.

MATALENI—This name does not appear in any Portuguese chronicle or map. Castro (pp. 39–48) refers to three rivers, between Dabhol and Danda, from south to north, the *Quelecim*, the *Beiçoim*, and the *Cifardam*. *Cifardam* corresponds to Srivardham or Shrivardham bay, which Castro rightly places five leagues south of Danda. *Quelecim* is the Bhária, which he locates seven leagues north of Dabhol and about one south of *Beiçoim*, saying that it is exactly in 18 degrees of latitude (correct lat. 17° 56′ N). *Beiçoim* is the Savitri River, the most important of the three, of which he gives an accurate chart, where Port Bánkot now stands. This must correspond to Pires' *Mataleni*, perhaps the river *Mandaba*, placed by Barbosa between Danda and Dabhol and identified by Dames (I, 164) with the Savitri River. *Mandaba* does not appear in any chronicle or map.

SANGIZARA—The *Cinguiçar* of Barbosa and *Zamgizara* of Castro, is the Sangameshwar or Shastri Joygad River.

CARAPATANAM—Kharepatan. Castro (pp. 23–31) gives a detailed description and an accurate chart of the *Rio de Carapatão* which corresponds exactly to the entrance of Vijaydurg or Vijayadurg harbour, at the entrance of the Vághotan River. He says that 'It is the noblest and best sheltered river of all those which flow on this coast of India, and its excellence is such that there are not enough words to praise it'. According to the *West Coast of India Pilot*, Vijaydurg is today a port of little importance. It must be related to the *Arapatam* referred to by Barbosa. Dames (I, 169) took the names *Arapatam* and *Muruary* as meaning two sorts of pulses which he tries to connect with two Indian plant names, *arburrah* and *mohrī* or *mahasūrī*. Dalgado (II, 455, 507) also says that *Arapatão* is the *arburrah* or the garden pea, *Pisum sativum* Linn., and that *Muruary* is *mulayari*, the Malayalam word for 'seed of bamboos, which is used in several parts as a foodstuff'. Although the defective punctuation of the 1821 Portuguese edition (p. 293) may justify this confusion, it seems more likely that Barbosa refers the words *Arapatan* and *Muruary* to 'other small places which are also sea ports', and not to 'pulses'. The name still survives in the village Kharepatan, on the left bank of the river, twenty miles from its mouth.

[1] In the Lisbon MS these names read as follows: 'badir vesapor çidapor solapor Rachull cugar/quell/ber guaquelher bain.' BIDER—Bidar, in the State of Hyderabad. Both Barbosa and Barros mention *Bider*. VISAPOR—Bijapur. *Bisapor* in Barros, *Visapor* in Castanheda. SOLAPOR—Sholapur, in Bombay

Name of the king and the chief lords.

The king is called Sultan *Mahamud Xaa*. Next in rank to the king are *Idalhan*, *Niza Malmulc*, *Cupall Mullc*, *Hodanan*, and *Miliqui Dastur*[1]. These four lords, and those who succeed to their titles, govern the kingdom. This *Idalhan* is a Turk from Turkey. His father was a slave of this king's father, and as the king considered him to be a man of worth he made him *Çabayo*[2]. This name of *çabayo* is a Siamese name like captain of the king's guard who governs half the kingdom. The man who holds this office is called the *çabayo*. The official *çabayo* holds a vital position in the kingdom. The one who has this dignity is a very great lord and he ministers to the king in all that he needs. This office was held by the father of its present holder.

The former *çabayo* was a knight of great esteem, and they say that he took part in forty pitched battles and was defeated in

Province. RACHULL—Raichur, in Hyderabad. ÇAGAR—Sagar, in Gulbarga District, Hyderabad. *Seguer* in Barros. QUELLBERGA—Kulbarga or Gulbarga, in Hyderabad. *Calbergá*, in Barros. QUEHER—Koyer or Kohir, in Bidar District, Hyderabad. *Querhij*, in Barros. BAYN—Bhaja, a small old town in Poona District, Bombay? Or Badami, another small old town in Bajapur District, Bombay? *Vay*, in Barros.

[1] MAHAMUD XAA—Mahmud Shah, Bahmani king of the Deccan. IDALHAM or *Idalcam*—Adil Khan, meaning 'The righteous Lord'. The usual form among the Portuguese chroniclers was *Idalcão, Adilchan, Hidalcão* and *Hidalchan*; but Orta (x) calls him Adelham, which seems more like Pires' *Idalham*. This title was extended by the Portuguese to all the kings of the Mohammedan dynasty of Bijapur. NIZA MALMULC—Nizam-ul-Mulk, 'The Regulator of the State.' Barros (II, v, 2) gives the names of the principal 'captains' of Mahmud Shah, who held power in the Deccan when the Portuguese came to India, among them the four mentioned by Pires. This one is called *Nizamaluco* by Barros as well as by the other chroniclers. CUPALL MULLC—Kutb-ul-Mulk,'The Pole-Star of the State'; called *Cotamaluco* by Barros and *Cotalmaluco* by Orta. HODANAN or *Hodan an han*. Perhaps Kwaja Mukaddan, the *Coje Mocadam* of Barros, and the *Mohadum Coja* of Orta. MILIQUI DASTUR or *Milic Dastur*—Malik Dastur or Malik Dinar Dastur-i Mamalik, *o Abexi capado* (the Abyssinian eunuch) of Barros, later referred to by Pires as an 'Abyssinian slave of the king'. In the Lisbon MS these names appear rather mixed up: 'mamedxa/ idalham niga/ mall malet/ odanam/ melique destur/'.

[2] *Çabaio*. There has been a good deal of speculation about the origin and meaning of this title *Çabaio*, or, as more often spelt by the Portuguese chroniclers, *Sabaio*. Barros (II, v, 1) says that when the Portuguese 'came into India the lord of this city of Goa was a Moor named Soay, captain of the King of the Deccan, whom we commonly call Sabayo'. Dames (I, 172–4) has already dealt extensively with this question.

thirty and victorious in ten. Shortly after his death, his son called himself *Idallcam*, which means captain general of the whole kingdom, and seized the king, and the king has to live where the *Idalcam* wishes and is more or less a prisoner. However, when the *Idalcam* sees the Sultan *Mahamud Xaa*, he does show him a certain amount of deference. *Idalcam* took this bold step against the wishes of the four and of the king, because all the white people in the kingdom came under his jurisdiction; and because he was a foreigner and a Turk and held this office, most of the mercenaries came to his support. With the exception of Bidar, all the towns in the kingdom are for the most part under the *Idalcam's* jurisdiction. As long as this man was *Çabaio*, these other lords were as powerful and important as he; but when he called himself *Idalcam* they all came under him; and, as this offended them, they are always at war, as we shall see later. All the seaports in this kingdom belong to the *Çabaio*, except Chaul and Dande.

The Lord of Chaul and Dande.

The Lord of Chaul and Dande is called *Niza mall mulec*. His father was a Turk by birth. He was one of the king of the Deccan's slaves and became a great lord, and holds many places inland. He has a thousand white warriors from Persia and a thousand horsemen.

Cupal mulec.

This *Cupall mulec* is a great lord. Others call him *Cutell mamaluqo*. He is a native of the kingdom of the Deccan and was not a slave. He is a man of great worth and greatly esteemed in the land. They say that he has nearly one thousand five hundred mounted white men.

Hodau an han.

This man is a native of the kingdom, like the above, and has as much land and people.

Milic Dastur.

This *Milic Dastur* is an Abyssinian slave of the king, and almost as important as each of these. His land borders on the Narsinga frontier, and he lives in Kulbarga where he has a garrison. The *Çabaio* took this city from him, and now they are at war.

When the above four lords join forces in agreement they have between twelve and fifteen thousand mounted men, counting natives as well as white men. These four have joined together against the *Çabaio*. The *Çabaio*, who is now *Idalcam*, has as

many men as they, and they are continually at war with one
Fol. 132v. another. The pay in this country is better than any in these | parts. They are sometimes badly paid. There are also many heathen natives and many esteemed Brahmans. Whenever a heathen of the country dies, it is the custom for his wife, if he has one, to burn herself alive, so that she may keep her husband company wherever he may be. If she does not do this, not only is she herself dishonoured, but all her relatives also; and sometimes the wives are not very willing and their relatives and the Brahmans persuade them to burn themselves, so as not to depart from the custom.

The kingdom of the Deccan is a land of chivalry. It must have about thirty thousand mounted men, besides countless foot soldiers. Those white people whom we call *Rumes* used generally to come to this kingdom and to Goa to earn wages and honour. This king used to bestow names like *miliques*[1], for instance, so-and-so *milic*, and the most honoured name is *han* or *can*[2] and they use to come to win these titles. The *cãns* are greatly esteemed and honoured here—I mean *cães* the plural of *can*, and not dogs [*cães* in Portuguese]. The people of this kingdom are full of pride and presumption. The king is addicted to opium and women, and spends all his time in this way. And his *Idalcam* is no less so. The king must be about forty years old and the *Idalcam* thirty. They are both fat men, and given to every form of vice. There must be about two hundred Turks, *Rumes* and Arabs in the kingdom of the Deccan, and from ten to twelve thousand Persian men-at-arms. The man who has the most white men in this kingdom is the most powerful. This kingdom must possess about fifty elephants, and it has Arab and Persian horses of unbelievable value.

Food-stuffs. There is an abundance of rice in the kingdom of the Deccan, and some wheat and meat. There is a great deal of areca and betel.

Trade in the kingdom of the Deccan. The Deccan used to do a great deal of trade, chiefly in Dabhol. It was a rich and honoured port of call, a good port, with many ships; and Your Highness treated these ports so ill that they

[1] *Mjlique* or *Mjlic—Malik*, which actually meant king, but was used as meaning ruler or lord.

[2] *Han* or *Can—Khan*, which means prince.

were destroyed, and Diu, from being a wilderness, became great, through Your Highness' favour. It still has great mechants and carries on trade, but not the tenth part of what it used to do. These used to be ports of call between Aden and Malacca. They used to deal in all kinds of merchandise in large ships belonging to many merchants. These were good halfway ports, set in fertile country with plenty of water. Most of the horses imported into the kingdom of the Deccan were landed here. These were rich ports, and the king of the Deccan and his *Çabaio* and *Nazimall mulec* had a right to the dues, and this enabled them to pay good wages; but now that the Captain-General[1] has made over this trade to the civilized kingdom of Goa, the kingdom of the Deccan will not be able to maintain its position much longer. The way is open for it to be lost beyond recall, or for Goa to become the greatest place in the world[2]. Time shows all these things as it passes; and there is reason to believe that it should be so, since it is plain beyond contradiction that there used to be a great deal of very rich trade in Dabhol. The port of Chaul was renowned throughout Asia, and so was Dabhol—Dabhol not so much, on account of the water there, which is brackish. The followers of Mohammed are apprehensive. These people who were so prosperous are watching their wealth fade away (?).

Merchandise.

This kingdom of the Deccan produces the following merchandise: calicos—cloths in white and countless colours—and *beatilhas*, which the Moors and Klings generally use for their turbans. They make enough of these two things to furnish the world. They also make black beads in this kingdom which are good for *Diua*[3] and Abyssinia. Most of the betel, which is called

[1] Afonso de Albuquerque.

[2] Time has indeed proved Pires to have been right in his prophecy—as far as the Orient was concerned.

[3] *Diua*—This single word is repeated further on (p. 84). It might mean Diu, which Barbosa calls 'a great town named by the Malabars *Deuixa*' (Port. ed. p. 282), and which appears as *Diuxa* in Ramusio's translation. Yule says that the town stands on an island, whence its name, from Skt. *dwīpa*. *Hobson-Jobson*, *s.v.* Diu. But it is more likely that *Diua* may mean the Maldive islands, whose etymology has been explained in so many ways, although it probably embodies the same Sanskrit word *dvīpa*. Further on Pires calls the Maldive Islands quite clearly *Ilhas de diva*. See note p. 82. In the Lisbon MS it is also *Diua*, but Ramusio transformed it into *Adem*.

folio Indo[1], goes from here to Cambay, Ormuz and Aden, although that from Goa is better. As the ports in this kingdom were conveniently situated, the merchandise from all over Asia and Europe was to be found there; and the port of Chaul was very famous, but it is already on the decline.

[GOA]

Fol. 133r. Now our road takes us to the magnificent kingdom of Goa—the key to the First and Second India. On the sea-coast it is separated from the Deccan by Kharepatan, the chief river in India; on the Honawar side it has *Cintacora*; and inland it is bounded by the kingdom of the Deccan and the kingdom of Narsinga. The language which is spoken in this kingdom is Konkani. The kingdom of Goa was always esteemed as the best of the king of Narsinga's possessions, for it was as important as it was prosperous. The people of the Deccan won part of this kingdom from him, and afterwards the old *Çabaio*, father of the present one, won the rest of it from the heathens. It is forty-five years since the *Çabaio* took over this kingdom, and as long as it formed part of the kingdom of the Deccan, Goa was the head of the whole kingdom of the Deccan and Goa. The language of this kingdom of Goa does not resemble that of the Deccan, nor that of Narsinga, but is a separate language. The people of this kingdom are strong, prudent and very hard-working, both on land and sea.

Kingdom of Goa (Guoa).

Seaports. Next to Kharepatan along the sea coast Goa has Devgarh (*Damdriuar*), Banda, Old Goa, New Goa, Liga (*Aliga*), *Ancoll*, Pale (*Vpale*), Sal River (*Rijo de Sall*), Cape Ramas (*Ponta*

[1] Pires repeats the same assertion later on, when describing Bachian (*Pacham*) island, and in his letter of 1516 Barbosa says also—'This betel we call *folio Indio*' (Port. ed. p. 292), a misconception which passed unnoticed by Dames, who simply translated *folio Indio* as 'the Indian leaf' (I, 168). This mistake was wide-spread in the sixteenth century, and Orta himself fell into it until he went to India, as he explains in the *Last Colloquy*. Then he corrected the error, showing that betel is one thing, and '*folio indo*' or '*folium indum*' something quite different. There is betel or *Piper Betele* Linn., and there is *Folio Indo*, which is the *Cinnamomum Tamala* Fries, 'cassia lignea' or 'cassia cinnamon', the bark and leaves (known also as *folia malabathri*) of which are applied in medicine, etc. See note p. 219.

Darrama), *Cimtacora*, Anjediva (*Amjadiua*)[1]. Between these ports there are rivers, which ships used to—and still do—navigate.

[1] In the Lisbon MS these names read as follows: 'damda/ mujbamda/ guoa a velha/ & a nova alimga/ amola/ paçe/ o Rio do Sall/ apomta da Rama/ çimtaçora/ amgediua/.'

DAMDRIUAR—Devgad or Devgarh harbour. Three leagues south of *Carapatão*, Castro (pp. 22–3) places the *Rio de Tamaraa*, with 'a very beautiful bay nearly round shaped', which corresponds to Devgarh harbour, or Pires' *Damdriuar*. About ten miles inland, on the right bank of the river that debouches at Devgarh, there is a village called Tamhara. The map of *c.* 1510 has *dendbasya*, between *dabull* and *goa*. One of the ports mentioned by Castro may be the *Muruary* of Barbosa (see note p. 49), perhaps Pires' *Damdriuar*.

BANDA—To the south, the only important port before Goa is Vengurla, sixteen miles east-south-eastward of which is the inland town of Banda. Banda is also referred to as a seaport by Barbosa and Barros, and appears as *bamda* on some Portuguese maps, always south of Goa.

GUOA VELHA—Old Goa.

GUOA NOUA—New Goa or Pangim. As early as 1433–4 Ibn Batuta wrote: 'There are in the island (of *Sāndabūr*, or Goa) two cities, one ancient built by the pagans; the second built by the Mussulmans when they conquered the island the first time.' Cf. *Hobson-Jobson*, *s.v.* Sindābūr.

ALIGA—This must be the Kalinadi or Liga River, called by Barros 'rio Aliga de Cintacora' (I, ix, 1), but coming immediately after Goa, it seems to be misplaced.

ANCOLL—Suggests the town of Ankola, in a creek thirteen miles south-east of the mouth of the Liga or Kalinadi River. Ankola is the *Ancôla* which Castanheda (III, xxxiii) says lay four leagues from Anjediva, and which is mentioned by other chroniclers. *Ancola* appears between *cintacala* and *mergeo* in D. Homem's atlas of 1558. But there is also, after Goa, on the south-east coast of Mormugão peninsula, a place called Colla or Culua, at the mouth of a small river in Colla Bay, which the Portuguese call Mar de Colla. Perhaps the *Ancoll* of Pires corresponds to the '*tanadaria* of Colator', a seaport in the Goa District, mentioned by Barros (II, v, 2).

VPALE—There is a small place called Pale, Palee or Paula on the eastern side of Colla Bay. As all these ports are indicated in succession, from north to south, it seems that *Ancoll* indeed corresponds to Colla, though it may be that there is some confusion with Ankola and the misplacing of *Aliga*.

RIJO DE SALL—Sal River, sixteen miles south-east of Pale. It appears on some early Portuguese maps.

PONTA DARRAMA—Cabo de Rama or Cape Ramas, four and a half miles south-west of Sal River. It appears also on several early Portuguese maps.

CIMTACORA—Castanheda says that 'one league from the island of Anjediva, at the mouth of a great river of fresh water, there was a great fortress of the Moors called Cintacora' (II, xiii). Almost all the chroniclers refer to Cintacora as a fortified place or as a river, very near Anjediva island. Barros (I, viii, x) calls this river *Aliga de Cintacora* and refers to the origin of the fortress. The river is the Kalinadi, formerly the Liga River. 'On the northern side of the river, just within the entrance, on the summit of a 218-foot (66·4m) hill, are the remains of an old fort, and on a hill about a quarter of a mile eastward are

And because these things belong to the kingdom of Goa, we will only speak of Goa itself. On the mainland it had cities and towns, many *tanadarias*[1] yielding large revenues and having highly cultivated lands, which are still in the hands of the Moors; but since the great city of Goa, which is the key to all [the rest], is now in the power and service of the most high God, it will not be long before the remainder follow it.

In the same way as doors are the defence of houses, so are seaports the help, defence and main protection of provinces and kingdoms; and once these are taken and subjugated, the provinces and kingdoms are put to great suffering, and if they have quarrels among themselves or with their neighbours, they are immediately lost because they have no help, especially as these kingdoms had no other protection but the city and port of Goa, which was their principal thing. Goa used to be a haunt of thieves, Turks, *Rumes* and people who die opposing our faith. Goa was preparing to inflict great losses on the Christians, but God's judgement turned the loss upon them, for there is no doubt that the Moors groaned when Goa was taken. Goa was a place so arranged that in the space of a year the Moors could easily get together armadas there, such as they could not get in Suez in twenty.

Who can doubt that in the rout of Goa, ships were taken which the Moors had made ready to fight against us, and which afterwards went to Banda to bring cargoes of mace for us? The judgement of our Lord is incomprehensible, and let every one

the ruins of another fort. The town of Sadashivgarh (Sadashivgad) is situated close northward of these hills.' *West Coast of India Pilot.* The whole of this place is still called Chitakuli or Chitakul which corresponds to the *Cintacora* of the Portuguese. This must be the *Cintabor* of the Medici sea atlas (1351) or the *Chintabor* of the Catalan map (1375–81), which rather perplexed Yule (*Cathay*, IV, 65, etc.) and Dames (I, 171-2, 182). It already appeared as *Rio de cimtacolla*, south of the *ilhas de goa*, on Rodrigues' map of the west coast of India, as *Cymtaquola* on P. Reinel's map of *c.* 1517, and *Cimtacola* on other early maps.

AMJADIUA—Anjediva Island. *aJadiua* on Rodrigues' map (fol. 28).

[1] *Tanadaria.* The post held by the *tanadar*, actually meaning 'chief of local police', in Hindustani. The word was adopted by the Portuguese in India who used it in a wider sense, for the military authority of a small town, or receiver of revenues and customs. *Tanadar* or *Thanadar* is still in use in British India in the civil sense.

take good note that the Moors suffered a greater loss in Goa than they will suffer when they lose Aden. Goa not only curbs the kingdom of the Deccan, but it stifles that of Cambay too. The Moors have a bad neighbour in Goa. Just as the Moors used to go on conquering kingdoms, they are now losing them. A kingdom without ports is a house without portals. It is Our Lord who decrees the downfall of Mohammed, and John the writer[1] is rapidly bringing it about. The time has already come. Let no one in India count on the Moors now, except on those who plough the hills. The kingdom of Goa is the most important in India, although they may not wish it to be so. It is civilized, having famous orchards and water. It is the coolest place in India, and it is the most plentiful in foodstuffs; so that it used to be customary among the *Rumes* and the white people to make a practice of going to the kingdom of Goa to enjoy the shade and the groves of trees and to savour the sweet betel. There is no doubt that the betel in Goa is better than that anywhere else, mild and pleasant to the taste and highly prized, and it is usually from Goa that betel is exported to Aden, Ormuz and Cambay. It has more and better areca or *avelana India*[2] than any other place. Cargoes of rice are taken from here, and great trains of oxen loaded with merchandise used to come in to Goa from very distant kingdoms in the interior. And if these things happened in the past, how much more reason is there to believe that from now on Goa will become a great port of call, greater than there has ever been; and the merchants will rejoice under our administration more than they did under the Moors.

The kingdom of Goa always had the advantage over Chaul. It *Fol. 133v.* traded lavishly. It had many merchants of all nationalities, people of large means. Its trade was large. It always had a great many ships. It has a good port, and not only that, but it was especially suited to the business of raising armadas which was carried on there, on account of the wood and of the craftsmen, and also because it had plentiful supplies and was very strong, and because there were always a large number of white people living there, full of pride, and not without cause, for the kingdom

[1] St. John, the writer of the Apocalypse?

[2] The nut of the *Areca catechu* Linn., areca-nut or betel-nut, was called by the Portuguese *avelã da India* or *avelana Indiae.*

of Goa lies in the heart of all India. Great festivals used to be celebrated here in honour of the profane Mohammed, and these have now been changed to the name of Jesus Christ. The city of Goa is as strong as Rhodes. It has four fortresses, very richly constructed, in the necessary places, to injure the name of Mohammed.

Trade. They used to bring horses to Goa from all the kingdoms in Arabia Petrea, from Ormuz, from Persia and from the kingdom of Cambay; and from Goa they were sent to the kingdoms of the Deccan and of Narsinga. After Goa was taken from the Moors Narsinga got its horses through Bhatkal. And Goa also collected all the merchandise of those parts and they took back calico, fine muslin, rice, areca, betel and many *pardaos* and *oraos*, because horses here are worth a great deal. A horse may be worth as much as eight hundred *pardaos*, coins worth three hundred and thirty-five *reis* each[1]. [Goa] used to receive many spices and quantities of merchandise from these other parts.

The kingdom of Goa had a large number of ships which used to sail to many different places; and the Goanese ships were esteemed and favoured everywhere, because the Moors had all their power in these parts, in the kingdom of Goa. The seamen who sailed the ships were natives of the country, because the kingdom of Goa produces good seamen who can stand hard work. And thus with men from Goa sailing to other places, and people from the other places sailing to Goa, its trade was great, so that large revenues were derived from the dues on the merchandise and anchorages, and also from the land dues and the *tanadarias*. I have often heard it said that Goa and the surrounding district yielded four hundred thousand *pardaos* a year from the duties on everything that came into the port, together with its own products. And according to the run of things, this seems to be correct.

Heathens of this kingdom. There are a great many heathens in this kingdom of Goa, more than in the kingdom of the Deccan. Some of them are very

[1] PARDAOS—Popular name among the Portuguese for gold or silver coins of Western India worth 360 *reis* and 300 *reis* respectively. The 335 *reis* indicated by Pires as the value of the *pardao* in his time would correspond to about thirteen shillings today, with four or five times its purchasing power. ORAOS—Coins also called *horaos* or *oras* by the Portuguese, equivalent to *pagodes* (*Hobson-Jobson*, *s.v.* Pagoda c) or gold *pardau* (Dalgado, *s.v.* Orá).

honoured men with large fortunes; and almost the whole kingdom lies in their hands, because they are natives and possess the land and they pay the taxes. Some of them are noblemen with many followers and lands of their own, and are persons of great repute, and wealthy, and they live on their estates, which are very gay and fresh. The heathens of the kingdom of Goa surpass those of Cambay. They have beautiful temples of their own in this kingdom; they have priests or Brahmans of many kinds. There are some very honoured stocks among these Brahmans. Some of them will not eat anything which has contained blood or anything prepared by the hand of another. These Brahmans are greatly revered throughout the country, particularly among the heathen. Like those of Cambay, the poor ones serve to take merchandise and letters safely through the land, because the rich ones rank as great lords. They are clever, prudent, learned in their religion. A Brahman would not become a Mohammedan [even] if he were made a king.

No torment will make the people of the kingdom of Goa confess to anything that they have done. They can bear a great deal, and when they are being tortured with different tortures they will die rather than confess anything they have made up their minds to keep to themselves. And the pretty women of Goa dress well, and those who dance do so better than any others in this part of the world.

It is mostly the custom in this kingdom of Goa for every *Fol. 134r.*
heathen wife to burn herself alive on the death of her husband. Among themselves they all rate this highly, and if they do not want to burn themselves to death their relatives are dishonoured and they rebuke those who are ill-disposed towards the sacrifice and force them to burn themselves. And those who will not burn themselves on any consideration become public prostitutes and earn money for the upkeep and construction of the temples in their district, and they die in this way. Each of these heathen has one wife by law. Many Brahmans make a vow of chastity and keep it for ever.

In the other ports in the kingdom they load quantities of rice, salt, betel and areca, in which they trade. Each of these rivers has towns, far from the water because they are afraid; and those who know them well navigate there, because if they do not know them well they are lost. They are under the authority of the *Çabayo*, with captains who collect the revenues from the land, and some of them have a garrison of horsemen because they are constantly at war with the lands of the province of Narsinga.

[KANARA]

Fol. 125v.

Kingdoms in the land of Kanara (terra Canarjm).

Now you are in the last kingdom of the First India, which is called the province of the Kanarese (*Canarijs*)[1]. It is bounded on one side by the kingdom of Goa, and by Anjediva (*Amgadiva*), and on the other by Middle India or Malabar India. Inland is the king of Narsinga, whose language is Kanarese, which is different from that of the Deccan and of the kingdom of Goa. There are two kings along the sea-coast and a few small regions. They are all heathens and vassals of the king of Narsinga. They are a civilized people, warriors, and practised in the use of arms both on sea and land. The land we are now describing is the only one remaining to the king of Narsinga of those he possessed in the First India. It is a cultivated land, with important towns.

Seaports.

In the land of the Kanarese from Anjediva to Mangalore [there are] Mirjan (*Mjrgeu*), Honawar (*Onor*), Bhatkal (*Baticala*), Basrur (*Baçalor*), *Baira Vera*, Barkur (*Bacanor*), *Vdipiram*[2], Mangalore (*Mamgallor*). All these are trade ports. From

[1] *Canarijs* or *Canarins* are the inhabitants of Kanara, but, according to Dalgado (*s.v.*), the Portuguese erroneously designated the people of Goa by this name. Dames says, without much ground, I consider, that the term is applied to the class we call Eurasians, and that the Anglo-Indian term *Karām* is probably derived from *Canarim*.

[2] In the Lisbon MS these names read as follows: 'mergeo batecala bacalor baira/ vera/ bacanor vydeperão mãgalu.'

MJRGEU—Modern Mirjan, at the mouth of the Gangawali River, north of Honawar. *Mergeu* in Barbosa, the Portuguese chroniclers and Reinel's map of *c.* 1517, *Mergueo* on Reinel's map of *c.* 1518, and *Mergeo* on later maps.

ONOR—Honavar or Honawar. Omitted in the Lisbon MS and in Ramusio. *Honor* in Barbosa and *Onor* in Portuguese chronicles and maps.

BATICALA—Bhatkal. *Baticalla* on Rodrigues' map (fol. 28).

BAÇALOR—Corresponds to Basrur, a village in Coondapur, or Kundapur, in south Kanara District, situated to the south of a large estuary into which three rivers run. The ruins of an old Portuguese fort are still there. *Braçalor* in Barbosa, *Barcelor* and *Bracelor* in the Portuguese chronicles and maps.

Honawar and Mirjan to Anjediva belongs to the king of Gersoppa (*Garçopa*) who neighbours on Goa [and is] for the king of Narsinga; Bhatkal, with Basrur and other inland towns, has a king; the other four ports have captains. They are all vassals of the king of Narsinga and pay their revenues to him.

The king of Gersoppa is an important man, with many mounted men—up to three thousand, so they say. Gersoppa stretches five leagues up the Honawar river. Inland there is a small, cool town, where *Timoja*[1] lives. He used to live in Honawar, because he was related to the king of Gersoppa. He is often at the king of Narsinga's court, and is his obedient vassal. This river of Honawar is thickly populated, and has ships, out of which *Timoja* made the armada with which he went pillaging from here to Cape Guardafui, where he took a great deal of booty. This *Timoja* was feared by the seamen and helped the king of Gersoppa.

Bhatkal (Baticala).

The king of Bhatkal is a Kanarese heathen and a greater king than those of Honawar and Gersoppa. His kingdom extends a long way inland. The port of Bhatkal comes next in importance to Goa and Chaul, and has a great deal of trade. It is the port which serves the kingdom of Narsinga, and through which the

BAIRA VERA—As Pires gives all these names in geographical order, it seems that *Baira Vera* should be between *Baçalor* (Basrur) and *Bacanor* (Barkur, on the Sitanadi River). But between the mouths of the Coondapur estuary and the Sitanadi River there is no break in the coast line that could be called a port. There is the small port of Baindur, at the entrance of the Baindur River, but that lies between Bhatkal and Basrur. *Bacanor* corresponds to the village of Barkur, on the north side of an estuary of several rivers, the more important being the Sitanadi on the north, and the Swarnanadi on the south. About one mile south of Barkur, between the two rivers, lies the village of Brahmawar, and it is possible that this may be Pires' *Baira Vera*, perhaps the *Barrauerrão* placed by Castanheda (II, xvi) between *Bacanor* and *Baticalâ*.

BACANOR—The old village of Barkur, in Kanarese, the traditional capital of Taluva (*Imp. Gaz. of India, s.v.*) corresponds to the Malayalam Fakanur or Vakkanur, the *Bacanor* of all Portuguese chronicles and maps.

VDIPIRAM—Udipi, the principal town near the river, lies inland, about two and a half miles from Malpe or Mulpi, which is at the entrance of Udiyavara Hole (Malpe River), about thirty miles north of Mangalore. It must be *Vdebarrão*, a 'very large and good port', that Castanheda (II, xvi) places near Mangalore.

[1] Timoja was a pirate, later employed by Albuquerque who appointed him bailiff (*Aguazil*) of Goa in 1510. He proved unfaithful and before his death in 1511 joined forces with the Adil Khan.

horses come. The city has many merchants, both heathens and Moors. It is a great port of call with many merchants and is a large port. The king is always inland. He has made *Damj*, a Chetti, governor of the heathens in his kingdom, as he has the most property and is a great merchant; and the governor of the Moorish people is *Caizar*, a Moorish eunuch who was a servant of *Cojatar*[1], the one of Ormuz. There are Moors of all nations in this city, which used to be very great before the capture of Goa by the Captain General, and which is now already of less importance.

Bhatkal used to be the most important of all the ports in the kingdoms of Kanara, on account of its many merchants, and many horses from all parts were landed here, and much other merchandise. These horses were bought for the kingdom of Narsinga, and heavy dues were paid on them. The merchants returned from this land of Kanara with quantities of the best rice there is in this part of the world, that is *giraçal* which is the finest and whitest and most expensive and considered the best; after this comes *chambaçal* and after *chambaçal* comes the *pacharil* from Goa and the kingdom of the Deccan[2]. They also took back iron and a great deal of sugar which there is in this country, and many sugar preserves which are made in Bhatkal; these [were products] of the land. And many of the merchants from Malabar used to go there so that its trade was of great account. This is the most important possession the king of Narsinga has in Kanara.

As for *Baira Vera*, Barkur, *Vdipiram* and Mangalore, they are all ports for ships and merchants, who trade with Cambay and with the kingdoms of Goa and the Deccan and Ormuz, taking the products of the country and bringing others [in exchange]. There are important captains in these ports, with garrisons of
Fol. 126r. men. Their revenues are paid to the king of Narsinga. | The king derives large revenues from this country of Kanara, both from the seaports and from the land, and he has fortresses, such

[1] *Cojatar* or *Coje Atar*—Khwaja Attar, wazir of Ormuz under the Sheikh Ismail.

[2] Many early Portuguese writers refer to these three kinds of Indian rice. Pires' description is very accurate. Dalgado (*s.v.* Arroz) deals at length with the several kinds of rice in India.

as they use, on the sea coast, but the most powerful fortresses are formed by the mouths of the rivers. The whole country is well cultivated, large, and good. It is very productive and has many people, both mounted and on foot. It has much betel and areca. The Kanara country has many large and important praying temples. There are many Brahmans of different kinds and orders, some of them chaste and some of them not. They are in the habit of burning the women as they do in the kingdom of Goa in the same way as is told of the other heathen.

These provinces are [as follows]: Dacanis of the kingdom of the Deccan; Konkani of the kingdom of Goa; Kanarese of the kingdom of Narsinga. Each one has its own separate origin. And because these lands belong to the king of Narsinga, I decided to deal with the kingdom of Narsinga here, as it would have been as convenient to talk about him when describing the Choromandel coast, where he is a greater lord. And because he rules here I will say a little now and I will tell the rest when I am describing Choromandel.

[NARSINGA]

The kingdom of *Narsinga*[1] is large and very important. It is bordered on one side by the kingdom of the Deccan and Goa, and that part is Kanarese, the chief city of which is Vijayanagar (*Bizanaguar*), where the king is in residence. On the Ganges side, where the river flows into the sea it marches with part of the dominions of the kingdom of Bengal and with the kingdom of Orissa, and inland it is bounded by the mountains of Delhi and

[1] *Narsinga*, *Bisnagar* or *Bisnaga*, is the name applied by the Portuguese—as similar forms were applied by many other Europeans after them, such as *Beejanugger*, *Bidjanagar*, *Bichenegher* or *Bijanagher*—in the sixteenth and seventeenth centuries to a large kingdom in Southern India. *Bisnagar* or *Bisnaga* is a corruption of *Vijayanagara*, the name of a dynasty that reigned until about 1487. The capital of the kingdom was the city of Vijayanagar, founded in 1336, the ruins of which still exist in the Bellary District, Madras, preserved by the British Government. In 1487 the dynasty of Vijayanagar was replaced by Narasinha, a prince who reigned till 1508. When the Portuguese first arrived in India they called that part of the country the kingdom of Narsinga, a name derived from that of its actual ruler.

on the ocean side by the provinces of Malabar and Choromandel and *Benua Quilim*[1].

In older times the kingdom of Narsinga was much greater than it is now and embraced almost the whole of the Deccan as far as Bengal, including Orissa and all the maritime provinces. Now it is not so big because[2] the Deccan, Goa, Malabar and Orissa have [each a] king; but still it is large. With the exception of the kingdom of Delhi, this is the largest province in these parts, and, they say, in India.

The king is a heathen of Kanara, and on the other hand he is a Kling; in his court[3] the language is mixed, but his natural speech is Kanarese. This King is a warrior and he often goes into the field with more than forty thousand mounted men and a large number on foot. He must have five hundred elephants, two hundred of which are for war[4]. He is always at war, sometimes with Orissa, sometimes with the Deccan and sometimes inside his own country. He has great captains and many mercenaries. When he rests it is in Vijaynagar, a city of twenty thousand inhabitants[5], which lies between two mountain ranges. The houses there are not usually very much ornamented. The king's houses or palaces are large and well built, and the king has a good following of noblemen and horsemen. He has great lords with

[1] *Choromandel* was the designation generally given by the Portuguese to the east coast of India, from Ceylon northwards to the Kistna River in the present Madras Residency. According to Dalgado (I, 313; II, 484) the right spelling is *Choromandel*, as written by Pires and Barbosa (though the latter prefers *Choramândel* and Yule *Coromandel*), the *ch* being pronounced as in 'church'. Pires does not give a special description of Choromandel anywhere in the *Suma*. Further on, dealing with Bengal he mentions five ports, from *Cultarey* (Nellore?) to Negapatam, 'all these ports in the *Bonuaquelim*, land of Narsinga'. See note p. 92. Dealing with the Malacca trade he refers to twelve 'ports of the coast of Choromandel' from *Caile* (Old Kayal) to Pulicat. See notes pp. 81 and 271–2. However, in his letter of 27 Jan. 1516, Pires says that '*Choromandell* is from the shoals (of *Chilã*) to *Cunjmeyra* (Pondicherry)'.

[2] In the Paris MS this word reads *que* (that); but in the Lisbon MS it is *porque* (because), and similarly in Ramusio. The transcriber of the Paris MS left out the *por* of *porque*, making the sentence unintelligible.

[3] The Paris MS has *arte* (art). But the Lisbon MS says *corte* (court), and similarly in Ramusio.

[4] The Lisbon MS says 300,000 mounted men and 800 elephants. Ramusio agrees with the Paris MS.

[5] The Lisbon MS says 50,000 inhabitants. Ramusio agrees with the Paris MS.

him and he is held in great respect. There are a thousand girl entertainers in his court, and four or five thousand men of the same profession. These are Klings and not Kanarese, because the natives of this province of Kalinga (*Talingo*)[1] are more graceful and more apt in mimicry than those of other parts. Many of these people are scattered from here all over the three Indias, and I will tell more about them in the description of his other dominion.

Middle India. As the First India ends at Mangalore in the land of Kanarese, you are now entering into the Second or Middle India, which begins at Manjeshwaram (*Mayciram*), the first port in Malabar, and ends at the river Ganges on the Bengal frontier. And the present account of this land will be divided into two parts: in the first part you will be told about the land of Malabar, how large it is, how many ports it has where there are ships, how many kings it has, what customs the people have, and who is the chief person in the province, and you will also be told about the trade in Malabar and about the number of ships there are there.

In the second part[2] you will hear about the king of Narsinga and his country, about the people with whom he fights, what horsemen he has, and something about his habits, and also the extent of the kingdom, with some account of the trade there is in his ports also.

And then we must deal with the kingdom of Orissa or *Odia*[3], *Fol. 126v.* and our Second or Middle India will have been as far as possible described.

[MALABAR]

Province of Malabar. The province of Malabar begins at Manjeshwaram (*Maycerã*), a port belonging to the king of Bisnagar, which neighbours

[1] *Talingo*, Telinga, Telingana or Kalinga, is a group of Telugu-speaking people of Dravidian race from Southern India. According to Yule (*Hobson-Jobson*) *Kalinga* is a very ancient name for the Telugu coast of the Bay of Bengal, i.e., that coast which lies between the Kistna and Mahanadi rivers.

[2] This is one of the many confusions in the division of the *Suma*; actually Narsinga had just been described, before Malabar.

[3] *Orixa* or Orissa, corresponding to the vernacular *Odisa*, whence *Odia*, as in this case, must not be confused with Ayuthia, which was written also as *Odia* by Pires and other sixteenth-century Portuguese writers. See note p. 103.

Mangalore in the land of Kanarese belonging to the king of Narsinga, and it ends at Cape Comorin in the king of Quilon's land, which borders on the province of Kalinga in the said kingdom of Narsinga. Inland the whole of this country is surrounded by mountains which divide it from the said kingdom of Narsinga. This country must extend from a hundred and ten to a hundred and twenty leagues along the coast, and inland to the mountains it is about five leagues wide in some places and fifteen in others, and so it goes on without getting narrower or wider.

Mountains which divide Malabar from Narsinga.

These lands are so high that they do not allow the north-east and east winds to penetrate to the Indian coast, nor on the other hand do the south-west and west winds blow in the kingdom of Narsinga—that is, if you are coming from Ceylon to the coast of India with fresh winds blowing from the above [quarters], they cease blowing when you reach the Choromandel coast. You set out with the west winds, and as soon as you enter the Ceylon channel they stop blowing. Whence it follows that since Malabar is lacking in dry winds it is fresh and gracious, while the province of Choromandel, which lacks wet winds, is sterile, without a single tree, large or small, as I shall tell in more detail when I describe it. Enough of this.

The faith of Malabar.

The whole of Malabar believes, as we do, in the Trinity of Father, Son and Holy Ghost, three in one, the only true God[1]. From Cambay to Bengal all the people hold this [faith], as I will tell in more detail in the description of the land where St. Thomas the Apostle lies.

I ought not to enter into an account of Malabar, which is already so well known to Your Highness, since you have three beautiful, large and important fortresses there, that is, that of Calicut, that of Cochin with a very large gateway made entirely

[1] Dames (I, 115; II, 37) says that the 'Trinity' described by Barbosa is related to the Hindu Trimurtti or the three-fold god of Brahma with Vishnu and Siva. When describing Cambay, Castro (p. 114) says that it 'is inhabited by a people called *Guzarates* . . . among whom there are some men, like philosophers and religious men, who are called *Bramenes*, who believe in the Holy Trinity, Father, Son, Holy Ghost, and many other things of our very sacred law'. Barros (I, iv, 9; II, v, I) also refers to the Brahman 'Trinity' but remarks that it is 'very different' from the Christian Trinity, and is also rejected by the Mohammedans.

of lime of cockle-shells, and that of Cannanore which is well situated with a good moat; but, to keep to the promised order I will mention everything in this voyage.

The people of Malabar are black and some of them dark brown. All the kings are Brahmans, which is the caste of their priests. The language is almost the same [throughout the country]. They differ in very little, as is the case in Italy. The whole country is thickly populated. There must be a hundred and fifty thousand Nayars (*Naires*)[1] in Malabar. They are fighters, with sword and buckler, and archers. They are men who adore their king, and if by chance the king dies in battle they are obliged to die, and if they do not they go against the custom of their country and they are made a reproach for ever. The Nayars are loyal and not traitors. Before a king of Malabar fights with another, he has first to let him know, so that he may prepare himself. That is their custom. No Nayar, when he is fit to take up arms, can go outside his house unarmed even if he be a hundred years old, and when he is dying he always has his sword and buckler by him, so close that if necessary he can take hold of them. They always make a deep reverence to the masters who teach them, so much so that if the best of the Nayars were to meet a Mukkuvan (*Macua*)[2] who happened to have taught him something, he would make him a reverence and then go and wash himself. If a Nayar meets another older than himself on the road, he does him reverence and gives place to him. If there were two, three or four brothers, the oldest would have to be seated while the others remained standing.

And because the chief people of Malabar are the Brahmans, from whom the kings are descended, and who are more noble by reason of their priesthood, I will talk about them first and afterwards about the Nayars and the other castes.

[1] The *Naires* were aborigines of South-Western India, where they formed the noble and military caste corresponding to the Kshatriyas, second in importance to the Brahmans. At present, 'Nair or Nayar is a title added to nearly all the names of the race, and it is, like Mister or Esquire, assumed as a birthright by any respectable member of the race who has no other'. Balfour, *The Cyclopaedia of India, s.v.*

[2] A caste name applied to the fishermen of Malabar coast, from the Dravidian *mukkuha*, 'to dive'. Mukkuvan is the name generally used, but Mucua (in the plural Mucuar) is also frequently met with.

Fol. 127r. Brahmans are priests who wear a cord hanging from the left shoulder and under the right arm[1]. This cord is composed of twenty-seven threads, made in three. The best of this people are the Kshatriyas (*Chatrias*); then come the Pattars (*Patadares*) and after these the Nambutiris (*Nambuderis*), and lowest of all come the Nambutiris (*Namburis*)[2]. These Brahmans are of very ancient birth. They are of purer blood than the Nayars. It is their duty to be in the *turucois*[3] praying. They are well versed in the things of their faith. The most important of these Brahmans are with the king of Malabar. They are men who do not eat anything which has been living [flesh and] blood; and for this reason the ancients said of them that no person in Malabar should have the power to eat beef on pain of death, and that this would be a great sin. The reason must be because the Brahman women ate the milk and afterwards refused the meat, whence comes the great esteem in which cows are held, for in many heathen places the cow is worshipped as a sacred thing. These Brahmans have the power of excommunication and absolution. None of them bears arms or goes to war; nor are they ever put to death for any reason whatever. They go freely wherever they like, even if there is war.

Many people in Malabar, Nayars as well as Brahmans and their wives—in fact about a quarter or a fifth of the total population, including the people of the lowest castes—have very large legs, swollen to a great size; and they die of this, and it is an ugly thing to see. They say that this is due to the water through which they go, because the country is marshy. This is called

[1] This sacred thread, called *punul,* is always worn by Brahmans.

[2] 'A few of the princely families of Malabar claim to be pure Kshatriyas . . . Racially, no doubt, Kshatriyas were originally Nayars'. C. A. Innes, *Malabar Gazetter*, p. 112, Madras, 1908. The Kshatriyas are immediately below the Brahmans in the caste hierarchy. The generic name for the Malabar Brahman is Nambúdiri. In addition to the Nambúdiris—who are mostly landlords, and are polluted by the touch of all castes below them, and by the approach of all lower than Nayars—there are two other classes of Brahmans, called Pattars and Embrándiris. The two forms *nambudiri* and *namburi* are both Malayalam for Nambutiri. Pires' remarks are rather confusing, though he is not far from the truth.

[3] *Turucol, Turicol* or *Turcol*—Temple or pagoda in Malabar, according to Dalgado, *s.v.* But Góis (I, lxxxix, cxii) says—'a *Turcol,* which are houses of prayer, where live religious men, as friars among us', suggesting a monastery.

pericaes in the native language, and all the swelling is the same from the knees downward, and they have no pain, nor do they take any notice of this infirmity[1].

In Malabar it is the custom for the woman to have her eyes on the bed during the act of coition and for the man to have his on the ceiling, and this is the general practice among great and small, and they consider anything else to be strange and foreign to their condition, and some Portuguese used[2] to the country do not find this ugly.

Malabar physicians.

When they are ill the patients do not eat meat; and have a diet of fish alone. The chief remedy is to play the kettle-drum and other instruments to the patients for two or three days—and they say this does good. If they have fever they eat fish and keep washing themselves; if they vomit they wash their heads with cold water and it is good, and it stops; and if they have a catarrh they drink *lanha* water—*lanha* is the young coconut—and it stops at once; if they want to purge themselves they take the crushed leaves, or the juice or the seeds of the *figueira do inferno*[3], and they are well purged, and they wash themselves; if they are badly wounded, they let warm coconut oil run over the wound twice a day for an hour or two, and they are cured. Our people when they have fevers eat fat chickens and drink wine and are cured. This happens to many, but those who go on a diet are used up.

Affronts in Malabar.

What is considered in Malabar to be the worst thing you can

[1] *Perical* or *Panicale*—From the Malayalam *perikkal*, 'big leg'—elephantiasis; also commonly called 'Cochin leg' or 'St. Thomas's leg' in India.

[2] Though in the Paris MS it is written *trosnados* (a meaningless word), the Lisbon MS has *custumados*, and Ramusio translated accordingly.

[3] Although several Portuguese-English dictionaries refer to *Figueira do inferno* as Palma Christi or castor-oil plant, this is incorrect. The Palma Christi or Castor-oil is *Ricinus communis* Linn., and the *Figueira do inferno* is *Datura Stramonium* Linn. Both plants are found in Portugal as well as in India, and though they belong to distant families, there is some sort of resemblance between them. The Datura, whose effects were so picturesquely described by Garcia da Orta (xx) in 1563, is sometimes mixed in India with intoxicants, which thereby become 'most reprehensible and even dangerous to life. Moreover, the seeds are known to enter into the composition of certain alcoholic beverages and render the consumers of these literally mad'. Watt, p. 488. Pires undoubtedly refers to *Ricinus communis*, though it seems rather strange that he should mistake one plant for the other.

do to anyone to whom you bear ill-will is to break a new saucepan at his door. This is a great insult. Or if you pass along the street and throw it so that it breaks against that person, that is worse. These things mean death for the man who does them, and anyone who lets them pass is for ever dishonoured.

The kings of Malabar are all Brahmans with these threads, some of them of more noble birth than others; because it is the custom in Malabar that the king's son does not succeed to the kingdom, but his brother or nephew; and because they are Brahmans and cannot marry Nayars, since that is forbidden, they choose the most honoured Brahmans of that generation to mate with the [king's] sisters, so that the eldest [son] may succeed; and thus the Brahmans sleep with the king's sisters and from them come the kings of Malabar. As the king of Cochin is of pure blood and there is no one on earth whom he can marry, if there are Brahman *Patamares* of Cambay—who were related of old to the Brahman king, who was once held to be a saint—these are chosen for the act of generation; and if there are more they take the noblest Brahmans in the land. They say that this has been their custom for thirty thousand years.

Fol. 127v.

Custom of the Kings of Malabar.

The kings of Malabar marry as often as they like; and after they have had the women they give them in marriage, according to the custom of the country, to important people. The king's sons are Nayars like the others. They do not inherit anything. Many of the kings marry for dowries and sometimes they keep them until their death. If any king of Malabar wants the wife of one of the most honourable men of his kingdom, who are the Kaimals (*Caimaes*), she comes willingly, and these Kaimals are greatly honoured[1]. Often the great lords give money to the *Patamares* to deflower their wives, and the *Patamares* argue about the price.

All the Brahmans are married. Their sons inherit their property. The Brahman women are chaste and do not lie with any

[1] *Caimal* or Kaimal—Duarte Barbosa says: 'certain earls (condes) whom they call Cahimal'. Dames (II, 13) translated *condes* more generally as 'nobles'. According to Dalgado (I, 172), sometimes it is the ordinary mode of address employed by the low classes when speaking to some Nayar or an individual of the military caste in Malabar. Further on Pires refers again to the *Caimaes* in more detail (pp. 81–2).

man but their husbands; and the Brahman woman always remains a Brahman and her children are of unmixed race. A Brahman woman must not sleep with a Nayar man, but a Nayar woman may sleep with a Brahman man at will[1].

Nayars of Malabar.

None of the Nayars have either father or son. They do not marry. The more lovers a Nayar woman has, the more important she is. So if a Nayar woman has a daughter, or two or three, she chooses a Nayar for her while she is a virgin, and he marries her. For the deflowering they make a feast, for which the Nayar pays according to his means; and he stays with her for four days, and as a sign that he has deflowered her he places a small piece of gold round her neck, worth about thirty *reis*, called *quete*[2]. This man goes, and other Nayars come; and they arrange among themselves—one gives her one thing, and one another, and the more she has the more honoured she is. And the Nayars are also put to expense with other women. For the most part the Nayars do not eat in the women's houses. And that is why no Nayar has ever had father or son, because each woman has from two to ten known [lovers], which is accounted a merit in her. There are also Nayars who sell oil and fish, and many are craftsmen.

If any Pulayan (*poleaa*) touches a Nayar woman with his hand or with a stone when she is out of her house, he runs the risk of being killed or sold, and if he touches her when she is walking with a Nayar she is not contaminated. This is done so that they shall not seek the company of people of low condition. If he who touches her is caught, he dies for this crime. The Nayar women of Malabar have no virtue, nor do they sew or work, but only eat and amuse themselves.

[1] The Paris and Lisbon MSS agree in this sentence. But Ramusio's translation, which I follow here, seems more correct than the two Portuguese texts.

[2] According to the Lisbon MS, which, as well as Ramusio, calls it also *quete*. Many sixteenth-century writers describe this marriage ceremony and this ornament, but no one else calls it *quete*. Some of them call it *tali* or *tale*. Dalgado records *quete* as meaning in Ceylon a handful or small portion. However, the *Talikettu* or *Tali-kettu Kalyanam* is the name given among the Nayars and some other Malayalam castes to the marriage ceremony gone through by girls, much on the lines described by Pires. Iyer, *The Cochin Tribes and Castes*, II, 22–8; Thurston, *Castes and Tribes of Southern India*, *s.v.*

Families in Malabar. In Malabar a son cannot be more important than his father, in the way the sons of a Brahman woman can; and a Nayar is always a Nayar, and in all the crafts, and among jesters, singers and sorcerers, the son has to follow his father's profession.

The lowest caste are the Parayans (*pareos*) who eat cows' flesh. They are lettered men and sorcerers. The Pulayans work in the fields and so do the Vettuvans (*beituãas*); the Vannathamars (*mainates*) are washermen; the *Yravas* are stone-masons; the Pulayans play music in the *turucoes* or at feasts; the *Canjares* dance in the temples and pagodas; the Mukkuvans are fishermen; the Kaniyans (*canacos*) make salt; and in addition to these there are carpenters, goldsmiths and craftsmen of all kinds; and then there are the *Irava* men who make the wine[1]. None of these may go along the roads frequented by the Nayars, and they all keep away from them on pain of death; and in case of need—such as war or sickness—and in fencing and jousts for sword and lance, the Nayars and the king may touch them, and wash themselves and be clean; and if a Nayar needs any thing from these people, it is not a sin for him to deal with them if it is for his own benefit. In all these castes the son inherits his father's property, and each man is married to one woman.

I will not enter into further details about this province, which is full of idolatry and witchcraft and other very heathen practices, because you already know about the conditions there, and because it is not a subject which comes within the scope of this account.

Fol. 128r. *Snakes.* There are *cobras de capello* in this province and also breath-snakes (*cobras de bafo*)[2]. The *cobras de capello* are small and black,

[1] Barbosa mentions eighteen different castes of Malabar, which Dames (II, 71) assembles in a table, comparing the names given by him with those in Ramusio's translation and the Spanish, together with the modern forms. The *Yravas* and *Canjares* are not among them, unless the latter are either the Chaliyans, weavers, referred to by Barbosa as *Caletis*, or the Kusavans, potters, referred to as *Cuiavem*. Although the *Yravas* or *Jrauaas* are mentioned as masons and wine-makers, Dalgado (*s.v.* Iravá) quotes them only under the latter craft. Barbosa refers to the *Poleas*, Poleahs or Pulayans as rice tillers only, to the *Betunes* or Vettuvans as salt-makers, and to the *Canaquas* or Kaniyan as astrologers.

[2] These 'breath-snakes' cannot be identified. They must be a product of the natives' imagination, and Pires says quite honestly that he had never seen them.

as thick as your thumb and three or four spans long. They have fangs, and the loose skin on their heads makes a kind of covering called a hood (*capello*) when they raise them. If these snakes bite, they kill at once. They say that the breath-snakes are the same length and as thick as a man's wrist, without hoods, and that their breath alone is deadly. I have never met a man who has seen one. Both heathen and Mohammedan sorcerers take the cobras about in jars, and by making a certain noise they make the snakes move about on the ground, and when they say certain words to them they take them fearlessly in their hands; but if by chance the snakes do bite them, they die. The sorcerers catch these [snakes] wild in the jungle and charm them. The Nayars and the Brahmans are forbidden by law to kill cobras, which they say are holy things, and they have special places for them in their gardens, where they give them cooked rice.

Christians in this province.

There are fifteen thousand Christians in this province of Malabar, dating back to the time of St. Thomas the Apostle. Two thousand of these are men of repute, noblemen, merchants, estimable people, and the others are craftsmen, poor people. They are privileged and are allowed to touch the Nayars. These Christians live in the district from Chetwayi (*Chetua*) to Quilon (*Coulam*). Outside this area there are none of the early Christians —I do not refer to those who have been converted in Your Highness' time, nor to those who are now being converted every day, and who are numerous.

Malabar country where there are rivers.

In one part of this land of Malabar there are large rivers, deep in some places and shallow in others, which make it strong, and where they fish, where they can go in large *tones*, to wit, from Ponnani (*Panane*) to Quilon. The other part of Malabar is dry and easy to travel over by land; but in this part [you have to go] in *tones catures*[1].

Kings in Malabar.

Going from Mangalore to Comorin, the following are the kings in the province of Malabar: the king of *Bangar*, the king of

[1] *Tone* or *tona* is a small boat with a sail and oars, used in Southern India. *Catur* is also a long narrow boat much used in India in old times. It seems probable that the modern English 'cutter' is derived from *catur*. Pires gives more particulars about this craft, further on, and always uses the two names together, apparently to represent a single craft.

Cota[1], the king of Cannanore, the king of Calicut, the king of Tanore (*Tanor*), the king of Kranganur (*Cramganor*), the king of Cochin, the king of Kayankulam (*Caya Coulam*), the king of Quilon (*Coulam*), the king of Travancore, the king of Comorin. There are great Kaimals in this country, some of whom are greater than many of these kings, though they have not the title of king. Some of them are Brahmans and some of them Nayars. The king who has the most land and the most people is the king of Quilon; the one who has more nobility is the king of Cochin; the king of Calicut has the greatest title. After Quilon in inhabitants comes Cannanore, and after Cannanore comes Kayankulam. The men of Calicut are the best fighters.

Sea ports in this province. The following are the inhabited seaports in this province where there are ships: Manjeshwaram (*Mayceram*), *Mayporam*, Kumbla (*Combula*), Kattakulam (*Coty Coulam*), Nileshweram (*Njliporam*), *Hyeri*, Baliapatam (*Balea Patanam*), Cannanore, Durmapatan (*Tarmapatam*), Madayid (*Marlarjanj*), Chombakulu (*Combaa*), Puthupattanam (*Pudopatanam*), Tricodi (*Tiricorij*), *Bairacono*, Kollam (*Coulam*), which they call Pantaláyini (*Pamdaranj*), Kappatta (*Capocar*), Calicut, Chaliyam (*Chaliaa*), Parappanangadi (*Para Purancorj*), Tanore (*Tanor*), Ponnani (*Panane*), Veleankode (*Bely Ancoro*), Chetwayi (*Chetua*), Kranganur (*Cramganor*), Cochin, Kayankulam (*Caya Coulam*), Quilon (*Coulam*), Vilinjam (*Bilinjão*), Comorin[2].

[1] BANGAR—*Bemgar* in the Lisbon MS. Probably Bandadkar, inland, between Mangalore and Cannanore. COTA—Probably Kottayam, the district east of Cannanore.

[2] In the Lisbon MS these names read as follows: 'maiçeram/ maiporam/ combula/ cotecoulão nilixorão/ eriballcaa/ patanam/ cananor tumapatam/ murlariom/ combaa/ pudy patanam/ tericori/ baicarom/ coulão a q̃ chamão pamdarane capocar/ calequiu chale/ parapurãocole/ tanor/ panane/ betiamcor/ chatuaa/ chamganor cochym caicoulão/ coulão/ belurgam & o comorym'.

MAYÇERAM—Probably Manjeshvar or Manjeshwaram, nine miles south-south-westward of Mangalore; the *Mangeiram* placed by Barros (I, ix, I) between Mangalore and Kumbla (*Cumbata*). It appears as *Mamgesirão* and *Magicera* on several sixteenth-century Portuguese maps.

MAYPORAM—No place can now be found between Manjeshwaram and Kumbla which could be called a port, the coast being unbroken, flat, and a continuous coconut palm grove.

COMBULA—Kumbla, seven and a half miles from Manjeshwaram; *Cumbola* in Barbosa, *Cumbata* in Barros.

There must be about four hundred cargo boats in the kingdom of Malabar, in the kingdoms and ports we have just

COTY COULAM—Kattakulam, a modern place in South Kanara, according to Dames, II, 79. *Cotecolam* in Barbosa, *Cóta-Coulão* in Barros.

NJLIPORAM—It may be 'represented today by the village of Nileshwar or Nileshweram, south of Kasaragod', as suggested by Cordier. *Cathay and the Way Thither*, IV, 74. *Minaporam* in Barbosa, *Nilichilão* in Barros.

HYERI—A place that existed in the bay south of Mount Dely, or Jelly Paud. It corresponds to Marco Polo's *Eli*, a name that Yule says survives 'in that of Mount *Dely*, properly Monte d'Ely, the *Yeli-mala*'. *Marco Polo*, III, xxiv. On the map of *c.* 1510 it appears as *ely*. On Rodrigues' map (fol. 28) it is recorded as *momte dally*; and the *Livro de Marinharia* (p. 224) says that *mõte dEly* is five leagues from Cannanore.

BALEA PATANAM—Baliapatam, Valarpattanam or Azhikkal, a small town and port on the south bank of the river of the same name, five miles north of Cannanore. *Balaerpatam* in Barbosa, *Bolepatan* in Barros and *Baleapatão* on some Portuguese maps.

TARMAPATAM—Durmapatan or Dharmapatna, seven miles south-west of Cannanore. *Tremapatam* in Barros and on Rodrigues' map.

MARLARJANJ—Perhaps the *Maranel* of Barbosa and the *Marabia* of Barros, Correia and the Portuguese maps, which Dames (II, 79) identifies with 'the place known as Madayid (also called Pazhayangadi)'.

COMBAA—Chombakulu, a little port two and a half miles south-east of Mahé, the French settlement at the mouth of the river of the same name.

PUDOPATANAM—Puthupanam or Puthupattanam, on the Kotta River. *Pedirpatam* in Barbosa, *Puripatan* in Barros.

TIRICORIJ—Tricodi. *Tircore* in Barbosa.

BAIRACONÒ—A place which no longer exists, possibly on the small bay between Kadalur Point and Vellarakkad, a hillock one and two-thirds miles westwards.

COULAM—PAMDARANJ—*Coulam* is the small port Kollam, about three miles from Kadalur Point, and *Pamdaranj* is Pandaláyini, a place near Kollam. *Pandanare* in Barbosa, *Pandarane* in the chronicles. Perhaps it is the *paudacar* on the map of *c.* 1510. It appears as *ilheos de pamdarane* on Rodrigues' map. In the *Livro de Marinharia* it is said that *Pamderanne* is five leagues from *Tramapatão*. *Pandarani* is already recorded on Reinel's maps of *c.* 1517 and *c.* 1518.

CAPOCAR—Must correspond to the small port of Kappatta, between Kollam and Calicut. *Capucate* in Barbosa, *Capocate* in the chronicles.

CHALIAA—Chaliyam, a place at the entrance of the Chalium or Chaliyar River, where the Portuguese had a fortress, four and a half miles south-south-east of Calicut Creek or Kallayi River. *Chiliate* in Barbosa, *Chála* in Barros.

PARA PURANCORJ—Parappanangadi, the small port eight and a half miles southwards. *Propriamguary* in Barbosa, *Parangale* in the chronicles.

TANOR—Tanore, Tanur or Tánniyúrnagaram, four and a half miles further south.

BELY ANCORO—Veleankode or Velijangod, at the entrance of the Kanniramukker River, four miles south-east of Ponnani. *Baleancor* in Barros.

described. Some of these are large and some small; they are *ladas*, ships of shallow draught[1] with flat bottoms, which will take heavy loads and draw less water than ships with keels. They are made like this because the Malabar people usually sail along the province of Kalinga, which includes the district from Comorin to Pulicat (*Paleacate*). As there is a channel between this land and Ceylon, where the water in the middle is only a fathom and a half deep at low tide, and which is called the shoals of *Chilam* (*Baixos Chilam*)[2], they had to make *ladas*. That is the reason why these people do not sail on the high seas, except in fear and trembling. They have still other small ships, which they call *pagueres*[3] and which take as much cargo as caravels.

Where the rice comes from. The whole of this province is lacking in rice, and it hardly produces any. In the district from Tanore to Manjeshwaram the rice comes from Goa and Narsinga on the Kanarese side. This rice is cold and can be used as far as Tanore. From Tanore to Quilon

CHETUA—Chetwayi, a modern town on an island within the mouth of the river of the same name. *Chatua* in Barbosa and the chronicles.

CRAMGANOR—Cranganor, Cranganur or Kranganur.

CAYA COULAM—Kayankulam, about fifty miles south-south-east of Cochin. *Cale Coilam* in Barbosa, *Caecoulam*, *Cale Coulão* and *Caicoulão* in the chronicles and maps.

BILINJÃO—Vilinjam, about forty miles south-east of Kayankulam. *Berinjam* in Barros, *Brimgão*, *Brijão* and *Brimgiam* on some maps.

[1] *Lada* was an old Portuguese word to designate a river bank or 'water way along which ships, or any other vessels (that were then indifferently called *ships*) could sail'. Cf. Viterbo, *Elucidario*, *s.v.* Lada. Pires' *naos ladas* may mean in this case *naus de pouco calado* (ships of shallow draught).

[2] *Baixos de Chilam* or *Chilão* was the name given by the Portuguese to the shifting sandbanks, with intricate channels, now known as Adam's Bridge, between Mannari island, off the west coast of Ceylon, and Pamban island, off the Indian coast. When referring to *os baixos de Chilão*, the *Livro de Marinharia* (p. 231) mentions 'the sandy *Chilão* point' which lies west-south-westward, when coming from the north; this corresponds to Chultram point, on the eastern end of Pamban island, now the terminus of the South Indian Railway. The passage through the *baixos de Chilão* was near this point, where the water is not so shallow. There is, however, on the western coast of Ceylon, though rather more to the south, the conspicuous point and port of Chilaw, which the Portuguese designated first as *Celabão* or *Celauam*, and later as *Chilam* or *Chilão*, obviously connected with the name of the *baixos*. Barros (III, ii, I) and Couto (V, i, 7) say, erroneously, that from the *baixos de Chilão* came the name of *Ceilão* to the island. (See note on Ceylon, p. 85.)

[3] Ancient cargo boats in Southern India, often mentioned by the chroniclers. Dalgado, *s.v.* Paguel.

they get their rice from the province of Kalinga by Choromandel. This rice is hot and is used up to Tanore whence it appears that where the Choromandel rice is used, that from Goa and the Kanarese is of no value, and on the other hand where the Kanarese is used, the other rice is worth a third part less or only half as much.

Fol. 128v.

Distribution of the ports among the kingdom.

The ports of Manjeshwaram and Mayporam belong to the king of Bandadkar (*Bangar*). Malabar begins here and this king is a neighbour of the Kanarese. It is a land with plenty of rice and plenty of fish. Although the people of this kingdom are few in number, they are warlike. They are great archers, and they use arrows with long and wide heads. They defend their country and sometimes make war on the Kanarese. It is a small kingdom. These two seaports have a few ships and some inhabited places, and they trade with those of this province.

The king of Kottayam.

The king of Kottayam has no seaport; all his power is on land. It is a kingdom like the one described above. It is at war with Cannanore. He mints coins against the will of the kings of Malabar and fears none of them. He and the king of Cannanore are great enemies. His people and his land are strong, and it is from here that the *Cota fanões*[1] come.

Kingdom of Cannanore.

The ports of Kumbla, Kattakulam, Nileshweram, Hyeri, Baliapatam, Cannanore, Durmapatan and Madayid belong to the king of Cannanore. All these ports are unimportant, except the port of Cannanore which is large, noble and important. This kingdom of Cannanore is large and has a large city and much trade and many people. The land is good; there is good air and good water; there are many Moors. The city of Cannanore has many wealthy merchants. If Your Highness had not taken this kingdom under your rule, it would be Moorish by now, because a certain *Mamalle Mercar*[2] was beginning to be very powerful. There are a great many musketeers in this country, bowmen and

[1] *Cota fanões* means '*fanões* from Kottayam'. The *fanão* was a small coin formerly used in Southern India, worth between twenty and forty *reis*, and of an average weight equivalent to six grains of gold.

[2] *Mamalle* or *Mamale* is a contraction of Mohammed Ali. Cf. David Lopes, *Historia dos Portugueses no Malabar por Zinadim*, p. 69 n. *Mercar* is the *Mercaire* that Pyrard de Laval says means 'lieutenant or viceroy'. *Voyage* I, 350. According to Dalgado (*s.v.*) *Mercar* or *Marcar*, from the Malayalam *marakkān*, means a pilot or helmsman, or figuratively a chief or commandant. Many contemporary documents and chronicles refer extensively, between

Nayars with sword and dagger. The king is a Brahman with a very long beard, which is the sign of a Moor rather than of a heathen priest of Malabar.

Kingdom of Calicut.

The ports of Chombakulu, Puthupattanam, Tricodi, Pantaláyini, Kappatta, Calicut, Chaliyam and Parappanangadi belong to the kingdom of Calicut. They are small ports. All these have ships and merchants and good towns. The king of Calicut is called the Zamorin, that is Lord of all the people of Malabar. This kingdom is bounded on one side by Cannanore and on the other by Tanore, that is by these kingdoms. The port of Calicut is not good because the land slopes up from the sea. The town is large and has many inhabitants, and a great deal of trading is done there by many merchants, natives of Malabar as well as Klings, Chettis and foreigners from all parts, both Moors and heathens. It is a very famous port and is the best thing in all Malabar. Many nations used to have great factories here; each country used to bring its merchandise here, and a great business of barter and exchange took place. It is a large place; it is renowned in all this part of Asia as an important place; this kingdom is smaller than Cannanore; it has better fighting forces; it is a well-shaded country. They make many kinds of silken cloths here, and preserves. Although this king has a great name, he is only obeyed inside his kingdom, and not always that; and because I am not writing history, I will not give the origin of this title; only the people of Malabar say that there used to be a king in this Malabar who reigned over the whole country of Malabar, and that, persuaded by the Moors, he became a Mohammedan and started along the road to Mecca, but died in the kingdom of Dhofar (*Tufar*)[1] before he reached the mouth of the strait[2]. He was already out of his mind when he left Malabar,

1501 and 1525, to this ambitious and adventurous *Mamale*, an important Moorish merchant in Malabar, and his hostility to the Portuguese. Eventually his hands were cut off and he was hanged on the wall of the Portuguese fortress of Cannanore in January 1525. Correia, II, 862–3; Castanheda, VI, lxxx, lxxxi. Barros (III, ix, 3) says that the hanged Moor was *Bala Hacem*, but this is obviously a mistake, in face of Correia's circumstantial description.

[1] Dofar, Diufar or Dhofar, on the southern coast of Arabia.

[2] This was king Cheruman Perumal, whose story is related with variants by Barbosa and other Portuguese chroniclers. Even Camoens mentions him in *Lusiadas* (VII, 32), when describing Malabar.

and had divided up the whole country, and after he had given it away, a relative of his arrived and asked for a portion. He gave him the land of the city of Calicut, which was a small thing, and the name has remained until today; but Calicut has grown in importance on account of the trade that is carried on there.

Tanur has many ships. There is no other seaport there. The king is important and has a good [amount of] land—though not so extensive as Calicut—and many subjects. The king is related to the kings of Cochin. His country has many inhabitants. He is an important Brahman king. *Kingdom of Tanore.*

The ports of Ponnani, Veleankode and Chetwayi, with the land belonging to each, are ports with ships and merchants and goodly towns. They belong to Brahman lords and Kaimals, important people, who sometimes seek the support of someone they like (?) and sometimes not. They used to be more attached to the Calicut faction, but now each one is for himself or acts as he pleases. Each of these chiefs is like a king of Malabar, and each one is called king by his own people, but not by the other kings and lords.

The kingdom of Kranganur is joined to the land of Chetwayi on one side and to the kingdom of Cochin on the other. Kranganur used to be a place of great repute. It is a good port and has many inhabitants and good land. The city of Kranganur was important and had a great deal of trade, before Cochin became prosperous after the arrival of the Portuguese[1]. This king is noble. Sometimes he seeks the support of Cochin—because Cochin receives part of the revenues of this kingdom—and sometimes that of Calicut, and sometimes he stands alone. He is related to the king of Cochin. The kingdom is not very large. *Kingdom of Kranganur.*

The kingdom of Cochin is very small and very great. The kingdom is no more than the Island of Vypin (*Vaipim*)[2] and that of Cochin, which together contain about six thousand Nayars. *Fol. 129r.* *Kingdom of Cochin.*

[1] The transcriber of the Paris MS missed out some words which appear in the Lisbon MS.

[2] I found this Island of Vypin, Vypeen or *Vaipim* mentioned for the first time, in a document dated 22 Feb. 1509, as *Vaypy*, a place where the Portuguese went from the fortress of Cochin to fetch timber to repair and build ships. *Cartas*, II, 430–8. However, the chroniclers relate how, in 1503, the king of Cochin, after being defeated by the Zamorin of Calicut, withdrew to

There are lords connected with this kingdom, whose lands are as large or larger than the kingdom itself; and all these are now vassals of the king of Cochin on account of the power he has received through Your Highness; and he is now the greatest of all, and the head of all the land of Malabar, and more important than any of them and more highly esteemed. He has a good city and a good port, and many ships, and does a great deal of trade. It is the best thing there is here. The Brahman king is the chief of them all and the pope of this country. He always takes about with him a great many Kaimals, people who are very important, as well as many Brahmans.

Kingdom of Kayankulam. The kingdom of Kayankulam is bounded on one side by the land held by the lords of the kingdom of Cochin and on the other by the kingdom of Quilon. The king has as much land as Calicut and more. There is a certain amount of trade in his land, and he has some ships and merchants, though not many. He is an important king with many subjects. He is held in esteem. He is rich and a great lord, and has more ships than Quilon.

Kingdom of Quilon. The kingdom of Quilon is bounded on one side by the kingdom of Kayankulam and on the other by the kingdom of Travancore. In addition to the port of Quilon it has the port of Vilinjam. This king is the greatest in Malabar in land and subjects. He has the city of Quilon. It is a great port of call where the ships of many merchants from different places do a great deal of trade in this kingdom. He is a great lord, and the principal king of Ceylon used to be his vassal, and used to receive forty elephants every year as a tribute; but these he now no longer receives, after Your Highness has made manifest your power in India. The kingdom of Quilon has great trade, and there are many ships.

Kingdom of Travancore. The kingdom of Travancore is bounded on one side by Quilon and on the other side it ends at Cape Comorin. He has only a few houses on the sea coast, but inland he is a great lord and an

the Island of Vypin with the Portuguese who were in the factory of Cochin 'This island of *Vaipim* is believed among them to be a holy land, as the land of Jerusalem is among us. . . . And because this island of *Vaipim* was the first land uncovered by the sea, it was honoured as the paramount (*senhora*) of all the others uncovered later'. Correia, I, 361–3. Castanheda, I, liii; Barros I, vii, I; Pyrard de Laval, I, 435.

important person with good land and warlike people. This [king] buys many horses, which go from this kingdom to the kingdom of Narsinga. He has many subjects, and good men at that. There are Mukkuvan villages on the sea-coast, and the Mukkuvans let the people of the interior know when ships are coming in, and help unload the horses.

Kingdom of Comorin.

The kingdom of Comorin is bounded[1] on one side by Travancore and on the other it extends as far as *Qaíle*[2] which belongs to it. The prince of Comorin becomes king of Quilon on the death of the king of Quilon. With exception of the land in the kingdom of Travancore, this land of Comorin is not so good as the others; it has no palm trees, or only very few.

All the kings who live in Malabar are always at war with one another—on land, because the Nayar's religion forbids him to eat at sea, except by permission of his chief Brahman in case of dire necessity. The Brahmans go to sea even less.

There are in Malabar *tones catures*, which are long rowing boats, covered over on top, leaving just room for a man to worm his way in. Each one of these takes from ten to twenty oars. They are light, and there are a great many of them, and archers go in them. They belong to Mukkuvan *Arees*[3], who have many people and wealth, and there are many along this coast, and if they find a ship that has been becalmed, by rowing they take it wherever they like, against the will of the ship's crew, because they are great archers. The low caste people in Malabar are very poor, and they are great thieves. There are more Nayars and Brahmans than people of any other nation in Malabar.

No one in the whole of Malabar is allowed to roof his house with tiles, unless it be a *turicol* or mosque or, by special privilege, the house of some great Kaimal; and this is to prevent them from becoming too powerful in the land. And the kings of Malabar

[1] According to the Lisbon MS and Ramusio.

[2] *Qaile* is later spelt *Caile*, and appears as *Calle* in the letter of 1516 and as *Cale* in the Lisbon MS. This place was often mentioned for its pearl fishery. Once a famous port near the extreme southern part of India, opposite Ceylon, it is to-day 'represented by the deserted site among the lagoons of the delta of the Tambraparni River now known as Palayakayal or Old Kayal'. Dames, II, 122–3; Yule, *Marco Polo*, II, 371–4.

[3] *Arees*, plural of *arel*, chief of the fishermen, pilot, or captain of the port, in Malabar. From the Malayalam *arayal*.

enforce this very firmly. They are called Kaimals in the same way as we say dukes, marquises, counts and other titles, because they are lords possessing much land and vassals[1]; and there are some Kaimals in Malabar with ten thousand Nayar [vassals], and there are others with a hundred or two hundred Nayars.

rade in Malabar. There are countless palm trees and arecas along the coast of Malabar; but they do not extend for more than a league and a half inland, or two leagues at the most. The fruit of the palm trees is called coconut; we call them *nuces Indiae*, and the fruit of the areca is called areca and we call it *avelana Indiae.* There are an enormous number of these. There is a great deal of betel. The merchants of Malabar trade as far as Cambay and the Rajputs on the Persian side, and as far as Pulicat on the Choromandel side, and also in Ceylon and the Maldive (*Diva*) Islands[2]. All the merchants in Malabar who trade on the sea are Moors, and they have the whole of the trade. They are great *Fol. 129v.* merchants | and good accountants. These merchants have paid Nayars who accompany them; and some of these Nayars are their secretaries and are better accountants than the Moors. Some of the people of Malabar turned Mohammedan at the beginning, but not now.

Merchandise of Malabar. Copra, which is the dried kernel of coconuts, ripe coconuts, areca, betel, palm sugar, which is called jaggery, coconut oil, coir, pepper, ginger, tamarind, myrobalan. There must be about twenty thousand bahars[3] of pepper in Malabar, and it

[1] Perhaps the transcriber of the Paris MS missed a line here, for in the Lisbon MS and Ramusio it reads as translated above.

[2] Pires is the only Portuguese writer who used the form *Diva* or *Diua* (see note p. 53) for the Maldive Islands. Barbosa calls them *Ilhas do Maldio*, and all the chronicles *Maldivas*. However, the form *Diva* was usual among earlier writers, from at least as early as the fourth century. From the sixteenth century down to the present day several writers have tried to explain the etymology of the word Maldives. No doubt *diva* means island and is derived from the Sanskrit *dvīpa*; but for *mal* or *male*, opinions are most divergent. The most likely of all explanations is that it is derived from the Sanskrit *mālā*, meaning 'a garland or necklace', which seems rather appropriate to the configuration of the Maldive Archipelago.

[3] *Bahar* is an ancient weight used in large trading transactions in India and the Indian Archipelago. Its value varied much with the locality, but it was generally reckoned as equal to four quintals or 400 lbs. avoirdupois, according to Yule (*Hobson-Jobson*). See pp. 277–8.

grows from Chetwayi to the kingdom of Kayankulam, and a little around Quilon; Kranganur and Cochin are the nearest ports of call for this pepper, and they take it to wherever they make the most profit, however difficult the journey. Pepper does not grow in either Kranganur or Cochin; but the lords who live near these two kingdoms gather it and sell it. That grown in the kingdom of Cochin is the best.

Upwards of two thousand quintals of ginger are produced in this part of Malabar every year. It grows from Calicut to Cannanore. That from the land of Calicut is larger, and better, and not stringy; that from Cannanore is inferior. The largest quantity comes from Calicut, and the least from Cannanore.

The jungles all over this province are full of myrobalans of all kinds—citrine, Indian, chebulic and belleric[1]; and there are also some tamarinds.

Coconuts—Palm trees are the most plentiful things in the kingdom of Cannanore as far as Vilinjam in the kingdom of Quilon; from Vilinjam onwards to Choromandel you can count them because they are so few—hardly any at all.

Many of these dried coconuts are sent out of the country. They are good merchandise. All the ships take them. Oil is made from them, and they are also eaten.

There is a great trade in areca, which is generally sent to Cambay; because most of that in Choromandel comes from Ceylon, as we shall see when we come to Ceylon. There is a great deal in Malabar, and dried [areca] is exported in quantities. The largest amount of it in these parts grows from Cochin to Cannanore, and the bulk of the trade is made up of this and coconuts.

Coir also comes from this country. What is known as esparto is also called coir here. But coir is the fibre or outer covering of

[1] In his letter of 1516 (Appendix I), Pires says that 'Myrobalans are of five sorts'. In the *Suma* he names only four of the five sorts he mentions in the letter. The fifth is the emblic myrobalan or *Phyllanthus Emblica* Linn. The citrine (*cetrino*) or yellow myrobalan is *Terminalia citrina* Roxb.; the Indian (*indio*) or black myrobalan is *Phyllanthus disticus* Muell.; the chebulic (*qũblico* or *quibuly*) myrobalan is *Terminalia Chebula* Retz.; the belleric (*beleriqo*) myrobalan is *Terminalia belerica* Roxb. Orta (XXXVII) deals at length with all the five sorts.

the coconut shell. Things made from this coir, beaten and spun in their way, are good and stand up to every kind of use without spoiling, except if they get wet in fresh water, when they rot. Nothing but coir is used in these parts for ship's rigging and cables, and it is an important trading item. A great deal comes from the Maldive (*Diva*) Islands, as we shall see in the proper place.

So the Moors of Malabar, who are sailors and merchants, bring their goods from the Diu coast, and also from the Choromandel coast, Ceylon and the Maldive (*Diua*), and do a good trade in Malabar. Calicut is the chief place where most of the merchandise goes.

[CEYLON]

Fol. 160r.

Account of the island of Ceylon (Ceilam).

As I followed the coast of the mainland, I had no mind to deal with the island of Ceylon, and afterwards I almost forgot about it; and it did not seem right to fail to speak of it even in a place inserted out of the proper order; but the scarcity of paper made me do this, and so as not to put in a leaf and break the original order.

The beautiful island of Ceylon is situated over against Comorin; it extends almost to Nagore (*Naõr*), which must be a good hundred and thirty leagues of coastline. Cape Comorin is thirty five leagues out to sea, and from there onwards it draws nearer until at the nearest point it is only fifteen leagues away. And all the Malabar ships sail between this island and the Choromandel coast; but those making for Bengal or Pegu or Siam, go round the island on the southern side.

The island of Ceylon is large; it must be three hundred leagues in circumference, much longer than it is wide. It is very populous; it has many towns and large houses of prayer, with copper pillars, and with roofs covered with lead and copper. The kings of Ceylon are five. They are all heathens. They stand between the people of Malabar and the Klings. The land is well provided with everything, except that there is a scarcity of rice. It has plenty of the other foodstuffs.

The best part of the island is from Galle (*Calee*)[1] up to the point opposite Comorin, and this is where the chief king is, and the best towns, and at this point rise great mountain ranges, and here are found precious stones in this king's land, where all the trade is. It is an island for trade and navigation.

Ports in the island of Ceylon.

The chief one is Colombo (*Columbo*), another is Negombo (*Nygumbo*), and Chilaw (*Celabão*) and Dewundara (*Tenavarq̃e*) and Weligama (*Balimgão*)[2]. The king has his residence near the

[1] Galle, already called *Gálle* by Barros, and *Gale* by Castanheda, corresponds to the modern Point de Galle and Galle harbour in the south-western end of the island. Recorded for the first time on the map of *c.* 1540 as *galte.*

[2] The map of 1502, so-called Cantino, is the first to represent Ceylon approximately in its right position. It has on the east coast three place-names: *morachitu* (Mullaitivu), *traganamelee* (Trincomalee), and *pananio* (Panawa?); off the south-east coast of the island it has the inscription: 'here grow cinnamon and many other kinds of spices, and here they fish for pearls and seed-pearls. The people of this island are idolaters and they trade together with Calicut'. Next comes Rodrigues' map (fol. 28), the first on which the island is called *Ilha de çeillam*; a supplementary inscription explains: *o propo nome destaa ilha se chama iranary* (the proper name of this island is Iranary). Barros (III, ii, 1) says that the proper name of the island is *Ilanáre*, which the Portuguese did not know, so they called it *Ceilão*, from the *baixos de Chilão*. See note p. 76. 'The Malabars and other Indians call this island *Hibendro* [the *b* being an obvious mistake for *l*], which means rank land'. Castanheda, II, xxii. *Illenáre* means 'the kingdom of the island' in the Malabar language. Couto, V, i, 5. But neither was right. It seems that *Iranary* or *Ilandre* comes from the Tamil *Ilan-nádu*, 'the country of Ceylon'. *Hobson-Jobson, s.v.* Ceylon; Ferguson, *The Discovery of Ceylon by the Portuguese* in *1506*, p. 380, and *History of Ceylon*, pp. 30–3; Dames, II, 109. Another note on Rodrigues' map of Ceylon says: *tẽ alifantes aRoz esta tem canella ɀ asi muytos Robis ɀ outra pedraria* (this has elephants, rice; it has cinnamon, as well as many rubies and other precious stones). This map has the following place names: *ticanamalee* (Trincomalee), *maticalab* (Batticaloa), *baligaoo este he iraua* (Weligama, this is *Irana*), *bagicancla* (Galle), *alicano* (Alutgama), *penotore* (Pánadure), *colunbo* (Colombo); between the last two names is written: *outros qatro falecẽ aq̃ pera por* (four others are missing here for lack of space [to write them down]). Another Rodrigues' map (fol. 33) represents the two northern thirds of the island, with the following inscriptions and names: *A Jlha de çeillam homde toda pedraria ɀ muyta canella ɀ muyt9 allifamtes//. ɀ o propo nõme desta ilha se chama Jranary//* (The Island of Ceylon where [there are] all precious stones and much cinnamon and many elephants. And the proper name of this island is *Jranary*); *Janapanapatatiam este tẽ alifantes este he baneane* (Jaffna; this has elephants; this is Banian); *ticanamalee este tẽ aRoz nele* (Trincomalee; this has rice in it); *maticalab este tẽ alyfantes/ he macua/* (Batticaloa; this has elephants; it is Mukkuvan); *desta Jlha a Jlha de gamysspolla ha duzemtas llegoas* (from this island to the island of *Gamispola* is two hundred leagues); *alicano* (the upper part of this word was cropped when the volume was bound) (Alutgana), *penotore* (Pánadure), *calitore*

port of Colombo, half a league from the port, and in the greater part of the island has the following merchandise:

Ceylon merchandise. It has all kinds of precious stones, except diamonds, emeralds, turquoises. It has all the others in quantities. The stones are not sold without the king's licence. Every stone in the country worth fifty *cruzados* belongs to the king. This is by decree under pain of death to whoever has it, and it is sold through the king's hands

Fol. 160v. to whoever goes there to buy it. | It has a great abundance of elephants and ivory; it has cinnamon. Elephants are sold by the cubit; they are measured from the tip of the fore-foot to the top of the shoulder. Cinnamon is usually worth a *cruzado* a bahar. The bahar is the same as that of Cochin—three quintals and thirty *arrates*. The country has a great deal of areca, which is called *avelana Indiae* in Latin. It is eaten with betel. It is a foodstuff and is very cheap. It is sold in Choromandel.

Ceylon trades elephants, cinnamon, ivory and areca with the whole of the Choromandel and Bengal, [and] Pulicat, taking rice, white sandalwood, seed-pearls, cloth and other merchandise in return.

Merchandise of value in Ceylon. Rice, silver, copper, a little quicksilver, rosewater, white sandalwood and Cambay cloths, a few *caçutos*, a great many *mantazes*, *vispices*[1]. All white cloth is of value, and some clothing—not much —from Pulicat, a little pepper, and also cloves and nutmeg.

Coinage of the country. They have silver *fanões*, four being worth one Cochin *fanam*, which are eighteen to the *cruzado*. Gold money is current everywhere in Ceylon at its value. Ceylon has good craftsmen—jewellers, blacksmiths, carpenters, and turners chiefly. The people of Ceylon are serious, well educated. The grandees do little honour to strangers, and they do not steal, [only] if they cannot. They have complete justice among them.

(Kálutara), *colunbo* (Colombo), *mogutuarã* (Maguhare?), *nygonbo* (Negombo) and *celauam* (Chilaw).

Besides *calee* (Galle), *columbo*, *nygumbo* (Negombo), *celabão* (Chilaw) and *balimgão* (Weligama), Pires mentions *tenavarq̃e*, which corresponds to Dewundara (or Devundara or Dewinuwara), on Dondra Head, the southernmost peninsula of Ceylon. This is Barros' *Tanabaré* (III, ii, 1) and Couto's *Tanavarè*, *Tancuarem* or *Tanaverem* (v, vi, 3; x, iv, 12; x, x, 15).

[1] CAÇUTO was an Indian cloth, perhaps black or dark, of Persian origin. MANTAZ was a Cambay cloth, perhaps of cotton. VISPICE was a coarse cotton cloth in India. Dalgado, *s.vv.* Caçuto, Mantaz and Bespiça.

The king is very arrogant in not allowing people to speak to him except from far off. He always used to be a tributary of the king of Quilon, sending forty elephants yearly; and since the affair of the factor whom they killed there in Quilon they say that the king of Ceylon did not pay him any more tribute. The land of Ceylon is beautiful, well shaded. It has many native fighting men, bowmen and lancers. It has a few ships of its own, and they trade from Quilon [and] from Bengal to Cambay. They trade mainly in the port of Colombo because it is the most important.

They do not trade with the other kings because they have no ports, and if some have them they are shallow; but the kings are wealthy, and they come and bring elephants and cinnamon to this king's land and there they arrange about their merchandise. These kings have some rice in their lands. They are all relations and friends.

The island of Ceylon has many religious men, such as friars, monks, beguines, under a vow of chastity; and every man of Malabar and gentile holds the observances of Ceylon in veneration. Their temples are richly adorned and the priests are dressed in white, not after the fashion of the people. They are ill-disposed towards Moors and worse towards us. The different peoples say that they are all ruled justly.

[*THIRD BOOK*]

[BENGAL TO INDO CHINA]

[Bengal—Arakan—Pegu—Siam—Burma—Cambodia—Champa—Cochin China]

[BENGAL]

Fol. 134r. THE Bengalees are great merchants and very independent, brought up to trade. They are domestic. All the merchants are false.

The Bengalees are merchants with large fortunes, men who sail in junks. A large number of Parsees, *Rumes*, Turks and Arabs, and merchants from Chaul, Dabhol and Goa, live in Bengal. The land is very productive of many foodstuffs: meat, fish, wheat, and [all] cheap. The king is a Moor, a warrior. He has great renown among the Moors. The people who govern the kingdom are Abyssinians. These are looked upon as knights; they are greatly esteemed; they wait on the kings in their apartments. The chief among them are eunuchs and these come to be kings and great lords in the kingdom. Those who are not eunuchs are fighting men. After the king it is to this people that the kingdom is obedient from fear. They are more in the habit of having eunuchs in Bengal than in any other part of the world. A great many of them are eunuchs. Most of the Bengalees are sleek, handsome black men, more sharpwitted than the men of any other known race.

Method of succession in the kingdom. They have now been following the Pase (*Paçẽe*) practice in Bengal for seventy-four years, that whoever kills the king becomes king. They hold and believe that no one can kill the king without the consent of God, and he therefore becomes king; and in this way the kings last a very short time. From that time up to now it has always been Abyssinians—those who are very near to the king—who have reigned. This is done in such a way that there is no surprise in the kingdom. The merchants live in peace. It is already the custom. Formerly it was not done in this way,

Rodrigues' map (fol. 29) showing Ceylon, the Nicobar Islands and the Malacca Strait (pp. 520-1)

PLATE XVI

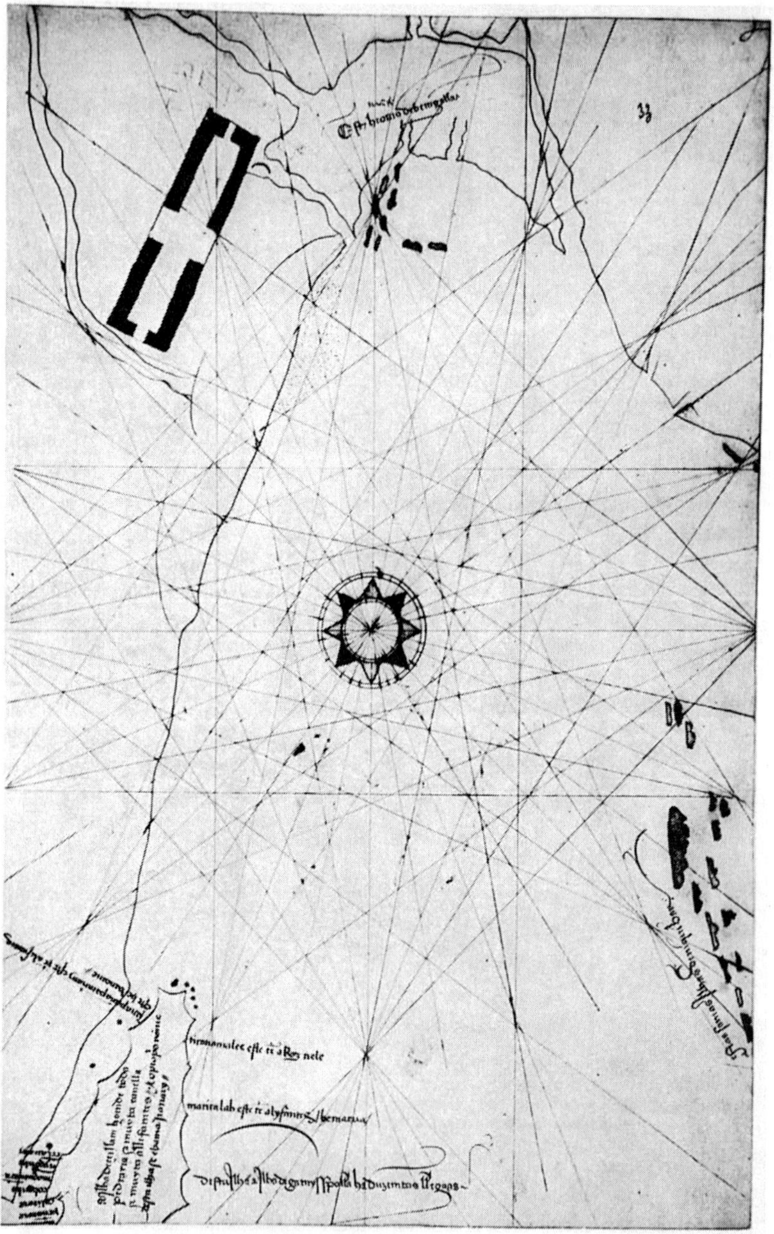

Rodrigues' map (fol. 33) of the Bay of Bengal, with part of Ceylon, and the Andaman and Nicobar Islands (p. 522)

but was from father to son. They borrowed this practice from Pase and they keep strictly to it.

The King's standing.

The king of Bengal is powerful[1]. He has many mounted men. There must be a hundred thousand mounted men in his kingdom. He fights with heathen kings, great lords and greater than he; but because the king of Bengal is nearer to the sea, he is more practised in war, and he prevails over them. He is much given to arms. He is a very faithful Mohammedan. The kings of this kingdom turned Mohammedan three hundred years ago. The land is very rich.

Tributary Kings to the King of Bengal.

The king of Orissa borders on Bengal on the Choromandel side. He is a great king and he is his tributary. He possesses a great many elephants and he is the chief king and rich. The good diamonds come from this country.

Arakan (*Raçam*)[2] borders on Bengal on the Pegu side. This [king] has many horses and is warlike and he is always at war with him. And this king is also tributary to the said king of Bengal.

The King of *Coos*[3] is a heathen. They say he must have seventy thousand horsemen, and he is also tributary to him. This kingdom of *Cõus* has much pepper and silk and opium.

The king of Tripura (*Típura*)[4] is also a heathen, in the interior, and a tributary of his. He possesses many elephants and [is] the lord over all these four kings. His vassals are great lords. The rich things there are in Bengal are made in these kingdoms, and

[1] In Pires' time the Mohammedan sovereign of Bengal was Alauddin or Ala-ud-Din II, who reigned from 1499(?) to 1521.

[2] This is the *Arcangil* of Barbosa, and *Arraçam*, *Aracam*, *Arracão*, *Aracão* or *Racão* of Portuguese chroniclers and maps.

[3] *Coos* or *Cõus*. *Caus* in the Lisbon MS. In his description of Bengal, Barros (IV, lx, 1), after referring to the *Reino de Arracam*, mentions the *Reino de Cou*. It is likely that *Coos* corresponds to Barros' *Cou*. He writes that 'The Bengalees say that [some time ago] . . . the *Tiporitas* [inhabitants of Tipóra or Tripura] made an alliance with those of the kingdom of *Cou*, also hostile to the Bengalees, whom they do not obey any more; and as this kingdom of *Cou* is great, has more horsemen than any of its neighbours, and is difficult country because of the many mountains, it alone could conquer Bengal, the more so if helped by the *Tiporitas*, who are a very warlike people'.

[4] The state of Tripura, in Bengal, which appears as *Reino de Tipora* on Lavanha's map of Bengal, added by him in 1615 to his first edition of Barros' *Decada IV*. Bocarro calls it *Tipara*, ch. xcix.

because they cannot live without the sea, they obey him, because he allows them an outlet for their merchandise. It must be three years now since they rose against Bengal. They are waging a fierce war and do not obey him. This *Tipura* has an infinite amount of cotton.

Fol. 134v. The king of Bengal is always at war with the king of Delhi, and the captains and men of one and the other are always fighting. The king of Delhi is a much greater lord than the king of Bengal, but he is fifteen days' journey away from Bengal and there is not much water along the road, and for this reason the said king of Bengal is not obedient to the said *Xaquedarxa*[1], king of Delhi. This king is a heathen, a great lord, much feared, with a very large number of horses, elephants and men.

Ports of Bengal. The principal port is that of the City of Bengal[2], whence the kingdom derives its name. It takes two days to go from the mouth of the river up to the city, and they say that at the lowest tide there are three fathoms. The city must have forty thousand inhabitants. The king has his residence in this city. They are all

[1] Sikandar Lodi, who reigned till 1517.

[2] 'The City of Bengal', was the ancient capital of Bengal, the great historic city of Gaur or Gour. Its ruins, extending over an immense area, still exist a few miles south of English Bazar, on the eastern bank of the old channel of the Ganges. When Pires wrote down his information, Gour was in full splendour; it had been, though with ups and downs, a great centre for some centuries. The identity of the so-called 'City of Bengal', mentioned also by Varthema and Duarte Barbosa, has given rise to much controversy. Opinions have been divided mainly between Gaur, Chittagong and Satgaon, besides several other places. Studying and discussing new data, mainly from Pires' *Suma*, Portuguese chronicles and early maps, I have dealt at length with this very interesting subject, together with that of Satgaon (*Sadegam*), in two articles—*The 'City of Bengal' in early reports*, and *A 'Cidade de Bengala' no século XVI*, published respectively in the *Journal of the Royal Asiatic Society of Bengal* and in *Boletim da Sociedade de Geografia de Lisboa.* I came to the following conclusions: (1) The 'City of Bengala' of the early sixteenth-century writers was Gaur. There are many reasons for this identification, but the decisive argument in its favour is the fact that Tomé Pires mentioned the 'City of Bengala' and Satgaon as different places, and said that the former, a great city of 40,000 hearths, lay two days' journey up the river, which excludes Chittagong. (2) Later on, however, when the Portuguese settled in Bengal, the designation 'City of Bengala' corresponded to Chittagong, as is shown by several mid sixteenth-century Portuguese chroniclers and cartographers. (3) As far as I know the designation 'City of Bengala' was never applied by the Portuguese to any other city or port of Bengal.

palm-leaf huts, but the king's house is of adobe and well built. This river is the Ganges—the Bengalees say that it comes from heaven.

The other port is Satgaon (*Sadegam*)[1] over against Orissa. It has a good port; it has a good entrance. It is a good city and rich, where there are many merchants. It must have ten thousand inhabitants. These are the chief trading cities in Bengal. There are others inland, but they are strongly fortified garrison towns, of no [commercial] importance, and there is constant war in the interior.

Orissa (*Orixa*), which is in the kingdom of Orissa, is the port of the city of Orissa. It lies near the sea.

Cultarey, Armagon (*Arjamom*), Pulicat (*Paleacate*), Nagore (*Naãor*), Negapatam (*Nagapatam*) of the great and famous *turucol* of Narsinga—all these ports in the *Bonuaquelim*, land of Narsinga[2].

[1] Satgaon is today a ruined city north-west of the modern town of Hugli, twenty-three miles north of Calcutta. It was the mercantile capital of Bengal from the days of Hindu rule until the foundation of Hugli by the Portuguese in 1579. The Portuguese speak of *O Goli* or *O Golim*, just as they say *O Porto*. From the latter resulted Oporto; so the former gave Hooghly or Hugli.

[2] In the Lisbon MS these names read: 'callcari/ ariamão paleacate na ornaga/ patamto/ turocoll/.'

PORT AND CITY OF ORIXA—As Gour corresponds to *Cidade de Bengala*, so Cuttack, the historical capital of Orissa, must correspond to *cidade dorixa* or City of Orissa. Cuttack, the chief city of Orissa is on the right bank of the Mahamadi River, fifty-five miles from its mouth, on the apex of the delta. It may have been a good port formerly, but the beds of the deltaic rivers have long been silted up and their outlets obstructed by shoals and sand bars. Barros (I, ix, I) says that the coast of the kingdom of '*Orixa*, owing to its roughness, has few ports, only *Panacote, Calingam, Bazapátan, Vixáopatan, Vituilipatan, Calinhápatan, Naciquepatan, Puluro, Panagate*, and *Cabo Segógora*'. Many early maps show at about the latitude of Cuttack (20° 29′ N.) a port named *Calecota* or *Casecota*; sometimes another name, *Casegate*, appears just on the north of *Calecota*.

CULTAREY—This must correspond to *Caleture* mentioned by Barros as one of the seven main places on the coast between *S. Thomé de Meliapor* and *Guadávarij* (Godávari). It appears with similar names on early maps, about 14° 30′ N, corresponding perhaps to Nellore (14° 27′) on the Penner River or to Allur at its mouth. However, the chief and safest natural harbour on the Choromandel coast north of Madras is Cocanada, in 16° 57′ N.

ARJAMOM—*Aremogam* in Barros and similarly on several early maps. Corresponds to the Armagon Shoal, 13° 55′ N; Blackwood harbour lies between Armagon Shoal and the coast.

A junk goes from Bengal to Malacca once a year, and sometimes twice. Each of these carries from eighty to ninety thousand *cruzados* worth. They bring fine white cloths, seven kinds of *sinabafos*, three kinds of *chautares*, *beatilhas*, *beirames*[1] and other rich materials. They will bring as many as twenty kinds. They bring steel, very rich bed-canopies, with cut-cloth work in all colours and very beautiful; wall hangings like tapestry; and also sugar preserves of various kinds in great plenty: all the myrobalans in conserve, ginger, oranges, cucumbers, carrots, rapes, lemons, quinces, figs, pumpkins, Indian gourds and many other fruits; some of these in vinegar. They bring an abundance of strongly scented vases in dark clay, which are highly esteemed in these parts and are very cheap.

These people sail four or five ships and junks to Malacca and to Pase every year, and this is still done to a large extent.

Bengali cloth fetches a high price in Malacca, because it is a merchandise all over the East. In Malacca they pay six per cent. They are people who know a great deal about merchandise. From here in Malacca they use all their money and other [money] which they take on the return [voyage] in [trade with] Bengal,

PALEACATE—It is spelt thus in every chronicle and early Portuguese map. Corresponds to Pulicat, 13° 25′ N.

NAÃOR.—*Aahor* in Barros. Corresponds to Nagore, a port three miles northwest of Negapatam.

NAGAPATAM—*Negapatam*. 'The great and famous *turucol*' cannot be in the town itself, where the oldest temple dates from 1777. 'The only other considerable town (in Negapatam Taluk) is Tiruvalur, noted for its temple and the idol car belonging thereto.' *Imp. Gaz. of India, s.v.* Negapatam Taluk. 'There is (in Tiruvalur) a richly-endowed temple, which is attended by pilgrims.' *Idem, s.v.* Tiruvalur. This may be the *turucol* or temple referred to by Pires. The idol on the car was annually drawn in procession through certain parts of the city of Negapatam, this being the occasion for scenes of self-immolation similar to those of the famous Juggurnaut festival at Puri in Orissa.

BONUA Q̃LIM or *Bonuaquelim*, spelt also *Benuaquelim*—*Bonua* corresponds to the Malay *banuwa*, which means land, country. *Qlim*, or *quelim*, from the Malayalam *Kĕling* or *Kling*, was the name given by the Portuguese to the natives who came from at least part of the Choromandel coast to trade or live in Malacca. *Bonuaquelim*, then, means 'Land of the Klings'. See note p. 64.

[1] SINABAFO—Shanbaff or Sinabaff. A white fine cotton cloth made in Bengal. CHAUTAR—A large piece of cloth, sheet or shawl, white or in colours. BEIRAME—Fine cotton cloth of several colours.

and make a great profit with it, which they cannot do in Pase, except with pepper and silk.

Return [voyage] from Malacca to Bengal.

The chief merchandise they take to Bengal is Borneo camphor and pepper—an abundance of these two—cloves, mace, nutmeg, sandalwood, silk, seed-pearls a large quantity, white porcelain in plenty, copper, tin, lead, quicksilver, large green porcelain ware from the Liu Kiu (*Leqios*), opium from Aden and some little from Bengal, white and green damasks, *enrolados*[1] from China, caps of scarlet-in-grain and carpets; krises and swords from Java are also appreciated.

Dues which are paid in Bengal.

Every merchant who goes to Bengal has to pay three on every eight, and they consider that this unreasonable tax is a right thing, because these goods are of so much value in the country, and the things they take back are of such high value and so small in bulk, that they affirm that when the goods are brought safely into harbour and sold, the profit on one is from two and a half to three.

Fol. 135r.

Time of the monsoon.

They leave here at the beginning of August and they reach Bengal in thirty days; they stay there trading; they leave there on the first of February and they take as long again to Malacca. When they want to insult a man they call him a Bengalee. They are very treacherous; they are very sharpwitted. There are a large number of Bengalees, men and women, in Malacca. The men are fishers and tailors—most of them—and some of the workmen do very bad work.

Coinage of Bengal with which they trade.

Gold is worth a sixth part more in Bengal than in Malacca and silver is a fifth part cheaper than in Malacca, and sometimes a quarter cheaper. The silver coinage is called *tanqat*. It weighs half a tael, which is nearly six drams. This coin is worth twenty *calains* in Malacca, and seven *cahon* in Bengal. Each *cahon* is worth sixteen *pon*; each pon is worth eighty cowries (*buzeos*); so that a *cahon* is worth one thousand two hundred and eighty cowries, and a *tancat* is worth eight thousand nine hundred and sixty cowries, [at the rate of cowries] four hundred and forty

[1] *Enrolado*. This word is very frequent in the chronicles, and some Portuguese dictionaries record it as meaning 'a kind of old Indian cloth' or 'a sort of woollen cloth'. Dalgado (*s.v.*) was unable to discover the nature of this cloth or the reason for the name. Resende mentions '*enrrollados* which are thin like *bofetas*' (a kind of zephyr fabric). *Livro do Estado da India*, fol. 321r.

eight to the *calaim*, which is the price for which they give a good chicken, and from this you can tell what you could buy for them. In Bengal the cowries are called *cury*[1].

Where these cowries are valid and current coinage.

Cowries are current coinage in Orissa and in all the kingdom of Bengal, and Arakan (*Raqã*), and in Martaban (*Martamane*)[2],

[1] TANQAT—The word *tucka* or *táká* is still usual in Bengal for a rupee. From the Sanskrit *tankaka*, 'stamped silver money'.

CALAIM—Calay, meaning tin in the Orient. Although generally used in this sense, it was also used as meaning a tin coin. Referring to the seizure of Malacca by Albuquerque in 1511, Barros (II, vi, vi) says that 'there were no other coins there but those of tin'. When describing the currency in the Cuama River (Zambeze, in Mozambique) Fr. João dos Santos writes: 'Tin is also currency: they call it *calaim*, which is shaped into loaves, each weighing half an *arratel*, and they call these *pondos*; each of these *pondos* is worth two *tangas*, which are worth six *vintens*.' *Ethiopia Oriental*, I, ii, viii. Pires say later on, when dealing with Pegu coinage, that 'The *calaim* is worth eleven *reais* and four cetis'; and when dealing with Sunda coinage he speaks of 'three hundred *calaims*, which are nine *cruzados*', making the *calaim* equal to twelve *reais* or *reis*; this he confirms when dealing with the Malacca coinage.

CAHON—Kahan. Cowry tables dated about 1778 and 1854 show the following values—'4 kauris = 1 ganda; 20 gandas = 1 paṇ; 4 paṇ = 1 āna; 4 ānas = 1 kāhan.' *Hobson-Jobson, s.v.* Cowry. This table of values agrees exactly with those given by Pires.

PON or *pone*—Pan, the old Bengali designation for eighty cowries, from the Sanskrit *paṇa*, 'to barter', whence the Malayalam and Tamil *paṇam*, 'money', and, according to Hobson-Jobson (*s.v.* Fanám), and Dalgado (*s.vv.* Fanão and Pone), the *fanam* or *fanão*, an old gold or silver coin used in India at least until the last century. Nunes (p. 37) says that the *Cauryns* 'are current in Bengal, 80 *cauryns* make one *pone*: 40 to 50 *pones* are given for one *tangua larym*.' Dealing with the 'Weights in China', Pires asserts that the *picoll* contains a hundred *cates*, the *cate* sixteen taels, the tael ten *mazes* and the *maz* ten *pons*.

BUZEO or *cury*—Cowry or kauri. Castanheda (IV, XXXV) says: 'There are in these islands (Maldives) . . . small white shells (*buzios*) which are called *caurís*, that serve as small currency in Bengal, because they are cleaner than the copper, which they say soils the hands.'

The transcribers of the Paris and Lisbon MSS, as well as Ramusio, all made the same rather careless mistake, in saying that the *tankat* is worth 8970 *buzeos*. Ramusio makes a further mistake when he says that the *calaim* is worth 458 *buzeos*.

[2] *Martaniane* further on; *Martabane* in the Lisbon MS and in Ramusio. It appears as *martabane* in the Cantino map, as *Martauão* in several middle sixteenth-century Portuguese maps, and as *cidade de martabam* in L. Homem's map of 1554. Although the usual form in the sixteenth-century chronicles was *Martabam*, Giovanni da Empoli, a contemporary of Pires, in a letter of 1514 wrote also *Martaman*. *Archivio Storico Italiano*, III, Appendice, p. 54. Firenze, 1846. 'This is the conventional name for a port on the east of the Irawadi Delta and of the Sitang estuary, formerly of great trade, but now in comparative decay', in Burma. *Hobsom-Jobson, s.v.* Martaban.

a port of the kingdom of Pegu. The Bengal cowries are larger, with a yellow stripe in the middle; they are valid throughout Bengal and they accept them for a larger number of commodities as they would gold; and in Orissa. They are not valid anywhere else and they are highly prized in these two places. We will speak about those of Pegu and Arakan when we talk of these places. These selected [cowries] come from the Maldive (*Diua*) Islands in large quantities.

The Bengal balance is called a *dala*[1]. This is a branch of wood without scales, and they tie the goods to the ends, and it is done like that. And with the merchants, if you take a balance, they work out the accounts, and so you do your trading. They say that ten or twelve people collect the dues, each one his own, and they are the officials for this, and that when they take their tithe they wrong the merchants and tyrannise over them greatly. *Method of weighing.*

The Bengalees merchants say that this king of Bengal, who is called Sultan *Vçem Xaa*[2], is not benevolent to the merchants, and that many of them are going to other places. This king has twenty-four sons by his concubines, and many daughters.

[ARAKAN]

The kingdom of Arakan is between Bengal and Pegu. The king is a heathen and very powerful in the hinterland. It has a good port on the sea, where the Peguans, the Bengalees and the Klings trade, but not much business. The port is called Myo- *Kingdom of Arakan (Racão).*

[1] *Dila* in the Lisbon MS; *dalla* in Ramusio. The Sanskrit *dāl* means 'to divide'. '*Dáli* [Hindi]. A tray, or a couple of trays, fastened by slings to each end of a pole, carried over the shoulders.' G. C. Whitworth, *An Anglo-Indian Dictionary*. According to D'Rozario's *Dictionary* a balance is *pallá* in Bengali.

[2] *Soltão bamxar* in the Lisbon MS; *Soltam vamxoa* in Ramusio. In this case, as in many others, we can hardly imagine what Pires originally wrote, or what he heard, and how he wrote it down. This *Vçem Xaa* may be one of 'the very powerful heathens whose generation are now called *venezaras*' (Orta, x), identified by Ficalho (I, 129–30) and Yule (*Hobson-Jobson s.v.* Brinjarry) as *Banjaras*, *Vanjaras* or *Brinjarries*, people who usually move about carrying their cattle and goods to different markets. The king or sultan of Bengal was also known as Alauddin Husain Shah in Pires' time.

haung (*Mayajerij*)[1]. Near this port the king has an adobe fortress, which for them is strong.

There are many horsemen in the land of Arakan and many elephants. There is some silver. There are three or four kinds of cotton cloth, which the natives wear. They are cloths of their manner and dressing, and there are more there than in other places, and people go there for them.

Where the musk and fine rubies come from.

The kingdom of Arakan is bounded far in the hinterland by the great mountain range which is called *Capelanguam*[2], where there are many places inhabited by a not very civilised people. These people bring the musk and rubies to the great city of Ava[3] which is the chief thing in the kingdom of Arakan, and from there they go to Pegu, and from Pegu they are distributed *Fol. 135v.* | to Bengal, Narsinga and to Pase and Malacca. The mine for the said rubies is in the *Capelamguã*, [and they are] the best there are in these parts. The musk comes from animals such as goats. They flay them and the flesh is pounded up with the blood. From the skins they make the little bags we call *papos*[4]; and this is the truth about musk, and it does not come from apostemes, and if you look at them closely you will find many that still have bones.

Cowries are current in this kingdom.

The coinage of this country is *cãça*, that is *fruseleira*[5] in

[1] *Malagery* (?) in the Lisbon MS; *Maiarani* in Ramusio. This must be Myohaung, in the Akyab District of the Arakan division of Burma. '*Myohaung Village* ('Old town'), formerly the capital of the ancient kingdom of Arakan. The ruins of the fort are still in existence.' *Imp. Gaz. India, s.v.*

[2] *Capelamgam* in the Lisbon MS; *Capelangam* in Ramusio. 'This is a name which was given by several sixteenth-century travellers to the mountain in Burma from which the rubies purchased at Pegu were said to come.' *Hobson-Jobson, s.v.* Capelan. *Capelam* in Barbosa. Yule refers to 'Capelang, the Ruby country north of Ava, a name preserved to a much later date, but not now traceable'. *Cathay*, I, 177.

[3] *Ava.* 'The name of the city which was for several centuries the capital of the Burmese Empire.' *Hobson-Jobson, s.v.* Ava.

[4] The expression '*papos de almiscar*'—pods or 'craws' of musk—was current in India. It is mentioned in the *Roteiro de Vasco da Gama* (1498), p. 112.

[5] When describing the Pegu coinage, Pires says that the *fresuleira* or *cança* of copper and tin is better than that of copper, tin and lead, and the worst is copper and lead. When he deals with China, the word is spelt *fuseleira*. Nunes (p. 38) writes: 'In Pegu there is no coined money, and what they use commonly consists of dishes, pans, and other domestic utensils, made of a metal like *frosyleyra*, broken in pieces; and this is called *gamça*.' 'In Pegu they do not mint coins, the currency being some old pans which they have used, and

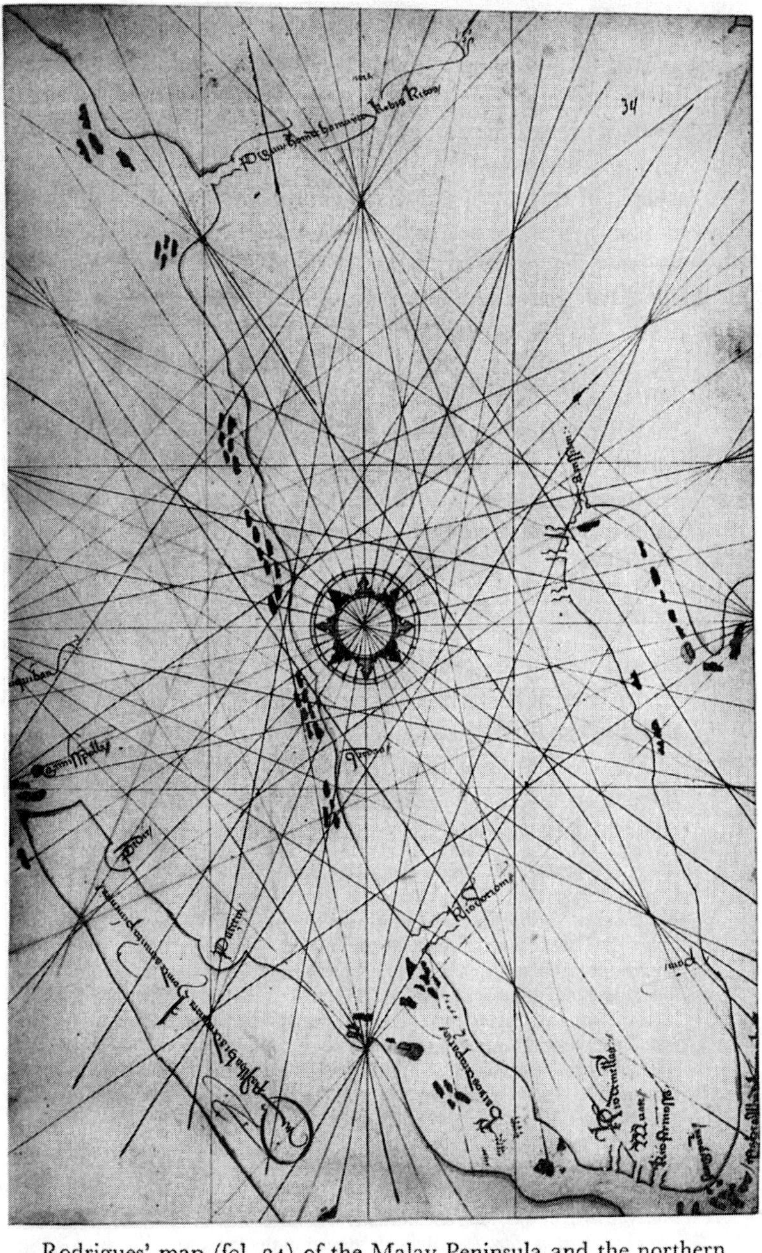

Rodrigues' map (fol. 34) of the Malay Peninsula and the northern part of Sumatra (p. 522)

with a large city and many merchants. The *Toledam* of it is greater than the others. The junks are made in this port because of the amount of good wood there. The other port is distant from Martaban; the people of Malacca and those of Pase go there, and it is also a good large city with merchants. The common people of this kingdom are naughty in their own country and outside it they are peaceable, good workers, simple folk.

Merchandise that comes from Pegu to Malacca and to Pase.

The principal [merchandise] is rice. There come every year to these two places and to Pedir fifteen to sixteen junks, twenty to thirty cargo *pangajauas*[1], like ships. They bring a great deal of lac and benzoin, musk, [precious] stones (?), rubies, silver, butter, oil, salt, onions, garlic, mustard (?)[2] and things to eat like that. They leave in February and arrive at the end of March and during the whole of April. They are men who sell their goods peaceably, according to the custom of the country. Seven or eight merchants value the merchandise, and they abide by this and sell it.

The duties they pay in Malacca.

Neither in Malacca nor in Pase are any duties paid on any foodstuffs, but they are given as a courtesy, because they are so accustomed in the country. On the rest they pay six per cent. There is great profit in bringing rice and lac and all the rest of it from Pegu to Malacca.

Return from Malacca to Pegu.

The chief thing is coarse china of various kinds and ornamented in red, a great deal of quicksilver, copper, vermilion, damask, dark *enrolados* with flowers—which come straight from

River as a branch of a large delta corresponding to the present Irawadi, Rangoon, Pegu and Sitang rivers, the whole under the name of *Cosmim* or *Rio Cosmim*, as appears more clearly on Eredia's map of the Bay of Bengal (fol. 73). This is why Castanheda, in another place, says that 'a city called *Cosmim*, the port of Pegú, lies eighteen leagues up a river on which lies Pegú ninety leagues from the sea' (IV, V). It is obvious that he is confusing Cosmin with the ancient Dagon or Rangoon. Correia (II, 474) makes the same mistake. Pinto (CXC) mentions in the same sentence the town of *Cosmim* and the river of *Digum* (Dagon) as quite distinct. The map of Fra Mauro records *Chesmi*. The earliest Portuguese map in which I find *Cosmj* is the anonymous one of *c.* 1540.

DOGÕ—Dagon, the original name of Rangoon. In the Lisbon MS it is written *Degoni*. It appears as *Digum* in Pinto's *Peregrinação*, CXC.

[1] *Pangajaua*, or *pangajava*, from the Malayalam *pĕnjajap*. It was an ancient Malayan man of war, long and of shallow draught.

[2] This word *mostarda* (?), difficult to read in the Paris MS, was suppressed in the Lisbon MS and in Ramusio.

China for them because they are of no use for others—quantities of tin, *freseleira*, some in broken pieces and some whole (?), especially that which is coinage. And they take an infinity of different kinds of china, seed-pearls, a little gold—they spend all their money, and more if they had it, on this—some cloves, nutmeg, mace, nothing much. They leave here on the first of July and go to Pase to load up with pepper and in August they go to Martaban.

Duties they pay in Pegu.

The duties which the said merchants pay in Pegu are twelve per cent, and none of these are remitted. If you have to speak to the governor, you must take a present, and that is the custom in Malacca: you have to pay a bribe according to what the affair is. The port of Martaban is dangerous. There are pilots of the bar who guarantee to take you safely in, if you pay them according to the custom of the country. They do not go in at full tide nor at low tide; they take it midway for safety.

Fol. 136r.

Pegu coinage.

The coinage of Pegu, which is used in trading is *freseleira*, which is called *cança*. Some of this *fruseleira* is better and some is less good. *Fruseleira* of copper and tin is better than that of copper, tin and lead, and the worst is that of copper and lead. The *cança* of Martaban is the best. This is current throughout the country at ten *calains*, three *arrates* and five ounces to the *viça*, which is a *cate* and a half on the big scales of Malacca. These are according to the new weight, and the other is worth less. The *calaim* is worth eleven *reais* and four *ceitis*, at the rate of a hundred *calains* to three *cruzados*[1].

[1] ARRATES—The *arratel* (pl. *arráteis*) is an old Portuguese weight equivalent first to 14 and then to 16 ounces. See note p. 277.

VIÇA—A weight used in Southern India and Burma, the value of which is given as from 40 ounces (Nunes, Castanheda, Bocarro, etc.) to 53 ounces. Yule (*Hobson-Jobson*, *s.v.* Viss) says that 'in Burma the *viss* = 100 *tikals* = 3 lbs. 5 5⅓', which is about the value given by Pires.

CATE—The *cate* or *catty* is a variable weight introduced from China into Malacca and now fixed at 625 grammes, or 22.9 ounces. The Portuguese considered it as equal to 20 or 28 ounces, but some authors even go as low as 4 ounces, or as high as 30½ ounces. The *cate* here indicated by Pires would be equal to 35.34 ounces; but further on, under the title 'Coinage and weights used in Pegu' and 'Coinage and weights used in Pase', he says that 5 *cates* are equal to 12 *arráteis*, which makes the *cate* equal to 38.4 ounces. When dealing with the Malacca weights and measures Pires says that 'the *cate* for merchandise weighs . . . 32¾ ounces and 25 grains'.

Value of the viça *of* cança.

A *viça* of the said *cança* is worth ten calains; so you say 'How many *viças* of such and such merchandise will you give me for a *viça* of *cança*?', or 'How many *viças* of *cança* do you want for a *viça* of such and such merchandise?'. And each of these *viças* contains a hundred *tiquas*[1]. These hundred *tiquas* are worth as much as a *viça*.

Gold and silver coinage.

The silver is in rounds marked with the mark of Siam, because it all comes from there. The piece in the round is called *caturna*[2]. The weight of it is a tael and a half which is two ounces and one eighth; and in Pegu one *quarto* is worth four *viças* and a half, and this side of Malacca it is worth a tael of *timas*[3] which is sixty-four[4] *calains*. Gold has the same value in Pegu as it has in Malacca. A great deal of silver is taken from Pegu to Bengal, where it is worth somewhat more.

Small currency.

The small currency of Pegu is small white cowries. In Martaban fifteen thousand are usually worth one *viça*, which is ten *calains*; when they are cheap sixteen thousand; when they are very dear fourteen thousand, and generally fifteen thousand. A *calaim* is worth one thousand five hundred. For four hundred or five hundred they will give a chicken, and things of that sort for the same price. If [you are] in Pegu the said cowries are not valid except in Martaban, and they are valid in the same way in Arakan. The cowries come from the Maldive (*Diva*) Islands, where they make large quantities of towels, and they also come from the islands of *Bagangã*[5] and of Borneo (*Burney*), and they bring them to Malacca and from here they go to Pegu.

CRUZADO—An old Portuguese gold (later silver) coin worth 390 reais in Pires' time. However, according to Pires' account it seems to be equal to 375 reais. The *cruzado* of Pires' time would be worth about 285 Escudos, or about £2 17s. today. Cf. Azevedo, *Épocas de Portugal Económico*, p. 488.

[1] *Tiqua*—'The quasi-standard weight of (uncoined) current silver' in Burma. A little more than three eighths of an ounce. *Hobson-Jobson* and Dalgado *s.v.* Tical.

[2] This sentence has been left out in the Lisbon MS and in Ramusio.

[3] Further on, when dealing with the Malacca coinage, Pires says that *timas* means tin.

[4] Eighty-four in the Lisbon MS and in Ramusio.

[5] *Bamgamjam* in the Lisbon MS; *Bandam* in Ramusio. Perhaps one of the small islands Balambangan or Banguey, the town of Bongon, or the port of Jabongon on the north coast of Borneo. See p. 522.

The *bahar* by the *dachim*[1] of Martaban is less than that of Malacca by twenty *cates*. The Martaban one contains a hundred and twenty *viças* which are a hundred and eighty cates, and the Malacca one contains two hundred, and these *cates* are according to the big scales. Rice is measured by *toõs*. Each *tom* contains ten Malacca *gantas*[2] tested in the country.

Weights and measures in Pegu.

One Gujarat ship comes to the port of Martaban and of Dagon (*Dogũo*) every year. They bring these goods: copper, vermilion, quicksilver, opium, cloth; and they take a large quantity of lac which is cheap in the country—sometimes four *viças* the bahar, sometimes five and six and seven; and they take benzoin, silver, [precious] stones and go back, and sometimes they are wrecked on the bar.

Gujarat ships in Pegu.

The king is always in residence in the city of Pegu, which is inland, and from the city to the port of Dagon (*Dagam*) is a day and night's journey, to Martaban four and to Cosmin (*Coximjm*) eight days. Next to the king in importance is the *Braja*[3], who is

King and chief people.

[1] It seems that *dachim*, *datchin* or *dachem* was a steelyard or balance, but it was taken also as meaning a weight (100 *cates* in Javanese). According to Nunes (p. 39), at Malacca 'The *baar* of the great *Dachem* contains 200 *cates*, each *cate* weighing 2 *arráteis*, 4 ounces, 5 eighths, 15 grains, 3 tenths. . . . The *baar* of the little *Dachem* contains 200 *cates*; each *cate* weighing 2 *arráteis*'. Marsden says that in Achin, for the payments in gold dust 'one is provided with small seals or steelyards, called *daching*'. *History of Sumatra*, p. 401. Further on, when dealing with the weights and measures of Malacca, Pires says that he verified the *dachim* and that it 'weighed exactly three quintals, three *arrobas* and twenty-six *arráteis*' (pp. 277–8).

[2] Toõs—The *mercal* or *mercar*, a grain measure in use in the Madras Presidency, is also known as *toom*. *Hobson-Jobson*, *s.v.* Mercáll. Nunes (pp. 36, 59) refers to the *mercar* as a rice measure in Negapatam, of variable capacity, but now estimated at 2.6 litres.

GANTA—The *guanta*, *ganta* or *ganton* is a measure of capacity in Malaya. Several sixteenth-century Portuguese writers give its value as a Portuguese *canada* (1.4 litres), but Nunes says that it was a rice measure equivalent to five *quartilhos* (1.75 litres, the *quartilho* being a fourth of a *canada*) in Malacca. *Ibid.* pp. 39, 40. Further on, when dealing with the weights and measures of Malacca, Pires says he found that the rice contained in one *ganta* 'weighed three *arráteis* and ten ounces of the new measure'. See notes p. 181 and 277.

As the Pegu *toom* mentioned by Pires contained ten Malacca *gantas*, it was about three times larger than the Negapatam *toom* or *mercar*. The *ganton* or *gantong* is still a measure of capacity in Malaya, equivalent to a gallon (4.543 litres) today. N. B. Dennys, *A Descriptive Dictionary of British Malaya*, p. 419.

[3] *Cobrajem* in the Lisbon MS; *Cobrai* in Ramusio.

his captain and governor of the kingdom, and next the *Toledam* of Dagon, and next the one of Martaban and next the one of *Xoij̃*[1]. He has a large number of elephants—there must be six or seven thousand in the whole kingdom.

Custom of the lords and other people. All the lords of Pegu, and the other people according to their wealth, make a habit of wearing little round bells in their privy parts. The lords wear as many as nine gold ones, with beautiful treble, contralto and tenor tones, the size of the *alvares* plums[2]
Fol. 136v in our country; and those who are too poor | to have them in gold and silver have them in lead and *fruseleira*; and the gold and silver ones make much more noise than these other lead and *fruseleira* ones[3].

Physical appearance and dress of the Pegu men and women. The men of Pegu are of medium height. They are on the stout side, stunted, and good workers with great strength. They are always shorn all round, leaving the hair growing in the middle of the head and longer on the top. Their teeth are always

[1] *Pesim* in the Lisbon MS; *Pizim* in Ramusio. Perhaps Pires wrote or intended *Cosmim*.

[2] A Portuguese variety of *Prunus domestica* Linn.

[3] Barbosa refers to this extraordinary practice with further details, ending however with these words: 'I say no more of this on account of its indecency.' II, 154. Galvão also mentions it: 'They haue delight to carrie round bels within the skin of their priuie members, which is forbidden to the king and the religious people.' Hak. Soc. ed., p. 113. In Garcia de Resende's *Miscellanea* there is this stanza:

'There is also this custom
in Pegu, that men vie [with each other
as to] which of them shall have
most bells in their privy member,
where they insert them,
cutting open their flesh,
and this healing up in time,
they remain fixed inside:
they say that they are better liked
by the women through this practice.'—St. 88.

Even Camoens in the *Lusiadas* alludes to this Pegu custom:

'Here sounding metal in their parts unseen
They fit, a trick invented by the Queen
Who, by this method, as she did intend,
To the accursed error put an end.'—Canto x, St. 122.

Pigafetta also gives a curious description of this practice, with most extraordinary details, but refers it to Java, a place to which he never went, evidently mistaking it for Pegu. Robertson's edition, II, 169. It seems that the practice—if it ever existed and was not 'a mere figment of imagination'—has never been recorded by any modern writer.

black with betel. They wear a great deal of white cloth round their thighs, and white cloth [round] their heads—almost like a mitre.

The women are fairer.

The women are fairer than the men are. They are of body beautiful, less shy, and wear their hair in the Chinese fashion, as we shall tell in the description of China. Our Malay women rejoice greatly when the Pegu men come to their country, and they are very fond of them. The reason for this must be their sweet harmony. Certainly they are much esteemed by them, and not without cause. These people are peaceable and well disposed here in Malacca. They say that in their own country they are proud.

As, in accordance with the arrangement of this book, we shall pass through Siam on the way to Malacca, it is right that we should speak of it, although we shall come upon it again on the China side at the river of *Odia*[1].

[SIAM]

Kingdom of Siam and its ports.

There are three ports in the kingdom of Siam on the Pegu side, and on the Pahang and *Champa* side there are many. They all belong to the said kingdom and are subject to the king of Siam. The land of Siam is large and very plenteous, with many people and cities, with many lords and many foreign merchants, and most of these foreigners are Chinese, because Siam does a great deal of trade with China. The land of Malacca is called a land of Siam, and the whole of Siam, *Champa* and thereabouts is called China.

The kingdom of Siam is heathen. The people, and almost the language, are like those of Pegu. They are considered to be prudent folk of good counsel. The merchants know a great deal about merchandise. They are tall, swarthy men, shorn like those of Pegu. The kingdom is justly ruled. The king is always in

[1] *Odia* or Ayuthia, former capital of Siam, was destroyed by the Burmese in 1767, after a two years' siege. Barros writes *Odia* and *Hudiá*. Couto (VI, vii, 9) gives an interesting description of 'the city of *Odia*, the principal of the kingdom of Siam, which lies forty leagues up the river' (Menam Chao Phaya). *Odia* was sometimes called *Judea* or *Iudia*. *Hobson-Jobson*, *s.v.* Judea.

residence in the city of *Odia*. He is a hunter. He is very ceremonious with strangers; he is more free and easy with the natives. He has many wives, upwards of five hundred. On the death [of the king] it has as king a person of the blood [royal], usually a nephew, the son of a sister, if he is suitable, and if not there are sometimes agreements and assemblies [to decide] who will be the best. Secrets are closely kept among them. They are very reserved. They speak with well-taught modesty. The important men are very obedient to the king. Their ambassadors carry out their instructions thoroughly.

Through the cunning [of the Siamese] the foreign merchants who go to their land and kingdom leave their merchandise in the land and are ill paid; and this happens to them all—but less to the Chinese, on account of their friendship with the king of China. And for this reason less people go to their port than would [otherwise] go. However, as the land is rich in good merchandise, they bear some things on account of the profit, as often happens to merchants, because otherwise there would be no trading.

There are very few Moors in Siam. The Siamese do not like them. There are, however, Arabs, Persians, Bengalees, many Kling, Chinese and other nationalities. And all the Siamese trade is on the China side, and in Pase, Pedir and Bengal. The Moors are in the seaports. They are obedient to their own lords, and constantly make war on the Siamese, now inland and now in Pahang. They are not very warlike fighting men. The said Siamese wear bells like the men of Pegu, and no less but just as many. The lords wear pointed diamonds and other precious stones in their privy parts in addition to the bells—a precious stone worn is according to the person or his estate.

Fol. 137r.

Duties and coinage in Siam.

The foreign merchants in Siam pay two on every nine, and the Chinese pay two on every twelve. The bahar weighs the same as it does in China, neither more nor less. The Siamese gold and silver *cate* is equivalent to a Malacca *cate* and a half. Cowries, like those current in Pegu, are current throughout the country for small money, and gold and silver for the larger coins. This money is worth the same as we have said for Pegu. And there seems to be no doubt that they pay one in fifteen on the goods going out, because the truth is that they pay duties of two in ten on everything in Siam.

Ports in Siam going towards Malacca on the Pegu side.

The nearest to the land of Pegu, to Martaban, is Tenasserim (*Tenaçarj*) and then Junkseylon (*Juncalom*) and then Trang (*Terrãm*)[1] and Kedah (*Quedaa*), and it is a port of the kingdom of Kedah which is tributary to it. And from Kedah to Malacca they are all tin places, as we have already said in the kingdom and district of Malacca.

This had to be [mentioned] before we speak of Kedah, so that it should be in order.

Ports in the kingdom of Siam on the China side.

Beginning from Pahang (*Pahãao*) and Trengganu (*Talimgano*), Kelantam (*Clamtam*), *Say*, Patani (*Patane*), Lakon (*Lugor*), *Martarã*, *Callnansey*, *Bamcha*, *Cotinuo*, *Peperim*, *Pamgoray*[2], are all ports belonging to lords of the land of Siam, and

[1] All fol. 137r. of the Paris MS was left out in the Lisbon MS and in Ramusio; so these names cannot be collated as in other instances.

JUNCALOM—Junkseylon, an island and old port off the west coast of the Malay Peninsula. It is referred to by Galvão and Pinto, and appears for the first time in Diogo Homem's atlas of 1558 as *jũsalã*.

TERRÃM—Trang, Tarang or Klong Trang, a river, port and town further south, in 7° 18′ lat. N. It is mentioned by Barros (I, ix, 1) as *Torrão*. The map of *c.* 1540 has *toram*. Some cartographers, as Dourado, placed *toraõ* south of Kedah; on the maps of D. Homem and Berthelot *torãque* or *Torram* is also south of Kedah. In this case they meant perhaps the present Trong, in 4° 40′, which appears on Rodrigues' map (fol. 34) as *Rio do trom*, i.e. Kuala Larut, bounded by Singa Besar Island on the north and Trong Island on the south.

[2] Later on, under the heading 'King and Lords of the kingdom of Siam', the names of these ports are written as follows: '*pahãm| talimgano| chantansay| patane| lugoumai| taram calnãsey banq^a chotomuj pepory pamgoray*'. Barros (I, ix, 1) says that along the coast up to the river *Menão* (Menam or Bangkok) there are the following notable towns: '*Pão*, which is the capital of the kingdom so called, *Ponticão*, *Calantão*, *Patane*, *Lugor*, *Cuy*, *Perperij*, and *Bamplacot*, which lies at the mouth of the river *Menão*.' He also mentions the following 'towns which are sea ports' from *Hudiá* (Bangkok) towards Malacca: '*Pangoçay*, *Lugo*, *Patane*, *Calantam*, *Talingano* or *Talinganor*, and *Pam*'. III, ii, 5.

CLAMTAM—Corresponds to Kota Bharu, at the entrance of the Kelantan River. The *Calantão* or *Calantam* mentioned by Barros. Dourado's atlas of 1580 has *R° de calamtão*, which is found also on later maps.

SAY—Corresponds to Saiburi at the entrance of the Telubin River, in 6° 42′ lat. N. The 1554 map of L. Homem has *sera patane* north of *calatam*; in D. Homem's atlas of 1558 there is *r. serra* between *catatã* and *patane*, and *tei* in Dourado's atlases. Then it appears again on an Eredia map (fol. 27) as *Sea. Rio*, between *calantan Rio* and *PATANE*; the atlas of *c.* 1615–23 has *Sea* between *calantam* and *patane*; Berthelot's map of 1635 has *Sey* between

some of these are kings. They all have junks; these do not belong to the king of Siam, but to the merchants and the lords of the places; and after these ports there is the river of *Odia*, where they go up to the city—a river where boats and ships can go, wide and beautiful.

River of Kedah (Quedaa). Kedah is a very small kingdom, with few people and few houses. It is up a river. There is pepper there, a matter of four hundred bahars a year. This pepper goes by way of Siam to China, with that which they bring from Pase and Pedir also. When any ship comes to Tenasserim and to the ports of Siam, it comes to Kedah to sell its merchandise also, and the people from the tin districts buy and take gold, because Kedah is a trading country; and they get to the land of Siam in three or four days by land, and they take the merchandise from Kedah to Siam.

The kingdom of Kedah is almost bounded on one side by Trang (*Terrão*), and on the other by the end of the kingdom of

R. de calantam and *Patane*. J. V. Mills says that the 'Sai River', as it appears on an ancient Chinese Wu-Pei-Chih chart, 'represents what is now called the Telubin River. The earliest European map to mark the river is that of Homem (1558) who calls it "Seiia" [a misreading for *r. serra* as noted above]. Similar names appear on all the maps on which the river is named, down to at least 1850: the name "Telubin" does not appear until after that date'. *Malaya in the Wu-Pei-Chih Charts*, p. 36. However, the name survived in Saiburi.

LUGOR—Lakon roadstead and town. The map of *c.* 1540 has *logor*.

MARTARÃ—The next important port to the north is Bandon. But still further north there is an islet called Matra near the coast, in 10° 24′ lat. N., southeast of M. Chum Pon. Is this connected with Pires' *Martarã*?

CALLNANSEY—Bang Kamma Sen, a small village on the coast, in 11° 2′ lat. N.?

BAMCHA—Bang-taphang or Bang Sabhan, in 11° 12′ lat. N.? *Banagh* in the *Mohit*. Pinto mentions several times this town or port of *Banchâ*.

COTINUX—Further on called *Chotomuj*. Koh Ta kut, in 12° 15′ lat. N.?

PEPERIM—Pechabury river and town. The *Perperij* of Barros. *Perpji* on the map of *c.* 1540, and *Peiper* on Berthelot's map. On several later maps it appears as *Piperi* (see maps in L. Fournereau, *Le Siam Ancien*). On an early sixteenth-century Portuguese map by Miranda (in Aires, *Fernão Mendes Pinto e o Japão*) it is *Piper*, corresponding to the town of Pechabury, in 13° 6′ lat. N. On the map published by Bowring, *The Kingdom and People of Siam*, end of vol. II, it still appears as *Phiphri*, on the north of the entrance of the river Pechabury in 13° 16′.

PAMGORAY—This must be the *Pangoçay* mentioned by Barros as the first port when going from Bangkok to Malacca. *Pangoçay* was identified as Bang Plassoy by Campos, *Early Portuguese Accounts of Thailand*, p. 11.

Malacca and by Bruas (*Baruaz*)[1]. Kedah trades with Pase and Pedir, and the people of Pase and Pedir come to Kedah every year. One ship comes from Gujarat to the ports of Siam, and comes to Kedah and takes in a cargo of the pepper there is in the country, and from there it sometimes goes back to Pase and Pedir to finish taking in its cargo, and it takes the tin from Bruas, Selangor (*Çalamgor*) and *Mjmjam*.[2].

Kedah is under the jurisdiction of the king of Siam, and they go to Siam by the Kedah river. Kedah has rice in quantities, and pepper. A great deal of merchandise from China is used in Kedah; and Kedah does not have junks, it has lancharas. It is a country. It does good trade. Because of their proximity, cloth in Kedah is worth the same as in Malacca.

Now we will go on to Siam on the China side, and after having finished talking about Siam, and about some of its ports, we will enter into the kingdom of Cambodia.

Merchandise in Siam which used to come to Malacca at the time when they traded with it. Foodstuffs.

There is a great abundance of rice in Siam, and much salt, dried salt fish, *oraquas*[3], vegetables; and up to thirty junks a year used to come to Malacca with these.

[1] The mouth of the river Bruas or Sungi Bruas is in 4° 28′ lat. N. One of the villages near the sea is called Pengkalen Bahru today, and higher up the river there is a village of Bruas. Pires says later, when describing *Baruaz*, that in the '*Baruaz* river there are two inhabited places (*povoações*)'. Pinto (CXLIV) states that in 1544 he 'saw all the coast of the Malay, which is 130 leagues (from Malacca) to *Junçalão*, entering all the rivers of *Barruhàs*, *Salangor*, *Panágim*, *Quedá*, *Parlés*, *Pēdão*, and *Sambilaõ Siaõ*'. Dealing with Malacca, in 1614, Bocarro (xliv) mentions *Barvas*. The map of *c.* 1540 has *broes*, between *queda* and *pulo cãbilam*; L. Homem's map of 1554 has *baruas* between *pemdam* (Penang) and *pulo sambilam* (Sembilan); Dourado's atlases and other Portuguese maps have *baruas* between *toram* (Trang) and *p. sambilaõ*; Eredia's map of the Malay Peninsula (fol. 27) has *baruas* immediately north of a cape corresponding to the Dindings; the Atlas of Janssonius (1658) still has *Baruas*. The *Malacca Strait Pilot* says that 'Sungi Bruas is a small river fronted by the mudbank extending from 5 to 9 miles off-shore' but navigable by canoes for nearly 60 miles. It appears that the former port of Baruas or Bruas disappeared through silting.

[2] *Mjmjam*—The map of *c.* 1540 has *micham* immediately north of *cãlagor* (Selangor, in 3° 21′). The name still survives in Mehegan Point, the south point of the mouth of Dinding River (4° 14′) which 'has a deep and clear entrance and is said to be navigable by vessels drawing 15 feet (4^{m} 6) . . . a distance of about 7 miles'. *Malacca Strait Pilot*. See below, p. 261.

[3] *Arrack*, here the distilled spirit from a palm. In some instances Pires seems to mean the palm-tree itself.

Merchandise. From Siam comes lac, benzoin, brazil[1], lead, tin, silver, gold, ivory, cassia fistula; they bring vessels of cast copper and gold, ruby and diamond rings; they bring a large quantity of cheap, coarse Siamese cloth for the poor people.

Fol. 137v. *Merchandise from Malacca for Siam.* They say that the chief merchandise they take from Malacca to Siam are the male and female slaves, which they take in quantities, white sandalwood, pepper, quicksilver, vermilion, opium, *azernefe*, cloves, mace, nutmeg, wide and narrow muslins, and Kling cloths in the fashion of Siam, camlets, rosewater, carpets, brocades from Cambay, white cowries, wax, Borneo camphor, pachak which are roots like dry rampion, gall-nuts (*gualhas*), and the merchandise they bring from China every year is also of value there.

How long it is that the Siamese have not been coming to Malacca. The Siamese have not traded in Malacca for twenty-two years. They had a difference because the kings of Malacca owed allegiance to the kings of Siam, because they say that Malacca belongs to the land of Siam—They say that it is theirs and that twenty-two years ago this king lost Malacca, which rose up against this subjection. They also say that Pahang rose against Siam in the same way, and that, on account of the relationship between them, the kings of Malacca favoured the people of Pahang against the Siamese, and that this was also a reason for their disagreement.

They also say that it was about the tin districts which are on the Kedah side, and which were originally under Kedah, and were taken over by Malacca; and they quarrelled for all these reasons, and they say that the chief reason was the revolt against subjection. After this the Siamese sailed against Malacca, and the Siamese were routed by the Malays, and [they say] that the *Lasamane* was the captain—who has therefore been held in great honour ever since.

Where the Simese trade now. The Siamese trade in China—six or seven junks a year. They trade with Sunda and Palembang (*Palimbaão*) and other islands. They trade with Cambodia and *Champa* and Cochin China

[1] Brazil-wood or sappan-wood, *Caesalpinia Sappan* Linn. In his description of Malacca, Resende refers to 'some sapam, which is a red wood for dyes not much inferior to that of Brazil'. *Livro do Estado da India*, fol. 377v. Two of the most important Brazilian species are *Caesalpinia Brasiliensis* Linn., and *C. echinata* Lam.

(*Cauçhy*), and with Burma (*Brema*) and *Jangoma*[1] on the main land, when they are at peace.

On the Tenasserim side Siam also trades with Pase, Pedir, with Kedah, with Pegu, with Bengal; and the Gujaratees come to its port every year. They trade richly outside and liberally inside the country, but they are great tyrants.

King and lords of the kingdom of Siam.

King *Prechayoa*[2] means lord of all, and after the king the *Aja Capẽtit*[3] is the viceroy on the Pegu and Cambodia side, and makes war on Burma (*Bremao*) and *Jangoma*. This *Aja Capẽtit* has many fighting men. Inside his own territory he is like the king of this land.

The second is the viceroy of Lakon (*Loguor*). He is called *Poyohya* (?)[4]. He is governor from Pahang to *Odia*; Pahang

[1] CAUÇHY, *Cauchij* or *Cauchy Chyna*—Cochin China, called by the Malays *Kuchi*, whence the Portuguese *Cauchi* and *Cochinchina*. Cf. *Hobson-Jobson*. On the eastern part of the Cantino map there is *champocochim* and *chinacochim*. Rodrigues' map (fol. 38) has *coçhim da çhina* at the head of a long and narrow gulf. See note on Champa (p. 112).

BREMA—Burma. Mentioned by Barbosa and other sixteenth-century Portuguese writers as *Berma*.

JANGOMA—Mentioned by several sixteenth-century Portuguese writers. 'The town and state of Siamese Laos, called by the Burmese *Zimmé*, by the Siamese *Xieng-mai* or *Kiang-mai*, &c.' *Hobson-Jobson*, *s.v.* Jangomay.

[2] *Rey pchayoa* or *prechayoa*. *Perchoaa* in the Lisbon MS; *Perchoa* in Ramusio. This might suggest King Phrachai or Prajai; but he reigned after 1534. In Pires' time the king of Siam was Rama Tibodi II, who died in 1529. *Phra*—'it is addressed at court to the king,' in Burma and Siam. It is supposed to be a corruption of Skt. *prabhu*, an honorific title meaning 'lord or chief'. *Hobson-Jobson*, *s.vv.* Pra and Parvoe; Dalgado *s.v.* Precheu. From Pinto (CLXXXIX) it seems that *Prechau* was a title of the king of Siam, which agrees with Pires' *Prechayoa*: 'The King's highest title is *Prechau Saleu*, which in our language means holy member of God.' Gerini says that Pinto's *Prechau* is 'P'hraḥ Chău, the Sacred Lord, *i.e.* His Majesty; something like "Holy Tzar".' *Historical Retrospect of Junkceylon Island*, p. 13.

[3] *Agii capitemte* in the Lisbon MS; *Aiam campetit* in Ramusio. Oya Kampengpet, the Governor of Kampengpet or Kamphengphet, the old Siamese city in 16° 30′ lat. N. A fairly complete Portuguese map by Miranda, of the early eighteenth century (in Aires, Fernão *Mendes Pinto e o Japão*) has *Campeng*.

[4] *Perajoa* in the Lisbon MS; *Peraia* in Ramusio. Perhaps Pra Oya, meaning 'Lord Governor'. According to Campos some cities and ports had a governor with the title of *Oya* or *Phya*. *Op. cit.*, p. 11. Pinto (CLXXXII) refers to the '*Oyâs*, *Conchalês* and *Monteos*, which are supreme dignities above all the others of the kingdom' of Siam. But referring to *Lugor* he says (XXXVI) there is there 'a viceroy whom they call *Poyho* in their language'.

(*Pahãm*), Trengganu (*Talimgano*), *Chantansay*, Patani, Lakon (*Lugou*), *Maitaram*, *Calnãsey*, *Banqa*, *Chotomuj*, *Pepory*, *Pamgoray* and other ports all have lords like kings, some of them Moors, some of them heathen. And in each port there are many junks and these navigate to Cambodia, Champa, Cochin China (*Cauchij*), and to Java and Sunda, and to Malacca, Pase, Pedir and to those of Indragiri (*Andarguerij*)[1], Palembang (*Palimbão*), and from these places to Patani. They have up to seven or eight hundred bahars of pepper every year, and everyone of these ports is a chief port, and they have a great deal of trade, and many of them rebel against Siam; and this viceroy very rich and a very important person—almost as important as the other, [of] Kampengpet (*Capemtit*).

The other is *Vya Chacotay*[2]. He is viceroy on the Tenasserim, Trang and Kedah side. He is the chief person. He has jurisdiction over them all. He is perpetual captain of Tenasserim. He is the lord of many people and of a land plenteous in foodstuffs.

Another is *Oparaa*[3]. He is secretary to the king. Everything passes through his hands and through the *Concusa* who is treasurer; and they say that both this *Oparaa* and the *Concusa* *Fol. 138r.* now have, | great authority with the king of Siam, although the *Concusa* is a man of low birth. It is customary in the kingdom of Siam for everything to go through these two people *Oparaa* and *Concusa*, and these two wrote to Malacca with the king of Siam.

[BURMA]

Kingdoms of Burma and Jangoma. The boundaries of the kingdom of Burma are in the hinter-

[1] All these names from *Camboja* to *Palimbão* were omitted in the Lisbon MS and in Ramusio. Barros (II, v, i), mentions *Andraguerij*, Albuquerque (*Comentarios*, III, xvii) refers to *Dandargiri*, and Castanheda (II, cxi) speaks of *Andragide* as a kingdom of Sumatra. Ribeiro's maps of 1527 and 1529 have *adaragire*. *Andarguerij* corresponds to the Indragiri River, which debouches on the east coast of Sumatra in 1° lat. S.

[2] *Ajaa chacotai* in the Lisbon MS, *Aia Chatoteri* in Ramusio. Oya Socotai, the Governor of Socotay, Sukotai or Sukhothai, the old Siamese city in 17° lat. N. The map of Miranda has *Socotay* north-west of *Campeng*.

[3] *Uparat* was a title meaning literally 'Second King' or 'Vice King' in the kingdom of Siam. He 'was, in fact, the Crown Prince', says Wood, *A History of Siam*, pp. 92-3.

land, on the side of Pegu and Arakan; and on the China side it is bounded by *Jangoma*, and *Jangoma* is bounded by Burma and by Cambodia.

These two heathen kings of the hinterland are at war with Pegu and Arakan and with Bengal and with Cambodia and chiefly with Siam because [Siam] killed certain of their sons. Others say that Burma has boundaries only from Pegu to Cambodia in the hinterland, and behind this kingdom of the *Edetrias*[1] and *Jangoma* they then enter into the land of China, and as the land narrows, there is no doubt that this is so.

Merchandise of these kingdoms.

They say that in Burma is the mine for the precious stones that go from there to the city of Ava, which is in Arakan, and that [Burma] has a great deal of benzoin and lac, which goes from there to Siam and Pegu; and that the musk comes from the kingdom of *Jangoma* and the kingdom of the [*blank*][2] and they say that musk also goes there from China.

They affirm, and it seems reasonable, that they can go overland from Pegu and Siam to take the pepper and sandalwood to China—on the hinterland side of China—because the people of Pegu and Siam trade with Burma in lancharas and *paraos*[3] up the rivers there are in the said kingdoms; and the merchants who go in this way say what they please and within a month they come back[4].

Merchandise that is traded in these Kingdoms of Burma and Jangoma.

Pepper, white sandalwood, wide and narrow *sinabafos*, quicksilver, vermilion, damasks, satins, brocades, white cloths from Bengal; and there are many men from these kingdoms in Siam, Pegu and Cambodia.

The men of these kingdoms are horsemen. They have horses and elephants. They wear boots. It is their custom to cut off the noses of all their prisoners, and specially of those from Cambodia, who started this custom.

[1] This word is omitted in the Lisbon MS and in Ramusio.

[2] There is a word missing here, and in Ramusio also. In the Lisbon MS it reads: 'and the musk comes from the kingdom of *Jangoma*; from there also musk goes to China'.

[3] A small Malay vessel. *Hobson-Jobson, s.v.* Prow; Dalgado *s.v.* Parau.

[4] This obscure sentence has been left out in the Lisbon MS and in Ramusio.

[CAMBODIA]

Kingdom of Cambodia (Camboja). Leaving Siam on the way to China along the sea-coast, is the kingdom of Cambodia, which is bounded along the said way by *Champa*. The said king is a heathen and knightly. This country extends far into the hinterland. He is at war with the people of Burma and with Siam, and sometimes with *Champa*, and he does not obey anyone. The people of Cambodia are warlike.

The land of Cambodia possesses many rivers. There are many lancharas on them, which sail to the coast of Siam on the Lakon side, and they often form into armadas against friends and foes (?). The land of Cambodia produces quantities of foodstuffs. It is a country with many horses and elephants.

Food-stuffs. The land of Cambodia produces quantities of rice and good meat, fish and wines of its own kind; and this country has gold; it has lac, many elephants' tusks, dried fish, rice.

Merchandise marketable in Cambodia. Fine white cloths from Bengal, a little pepper, cloves, vermilion, quicksilver, liquid storax, red beads.

In this country the lords burn themselves on the death of the king—as do the king's wives and the other women on the death of their husbands. And they go shorn around their ears as a sign of elegance.

[CHAMPA]

Kingdom of Champaa[1]. Beyond the land of Cambodia, following the sea-coast, inland, is the kingdom of *Champa*. The country is large and produces a great deal of rice, meat and other foodstuffs. | There are no
Fol. 138v. ports in this country for large junks. It has a few towns on

[1] *Champaa* or *Champa*—'The name of a kingdom at one time of great power and importance in Indo-China, occupying the extreme S.E. of that region. A limited portion of its soil is still known by that name, but otherwise as the Binh-Thuān province of Cochin China.' *Hobson-Jobson, s.v.* Champa. Barros (I, ix, I) says: 'Beyond this Kingdom of Camboja comes the other Kingdom called *Campá* . . . which our people call Cauchij China, and the natives Cachó.' Camoens (x, 129) also mentions 'the coast called Champà'. The Cantino map has *champocachim* on its eastern part. Then the name disappeared from Portuguese maps, to be found again on the atlas of *c.* 1615–23: *CHAMPA*, east of *CAMBOIA*; on Berthelot's map of 1635: *COSTA DE CHAMPA*, east of *CAMBODIA*. Similarly on other later maps.

PLATE XIX

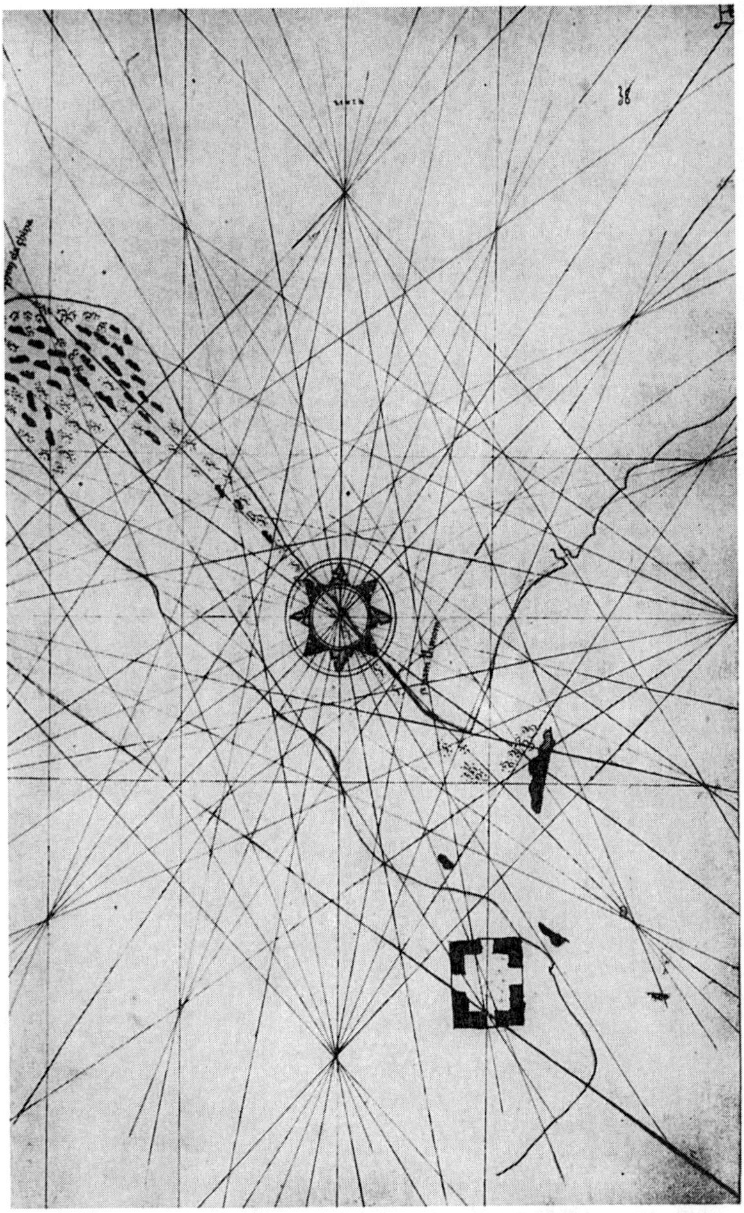

Rodrigues' sketch (fol. 38) of the Gulf of Tong-King, with Hainan
(p. 523)

PLATE XX

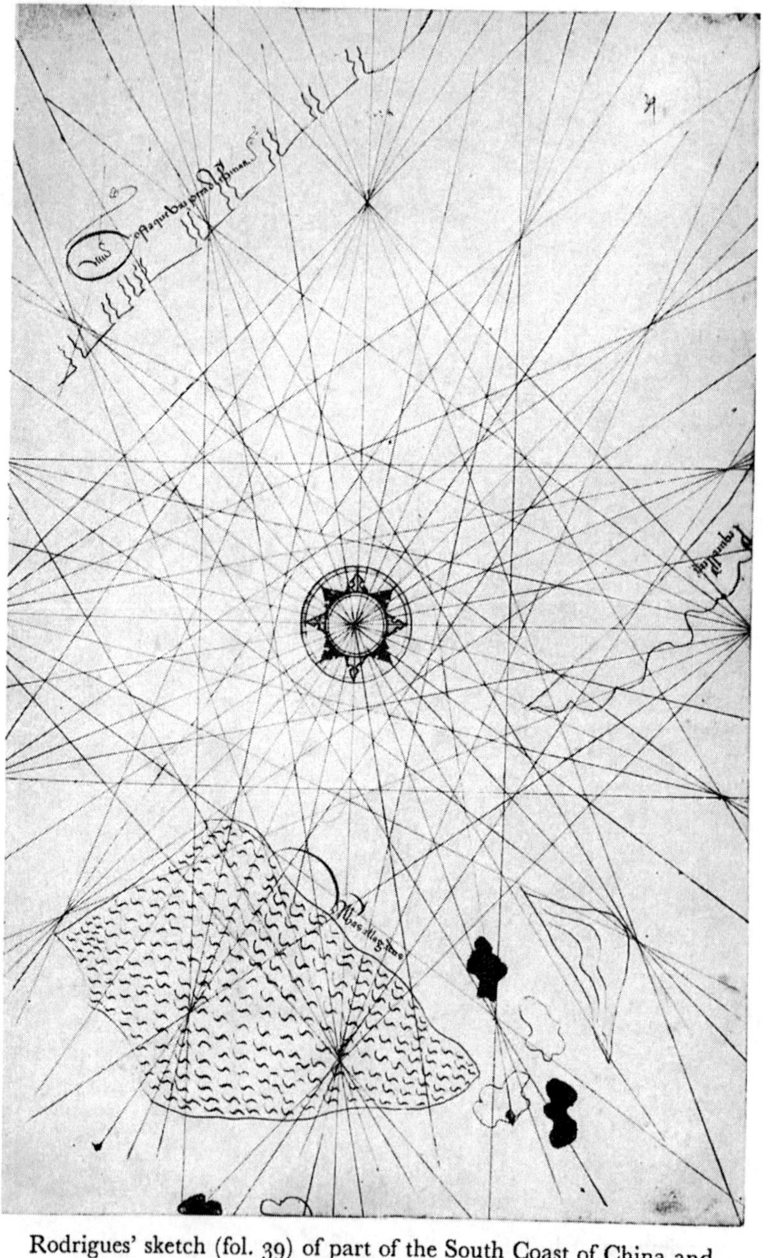

Rodrigues' sketch (fol. 39) of part of the South Coast of China and some islands, possibly the Philippines (p. 523)

rivers. Ships that draw a fathom and a half of water go in at high tide; at low tide they are dry at the entrance. Many lancharas navigate in Siam up to Pahang.

The king is a heathen. He has many subjects. He is rich and lives by husbandry. They all have horses. He is at war with other kings, and chiefly with the king of Cochin China.

The chief merchandise of *Champa* is calambac[1], which is aloes-wood, the true and best kind of it, for the kind that is used in Portugal is *guaro*, and here there are forests of it. There is a great difference in the taste and smell of calambac, and [there is as much difference] in its value as between gold and lead; and the best of this calambac, and the source of it, is in *Champa*. It is gummy with black and white veins. It is a soft wood. In Malacca two *arráteis* fetch six or seven *cruzados*, and there is some worth twelve; and the more perfect and the larger the wood the higher it rises in value, as against the small [wood], although they may both be equally good. *Calambac.*

It has a good quantity of tried gold from Menangkabau (*Menancabo*)[2], which comes from the mine, [and] which ever goes to Cochin China. The people of *Champa* hold gold to be a merchandise of its true value. It is gold in big pieces.

From [*Champa*] they take dried salt fish, rice and gold to Malacca, [and] some pepper, because there is no other merchandise in the country. The country does not have much trade in Malacca, because merchandise goes there from Siam. *Foodstuffs.*

[1] *Aquilaria Agallocha* Roxb., Calambac, Agallochum, Aloe or Eagle-wood. See Burkill, pp. 197–205.

[2] *Menancabo* is the ancient inland Kingdom of Menangkabau, in Sumatra. The letter to Albuquerque, written from Malacca on 6 Feb. 1510, by Portuguese captives, mentions for the first time 'the gold that comes to Malacca from a mine in *Menamcabo* on the side of *Çamatra*, and they go there from here by sea and a river in nine or ten days'. *Cartas*, III, 10. On the Cantino map there is *manjcabo* at the N.W. of Taporbana Island. The map of *c.* 1540 as *manacãbo* across Sumatra, in 2–3° lat.S. Dourado's atlases and the atlas of *c.* 1615–23 have *manãcabo* naming a river on the south-west of Sumatra. One of Eredia's maps (fol. 24v.) has *MINAS: DE: ORO do Monancabo* on the S.W. of Sumatra. Ferrand (*Malaka, le Mayalu et Malayur*, XII, 51–82), and Dames (II, 170–1, 186–7) have dealt extensively with Menangkabau and the Menangkabos. Tomás Dias, a Portuguese, was the first European to visit the hinterland of Menangkabau, in 1684, and a modern Dutch writer calls him 'the greatest explorer of Sumatra'. Schnitger, *Forgotten Kingdoms in Sumatra*, pp. 55–64.

Merchandise marketable in Champa.

The chief is areca, with which they eat betel, with cloth from Bengal, large and small *sinabafos*, *panchavilizes*[1], a few Kling cloths, pepper, cloves, a little nutmeg, catechu, a little pachak, liquid storax.

Coinage of the country.

Cashes (*caixas*)[2] from China are used for the small money, and in trade gold and silver [are used]. Gold in *Champa* is worth a fifth part less that in Malacca and silver a sixth part.

People and ships.

It is weak on the sea. It has many lancharas which need little depth, because there is little water. They sail through the country, which is large. With the merchandise of the country and with the cloth produced in the country for their clothes they go to Siam and Cochin China. It has no port of note. There are no Moors in the kingdom.

[COCHIN CHINA]

Kingdom of Cochin China (Cauchy Chyna).

The king of Cochin China is king of a larger and richer country than *Champa*. The kingdom is between *Champa* and China. He is a powerful warrior in the land. He has a great many lancharas and thirty or forty junks[3]. The country contains large navigable rivers. There are no settlers by them; near the sea [there are] many. His country extends a long way inland. In Malacca his country is called Cochin China (*Cauchy Chyna*), on account of *Cauchy Coulam*.

The king is a heathen, and so are all his people. They are not friendly to Moors. They do not sail to Malacca, but to China and to *Champa*. They are a very weak people on the sea; all their achievement is on land. They have great lords. This king is joined to the king of China by marriages; and as this king does not make war with China, he always has an ambassador at the king of China's court, even though the king of Cochin China be unwilling, or though it breed discontent in him, because he

[1] Perhaps the same as *pachavelões*, a printed cloth in Choromandel. Dalgado, *s.v.* Pachavelão.

[2] *Caixa*—cash. 'A name applied by Europeans to sundry coins of low value in various parts of the Indies.' *Hobson-Jobson*, *s.v.* Cash; Dalgado, *s.v.* Caixa.

[3] Although the Paris MS says 'four junks', this is obviously a mistake; the transcriber wrote 'terra atee q̃oat°' where Pires had written 'trinta ou quarenta'. The Lisbon MS and Ramusio have 'thirty or forty'.

is his vassal, as will be told in the account of China. Cochin China is a land of many horses.

This king is much given to war, and he has countless *Fol. 139r.* musketeers, and small bombards. A very great deal of powder is used in his country, both in war and in all his feasts and amusements by day and night. All the lords and important people in his kingdom employ it like this. Powder is used every day in rockets and all other pleasurable exercises, as we shall see in the merchandise which is of value there.

Merchandise there is in the land of Cochin China.

Chiefly gold and silver, much more than in Champa; the calambac is not so much as in *Champa*. They have porcelain and pottery—some of great value—and these go from there to China to be sold. They have better, bigger and wider and finer taffeta of all kinds than there is anywhere else here and in our [countries]. They have the best raw (?) silks in colours, which are in great abundance here, and all that they have in this way is fine and perfect, without the falseness that things from other places have, and also seed pearls and not much.

Merchandise of value in Cochin China.

At the head of the merchandise appreciated in Cochin China is sulphur, and [they would take] twenty junks of this if they would send them as many as these; and sulphur from China is greatly valued. A very great deal comes to Malacca from the islands of Solor beyond Java, as will be told when they are described; and from here it goes to Cochin China.

Saltpetre and precious stones.

A large quantity of saltpetre is also of value, and a large quantity comes there from China, and it is all sold there. Rubies, diamonds, sapphires and all other fine precious stones are of value, and some opium, but little, a little pepper, and so with the other things that are of value in China. Liquid storax is of fair value.

They rarely come to Malacca in their junks. They go to China, to Canton (*Quamtom*), which is a large city, to join up with the Chinese (?); then they come for merchandise with the Chinese in their junks, and the chief thing they bring [to Malacca] is gold and silver and things they buy in China.

Coinage of the country.

The money they use for buying food is the cash from China, and for merchandise gold and silver.

[*FOURTH BOOK*]

[CHINA TO BORNEO]

[China—Liu Kiu—Japan—Borneo—Philippines]

[CHINA]

Kingdom of China. ACCORDING to what the nations here in the East say, things of China are made out to be great, riches, pomp and state in both the land and people, and other tales which it would be easier to believe as true of our Portugal than of China[1]. China is a large country with beautiful horses and mules, they say, and in large numbers.

The king of China is a heathen with much land and many people. The people of China are white, as white as we are. Most of them wear black cotton cloth, and they wear sayons of this in five pieces with gores, as we do, only they are very wide. In the winter they wear felt on their legs by way of socks, and on top well-made boots which do not reach above the knee, and they wear their clothes lined with lambskin and other furs. Some of them wear pelisses. They wear round silk net caps like
Fol. 139v. the black sieves we have in Portugal. | They are rather like Germans. They have thirty or forty hairs in their beards. They wear very well-made French shoes with square toes.

All the Chinese eat pigs, cows and all other animals. They drink a fair amount of all sorts of beverages. They praise our wine greatly. They get pretty drunk. They are weak people, of small account. Those who are to be seen in Malacca are not very truthful, and steal—that is the common people. They eat with two sticks, and the earthenware or china bowl in their left hand close to their mouth, with the two sticks to suck in. This is the Chinese way[2].

[1] Prof. A. C. Moule pointed out to me how this modern assumption of western superiority is an interesting contrast to the medieval wonder at the superiority of the East.

[2] This is the earliest known European description of the chopsticks. 'A very good description too', comments Prof. Moule. *Hobson-Jobson*, *s.v.* Chopsticks, has nothing earlier than F. Mendes Pinto's description, *c.* 1540.

The women look like Spanish women. They wear pleated skirts with waistbands, and little loose coats longer than in our country. Their long hair is rolled in a graceful way on the top of their heads, and they put many gold pins in it to hold it, and those who have them put precious stones around, and golden jewelry on the crown of their heads and in their ears and on their necks. They put a great deal of ceruse on their faces and paint on the top of it, and they are so made up that Seville has no advantage over them; and they drink like women from a cold country. They wear pointed slippers of silk and brocade. They all carry fans in their hands. They are as white as we are, and some of them have small eyes and others large, and noses as they must be. *Chinese women.*

China has many cities [and] fortresses, all masonry. The city where the king lives is called *Cambara*[1]. [In the margin of this paragraph there is an addition to the text, in the same hand—perhaps a couple of lines left out here by the transcriber. The manuscript was badly cropped in binding, part of the words having been cut away. The text may, however, be reconstituted as here given in italics:] *This city is in the kingdom of China, the king of which is there sometimes as . . . Cambarra, which is called Peking* (Peqim). *These cities are inland, far from Canton* (Qãto). It has many inhabitants and many nobles with innumerable *Where the king is.*

Barbosa (II, 213) also refers to the chopsticks; Pires' account is better, however, perhaps because he had actually seen Chinese eating in Malacca.

[1] *Cambara* or *Peqim*—Peking. The *Cambalu* or *Cambaluc* of Marco Polo, and *Cambalech* of other medieval writers. Though several cities had stood on or near the site of Peking, this name was first used in 1403 by the Ming Emperor Chêng Tsu (better known by his reign-title Yung-Lo), who moved his court thither in 1420. Peking, of course, means 'northern capital'. It seems likely that Tomé Pires was the first European to call it by that name. It must be said, however, that the *Comentários* (III, xxx), compiled from documents contemporary with Pires, also refers to *Pequim* as the city where the king of China was. In their two long letters of 1524, Cristóvão Vieira and Vasco Calvo often refer to *Pequim.* The survival at that date of *Cambara* (Polo's *Cambalu*) is of considerable interest. It might suggest that Pires knew of Marco Polo's *Book,* though *Cambara* and *Cambalu* are so different in spelling, and he does not mention the famous Venetian traveller anywhere in the *Suma.* More remarkable still is the identification of *Cambara* with Peking. Nearly a hundred years later Ricci reckoned as a discovery 'il Cataio esser la Cina e la corte del re del Cataio esser Pachino'. *Opere storiche,* vol. I, p. 546. On the probable representation of Peking on Rodrigues' map (fol. 40), see p. 523.

Vassal kings of the king of China, his tributaries who pay him tribute

horses. The king is never seen by the people, or the grandees, except by very few, because that is the custom. They say he has countless mules—as if it were in our country.

The king of Champa, the king of Cochin China, the king of the Liu Kiu (*Lequjos*), the king of Japan. Mention will be made of these later.

Vassal kings without obligation of a tribute [who] only [give a] present.

The king of Java, the king of Siam, the king of Pase, the king of Malacca. These send their ambassadors with the seal of China to the king of China every five years and every ten years, and each one sends him the best there is in his country of what he knows they like there.

From Malacca they sent him pepper and white sandal-wood, good-sized wood, and also *garo*[1], which is apothecary's aloes, rings with precious stones, birds[2] which come in quantities dead, and things like that, camlets; and each one according to what he has. These ambassadors can enter and leave China.

How the ambassadors [are received] by the king.

When these ambassadors go to the king, they do not see anything but the vague shape of his body behind a curtain, and he answers from there, and seven scribes write down the words as he says them; the mandarin officials sign this without the king's touching it, nor being seen, and they return; and if they take a present of a thousand he presents them with double, and the ambassadors leave everything there as bribes and go away without seeing the face or the person of the king. This is the truth, and not, as they used to say, that four men were seated in view and that they talked to all of them without knowing which was the king. And these ambassadors can cast anchor in the port of Canton, as will be told later.

[1] *Garo*, which further on is spelt *garuu*—The Malay *garu* or *gaharu*, for the calambac, eagle-wood or aloes. Orta (xxx) says that the Malays call the inferior quality *garro*, and the very fine one *calambac*. 'Valentyn pronounces the *gahru* to be an inferior species . . . and different from the genuine *kalambak*'. Marsden, *History of Sumatra*, p. 160. Gaharu—from the Skt. *garu*, 'heavy'—is a word of trade and indicates the fragant heavy wood. Burkill, pp. 198–9, 202. Dr. Lionel Giles informs me that the Chinese name for *garo* is *ch'ên-hsiang*, 'sinking incense', so called because it is heavier than water.

[2] Perhaps the birds of paradise from Aru and New Guinea, and the brilliant-coloured parrots from the Moluccas, which were brought to Malacca as referred to by Pires further on. The Chinese also imported the hornbill and used the bill for various carved ornaments. Cf. Moule, *Some Foreign Birds and Beasts in Chinese Books*, p. 259.

Fol. 161r.

How they make a king.

The kings of China do not succeed from father to son or nephew, but by election in council of the whole kingdom. It always takes place in the city of *Cambara* where the king resides, and the mandarin who is approved by them becomes king[1].

Law of the realm concerning those who sail to other kingdoms.

No Chinese may set out in the direction of Siam, Java, Malacca, Pase and beyond, without permission from the governors of Canton, and they charge so much for signing the licence to go and come back that they cannot afford it and do not go; and if any stranger is in the land of China he may not leave without a licence from the king, and for this licence, if he is rich, he is reduced to nothing. And if any junk or ship passes beyond the bounds allotted to it for anchorage, its goods are confiscated to the king; and the people are put to death for it.

Places by the sea in the kingdom of China.

Beginning from the Cochin China (*Cauchy*) boundaries towards the coast of China, there are fortresses: first Hainan (*Aynam*)—where they find the seed-pearls that go to China—and Nan-t'ou (*Nantoo*) and Canton and Chang-chou (*Chamcheo*)[2] and other places. Let us speak only of Canton, which is the largest of all and the trading centre for these parts.

[1] All this information is, of course, wholly incorrect.

[2] There has been some discussion about the *Chamcheo* or *Chincheo* of the Portuguese, which has been identified with Marco Polo's *Zayton*, the *magnifico porto de Zaiton* of Fra Mauro's map (1459), corresponding either to Ch'üan-chou or Chang-chou, or to both, in the province of Fukien. T'ien-tsê Chang asserts that by the name of *Chincheo* 'the Portuguese evidently meant to include both the perfectures of Ch'üanchow and Changchow'. *Sino-Portuguese Trade from 1514 to 1644*, pp. 70, 85. Other authorities, however, are not so sure that the *Chincheo* of the Portuguese corresponds to any other place than Chang-chou; cf. Paul Pelliot, *Un ouvrage sur les premiers temps de Macao*, pp. 66, 92, where he analyses Chang's book. Prof. Moule tells me that '*Zayton* or *Zaitun* was certainly Ch'üan-chou, not Chang-chou; but that does not prevent *Chamcheo* being Chang-chou. One would think that originally *Chamcheo* was Changcheo, and that *Chincheo* was Ch'üan-chou; but they were naturally and immediately confused. For the Chinese at a rather earlier date, Ch'üan-chou was the port for foreign trade'. Yule had already remarked that on 'the old maps of the seventeenth century . . . Chincheo is really Changchau'. *Marco Polo*, II, 239. It may be added that sixteenth century Portuguese maps, such as Homem's of 1554, Dourado's of 1568–80, and others, show clearly that *Chincheo* is Chang-chou, situated at the inner end of a bay dotted with several islands. The spelling of Pires' *Chamcheo* rather suggests Chang-chou. The map of *c.* 1540 is the first on which I find *C. de chimcheo*; Mercator's globe of 1541, reproducing an earlier Portuguese map, has also *C do chimcheo*. Later maps have *chimcheo* or *o chimcheo* inscribed at the end of the bay.

This Hainan is a bay[1] on the coast, without a river. Near it are some islands in the sea, where they fish for seed pearls. There are large quantities of these.

The city of Canton (*Quamtom*)[2] is where the whole kingdom

[1] The Catalan map of 1375–81 is the earliest to represent Hainan Island, which is called *caynam*, from Marco Polo's *Cheynan*. The Cantino map has an *ylha ana* at the end of what may correspond to Polo's gulf of *Cheynan*, bounded on one side by *Amu* (which in some texts is *Ania*); but neither *Ana* nor *Amu* can be Hainan. One of Rodrigues' maps (fol. 38) shows the Gulf of Tong-King, with Hainan duly placed to the east of the entrance to the Gulf; on Lei chou peninsula is written *znam llimom*. *znam* stands for Hainan. *llimom* must correspond to King-Mên or Lin-mũn (Cantonese pronunciation), which means 'Gate of the mountain range', the name of a town in Hainan. In a *Lexique géographique des noms de lieux du Lei-K'ioung Tao*, published by Cl. Madrolle, we find '*Ling-Mên.*—Porte de la montagne. *Ling-Moun* (Cantonais); *Neing-Moun* (local). Bourg dans la région montagneuse de Hai-nan, district de Ting-an, hien'. *Hai-nan et la côte continentale voisine*, p. 113. Lei-K'ioung Tao, or Lei-ch'iung Tao, is the circuit (*tao*) comprising the departments (*fu*) of Lei chou, i.e. the peninsula of Kuangtung opposite to Hainan, and Ch'iung chou, the northern part of Hainan itself. Lei chou and Ch'iung chou were so called throughout the Ming and Ch'ing dynasties. Ting-an is a district (*hsien*) south of Ch'iung chou city, apparently on the western slopes of Ch'iung mountain. Ribeiro's maps of 1527 and 1529 have *C. daytam*—an obvious mistranscription from some earlier Portuguese map—written on a peninsula corresponding to Hainan Island, which appears as a prolongation of Lei chou peninsula. The same happens on the *c.* 1540 map, which has *Y. daniã*, and near it *a tinhosa* (Scurfy). The Gulf of Tong-King is fairly well drawn on this map, much better than on later sixteenth century maps. L. Homen's map of 1554, D. Homem's atlas of 1558, and Luís' atlas of 1563 represent Hainan as a separate island, but without name; however, they have *J. tinhosa*. Two ridges united by a sandy isthmus form the island still called Tinhosa or Tai chau, separated from the east coast of Hainan by a three-mile wide channel. Tinhosa, which afforded good shelter and supplies of water, firewood and fish, was an almost obligatory port of call for the ships sailing to and from Canton or any port further north. This still applies today, in some degree. Cf. *China Sea Pilot*, III (1923 ed.).

[2] This is the earliest document known in which Canton, the modern form of the name of the great city in southern China, occurs. It had been mentioned as *Hânfû* (probably = Chinese *Kuang fu*, i.e. *Kuang* [*chou*] *fu*) by Sulayman, and *Sîn-ul-Sîn* by Idrisi, in the twelfth century, and as *Sinkalán* by Ibn Batuta, and *Censcalan* (Chinkalan) by Friar Odoric, in the fourteenth century. One of Rodrigues' maps (fol. 40) represents the Canton River. See note on *Pulo Tumon*, p. 121. The first maps to record the name *Cantam* are, however, those of Ribeiro of 1527 and 1529. It was thought until recently that the voyage of Jorge Álvares in a junk to the Canton River, the first Portuguese visit to China, was in 1514. There are, however, several documents showing categorically that Álvares' voyage took place in 1513. Pires also confirms the year of this voyage when, writing before or at the beginning of 1514, he mentions China as one of the 'places where our junks and ships have been' (p. 283).

PLATE XXI

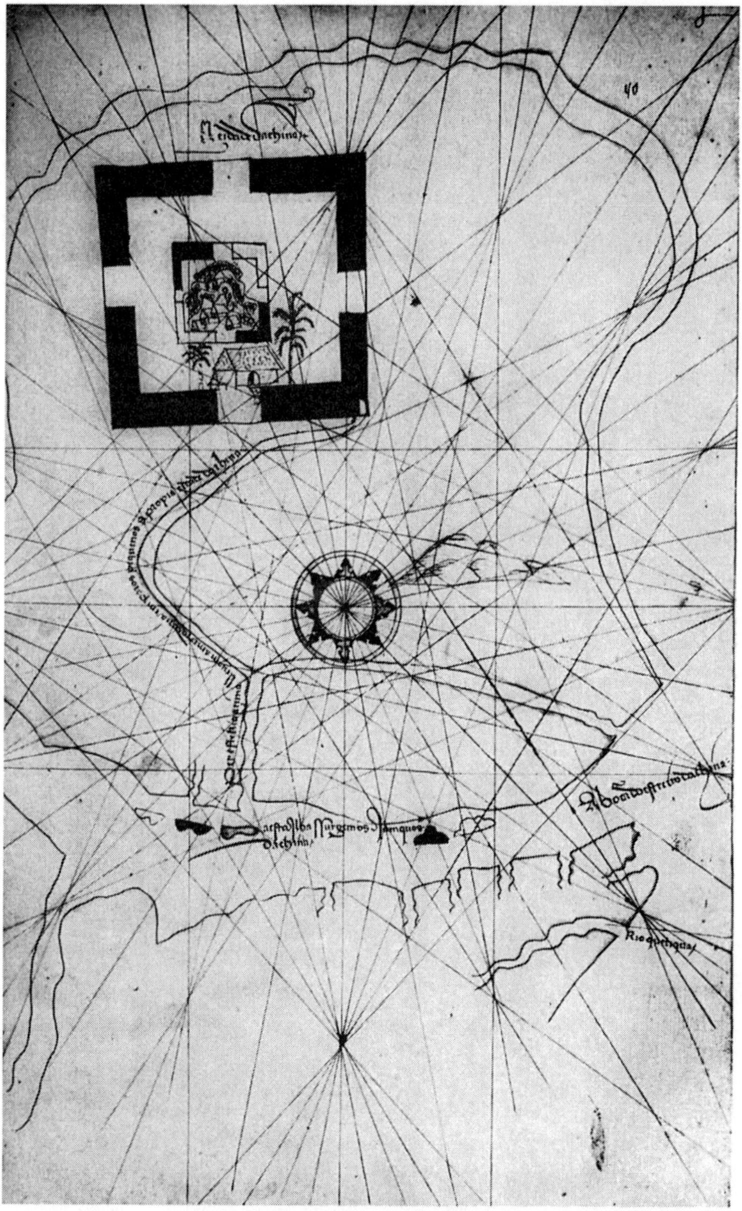

Rodrigues' sketch (fol. 40) of the entrance of the Canton River and probably Peking (p. 523)

PLATE XXII

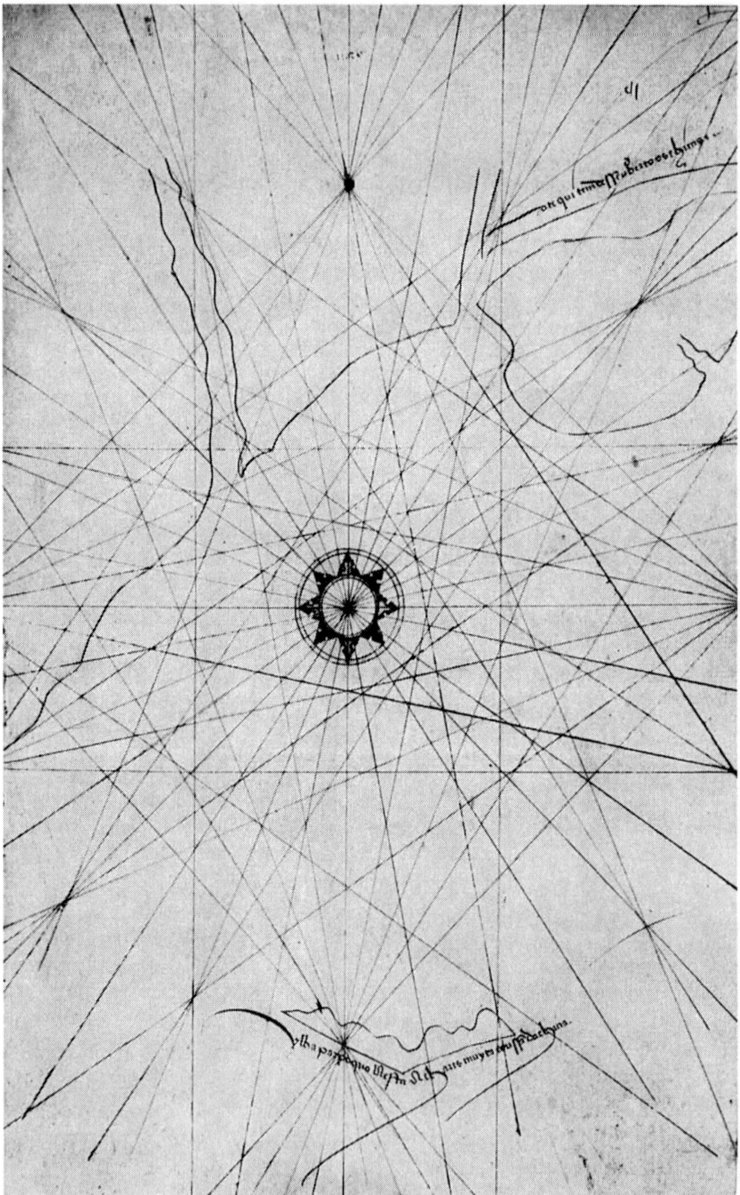

Rodrigues' sketch (fol. 41) of the North-east Coast of China, with an island, *Parpoquo*, which may correspond to Japan (pp. 523-5)

of China unloads all its merchandise, great quantities from inland as well as from the sea. The city of Canton is at the entrance of the estuary of a large river which is three or four fathoms deep at high tide. The city, which can be seen from the estuary, is situated on flat ground without any hills. All the houses are of stone and surrounded by a wall which they say is seven fathoms thick and as many high, and they say that it is steep on the city side. So the *Luções* say who have been there. And it has ports where there are many large junks. The city is guarded; the gates are closed. They are strong, these kings of whom we spoke; they have seals when they send their ambassadors. They trade inside the city, and if not, they do it outside, some thirty leagues from Canton, and take the merchandise there from Canton. Some say that the city [where the king lives] is about four months' journey from Canton, and others say four [weeks?] and others—and this is true—that they can do the said journey in twenty days good going.

Islands where the junks from Malacca anchor.

Thirty leagues on this side of Canton, towards Malacca, there are some islands near the mainland of Nan-t'ou (*Namtoo*)[1], where are the ports already allotted to each nation, viz., *Pulo Tumon*[2] and others. And as soon as the said junks anchor there,

[1] *Nantoo*, or *Nantó*, as it is called by other early Portuguese writers, is Nan-t'ou or Nam-t'au (Cantonese pronunciation), 'an important town in the San On [Hsin-an] District, just outside the present British boundary'. J. M. Braga, *The 'Tamão' of the Portuguese Pioneers*, pp. 428, 429. By San On, Braga means the District of Hsin-an which was anciently, and is now, called Pao-an. Nan-t'ou is either (*a*) the District of Pao-an, or (*b*) the military post 'in the Pao-an District'. See next note.

[2] *Pulo Tumon*, *Timon*, *Tamon*, and *Tamão*, or *Ilha da Veniaga* (Island of Trade), of the early Portuguese writers, was for long identified with San-chuan Island, but so unsatisfactorily that the problem has always provoked a good deal of controversy. J. M. Braga showed more recently that *Pulo Tumon* is Lin Tin Island, which lies about the middle of the Chukiang, the Canton, or the Pearl River entrance, nearer to the north bank. It seems likely that the *Tumon* or *Tamão* of the Portuguese corresponds to *T'un-mên* or *Tuen Moon O*, an old Chinese name for an anchorage off Lin Tin Island, the pronunciation of which in Cantonese has a sound similar to the Portuguese version. 'This would be the name given to the entire anchorage, and the Portuguese could very easily have applied the name of the anchorage to the island off which they anchored'. *The 'Tamão' of the Portuguese*, p. 431. Prof. Moule tells me, however, that 'A recent and on the whole reliable Geographical Dictionary (*Ku chin tĭ ming ta tz'ŭ tien*) gives Nan-t'ou city as a name of the district city of Pao-an on the mainland. T'un-mên (also called

the lord of Nan-t'ou sends word to Canton and merchants immediately come to value the merchandise and to take their dues, as will be told later. Then they bring them the merchandise made up from one part and another. Each one returns to his home.

The custom of land and sea captains in Canton. They affirm that all those who take merchandise from Canton to the islands make a profit of three, four or five in every ten, and the Chinese have this custom so that the land shall not be taken from them, as well as in order to receive the dues on the merchandise exported as well as imported; and the chief [reason] is for fear lest the city be taken from them, because they say that the city of Canton is a rich one, and corsairs often come up to it. *Hi Tação*[1], one of the chief people, is captain of this city, and there is a captain every year by the king's decree, and he cannot remain [in office] longer. There is another sea-captain almost like the land one, with separate jurisdiction. Both are changed yearly.

Fol. 161v. They say that the Chinese made this law about not being able to go to Canton for fear of the Javanese and Malays, for it is

Pei-tu) is the name of an *island* south of Pao-an; and there was a military post called formerly T'un-mên, but in the Ming dynasty Nan-t'ou, which was at the anchorage or harbour south-east of Pao-an. So the text seems to be correct in calling *Tumon* an island, and it is more likely that the harbour was named after the island than *vice versa*. The 'Lord of Namtou' may be the magistrate of Pao-an (=Nan-t'ou), or the commander of the garrison at Nan-t'ou military post'. Further on Pires says that *Tumon* is 20 or 30 leagues distant from Canton (Correia and Castanheda say 18 leagues): Lin Tin Island is really about 65 miles or 20 leagues from Canton by river. Pires says also that *Tumon* lies one league (3.2 miles) from Nan-t'ou on the mainland. The shortest distance between Lin Tin and Nan-t'ou Peninsula is about five miles. Castanheda, Barros, and Góis say that *Tamão* or *Tumon* was three leagues from the mainland, but as the anchorage was on the western side of the island and Nan-t'ou is eastwards, Pires' information is not so far out as it seems at first sight. Rodrigues' map (fol. 40) is the first to show this island, but bearing only the inscription: 'off this island anchor the junks of China', meaning the junks which went from Malacca to the Canton River. It is situated nearer to the north bank of a large river, which has written at its mouth: 'The mouth of the strait of China'. I do not know of any map with the name *Tumon*, or the like, though *Jlhas da veniaga* and *Jlhas de Cantam*, which include *Tumon*, appear for the first time on L. Homem's map of 1554. Pires' information shows that before being the anchorage of the Portuguese ships, *Tumon* was already the anchorage of the ships from Malacca; in this he is confirmed by Rodrigues' map.

[1] *Hi Tação*, i.e., the Hai Tao, an officer charged with coast defence. Chang (p. 54) says that he was the commander of the fleet at Canton. It seems that Pires mixed up the information he obtained.

certain that one of these people's junks would rout twenty Chinese junks. They say that China has more than a thousand junks, and each of them trades where it sees fit; but the people are weak, and such is their fear of Malays and Javanese that it is quite certain that one [of our] ship[s] of four hundred tons could depopulate Canton, and this depopulation would bring great loss to China.

Not to rob any country of its glory, it certainly seems that China is an important, good and very wealthy country, and the Governor of Malacca would not need as much force as they say in order to bring it under our rule, because the people are very weak and easy to overcome. And the principal people who have often been there affirm that with ten ships the Governor of India who took Malacca could take the whole of China along the sea-coast. And China is twenty days' sail distant for our ships. They leave here at the end of June for a good voyage, and with a monsoon wind they can go in fifteen days. From China they have recently begun sailing to Borneo (*Burney*), and they say that they go there in fifteen days, and that this must have been for the last fifteen years.

Merchandise of value in China that goes from Malacca.

The chief merchandise is pepper—of which they will buy ten junk-loads a year if as many go there—cloves, a little nutmeg, a little more pachak, catechu; they will buy a great deal of incense, elephants' tusks, tin, apothecary's lignaloes; they buy a great deal of Borneo camphor, red beads, white sandalwood, brazil, infinite quantities of the black wood that grows in Singapore (*Syngapura*); they buy a great many carnelians from Cambay, scarlet camlets, coloured woollen cloths. Pepper apart, they make little account of all the rest.

The said junks from Malacca go and anchor off the island of *Tumon*, as has already been said, twenty or thirty leagues away from Canton. These islands are near the land of Nan-t'ou, a league to seaward from the mainland. Those from Malacca anchor there in the port of *Tumon* and those from Siam in the port of *Hucham*[1]. Our port is three leagues nearer to China than

[1] Perhaps some of the islands forming or adjoining the Lantau Channel, such as Chung-chou, which lies about four and a half miles south of Lin Tin, towards the sea.

the Siamese one, and merchandise comes to it rather than to the other.

As soon as the lord of Nan-t'ou sees the junks he immediately sends word to Canton that junks have gone in among the islands; the valuers from Canton go out to value the merchandise; they receive their dues; they bring just the amount of merchandise that is required: the country is pretty well accustomed to estimate it, so well do they know of you the goods you want, and they bring them.

Dues levied in China on merchants coming from Malacca.

They pay twenty per cent on pepper, fifty per cent on brazil, and the same amount on the Singapore wood; and when this has been estimated a junk will pay so much in proportion. They receive their dues on the other merchandise at ten per cent; and they do not oppress you; they have genuine merchants in their dealings. They are very wealthy. Their whole idea is pepper. They sell their foodstuffs honestly; business over, each returns to his own country. The common people are not very near to truth, and the commoner things in their business are all false and counterfeit.

Weights in China—large and small.

Once in China, a hundred catties are called a *piquo*; then you make your price: so many *piquos* of pepper for one of silk or so many of such and such goods for one of pepper; and it is just the same with musk, so many catties of pepper for one of musk, [or] seed-pearls. A *picoll*[1] contains a hundred catties; each catty contains sixteen taels; each tael contains ten *mazes*; each *maz*[2] contains ten *pon*. Each catty contains twenty-one ounces of our measure. Three hundred and twelve catties of twenty-one ounces each make a Malacca bahar on the small scales.

Fol. 162r.

Food-stuffs: rice, wheat, meat, chickens. fish.

All these goods are sold by weight, to wit, so many measures of such and such for one of pepper; and when the merchants take it there is [an arrangement] among them in the country—so

[1] *Piquo* or *pico, picoll* or *picul*, is the Malay and Javanese *pikul*, 'a man's load', for the Chinese weight of 100 catties, equal to 133⅓ lb. or about 60 kg.

[2] The value of the *maz* was variable in the different far-eastern countries. *Maz* or '*mace* was adopted in the language of European traders in China to denominate the tenth part of the Chinese *liang* or *tael* of silver'. *Hobson-Jobson, s.v.* See note p. 145. These weights are given quite correctly by Pires. *Catty* is the Malay *kati*, *tael* the Hindi *tola* (through the Portuguese), *mace* the Hindi *masha*, and *pon* the Chinese *fên* (also called *candareen*, from the Malay *Kondrin*).

many weights of such and such a foodstuff for one of *fuseleira* cash, which are current in the country like *ceitis*, and for large merchandise and other purchases gold and silver [is used] for money.

Merchandise that come from China.

The chief merchandise from China is raw white silk in large quantities, and loose coloured silks, many in quantity, satins of all colours, damask chequered *enrolados* in all colours, taffetas and other thin silk cloths called *xaas*[1], and many other kinds of all colours; an abundance of seed-pearl in various shapes, mostly irregular; they also have some big round ones—this in my opinion is as important a merchandise in China as silk, although they count silk as the chief merchandise—musk in powder and in pods, plenty of this, and certainly good, which yields in nothing to that from Pegu; apothecary's camphor in large quantities, *abarute*, alum, saltpetre, sulphur, copper, iron, rhubarb, and all of it is worthless—what I have seen up to the present has been rotten when it arrived; they say it used to come fresh; I have not seen it—vases of copper and *fuseleira*, cast iron kettles, bowls, basins, quantities of these things, boxes, fans, plenty of needles of a hundred different kinds, some of them very fine and well made, these are good merchandise, and things of very poor quality like those which come to Portugal from Flanders, countless copper bracelets; gold and silver come and I did not see much, and many brocades of their kind, and porcelains beyond count. Of the things which come from China some are products from China itself and some from outside, some of them from places renowned as being better than others. You can spend your money on whatever of this merchandise you fancy, except that there is not so much musk to be found. They say that not more than one bahar comes from China each year in all junks. The land of China produces plenty of good sugar. There is a place called *Xamcy* where there is musk; it has a little and it

[1] *Xaas*, sash or shash, from the Arab *shāsh*, muslin—'A band of a fine material worn twisted round the head as a turban by Orientals'. *Oxford English Dictionary*, *s.v.* Sash. Prof. Moule tells me, however, that the Chinese *sha* 'gauze' is at least as old as the Han dynasty (206 B.C.—A.D. 200). The *s* of *xaas* in Pires' version is probably a plural. Is there any connexion between the Arabic *shash* and the Chinese *sha*? Apparently no; but *xaas* (if *s* is plural) may be simply Chinese.

is good. [*In the margin in the same hand are the words:*] 'The city whence the musk comes is called *Xãnbu*, which is in China, and they say that the animals from which they get the musk are in *Çancy*[1].'

The said junks come from China to Malacca and they do not pay dues, except for a present; and these presents they give in accordance with the decrees of the *Xabandares* of the different nations: the *Xabandar* of China, *Lequios*, Cochin China and *Champa* was the *Lasamane*; and the *Xabandares* have become rich through this function, because they greatly overtax the merchants; and these put up with everything because their profits are large and also because it is the custom of the country to do so and endure it.

Places where the merchandise comes from: the raw white silk is from *Chancheo*; coloured silks from Cochin China (*Cauchy*); damasks, satins, brocades, *xaas, loos*[2] from Nanking (*Namqim*) and from *Amq̃m*[3]; seed-pearl from Hainan (*Aynã*); apothecary's camphor from *Chamcheo*. [*In the margin in the same hand:*] 'In

[1] XAMCY and *Çançy* both seem to represent the province of Shensi, the characters for which are pronounced *Shansi*. In English it is written *Shensi* for the province in North-west China, simply in order to distinguish it from Shansi, the province in North China, separated by the Yellow River where it flows north-south. Prof. Moule tells me that this is derived from the early Missionaries—Portuguese (?) and certainly French—to whom *Chen* and *Chan* provide a convenient distinction without seriously distorting the sound.

XÃNBU may very well be Si-an-fu, capital of Shensi, the *Kenjanfu* of Marco Polo (II, xli), who emphasises its importance as 'a city of great trade and industry'. Several early writers refer to the musk of China as coming from regions neighbouring on Shensi, such as the Szechwan province, and from Tibet. See Yule, *Marco Polo*, I, 279, II, 35, 49; *Cathay*, I, 246, 316, etc.

[2] Crooke mentions a reference, in a Madras list of 1684, to 'gold flowered *loes*', which is supposed to be a 'name invented for the occasion to describe some silk stuff brought from the Liu Kiu Islands'. *Hobson-Jobson*, p. 514. But no doubt the word really existed, as the pronunciation of *loes* in English and *loos* in Portuguese has the same value. The Chinese *lo* means 'coarse silk'. The *s* of Pires' *loos* may be the Portuguese plural, the same as with *xaas*. Dr. Lionel Giles suggests that the word *loos* might be derived from the Chinese *lo-ssŭ*, meaning a thin kind of silk.

[3] *Damq̃m* or *de Amquem* might suggest Marco Polo's *Unken*—or *Vnquem*, as it appears in the first Portuguese *Marco Paulo* (Lisbon, 1502). *Unken*, however, has not been identified with any similar Chinese name, so the chance likeness of *Amquem* does not seem to have much significance. This part of the Chinese coast is called *costa de ucheu* on Homem's map of 1554. See note on *Foqem*, pp. 129–30.

this Nanking there are all the cotton cloths and big merchants; it is a month's journey from Peking (*Peqim*) to Nanking (*Nãnqy*) by river.' And because [our knowledge of] these places is unsatisfactory, and because this merchandise is recognizable at sight, I will not discuss them any more.

Salt is a great merchandise among the Chinese. It is distributed from China to these regions; and it is dealt with by fifteen hundred junks which come to buy it, and it is loaded in China to go to other places. Traders in this are very rich and they say to one another among themselves 'Are you a salt merchant to speak of?'

Beyond the port of Canton there is another port which is called *Oquem*[1]; it is three days' journey by land and a day and night by sea. This is the port for the *Lequjos* and other races. It has many other ports, which it would be a long business to tell of, and they do not concern us at present, except up to Canton (*Q̃mtom*), because this is the key to the kingdom of China.

They say that there are people from Tartary (*Tartaría*) in the land of China and they call them Tartars (*tartall*), and these people are very white with red beards. They ride on horseback; they are warlike. And they say that they go from China to the land of the Tartars (*tartaros*) in two months, and that in Tartary they have horses shod with copper shoes, and this must be because China extends a long way on the northern side, and our bombardiers say that in Germany they heard tell of these people and of a city named by the Chinese *Quesechama*[2], and it seems to them that by this route they could go to their lands in a short time; but they say that by reason of the cold the land is uninhabited. Between the Chinese and the Tartars are certain

[1] *Oquem* corresponds to *Foquem*, or Fukien. Prof. Moule tells me that the local sound of *Fu* is *Hok*, with an *h* which might easily be dropped, as the *h* of Hainan was dropped. The Italian traveller Francesco Carletti brought home in 1603 a *Chinese Atlas* in which Fukien was transcribed by him as *Ochiam*. Cf. Moule, *A Note on the Chinese Atlas in the Magliabecchian Library*, p. 393.

[2] *Que se chama* or *q̃ se chama*, as it appears in the manuscript, means 'which is called'. It is possible that Pires wrote some word or words corresponding to the Chinese name for a city in Tartary, which the transcriber transformed into *q̃ se chama*.

places where there are the *Guores*[1], and after Tartary [is] Russia (*Roxia*), say the Chinese.

Fol. 162v. And as no inland countries beyond China which deal with Malacca are at present known, I make a stop. [*A line here marks the beginning of an addition to the text which is written in the margin, in the same hand—perhaps a couple of lines at first left out by the transcriber. The manuscript was badly cropped in binding, the greater part of the words having been cut away beyond possibility of reconstitution. See Portuguese text*, p. 460.] From here onwards we will speak of the islands and only of those to which [the people of] Malacca sail, because if they all had to be mentioned there would be no end because of their infinite numbers. And now we will speak of the *Lequjos* and Japan (*Jampom*), *Burneus* and *Luçoees*.

[LIU KIU]

The Liu Kiu (Lequeos) *Island.* The *Lequeos* are called *Guores*—they are known by either of these names[2]. *Lequíos* is the chief one. The king is a heathen and

[1] Who are these *Guores*? In this case they could hardly be the *Lequeos*. Prof. Moule wonders whether they are not the Mongols (Moguors).

[2] The earliest European reference to the *Gores* is in a letter written 6 Feb. 1510 from Malacca to Albuquerque, by Rui de Araújo who had been taken prisoner when the treacherous attack was made against the first Portuguese to go there in 1509. *Alguns Documentos*, p. 223. Ferrand mentions two Arab manuscripts, dated respectively 1462 and 1489, where the island *Ghūr* is referred to as meaning Liu-Kiu or Formosa (L'île de Ghūr = Lieou-K'ieou = Formosa). According to Ferrand the 1462 MS says: 'Parmi les îles célèbres [du monde habité], on compte l'île de Likyū, qui est généralement connue sous le nom de Al-Ghūr'; the 1489 MS has: 'On y trouve des mines de fer [appelé] al-ghūrī . . . Son nom en langue djāwī (in this case the Chinese) est Likīwū'. *Malaka*, II, 126 *seqq*. This would explain the association of the name *gores* with *lequeos*. As far as we know, the first Europeans to visit the *Lequeos* islands were Fernão Mendes Pinto, Diogo Zeimoto and Simão Borralho, when they went to Japan in 1542. *Peregrinação*, cxxxii. Some months later Pinto went again from China to the *Lequeos*, where he was shipwrecked: he gives a description of the *Ilha Lequia* and his adventures there in ch. cxxxvii-cxlvii of his famous book. C. R. Boxer supposes that the *Gores* who went to Malacca, as mentioned in the *Comentarios*, were meant to be the Japanese. *Some Aspects of Portuguese Influence in Japan, 1542–1640*, p. 14. Crawfurd, *Dictionary*, *s.v.* Japan. Denucé says that *Gores* is a 'nom d'origine probablement chinoise et qui paraît dériver de Coriai, les Coréens' (*Magellan*, p. 164); according to Chassigneux, during the first half of the fifteenth century numerous Koreans sought refuge in the Liu-Kiu archipelago. *Rica de Oro*

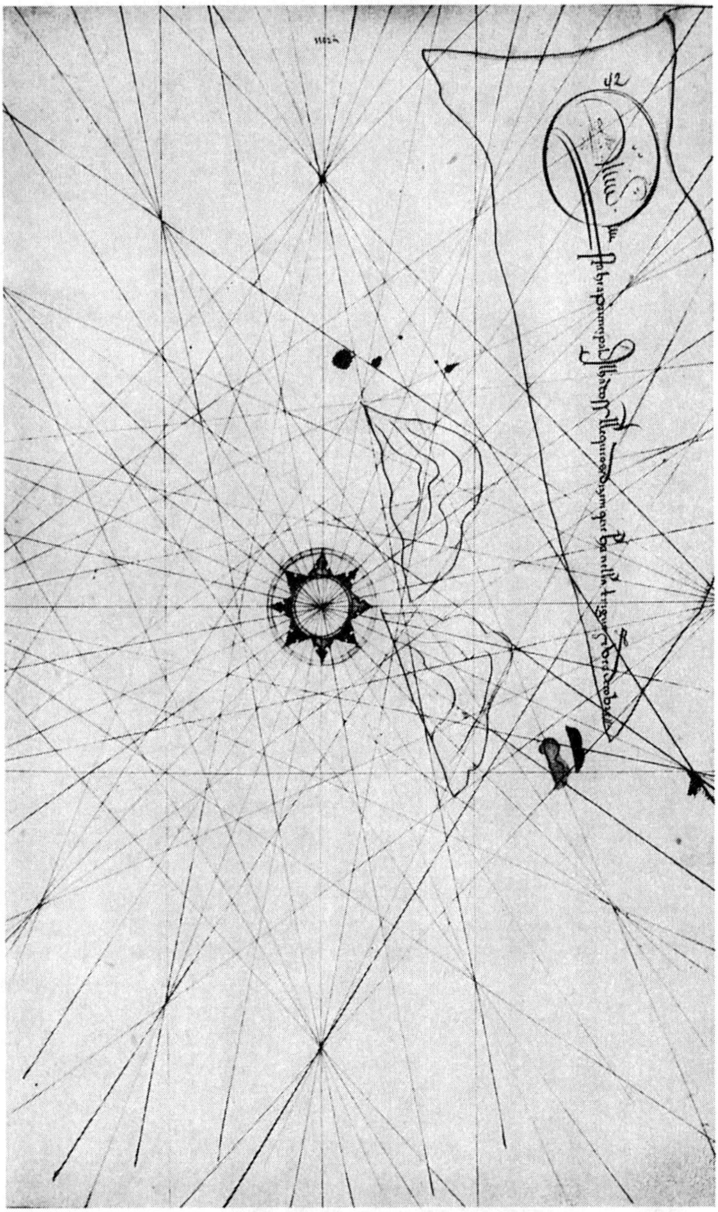

Rodrigues' sketch (fol. 42) of an island which must represent Formosa (p. 525)

PLATE XXIV

Rodrigues' map (fol. 35) showing the eastern end of Sumatra, the western end of Java, south-western end of Borneo and Banka Island (p. 522)

all the people too. He is a tributary vassal of the king of the Chinese. His island is large and has many people; they have small ships of their own type; they have three or four junks which are continuously buying in China, and they have no more. They trade in China and in Malacca, and some times in company with the Chinese, sometimes on their own. In China they trade in the port of *Foqem*[1] which is in the land of China near

et Rica de Plata, pp. 76 *seqq.* Whatever the origin of the word *Gores*, Pires was the first European to identify it with the *Lequeos*, or the inhabitants of the Liu-Kiu archipelago, from the Chinese name for the present Japanese Ryukyu or Loochoo Islands. Formosa is, however, included among these islands on old Chinese and some early Portuguese maps; and much of what is said here seems to refer to Formosa rather than to Loochoo proper. In his letter of 10 Aug. 1518, S. P. Andrade says: 'There are in the sea [far] from India other lands, which are isles called the Islands of the *Lequeos*, reaching as far as the Tartars, where there are great gold mines, and all the merchandise that exists in China, off [the coast of] which they lie two hundred leagues away; they are white people like Germans.' *Tôrre do Tombo, Gaveta 15, Maço 17, No. 27.* On the representation of the *Lequeos* on Rodrigues' maps (ff. 39, 42), see Appendix II. Ribeiro's maps of 1527 and 1529 have, west of Paragua Island, the inscription: 'These shoals have channels through which the *Lequios* go to Borneo and other parts.' Penrose's map has a round mass of islands called *as lecquas* east of Canton, between 17° and 20° (correct latitude 24°—30° N.). Homem's map of 1554 has east of *J. fremoza* a group of three islands called *Jlhas dos lequios*, and north-north-east of these another island called *lequios*; in addition, all these islands and an imaginary vast archipelago to the east are named, in large letters, *Os lequios*. Homem's atlases of 1558 and 1568 have a similar representation, except for the imaginary archipelago and large letters naming the whole. The atlases of Luís and Dourado have a group of three large islands, running SSW—NNE, which seem to correspond to Formosa, the northernmost called *lequio pequeno*; further north-east other islands, corresponding to the Tsubu Shoto group, are called *lequio gramde*; between the two groups there are some small islands named *Reis magos*, corresponding to the Nambu Shoto group, north of *lequio gramde* is the *J. do fogo*, corresponding to Nakano-shima or Suwanose-shima, two islands with active volcanoes. The islands *Reis magos* and *J. do fogo* appear for the first time on the map of 1554, and then on the others mentioned above.

[1] *Foqem*, or *Foquem*, must certainly be Fukien, the capital and main port of which is Foochow. But the port intended need not necessarily be Foochow, which lies some distance up the River Min, and would be less convenient for traders than places like Amoy, for instance. From Canton to the nearest point of the seacoast of Fukien province is about 350 miles by sea and about 250 miles by land as the crow flies; Foochow is still 250 miles farther. On the other hand, the main group of the Liu Kiu islands is 500 miles away, on the same latitude as Foochow, which seems to point to this important Chinese port, or some other port of Fukien province, as the more likely to be frequented by the *Lequeos*. Furthermore, in his two letters written from Canton in 1526, Vasco Calvo refers to the trade of the *Lequeos* with Fukien, but does

Canton—a day and a night's sail away. The Malays say to the people of Malacca that there is no difference between Portuguese and *Llequjos*, except that the Portuguese buy women, which the *Leq̃os* do not.

The *Lequjos* have only wheat in their country, and rice and wines after their fashion, meat, and fish in great abundance. They are great draftsmen and armourers. They make gilt coffers, very rich and well-made fans, swords, many arms of all kinds after their fashion. Just as we in our kingdoms speak of Milan, so do the Chinese and all the other races speak of the *Lequjos*. They are very truthful men. They do not buy slaves, nor would they sell one of their own men for the whole world, and they would die over this.

The *Lequjos* are idolators; if they are sailing and find themselves in danger, they say that if they escape they buy a beautiful maiden to be sacrificed and behead her on the prow of the junk, and other things like these. They are white men, well dressed, better than the Chinese, more dignified. They sail to China and take the merchandise that goes from Malacca to China, and go to Japan, which is an island seven or eight days' sail distant, and take the gold and copper in the said island in exchange for their merchandise. The *Leqios* are men who sell their merchandise freely for credit, and if they are lied to when they collect payment, they collect it sword in hand.

Merchandise which the Lequeos *bring to Malacca.*

The chief is gold, copper, and arms of all kinds, coffers, boxes (*caxonjas*) with gold leaf veneer, fans, wheat, and their things are well made. They bring a great deal of gold. They are truthful men—more so than the Chinese—and feared. They bring a great store of paper and silk in colours; they bring musk, porcelain, damask; they bring onions and many vegetables.

Merchandise they take from Malacca to their country.

They take the same merchandise as the Chinese take. They leave here in [*blank*], and one, two or three junks come to Malacca every year, and they take a great deal of Bengal clothing.

not mention Canton (pp. 156, 163). It seems as if Pires mixed up the information he received, and his *Amq̃m*, *Oquem* and *Foqem* correspond to Fukien, perhaps Foochow, which is called *Fucheo* by Pinto and in the atlases of Luís and Dourado. It is curious that Mercator's world map of 1569 and Ortelius' *Atlas* of 1570 have a place called *Fuquian*, near the coast but not a seaport, between *Cantan* and *Chincheo*.

Among the *Lequjos* Malacca wine is greatly esteemed. They load large quantities of one kind which is like brandy, with which the Malays make themselves [so drunk as to run] amuck. The *Lequjos* bring swords worth thirty *cruzados* each, and many of these.

[JAPAN]

The island of Japan (*Jampon*[1]), according to what all the Chinese say, is larger than that of the *Lequíos*, and the king is more powerful and greater, and is not given to trading, nor [are] his subjects. He is a heathen king, a vassal of the king of China. They do not often trade in China because it is far off and they have no junks, nor are they seafaring men. *Island of Japan* (Jampon).

The *Lequjos* go to Japan in seven or eight days and take the said merchandise, and trade it for gold and copper. All that comes from the *Lequeos* is brought by them from Japan. And the *Lequeos* trade with the people of Japan in cloths, fishing-nets[2] and other merchandise.

[1] *Jampon*, or Japan, is only one of the many far-eastern names which are found in a European form for the first time in Pires' *Suma*. Dahlgren, following Teleki and Gezelius, wrote in 1911: 'La première fois que le nom du Japon (Giapam) se retrouve en Europe, est sur la carte de Gastaldi de 1550. *Les débuts de la Cartographie du Japon*, pp. 13–15. Yule (*Hobson-Jobson*) quotes a letter of 1505, from the king of Portugal to the king of Castille, which mentions an island *Saponin*, whither the king of Calicut sent a ship to fetch some astrological instruments; he thinks, though without any apparent ground, that the island in question was Japan. It is extraordinary that between Pires and Gastaldi no extant document mentions the word Japan. According to Yule, 'our *Japan* was probably taken from the Malay *Japún* or *Japáng*'. Marco Polo's '*Chipangu* represents the Chinese *Jih-pên-kwé*, the kingdom of Japan, the name *Jih-pên* [literally, Sun-root, or Rising Sun] being the Chinese pronunciation'. *Marco Polo*, II, 256. See Crawfurd, *Dictionary*, *s.v.* Japan. Thus the origin of Pires' *Jampon* is obvious. On the possible representation of Japan on Rodrigues' map (fol. 41), see Appendix. II. Homem's map of 1554 is the first Portuguese document where the word *japam* appears after Pires. The first special map of Japan by a European is found in Dourado's atlas of 1568. In spite of all the controversy about the names of the first Europeans who visited Japan, it can be asserted that the discoverers were Fernão Mendes Pinto, Diogo Zeimoto and Simão Borralho, and that the discovery was made in 1542, as I have shown elsewhere.

[2] *Panos lucoees* might mean '*Luções* cloths'; but in his description of the *Luções* Pires does not mention any cloths, which, in any case, were not likely to be taken by the *Lequeos* to Japan. It seems more probable that *luco ees*, i.e. *lucões*, is the plural of *lucão*, an old Portuguese word for fishing-net.

[BORNEO]

The Island of Borneo (Burney). Borneo is made up of many islands, large and small[1]. They are almost all inhabited by heathen, only the chief one is inhabited by Moors; it is not long since the king became a Moor. They seem to be a trading people. The merchants are men of medium stature, not very sharpwitted. They trade direct with Malacca every year. It is a country with plenty of meat, fish, rice and sago.

Fol. 163r. *Merchandise which the Borneans bring to Malacca.* They bring gold, which is of low assay value, lower than any other gold in these parts; they bring every year up to two or three bahars of very valuable camphor. A catty of this varies in value according to the size [of the lumps]: the *cate* [is worth] from twelve to thirty or forty *cruzados* according to the kind and quality. They have a great many chebulic myrobalans which they bring to sell.

They bring wax, honey, rice and sago, [which] is a foodstuff for the lower classes—a sort of bread crumbs made up like sweetmeats—and is of value. They bring *orracas*.

They do not pay duties in Malacca; they hand over a present, which comes to the same thing, because the man who has to produce it is told by the xabandar what present he has to give.

[1] When Pires mentions several islands around Borneo, and *Tamjompura, Laue, Quedomdoam, Samper, Cate* and *Pamucã* as separate islands—though the latter are probably parts of the island of Borneo itself—he shows that he really thought he was correct in saying: 'Borneo is made up of many islands, large and small'. In most cases, however, when Pires mentions *Burney* he means simply the port of Brunei. On the representation of Borneo on Rodrigues' maps (fols. 35, 36), see Appendix II. In his letter to the king of Portugal from Malacca, 6 Jan. 1514, Rui de Brito wrote, perhaps after Pires had written his references to *Burney*: '*Borneu* is a large island, it lies between China and the Moluccas, in the open sea of the islands; the people of the island are called Luzons (*lucoeẽs*)'. *Cartas*, III, 92–3. Barbosa refers to the 'Isles of Borneo', also placing them too much to the north, beyond the island of *Solor* (Sulu archipelago). Torreño's map of 1522 has an *ysla de burney*, obviously inspired by some drawing similar to that of Pigafetta (see note on *Laue*, p. 224), and the same applies to the Turin map of *c.* 1523, on which there is also the port of *bruney*, on the *isla de bruney*. Most of the sixteenth-century Portuguese maps do not show the east coast of Borneo, and others, in which the coastline of the island appears complete, are very fanciful. The first fairly accurate and complete cartographical representation of Borneo is found on Berthelot's map of 1635, where the eastern coast of the island bears the inscription: 'This Island of Borneo was circumnavigated by Pedro Berthelot in the year 1627.'

They take clothing from the Kling and from Bengal, viz. chequered *enrolados*, certain kinds of *puravas*[1], *synabafos* of all kinds, *panchauilizes* and *synhavas*; they take Chinese armlets of brass; they take a great deal of coloured glass beads from Cambay, and pearl beads; they ask for red beads; and with these they go about the islands where there is gold and take it in exchange for the cloth, and for the beads only. *Merchandise they take from Malacca to Borneo.*

They have every year two monsoons to bring them and two others to take them back. They go from Malacca to Borneo in a month and their junks make the return voyage in another. The Borneans seems to be peacable men.

[PHILIPPINES]

The *Luções* are about ten days' sail beyond Borneo. They are nearly all heathen; they have no king, but they are ruled by groups of elders. They are a rubust people, little thought of in Malacca. They have two or three junks, at the most. They take the merchandise to Borneo and from there they come to Malacca. Luções *Islands*[2].

[1] *Puravá*, or *purauaa* as written by Pires, is an Indian cotton cloth.

[2] This is the first European reference to the Philippine Archipelago, called *Luções* from its largest and north-westernmost island, Luzon. The Philippine Islands are called 'by the Indians *Luçon*, from the principal island which is called *Luçon*', as Pyrard de Laval (II, 171) says he learned from the Portuguese. Galvão (p. 239) informs us that in June 1545 a Portuguese called Pero Fidalgo left the city of *Borneo* on a junk, and by contrary winds was driven towards the north, where he found an island in nine or ten degrees, which they called *dos Luções*, because its inhabitants were thus named. This voyage is recorded in the atlases of Luís and Dourado, in an inscription on a fanciful drawing named *Costa de lucões* (Luís, 1563) or *OS LVCOIS* (Dourado, 1580), which reads: *costa de luçoes e laos por omde p° fidalgo vimdo de borneo num Jumco de chis e coreo com temporal ao lomgo della foi tomar llamao* (Luís; similarly in Dourado). Leaving aside the possible representation of Luzon by the *Llouçam* inscribed by Rodrigues (map fol. 36) as a port on the north coast of Borneo (see Appendix II), this is the first time *Luçoes* appears on a map, though the south-east part of the Philippines had already been represented on Torreño's map of 1522, as a consequence of Magellan's expedition. After that the Penrose map and the map of *c.* 1540 have a much better representation of the southern part of the archipelago, which gradually improved in successive maps. Galvão gives the date of the first known Portuguese visit to Luzon, but it is quite likely that some other Portuguese ship on the China voyage had called before at the *Luçoes*, either on purpose or by accident. The 'Account of the Genoese Pilot' (Leone Pancaldo) says that when, in March 1521, Magellan's expedition arrived at the small island

The Borneans go to the lands of the *Luções* to buy gold, and foodstuffs as well, and the gold which they bring to Malacca is from the *Luções* and from the surrounding islands which are countless; and they all have more or less trade with one another. And the gold of these islands where they trade is of a low quality —indeed very low quality.

The *Luções* have in their country plenty of foodstuffs, and wax and honey; and they take the same merchandise from here as the Borneans take. They are almost one people; and in Malacca there is no division between them. They never used to be in Malacca as they are now; but the *Tomunguo* whom the Governor of India appointed here was already beginning to gather many of them together, and they were already building many houses and shops. They are a useful people; they are hard-working.

Of this family there are now the sons of the *Tumunguo* and his wife in Malacca, as well as his mother-in-law, and *Curia Raja* and *Tuam Brajy* who married the *Tumunguo's* wife. In *Minjam* there must be five hundred *Luções*, some of them important men and good merchants, who want to come to Malacca, and the people of *Mjjam* will not grant them permission, because now they have gone over to the side of the former king of Malacca, not very openly. The people of *Mjmjam* are Malays.

I have told all about the mainland from Cambay to China, including some islands near China. Now I will begin to tell of the great island ofSumatra, going from Malacca to the Moluccas.

The first will be the island of Sumatra and round *Gamispola* on the channel side and turning along the *Panchur* side back to *Gamispola*.

And then will come the account of the island of Java (*Jaaõa*) and of the kingdom of Sunda (*Çumda*), mentioning the ports and their lords, [and the] junks and *pangajavas* there are in each.

And afterwards [the account] of the island of Solor, and of Timor, and of Bima, Sumbawa (*Cimdaua*), Sapeh (*Çapee*) and then going towards the Moluccas, etc.

of Malhou, in the south-eastern Philippine Islands, the natives informed them that 'they had already seen there other men like them', which suggests that possibly even before 1521 the Portuguese had visited the archipelago. (Cardeal Saraiva edition, *Obras completas*, VI, 126).

[*FIFTH BOOK*]

[INDIAN ARCHIPELAGO]

[Sumatra—Java—South-eastern Islands—Banda, Ceram, Amboina—Moluccas—Central Islands]

[SUMATRA]

DESCRIPTION or account of the great, rich and populous Island of Sumatra (*Camotora*) and of the islands which are around it, and it will be described all the way round, beginning at *Gamispola* along the channel and going round by *Pamchur* back to *Gamispola*. *Fol. 163v*

And first I will tell how many kingdoms it has, and then what each is like and the trade and the kind of merchandise there is in the said island and how big it is and what it has in the way of lancharas and junks.

Kingdom in the Island of Sumatra

Beginning from *Gamispola* there is the kingdom of Achin (*Achei*) and *Biar Lambry*, the kingdom of Pedir, the kingdom of *Pirada*, the kingdom of Pase (*Paçee*), the kingdom of *Bata*, the kingdom of Aru, the kingdom of *Arcat*, the kingdom of Rupat, the kingdom of Siak (*Ciac*), the kingdom of Kampar (*Campar*), the kingdom of Tongkal (*Tuncall*), the kingdom of Indragiri (*Amdargery*), the kingdom of *Capocam*, the kingdom of *Trimtall*

[1] In his description of Sumatra Pires mentions, besides the *Gamispola* and other islands, nineteen *reinos* (kingdoms) and eleven *terras* (lands or countries): *Reino de Achey e Lambry, Terra de Biar, Reino de Pedir, Terra de Aeilabu, Reino de Lide, Reino de Pirada, Reino de Pacee, Reino de Bata, Reino de Daru, Reino de Arcat, Terra de Yrcan, Reino de Rupat, Terra de Purim, Reino de Ciac, Reino de Campar, Terra de Campocam, Reino de Andarguerij, Terra de Tuncall, Terra de Jamby, Terra de Palimbão, Terra de Tana Malaio, Terra de Çacampom, Terra de Tulimbavam, Reino de Andallos, Reino de Piramã, Reino de Tiquo, Reino de Barus, Reino de Quinchell, Reino de Mancopa* or *Daya, Reino de Menancabo*. In his description of the island, Barros says: 'When we entered India this great Island was divided into 29 kingdoms. . . . Beginning from the westernmost and northernmost (though Barros by mistake says *austral*) point of the Island, and going round from the North, the first is called *Daya*; and those that follow, as the coast continues, are *Lambrij, Achem, Biár, Pedir, Lide, Piradá, Pacem, Bára, Darú, Arcat, Ircan, Rupat, Purij, Ciáca, Campar, Capocam, Andraguerij, Jambij, Palimbam, Taná, Malayo, Sacampam, Tulumbauam, Andalóz, Piriáman, Tico, Bárros, Quinchel, Mancópa*, which brings us to *Lambrij*, bordering on *Daya*, the first we named'

[Tongkal?], the kingdom of Jambi, the kingdom of Palembang (*Palimbão*), the lands of Sekampung (*Çaçanpom*), Tulang Bawang (*Tulimbavam*), Andalas (*Andallos*), Priaman (*Pirjaman*), Tico (*Tiquo*), *Panchur*, Baros (*Baruez*), Singkel (*Chinqele*), Melabah (*Mancopa*), *Daya*, *Pirim* [Pedir?]—this borders on Lambry and the islands which are off *Gamispola*. And from Siak to Jambi, and from Priaman to *Panchur* on the other side, is the land of Menangkabau (*Menamcabo*), which has three kings. They are in the interior of the island, and there is a lake of sweet water in this land of Menangkabau, as will be told when Menangkabau is dealt with.

Islands that form a channel from Kampar to Palembang, along which one sails to Java, Banda and the Moluccas.

Pulo Pisang (*Pullo Piçam*), Karimun (*Carimam*), islands of the Celates which are called *Çelaĝuym gum*, Kundur (*Sabam*), Buaya, Linga, Tiga (*Tigua*), Pulo Berhala (*Pullo Baralam*), Banka (*Bamca*) and *Monomby*. These will be described in their place.

This is the merchandise which is produced in the Island of Sumatra itself.

It has gold in great quantities, edible camphor of two kinds, pepper, silk, benzoin, apothecary's lignaloes; it has honey, wax, pitch, sulphur, cotton, many rattans, which are canes from which they make mats. It is used like coir or esparto and serves as string with which they tie everything up.

(III, V, I). All these are given as 'kingdoms', though Pires discriminates between 'kingdoms' and 'lands'. Besides some spelling variations—like *Bata*, which appears in Barros as *Bára*—Pires' *Terra de Aeilabu* and *Terra de Tuncall* are suppressed in Barros, *Tana Malaio* is given as two separate kingdoms, and *Mancopa* and *Daya* seem to be different kingdoms. The kingdom of *Menancabo* is mentioned by Barros in other places. However, the similarity between the two lists of names (even *Daru*, which Barros in other places writes *de Aru*, is here given as Pires wrote it) is sufficiently striking to suggest that Barros used Pires' work, directly or at second hand. Some of the places here called *reinos* or *terras* were simple towns of some trading importance, like *Pedir*, *Aeilabu*, *Lide*, *Pirada* and *Pacee*, on a coast of only eighty-four miles as the crow flies. Many of them have either totally disappeared or only survive in the name of some little river or unimportant village. Although Pires visited many ports on the coast of Sumatra, he knew but little of the hinterland, and formed his opinion mostly from the information he gathered in Malacca. But his account is none the less valuable. All other writers before Pires, Europeans as well as Asiatics, mention only a few places when they deal with Sumatra; even Barbosa, who wrote a little later, mentions no more than seven places—*Pedir*, *Pansem*, *Achem*, *Compar*, *Andiagao* (Indragiri), *Macaboo* (Menangkabau) and *Ara* (Aru); a couple of centuries had to elapse before a more complete and accurate description of Sumatra was written.

It has plenty of rice—white and in the husk; it has much meat and fish, including shad in quantities as large as in Azamor; it has oils, many wines of their kind, including *tampoy*[1], which is almost like our wine; they have fruits in large numbers, including durians, certainly lovelier and more delicious than all the other fruits. *Food-stuffs of the country.*

In the island of Sumatra most of the kings are Moors and some are heathens; and in the heathen country some men make a practice of eating their enemies when they capture them. The kings on the channel side from Achin to Palembang are Moors, and from Palembang going around *Gamispola* are mostly heathens, and those of the hinterland and who live inland are heathens also. *Sects and beliefs of the Island of Sumatra.*

Fol. 140r.

The islands which are called *Gamispola* are two or three and more, near the land of Achin and *Lambry*. There must be about ten or fifteen islands three or four leagues round and the sea between them is two, three or four leagues, and it is twenty or thirty fathoms near the land[3]. *Islands in front of Pase and Achin near the point*[2] *of the Island of Sumatra.* Gamispola.

[1] *Tampoy* is the fruit of the tampoi-tree, a species of *Baccaurea*, (Euphorbiaceae), with roundish, thick-skinned fruit borne only a few in a bunch. Among the several species of this genus, Burkill mentions '*B. malayana* King, a big tree found in Sumatra, and in the Malay Peninsula in most parts. . . . The jungle tribes make its fruiting-season an occasion of feasting, and prepare a fermented liquor from the fruit'. *Op. cit.*, p. 279. The fruits of another species, *Baccaurea Motleyana* Muell.-Arg., found throughout western Malaysia, may also be fermented and made into a liquor. *Ibid.*, p. 280. Corner identifies the tampoi with *Baccaurea Griffithii*, a Malaya tree. *Wayside Trees of Malaya*, I, 240. Dalgado (*s.v.*) says that tampoi is the name of the fruit of a Malacca tree, *Artocarpus Gomeziana*, from which a very sweet liquor is made. *A. Gomeziana* Wall., however, is the native *tampang* or *tapang*, not the tampoi. See Burkill, p. 253. Eredia, just a hundred years after Pires, describes the tampoi thus: 'And the *Tampôe* is another tree of the same height (as the Mangosteen), and it has a thick-skinned fruit of the colour of cinnamon, and in the hollow inside there are sweet seeds like cloves or a head of garlic with a stone, and as it is sweet and strong they distil from it a wine like muscatel.' Fols. 16r. and 19v.

[2] Although in the Portuguese text this reads 'Junto com pom atrã de Jlha de çomotora', it must be a transcriber's mistake. Pires probably wrote 'Junto com a ponta da Jlha de çomotora', as translated.

[3] Marco Polo (II, 300, 307) mentions 'a very small Island that is called Gauenispola'. But *Gamispola* was the name given to the little archipelago immediately off the northernmost point of Sumatra. 'These *Guanispola* islands are many', says an early Portuguese rutter. *Livro de Marinharia*, p.

Some of these islands are inhabited by a few people. They have water and a great deal of fish and firewood. They all have quantities of sulphur, which supplies Pase and Pedir.

These islands belong to the king of Achin and their inhabitants—few as they are—obey him, chiefly [those of] the largest [island], which has more inhabitants (?); and there is some trade in these islands. They come from the island of Sumatra to do fishing and they catch a great deal of fish which is traded in some parts of Sumatra.

Kingdom of Achin and Lambry *and the land of* Biar.[1]

Achin is the first country on the channel side of the island of Sumatra, and *Lambry* is right next to it, and stretches inland, and the land of *Biar* is between Achin and Pedir, and now these countries are subject to the king of Achin and he rules over them and he is the only king there.

243. The modern names of the four larger islands are Wé, Bröeh or Bruas, Dobad and Bunta, and there are several islets. The Cantino map has *Gãspola*; then Rodrigues' map (fol. 29) has *as ilhas de gamispolla*; *ganyspora* on Reinel's map of *c.* 1517, and similarly on later maps. In Luís' atlas of 1563 and Dourado's atlases of 1568–80, *gamispola* appears already transformed into *gomes pola* or *gomes polla*, which is found as well on later maps down to the eighteenth century. Bowrey (pp. 227–8) mentions *Pullo Gomus.* The four larger islands are called either *Gomes Pulo* or *Pulo Gomes* on the later maps. The map in Marsden's *History of Sumatra* still has *P°. Gomez* as the name of Bunta, the south-westernmost islet of the group.

[1] ACHEY—Atjey or Achin, forms today an autonomous government embracing all the northern part of Sumatra except for the northernmost tip of Kuta Raja, through which flows the river Achin. Pires is the first European writer to mention Achin, and the map of *c.* 1540 is the first to record *achey*, with exactly the same spelling as in Pires.

LAMBRY—The *Lamuri*, *Lamori* or *Lambri* of the Arabs, Marco Polo, Friar Oderic and other medieval travellers. Couto refers to the *Lambri* mentioned by Polo, saying that it 'still preserves its name in Sumatra'. IV, iii, 1. Yule says in a note that 'most of the data about Lambri render it very difficult to distinguish it from Achin', but in the same note Cordier quotes Groeneveldt's opinion (*Notes on the Malay Archipelago*, 98–100) that Lambri was 'on or near the spot of the present Achin'. *Marco Polo*, II, 300–1. Dames, however, is of opinion that 'it may have been near Achin, but not so near as to be confounded with it' (II, 182–4), in which he is confirmed by Pires. Cordier suggests that a village called Lamreh, situated at Atjeh, near Tungkup (mentioned by Captain M. J. C. Lucardie, *Merveilles de l'Inde*, p. 235) 'might be a remnant of the country of Lãmeri'. *Marco Polo*, II, 301; *Cathay*, II, 146. See G. Schlegel, *The Old States in the Island of Sumatra*, p. 79.

BIAR—I cannot find any clear trace of the name of this land, situated by Pires between Achin and Pedir, with a seacoast corresponding to the present Krung Raya Bay and Blang Raya.

This king is a Moor, a knightly man among his neighbours. He uses piracy when he sees an opportunity. He must have about thirty or forty lancharas in which he goes to sea. When he is in his own country he lives on the crops of his rices and foodstuffs. He has rivers which flow through his country into the channel and they are of little depth at the mouth.

These lands produce meat, rices, and wine of their kind, and other foodstuffs. They have pepper—not much. The king of Pedir is always at war with him, and he [the king of Achin] does him a great deal of damage in his country.

Kingdom of Pedir[1].

Pedir in the island of Sumatra used to be important and rich and a trading place, and it had dominion over all the above mentioned kingdoms and also over the land of *Aeilabu* and the kingdom of *Lide* and the kingdom of *Pirada*; and it was at war with Pase; and Pedir once held the mouth of the channel. And it had all the trade, and they sailed there more than to Pase.

Until the year fifteen hundred and ten it always had trade. Its city is about half a league up a river. The bar is two fathoms deep at high tide. The city contains merchants of all nations even now. Although it has always war with its neighbours, it has not yet fallen away much from what it used to be.

As many as two ships from Cambay and Bengal trade with Pedir every year, and one from *Benua Quelim* and another from Pegu; with the first winds up to twenty small junks and lancharas set sail with rice. Trang trades with them and Tenasserim, Kedah [and] Bruas. After the taking of Malacca there was not so much trade, because of the war they had, especially after the death of king Muzaffar Shah, who died leaving | two small sons, when others rebelled inside the kingdom and it was always at war—which is against trade. *Fol. 140.*

[1] *Pedir.* The name survives in Pedir Point (Lat. 5° 30′ N), Kuala Pedir, which is the mouth of the principal stream on this part of the coast, and the large village of Pedir, where there is still 'an old ruined Portuguese fort'. *Malacca Strait Pilot*, p. 40 (1924 ed.). 'Pedir Point lies in 5½ degrees and helps to form a bay which extends southwards for one league and a half to the port of Pedir, and the west side of *Pasem* lies 17 leagues south-east of Pedir. The port of Pedir is in 5½ degrees and has a bar, which runs south-eastwards for one league and a half. . . . The coast is rocky up to one league from the shore as far as *Pasem*. This point and river are called *Jambuar*' (Jambu-Ayer). *Livro de Marinharia*, p. 243.

The merchandise that Pedir had, and will have in the future when the war is over and it comes into its own again: from six or seven to ten thousand bahars of pepper a year—they say that it has had as much as fifteen thousand bahars—there is white silk, benzoin in the country and its neighbours; there is gold, which also comes to Pedir through the interior; and on account of the pepper it used to receive a great deal of merchandise, and returns of one thing and another, which enriched the kingdom and its city.

And the last four years Pedir must have had from two to three thousand bahars of pepper a year, and no more. They say that the land is already returning to what it was before (?); on account of the war that broke out and of the war that has been going on up till now, many merchants have left. One of the king's captains is now reigning in Pedir, and he threw out one of the king's sons, who is now in Pase, out of his kingdom. Pedir uses tin coins like *ceitis* for small money; it has gold *dramas*[1], nine of which are worth one *cruzado*; it has silver *tangas*[2] like those of Siam, Pegu and Bengal, and they are current in the country at their value, and for merchandise in great quantities [they use] gold dust. The weight of the bahar is the same as in Pase.

Aeilabu[3] The country called *Aeilabu* is on the sea coast beyond the

[1] There was in India an old coin of little value called *dramo*, recorded in some Portuguese dictionaries and in Dalgado (*s.v.* Dama). Pires' *dramas* might suggest *drachmas*, but further on, under the heading 'Coinage and weights used in Pase', he clearly specifies that *dramas* is the local name for certain small gold coins. In a Chinese book, *Ying-yai Shêng-lan* (General account of the shores of the Ocean), written in 1416 by Ma Huan, it is stated 'the money used (in Sumatra) are coins of gold and tin. The golden coins are called *dinar* and contain seven tenths of pure gold, they are round, have a diameter of 5 *fên* official measure (1.6 centimetres) and weigh 2 *fên*, (otherwise *ch'ien*) 3 *li* (about 10 grammes)'. Groeneveldt, *Notes on the Malay Archipelago and Malacca*, p. 87. It is perhaps not impossible that the Chinese character here transliterated as *dinar* sounded rather like what Pires wrote as *drama*.

[2] *Tanga*. The name of a coin used in India and other eastern countries. It was made of different metals and was of varying value. The *tanga* is still a monetary unit in Portuguese India, equivalent to sixty *reis*. *Hobson-Jobson* and Dalgado, *s.v.* See note p. 20.

[3] *Aeilabu* corresponds to Kuala Ayer Lebu, the mouth of the river Tiro, fifteen miles south-east of Pedir.

frontiers of Pedir. This place used to have a king and now it has a mandarin, a captain vassal to the king of Pedir. This place of *Aeilabu* has a city, where there is a little trade. This place has quantities of pepper and the city is on the sea. It has foodstuffs for its own use.

The kingdom of *Lide* is beyond Aeilabu and borders on *Pirada.* The king of this country used to be from Pedir; but not now. It has places by the sea where some merchandise is traded. It has merchants. Pegu trade with it, and other places. There is a good amount of foodstuffs in the land of *Lide.* There is pepper and silk in its land. It is friendly with the king of Pedir. This kingdom now has lancharas which navigate and trade in merchandise. It defends itself against its neighbours; it is strong in its land. This country is always dependent (?) on Pedir. The kings are related. This one is a Moorish king. It has foodstuffs for its own use. Lide[1]

The kingdom of *Pirada* has more people than the land of *Lide* and the king is more powerful. He used to be a vassal of Pedir, but not now. It has two towns by the sea; one of them is called Medan (*Medina*)[3] and the other [*blank*]. They deal in merchandise. They have pepper and silk which they take to Pedir, and Lide also takes its [pepper and silk] there. They have factors in Pedir and are supplied from there. They are related to the Pirada[2]

[1] Sixteen miles east-south-east of Ayer Lebu debouches the river Ulim or Olim; the small village of Ulim is situated a mile from its mouth. This may suggest a survival from Pires' *Lidee.* E. H. Parker, following Groeneveldt, writes—'east and adjoining Lambri the Ming Records say there was a state subordinate to Sumoltra called Li-fah (or Li-tai) lying to the west of Nagur and Sumoltra [or Nakur and Samûdra]. This is the exact position of Lide according to De Barros' enumeration of the Petty states he visited' (*sic*). *The Island of Sumatra*, p. 141. According to Schlegel the Chinese *Li-fah* is a misprint for *Li-tē* (in A.D. 1416), i.e., Barros' *Lide* or Pires' *Lidee.* He shows also that 'west' is an obvious mistake for 'east'. *Op. cit.*, pp. 65–8.

[2] Five miles east of Ulim lies Cape Pedada, and a mile eastward is the river Pedada with a village of the same name near the coast. Seven miles south-east there is another river Pidada and a place of the same name. Some of these may correspond to Pires' *Pirada.*

[3] The *Mohit* (p. 72) mentions the harbour of *Mandara* on the east coast, about the same latitude as Pedada and Pidada. Another place, *Madina*, is situated by the *Mohit* (p. 87) much farther to the south-east, corresponding to the present Medan. It is possible that Pires confused the order of the places when he was gathering his information.

king of Pedir. They have gold. Pirada produces foodstuffs in its [own] land. They trade with it from many parts. It has trade—not much. It is powerful enough to defend itself against Pase, *Fol. 141r.* although the people of whom we are speaking | are more cunning than powerful, and they say that the people of Pirada are extremely malicious, treacherous and untrustworthy. They sometimes go robbing at sea. They are at war with the *Cafres*[1] on land.

Kingdom of Pase (Paçee)[2]. The rich kingdom of Pase has many inhabitants and much trade. On one side it is bounded by the kingdom of *Pirada*, as I have already said, and on the other by the land of *Bata*, the king of which is the *Tamjano*. The land of Pase stretches along by the sea coast. Its frontiers on the inland side of the island coincide with those of the king of *Manicopa*, which goes out to the sea on the other side, and with whom they are sometimes at war.

And now, since Malacca has been punished and Pedir is at war, the kingdom of Pase is becoming prosperous, rich, with many merchants from different Moorish and Kling nations, who do a great deal of trade, among whom the most important are the Bengalees. There are *Rumes*, Turks, Arabs, Persians, Gujaratees, Kling, Malays, Javanese and Siamese.

The people of Pase are for the most part Bengalees, and the natives descend from this stock; and because they are of this seed, there is a custom in the country which will be described later, for beyond doubt there is not in the world so vile a way as that of Pase in dealing with its king.

City of Pase. The kingdom of Pase has the city which is called Pase, and some people call it *Çamotora* (Sumatra). Because there is nothing else so important in the whole island, the city has thus given

[1] From the Arab *kafir*, 'unfaithful or unbeliever', meaning any person not Mohammedan. 'A heathen or *Cafre*', says Pires farther on (p. 159). 'The Heathen whom the Moors name Cafres', says Barbosa (I, 10). Even the English, at least once in 1799, have been called 'Caffers'! Cf. *Hobson-Jobson, s.v.*

[2] The name survives in the Pase river, in Lat. 5° 9′ N. It appears for the first time on Rodrigues' maps (fol. 34), as *Paççem*, and then on almost every map down to the eighteenth century. Castanheda refers to 'the town of Pacẽ, twenty leagues from Pedir, which lies a league up a river, situated upon its marshy land'. II, cxii. There are in fact 84 miles between Pedir and the modern Pase, which is 20 miles more than Castanheda's 20 leagues. See above note on Pedir.

its name to the whole island, being called by either of these names. This city has not less than twenty thousand inhabitants.

Thus the kingdom of Pase has large towns with many inhabitants towards the interior, where important people of good breeding live (?). These sometimes disagree with Pase because of the crops of pepper, silk and benzoin; but they affirm that in the quarrels their wishes prevail over Pase; and in these towns there live great nobles of the kingdom, who are called mandarins, and the men-at-arms.

How they reign and how long they have had kings and of what sects.

Pase used to have heathen kings, and it must be a hundred and sixty years now since the said kings were worn out by the cunning of the merchant Moors there were in the kingdom of Pase, and the said Moors held the sea coast and they made a Moorish king of the Bengali caste, and from that time until now the kings of Pase have always been Moors; except that up till now they have been unable to convert the people of the interior; and yet in these kingdoms there are in the island of Sumatra, those on the sea coast are all Moors on the side of the Malacca Channel, and those who are not yet Moors are being made so every day, and no heathen among them is held in any esteem unless he is a merchant.

As, when the Bengalees made their king, it was on condition that anyone who could kill the king should become king | whatever his estate and condition as long as he was a Moor, the grandees of Pase have from that time agreed that whoever kills the king becomes king; and they say that on one day there were seven kings in Pase, because one killed the other and another the other; and they consider it glorious to die kings and they are not guarded, because they say that that is God's command, so that the kings do not last long in their estate, and whenever one kills another, he buries the dead one with all royal solemnity, because that is the custom of the country; and there is no disturbance whatever in the city or among the people and merchants whether king be killed or live. *Fol. 141v.*

And because the Bengalees started this rule, the land of Bengal desired to do the same thing, as it will be seen in the account of Bengal that for the last seventy years they have been doing this in Bengal. And there is no country where this practice exists and lasts except in Bengal and Pase.

Because on two occasions two kings in Pase had died, ambassadors from Pase came twice in three months to show vassalage and obedience to Malacca, asking for Portuguese support as the land and people and kings were slaves of the king our lord; and they keep on coming to ask this as other kings succeed. And the king who is now reigning is the son of the king of Pirada.

The city of Pase lies about half a league up the river. And the river is like the one in Pedir, of that kind, a little wider but not much. Both rivers have stone pillars (*padrões*) of ours at their entrance.

Merchandise of Pase.

It has from eight to ten thousand bahars of pepper every year. The pepper from this island is not as good as that from Cochin: it is larger, hollower and lasts less; it has not the same perfection of flavour and it is not so aromatic. It produces silk and benzoin, and in Pase you will find all the merchandise there is in all the island, because it is collected there.

Coinage and weights used in Pase.

There are small coins like *ceitis*. They are tin coins bearing the name of the reigning king. There are very small gold coins which they call *dramās*. Nine of these are worth one *cruzado*, and I believe that each one of them is worth five hundred cash. Above this they have gold-dust and silver. Their bahar of pepper is less than that of Malacca—five *cates*, that is twelve *arráteis* less.

Merchandise which is traded in Pase in junks and *ships.*

The merchants who trade in Pase are Gujaratees, Kling, Bengalees, men of Pegu, Siamese, men of Kedah and Bruas, and these are already divided up, so many in | Pase and so many in Pedir and the remainder in Malacca. They do not trade with Pase from the east, only with the populous city of Malacca, for you could make ten cities like Pase out of the city of Malacca at the time of its punishment—when it received correction for the blunder it had made.

Fol. 142r.

As for this improvement which Pase received through what happened in Malacca, when Malacca is reformed—as it is becoming every day—Pase will return to its former state, and [so will] Pedir. With the help of God Almighty, the kings firstly of Pase and Pedir and also all those in this island will be tributaries and vassals to him who now owns Malacca, because otherwise in a year's time there will be no Pase and Pedir, and those who realise it are making themselves vassals before they are required to do so.

Pase has the right to one *maz*[1] on every bahar of merchandise that goes out, and it levies anchorage according to whether it is a ship or junk. They do not pay anything on foodstuffs, only give a present; on the other merchandise that comes from the west six per cent, and on every slave they bring there to sell five *mazes* of gold; and all merchandise they take out, whether it be pepper or anything else, they pay one *maz* per bahar. Neither Pase nor Pedir has a single junk; they have lancharas—as many as two, three or four for cargo. They used to come and buy junks in Malacca. The merchants of Pase buy junks from other merchants who go there from other places to trade, because they are not made in Pase on account of the scarcity in the country of *jaty* wood[2], which is strong for junks. *Duties in Pase.*

The kingdom of *Bata* is bordered on the one side by the kingdom of Pase and on the other by the kingdom of Aru (*Daruu*). The king of this country is called *Raja Tomjam*[4]. He is *Kingdom of* Bata[3].

[1] A gold weight used in Sumatra, equivalent to one sixteenth of a *tael* or ounce. Further on, when dealing with the Malacca coinage, Pires says also that the *tael* weighs sixteen *mazes*. But the value of the *maz* was variable in the Far-East. See note on *maz* p. 124.

[2] *Jaty*. *Tectona grandis* Linn., or teak, 'the pride of Indian forests'. The words *Kayu jati* mean 'the true, or real wood'. Burkill, *op. cit.*, p. 2127. Though Corner (*op. cit.*, I, 706) says that the teak tree was introduced into Malaya from Burma, Siam, E. Java, and the Philippines, it seems that in Pires' time it had long been known in Malacca.

[3] The *Batas*, Battas or Bataks were the inhabitants of the hinterland of northern Sumatra. Barros refers to the *Bátas* who dwell in the part of Sumatra over against Malacca and 'who eat human flesh, the wildest and the most warlike people in the whole world' (III, v, i). Galvão (p. 108) and Eredia (fol. 23v.), among others, also refer to the cannibalism of the Batas. The anonymous Portuguese atlas of *c.* 1615–23 has *bata* on the north-west, and Berthelot's map of 1635 has *R. dos batas* on the north-east coast of Sumatra, in Lat. 3° N.

[4] *Raja Tomjam*, or *Tamjano* as written before, must mean 'Raja of Tomjam'. Pinto refers to 'Timorraja, king of the Batas' (XIII). Castanheda says that the survivors of the *Frol de la Mar* went to the 'town of *Temião* in the island of Sumatra (III, lxxviii), and Barros informs us that the shipwreck was in front of 'a point called *Timia* in the kingdom of Aru' (II, vii, i). 'The river *Tomão* is in 4⅓ degrees', correctly states the *Livro de Marinharia*, p. 243. This must

a Moorish knight. He often goes to sea to pillage. He is the son-in-law of the king of Aru. He brought in (?) the ship *Frol de la Mar*[1] which was wrecked in a storm off the coast of his country, and they say he recovered everything water could not spoil, wherefore they say he is very rich. From what they say this *Tomjano* is rather wealthy. This *Tomjano* is often at war in the hinterland. Sometimes he fights with his father-in-law, sometimes with Pase, and he helps whichever he sees to be the stronger, and he receives [something] from them all. They say that the kings of *Bata* (*Batar*) have always had this habit.

He must have as many as thirty or forty well-equiped lancharas, which get out into the channel by the rivers there are in his country, because no one lives on the coast except watchers to see who goes by. The said land of *Bata* produces rice and wine and fruit. It has pitch from which they make many lamps, and they go there for cargoes of them. It also produces a great deal of honey and wax and a little edible camphor. The chief merchandise is canes in large quantities which they call *rotaãs*[2], and these are good merchandise because they serve for cable and threads in every way.

The kingdom of Aru is a large kingdom, bigger than any of

correspond to *teinaoa* on the map of *c.* 1540, and *R. themiam* on Berthelot's map, in the north-east of Sumatra—the small river Tamian or Tamiang (there are also a point and a hill called Tamiang, Lat. 4° 25′ N). Apparently the name occurs as *Dalmyan* in a Persian MS of 1310 and as *Tumihan* in a Javanese MS of 1365. Ferrand, *Relations de voyages*, pp. 261 and 652. A Chinese account of 1436 says: '*Tamiang* is connected with the territory of *Aru*. It is surrounded everywhere by mountains, and possesses a harbour leading to a large inland stream, surgy and boisterous for a thousand miles, which rushes into the sea.' Schlegel, *op. cit.*, p. 86.

[1] After the conquest of Malacca, Albuquerque sailed back to India, with a small fleet of four ships, on 1 Dec. 1511 on board the *Frol de la Mar* (Flower of the Sea). When the ships were sailing along the north-east coast of Pase they were caught in a fierce storm and the *Frol de la Mar*, an old ship, was wrecked on some shoals, with great loss of life and of all the treasures brought from Malacca. Albuquerque himself escaped with the utmost difficulty. The chronicles do not quite agree about the place where the *Frol de la Mar* was wrecked, but Albuquerque himself says in his letter of 20 Aug. 1512, written from Cochin to the King of Portugal, that *Frol de la Mar* was wrecked near Pase'. *Cartas*, I, 67.

[2] Rattan, the Malay word *rotan*, a cane. These canes are made from certain kinds of palms, mainly of the genus *Calamus* Linn.

those mentioned up to now in Sumatra, and it is not rich through merchandise and trade, for it has none. This [king] has many people, many lancharas. He is the greatest king in all Sumatra, and the most powerful in plundering raids. He is a Moor and lives in the hinterland, and has many rivers in his country. The land in itself is marshy and cannot be penetrated. *Fol. 142v* *Kingdom of Aru* (Daru)[1].

This [king] is always in residence in his kingdom. His mandarins and his people go robbing at sea, and they share with him because some part of the armada is paid by them. Since Malacca began, he has always been at war with Malacca and has taken many of its people. He pounces on a village and takes everything, even the fishermen; and the Malays always keep a great watch for the Arus, because this quarrel is already of long standing and it has always remained, whence comes the saying 'Aru against Malacca, Achin against Pedir, Pedir against Kedah and Siam, Pahang against Siam on the other side, Palembang against Linga, *Celates* against Bugis (*Bajus*)[2], etc.', and all these nations fight one against the other and they are very rarely friends.

The people of Aru are presumptuous and warlike, and no one

[1] *Daru* is the contraction of the genitive *de* and *Aru*. Pires also used the form *Daru* in his letter written from Cochin 27 Jan. 1516, where he refers to the *Regno de daru*; but it is erroneous to write 'de daru'. The kingdom or state of *Aru*, like most of those mentioned by Pires, has long ago disappeared from the maps. But the name survives in Aru Bay, on the north-east coast of Sumatra, and in Aroa Islands, a group of islets lying nearly in mid-channel between the Sumatran coast and Cape Rachado. Reinel's maps of *c.* 1517 and *c.* 1518 are the first to show *aRu* and *tr̃ra daRu*, immediately north and south of the equator; L. Homem's map of 1554 and D. Homem's atlas of 1558 have *R. daru* and *trra daru* situated in the region of the modern Rokan River. The *Aru* river corresponds to the modern Deli River, on which stands the city of Aru.

[2] '*Cellates* est un néologisme portugais formé avec le mot malais *sélát* "détroit". Il a le sens de "gens du détroit, population maritime vivant dans le détroit'," says Ferrand. *Malaka*, XI, 434. However Pires is quite explicit when he says a little further on that 'Celates is the Malay for sea-robbers'. Crawfurd is milder, calling the Celates 'the sea-gipsies'. *Dictionary*, p. 50.

Bajus or Bugis was the name given by the Malays to the dominant race of the Celebes. In the seventeenth and eighteenth centuries the Bugis established themselves in the Malay Peninsula and other places of the Malay Archipelago. Crawfurd remarked that 'the Bugis, now the most enterprising of all the native tribes of the Archipelago, are never mentioned by the earlier European writers', such as Barbosa and Barros; and that they 'are among the most advanced people of the Archipelago'. *Dictionary, s.v.*

trusts them. If they do not steal they do not live, and therefore no one is friendly with them. They must have a hundred *paráos* and more whenever they want them, not very big things, more adapted for speed than for taking cargo.

Food-stuffs. The land of Aru has plenty of rice, and very white and good and in large quantities; it has plenty of meat, fish and wines such as they use, and fruit in great abundance.

Merchandise. It has edible camphor in good quantities; it has gold; it has a great deal of benzoin, and good; it has apothecary's lignaloes; it has rattans, pitch, wax, honey, slaves (men and women); it has a few merchants. Some of this merchandise is sold by way of Pase and Pedir and some by way of *Panchur*, because some of the land of Aru is in the land of Menangkabau, and there they have great rivers inland along which the whole island of Sumatra can be navigated, and from these places they get the cloth for their clothes and other things.

Fair in this country. Aru has a town in the land of *Arqat*, where a slave market (of men and women) is held in certain months, and [it is] open to all. Anyone who likes can go there in safety; and many people go there to buy slaves, and some people send there to buy their sons, and daughters their mothers, and husbands their wives; and they also deal in other merchandise there; and that is the way it happens with the *Celates*, as will be told when we speak of the *Celates* robbers in their proper place.

Kingdom of Arcat[1]. The kingdom of *Arcat* is bounded on one side by Aru and on the other by Rokan (*Yrcan*). The king is a Moor. He has a small country. He has small *paráos*. He does not do much trade. He is a vassal of the king of Aru. The people of this kingdom on the sea coast are *Celates* robbers and those inland live on their crops.

Fol. 143r. This country has gold; it has rice, wines, and fish; and they load dried salt fish here. Only very small *paráos* can come into this country along inlets. The king is related to the king of Aru.

[1] The most important anchorage between the rivers Deli and Rokan is in a bay where three rivers—Kualu, Bila and Panai—debouch. This bay is limited on the west by a point called Pertandangan or Perapat. Is it perhaps reminiscent of Pires' *Arcat*?

The land of Rokan is between *Arcat* and the kingdom of Rupat. This country has no king; it has a mandarin. He is a vassal of the late king of Malacca. He helped him during the war with rowers and men-at-arms, who had to serve gratis, just for their food. Many of these people are *Celates*, which is the Malay for sea robbers.

Land of Rokan (Jrcan)[1].

The land of Rokan[2] has gold and rice. This [land] has the shad fisheries, whence they take them to Malacca in large quantities. And there is also in this country a market of slaves whom they and other robbers steal, and they come to sell them here and also in *Purim*.

The kingdom of Rupat is bounded on one side by Rokan and on the other by *Purim*. It is a small kingdom. Most of the people are robbers in small *pardos*. This kingdom has the same obligations to Malacca as the land of Rokan. It helps with people in war. It also has a little rice, wines, fruit, and they fish for shad in great quantities and for other fish.

Kingdom of Rupat[3]

The land of *Purim* is bounded on one side by Rupat and on the other by Siak. This country has a mandarin, a powerful person. He is a vassal of the king of Malacca, in the same way as was said of Rokan and Rupat, and he helps with rowing men in great numbers. And most of the people in this place are *Celates*, robbers, and they are brought up on the sea and are great rowers.

Land of Purim[4].

This *Purim* has a larger market for stolen slaves than there is in the two places of which we have spoken—leaving out *Arcat*. This *Purim* also has many shad and other fish in large quantities. It has some gold, rice, wines, meat and other foodstuffs. This mandarin of *Purim* is an important person and a great warrior.

The kingdom of Siak is bounded on one side by *Purim* and on

Kingdom of Siak (Ciac)[5].

[1] *Jrcan* corresponds to the Rokan River. The first maps on which I find this river are Eredia's (1613) and Berthelot's (1635), where it is given as *Aracan*.

[2] Though the MS has Purim, it is obviously a mistake for *Jrcan*.

[3] Pulo Rupat, a large island just opposite Malacca.

[4] The next island south-east of Rupat is Pulo Bengkalis (the *Bamcallis* of Dourado's atlas of 1580 and other later maps). The north-east point of this small island is called Parit, perhaps reminiscent of Pires' *Purim*, which farther on is also spelt *Porim*.

[5] *Ciac* corresponds to the Siak River. The map of *c.* 1540 has *Cjace*; similarly on later maps.

the other by Kampar (*Campar*). The king of this place is a Moor. This country has trade and some merchants. Siak is a country that has rice, honey, wax, rattans, apothecary's lignaloes. It has more gold than the three places we have mentioned; it has wines and other foodstuffs.

This king is respected in the country. He is related to the king of Malacca and to the king of Kampar. He is a tributary to him, and the king of Kampar is a tributary to Malacca for himself and for the other, and is defended. His country contains large rivers which come from far inland. This king has many *paráos*, and they are made in his country, because of the amount of wood there is there.

Fol. 143v.

Kingdom of Kampar (Campar)[1].

The kingdom of Kampar is bounded on one side by Siak and on the other by *Campom*. In front of this country are the Islands of Karimun (*Carjmom*) and of *Çelaguy guy* and of Kundur (*Sabam*)[2], which form the beginning of the channel to Java and other

[1] *Campar* corresponds to the Kampar River. Reinel's maps of *c.* 1517 and *c.* 1518 have *campar*; similarly on later maps.

[2] CARJMOM—Karimun islands. There are two, Great Karimun and Little Karimun, separated by a deep channel half a mile wide.

ÇELAGUY GUY—The Sugi islands, east of Kundur island? Between Karimun and Kundur lies the small Temblas island, the *Ambelas* of early Portuguese rutters (Lat. 1° N), and several others, but none suggests *Çelaguy guy* or *Çelaguym gum*. Pires, however, identifies these islands with the *Celates* (p. 136).

SABAM—Kundur island. Following on a modern chart the sailing directions in *Livro de Marinharia*, pp. 244–67, we find that the island of *Sabam* is unmistakably Kundur island. There is still a small place called Sawang on the west coast of Kundur, facing the channel. Reinel's maps of *c.* 1517 and *c.* 1518 have *sabã* south of the equator, at the northern entrance of a channel between Sumatra and a large archipelago (the present Rhio Archipelago) south of *sangapura*. The maps of L. Homem (1554), D. Homem (1558), Dourado and others, have 'way out of the *canal de sabam*' written on the coast of Sumatra, also south of the equator. However, the *Canal de Sabam*, between the Sumatran coast and the islands of Karimun and Kundur, lies well northward of the equator. But one of Eredia's maps (fol. 45) has the islands *cariman*, *ambilas* and *SABAM* forming with Sumatra the *ESTRETO: SABAM* (marked with dotted lines), situated north of the equator only some minutes short of the correct latitude. In spite of modern opinions to the contrary, there is no doubt that this was the route of the Portuguese ships sailing from Malacca to the south-east coast of Sumatra and beyond. Actually the soundings in the shallowest part of the channel, between the south-west of Kundur and Mendol, are four and three quarter fathoms; farther south-east, between the Sumatran coast and Pulo Wahu (N.W. of Pulo Durei), the shallowest part is only three and one quarter fathoms.

places. The channel between the islands and the land of Kampar is called Kampar because it begins there.

These kings of Kampar are related to the ex-king of Malacca, and the present one is married to one of his daughters; he is called Rajah Audela. His kingdom has no villages on the sea. It goes in by a river of five, six, or seven fathoms, and there is a great bore (*macareo*) in this river: the waters of many rivers meet in the estuary, and in a short time rises to a great height, and as it rises it produces waves, so that it overthrows and breaks up anything it finds; and if those who enter in are not warned to watch their moment for entering, they are often lost[1].

This land of Kampar is sterile and of little profit. Run up the river seven or eight days and there are the villages—not many of them. The river flows violently and is difficult to navigate on account of the currents. Almost at the end, by the last village belonging to the said king, the rivers divide—that of Kampar, that of Menangkabau and that of Siak; and at the entrance to the mouth of another river in Kampar another large river[2] is found which makes Siak, *Purim*, Rupat and Rokan into islands, and comes out opposite Malacca. *Pate Unus* came along this with the tide, because the winds in the channel were already contrary for getting to Malacca. However he turned the poop into the freshening wind and fled in the junks. This deed shall long be remembered[3].

[1] The *Malacca Strait Pilot* says that 'owing to the bore which takes place and the rapid tidal stream, local knowledge is necessary' in the Kampar River.

[2] There is no other river between the Siak and the Kampar. It is possible that by this 'other large river' Pires meant the narrow and long channel between the islands Bengakalis, Padang, and Tebing Tinggi on one hand, and the mainland of Sumatra on the other, which might look like a large river. He thought that the large island very close to the coast of Sumatra, in front of Malacca, with narrow channels and the rivers Rokan, Siak and Kampar, formed the enormous delta of a single river. This misconception was common to many cartographers and geographers, as is seen in early maps and descriptions of Africa, Asia and America, when their hinterlands were almost or entirely unknown.

[3] In January 1513 *Paty Onuz*, *Patih Yunus* or *Pate Unus* tried to surprise Malacca, bringing a 100 ships with 5,000 men, Javanese from Japara and Palembang; 'defeated, Patih Unus sailed home and beached his warship as a monument of a fight against men he called the bravest in the world, his exploit winning him a few years later the throne of Demak.' Winstedt, *A History of Malay*, 70–1 (following Castanheda, III, cii). When Alvim in 1513

Merchandise. This kingdom has a great deal of apothecary's lignaloes. It is called *garuu* in Malay and *agujlla* in India. It has gold, pitch, wax, honey. It is bounded inland by the [land of] the kings of Menangkabau, and trades with them.

Foodstuffs. It has rices, meats, *tampões* wines—all these in moderation, to feed their land. They take their merchandise to Malacca and bring back Kling and Gujarat cloth, which is valued throughout the island, and red cotton cloth is valued the most in Menangkabau.

Land of Campocan[1]. The land of *Campocan* is between Kampar and Indragiri. This country used to have a king. For the last ten years it has had

visited Japara, *Pate Unus* sent him presents, asking the Portuguese not to burn the famous junk, and no harm was done. In a letter to Afonso de Albuquerque, from Cannanore, 22 Feb. 1513, Fernão Peres de Andrade, the Captain of the fleet that routed *Pate Unus*, says: 'The junk of *Pate Umuz* is the largest seen by men of these parts so far. It carried a thousand fighting men on board, and your Lordship can believe me . . . that it was an amazing thing to see, because the *Anunciada* near it did not look like a ship at all. We attacked it with bombards, but even the shots of the largest did not pierce it below the water-line, and [the shots of] the *espera* [an old large kind of cannon] I had in my ship went in but did not pass through; it had three sheathings, all of which were over a *cruzado* thick. And it certainly was so monstrous that no man had ever seen the like. It took three years to build, as your Lordship may have heard tell in Malacca concerning this *Pate Umuz*, who made this armada to become king of Malacca.' *Cartas*, III, 59. Barros, II, ix, 4. Correia says that *Pate Unus* appeared before Malacca 'on a morning of January 1512 (II, 277), and Castanheda describes the event as having taken place in 1512 (*loc. cit.*); but they are obviously mistaken, unless here the year was exceptionally reckoned as beginning at Easter, which does not seem to be the case. Malacca was taken in the middle of August 1511, and Albuquerque sailed back to India in December; between the departure of Albuquerque and the coming of *Pate Unus* many other well-known events took place (described by Barros, II, ix, 1 and 2, Castanheda, III, lxxxi-lxxxvi, and Correia himself). Moreover, Andrade says in his letter that they had the first news of the coming of *Pate Unus* on Christmas Day 1512, and Barros rightly says that the enemy fleet appeared before Malacca 'at the beginning of January 1513'. Further on, when describing the 'Land of Demak', Pires says that *Pate Unus* 'came to fight (against Malacca) in the year 1512'; though not expressly stated, this refers to his departure from Java, of course. When describing Japara (p. 188) and the early establishment of the Portuguese in Malacca (p. 282), Pires refers to this case with more detail. Dames thinks that *Pateudra* or *Pate Udora* mentioned by Barbosa is identical with Pate Unuz (II, 190–1); but later on Pires' account shows clearly that *Pate Unus* and *Pateudra*, or *Pate Andura*, were different persons.

[1] Between the rivers Kampar and Indragiri there is the small river Kateman, the upper part of which is called Simpang-kana; this may correspond to Pires' *Campoquan*, *Campom* or *Campocan*.

a mandarin. It is a small country and this mandarin is a vassal of Malacca. This country has a few merchants. They take gold to Malacca, and bring back Kling or Gujarat cloth.

This country of *Campocan* has gold; it has apothecary's lign-aloes; it has wax, honey, pitch, rattans, and things that Kampar has. It is a small country and good. In front of it are | the islands of Buaya[1], which form the channel, because all along the coast of Sumatra the different places follow each other and so do the islands (?). It has plenty of foodstuffs for its needs: rices, meats, fish, wines, fruit, and many mats, dried fish in quantities. *Fol. 144r.*

Kingdom of Indragiri (Andarguery).

The kingdom of Indragiri is bounded on one side by the land of *Campocan* and on the other by the land of Tongkal (*Tunqall*). Indragiri is an important kingdom. It has a fair number of trading people, and people go there from many places to trade. It is the chief port of Menangkabau.

The kings of Indragiri are related to the kings of Malacca and of Kampar and of Pahang. The country is not very large, but the people are accustomed to trade. The merchants who go there are not badly treated. They come to Malacca from Indragiri, because Indragiri comes under Malacca like Kampar.

Indragiri does business and trade with a certain part of the land of Menangkabau in the interior, where they collect great deal of gold by hand with which they buy many cloths, and in this way they do their trade. It produces the same merchandise as Kampar, but in greater abundance, and also foodstuffs and meat. Opposite Indragiri are the Linga islands.

Land of Tongkal (Tuñcall)[2].

The land of Tongkal is joined on one side to Indragiri and on the other to the land of Jambi (*Jamby*). This country has no king nor mandarin. It is a country which is obedient to Malacca as a tributary. It is a small country. It also borders on Menagkabau. It has the same merchandise as Indragiri, but not in such quantities. It has enough foodstuffs for itself and for others. Opposite are the islands of *Calantiga*.[3]

[1] Pulo Buaya lies north-west of Linga, in the middle of several islets (Lat. 0° 10′ N).

[2] *Tuncall*—There is a river Tongkal between Indragiri and Jambi. Berthelot's map of 1635 has *Toncal*.

[3] Twelve miles westward of Pulo Singkep there is a group of three small islands, each with some islets around it, the central one of which is Pulo

Land of Jambi (Jamby)[1]. The land of Jambi is attached at one end to the land of Tongkal and at the other side to the land of Palembang (*Palimbão*), inland to Menangkabau, and opposite are the islands of Pulo Berhala (*Berella*)[2]. This country used to have a king. It is like Indragiri, and after the Javanese Moors began to grow powerful and took Palembang, they took Jambi, and they were called kings no longer, but they are called *pates*[3], which means mandarins in Malacca, and in our languge really [means] governors with capital powers, both civil and criminal over every person in their lands. They have full jurisdiction, only they have lost the name of kings, and have become *pates*, as will be told in speaking of the great Java. The said land of Jambi produces apothecary's lignaloes, and gold, and the merchandise of Tongkal and the other places. And there are already more foodstuffs here. It is under *Pate Rodim*, lord of Demak (*Demaa*). The people of the land of Jambi are already more like Palembangs and Javanese than Malays. The land is fertile and rich in its way.

Fol. 144v. All the kingdoms we have mentioned from Arcat up to here have a great many lancharas. They all trade in Malacca, all the year round, and it is all Menangkabau land and they are all Malays.

Land of Palembang (Palimbam)[4]. The large country of Palembang is bordered on one side by Jambi and on the other by the point and end of the island of

Alang Tiga. These are Pires' *Jlhas de Calamtigua,* which he referred to before as *Tigua*. They appear clearly marked on Rodrigues' map (fol. 30) as *carãtiga*.

[1] The Jambi territories, through which flows 'the largest and most beautiful' river of Sumatra, the Jambi River, form today a province with the city of Jambi as capital. L. Homem's map of 1554 is the first to show it as *jamvim*.

[2] This *Pullo Berella* seems to correspond to Pulo Singkep, the southernmost island of the Linga group. The name survives in the Berhala Strait, between Singkep and Sumatra. There is, however, a Pulo Berhala in the north part of the Malacca Strait, which was called *Ilha da Polvoreira* by the Portuguese. 'An island, which our men call Poluoreyra and the natives *Barala*', says Barros, II, vi, 1 and 2. *A polluoreira* appears for the first time on Rodrigues' map (fol. 29).

[3] This is the first explanation of the word *pate* or patih, at least by an European writer. Many later sixteenth-century writers define this term, but no one so completely as Pires. The title is still in use for some native Java dignitaries.

[4] The territories of Palembang form today a province of southern Sumatra through which flows the Palembang or Musi River. It has the city of Palem-

Sumatra which is called *Tana Malayo* and from the interior and the sea along the way to *Pansur* or *Panchur*, it is bordered by Sekampung (*Caupõ*), Tulang Bawang (*Tulumbavam*), Andalas (*Andallõs*), and in the interior by the land of Priaman (*Pyramam*) which is in the land of Menangkabau. Palembang has the islands of *Monomby*[1] and the islands of Banka (*Banca*) in front of it in the channel. Palembang belongs to *Pate Rodim*, lord of Demak. Most of the people of Palembang are heathens of low class, and [there are] also many heathen *pates*.

The land of Palembang used to have heathen kings of its own and it was subject to the *cafre* king of Java, and after the Moorish *pates* of Java had made themselves masters of the sea coasts, they made war on Palembang for a long time and took the land, and it had no more kings, only *pates*, and Palembang has ten or twelve chief *pates*. Palembang has about ten thousand [men ?] many of whom lost their lives in the Malacca war against us.

The land of Palembang is the best thing *Pate Rodim* has, better than his own country, and it has now been destroyed by us, [and so have] all his junks and *champanas*[2], and all the lords of Palembang were killed in the defeat of *Pate Unus*. Even though the Palembang people came to fight at Malacca very unwillingly, all those who came died. And because this fact does not belong to this place I will return to the description and account of Palembang.

Palembang trades in Malacca and it trades largely with Pahang. Palembang has many junks and cargo *pangajavas*. Ten

bang as capital and seat of the Government Resident. Rodrigues' map (fol.30) is the first to record Palembang as *as tres bocas de pallambam*, placing them accurately. The Palembang River has really three mouths—the main entrance is Sungi Sunsang (Musi), navigable as far as Palembang for vessels that can cross the bar, a distance of fifty-four miles; the two eastern mouths, Sungi Saleh and Sungi Upang, are not navigable. The *Comentários de Afonso de Albuquerque* (III, xvii) and Barros (II, ix, 4, etc.) mention another *Polimbão* or *Polimbam* in Java, (see G. Ferrand, *Malaka*, I, 412–4); several Portuguese cartographers, like the anonymous author of the *c.* 1540 map, L. Homem, D. Homem, Luís, Dourado and Lavanha, insert also a *Polimbam* in the north-east of Java. Pires knew better.

[1] Near the west end of Banka island rises the Menumbing or Monopin hill (455 metres); this conspicuous elevation appears for the first time on Rodrigues' map (fol. 30) as *monõpim*.

[2] *Champana*, from the Malay *sampan*, is a small East Indian craft.

or twelve junks would come to Malacca every year [laden with] white rice and many good vegetables, and this rice is the chief merchandise. They also have many slaves for merchandise; they have plenty of cotton; they have rattans in large quantities; they have some gold, a great deal of rice in the husk; they have pitch, iron; they have a great deal of wax, honey, many wines, meats; they even bring an infinite quantity of garlic and onions, which are good merchandise; they have a great deal of black benzoin in large quantities, which is used in *Bonuaquelim* and in Macassar (*Marcaçar*), *Tanjompura* and in the other islands.

In Palembang they use a large amount of clothing of the coarse [kind] from the Gujaratees and from the Kling. They spend all the money they get for the merchandise in Malacca, as well as what they bring in gold, as all those who come to Malacca do; they load up with merchandise taking a large quantity of Kling clothing.

Islands which form the channel. In front of Siak the islands of Pulo Pisang (*Piçã*); in front of Kampar the islands of Karimun (*Carimam*) and the Selat (*Çelates*) and Kundur (*Sabam*). These produce a few foodstuffs and are inhabited. Opposite *Capitam*[1] the islands of Buaya; opposite Indragiri the islands of Linga (*Lingua*).

As I have already said of the islands of Linga in [the account of] the lands under the jurisdiction of the kingdom of Malacca, they are thickly populated; they have a king; they are perfect knights; they have up to forty lancharas; they have many *lancarias*[2]; Linga has apothecary's lignaloes ; it has a great deal
Fol. 145r. of rice and foodstuffs; the land is good, | it defends itself against enemies. This [king] is like a king of the Celates. He is feared and powerful—more than Kampar; the land is similar; his country has some trade. These islands must have four or five

[1] It is possible that the river Kateman, which in fact debouches in front of Pulo Buaya, corresponds to *Capitam*; or perhaps this is simply another spelling of *Campocan*.

[2] *Lancarias* or *lançarias*, from *lança*, may mean lancers. However, there is a fruit-tree in the East Indies called *lanceira* (*Lansium domesticum*). Further, Orta (XXIV) refers to the *lancuaz* that is found in Java. This is the *Alpinia gaianga* Willd., the Greater or Java-galangal. But this could hardly be Pires' *lancarias*, as in his later letter of 27 Jan. 1516 he refers to the *galanga* and its countries of origin, without mentioning either the name *lancuaz* or any of the East Indies regions.

thousand men, and from the point of them opposite the islands of Buaya lies the channel to Pahang and Bintang (*Byntã*) and to Siam and all these other parts.

And in front of Tongkal are the three islands which are called *Calantiga*. These are desert and have no inhabitants; they have good water.

And in front [of Jambi] the islands of Berhala are also uninhabited. Some Celates sometimes take shelter there; they have plenty of water.

And in front of the first land of Palembang [are] the islands of *Monomby*. These islands are as thickly populated as Linga, and they are to some extent subject to *Pate Unus*, but not entirely. They have mandarins; they have a great many lancharas; they have apothecary's lignaloes; they have wax and honey; they have many foodstuffs in plenty. *Monomby* and Banka are all one land which belong to *Pate Unus* of Japara (*Japera*). Beyond *Monomby* in front of the latter part of Palembang are the islands of Banka. These have a *pate*; they belong to *Pate Unus*, a Javanese Moor. These islands have about a thousand inhabitants; they used to have seven or eight thousand. They have apothecary's lignaloes; they have wax, honey, iron, cotton; they have many foodstuffs.

In front of Tana Malaio is the island which is called Lucipara (*Luçeparij*)[1]. This is at the end of the channel. To the east-north-east of this island it is all islands and shoals, and to the east is the channel to the Moluccas (*Maluqo*), and from the south-west to the east-south-east is Java, and from the south-west to the east is the kingdom of Sunda; and from Lucipara to the first land of Java, which will lie to the east-south-east or to the south-east, will be a hundred and twenty leagues to the first land to be reached in Java and the island of Mandelika (*Mandalica*), which is over against the land of Japara (*Jarapara*), three or four leagues from the port of *Pate Unus*. If I am not very accurate in this chapter I refer to the [proper] chapters, so as not to digress. Our ships can go from Lucipara to the land of Japara in three days and nights with a monsoon wind.

[1] *Luçeparij*—Lucipara. Rodrigues' map (fol. 30) has *nuçapare* (*Mas Pari* in Malay).

Tana Malaio[1]. At the end of the land of Palembang is the land which is called *Tana Malaio*. It has the islands of Lucipara in front of it, and there are two channels formed with this island: one on the Palembang side, and another better one against the islands of Banka. And this land borders on the land of Sekampung. This land has a *pate*; it has a great deal of cotton; it has rattans, pitch; it has many foodstuffs in plenty; it has some gold. They say that *Paramiçura*, the founder of Malacca, came from this land, as has already been said.

Land of Sekampung (Çacampom)[2]. Now we begin to round the island almost in a westerly direction. Sekampung is a large country. It has on one side the land which is called *Tana Malaio* and on the other Tulang Bawang. This country is plenteous; it has a *pate*; he trades in Sunda and in Java; and this country's trade with Sunda is large. They say that it is in sight of Sunda. This country has a great abundance of cotton; it has a little gold; it has plenty of honey, wax, pitch, rattans; it has some pepper, and good they say; it has plenty of rice, meat, fish, wines, fruit. According to what they say, this *pate* is a *Cafre*, and his people are. | *Fol. 145v.* In the hinterland they are *Cafres*, as it is certain that they are almost all heathen in the hinterland of Sumatra, and they are not subject to anyone. They cross to Java in three days in lancharas, and they say that they go to the land of Sunda in one day.

Land of Tulang Bawang (Tulimbavam).[3] The land of Tulang Bawang borders on Sekampung on

[1] *Tana malaio* or *Tana Malayu* means the Malay country. Ferrand seems to decide on 'l'identité de l'ancien Malayu et du Minankabaw actuel. Plus vraisemblablement encore, le Minankabaw était l'État souverain de l'ancien royaume de Malayu dont faisait également partie Palemban. . .' *Malaka, le Malayu et Malayur*, II, 79. According to Pires' account, *Tana-Malayu* corresponds to the south-eastern part of the present Palembang Residency

[2] *Çacampom* corresponds to Sungi Sekampung (Lat. 5° 35′ S.) 'the largest stream of the south-east coast of Sumatra' southward of Tanjong Sekopong (Lat. 4° 56′ S.), 'a rounded prominent point'. *China Sea Pilot*, II. Lavanha's map of Java in his first edition (1615) of Barros' *Decada Quarta da Asia*, shows the south-east corner of Sumatra, where *Çacampã* is situated south of *Palimbã*. Actually the coast runs due south, not almost 'in a westerly direction' as Pires asserts.

[3] *Tulimbavam* corresponds to the Tulang Bawang (Lat. 4° 24′ S.), about the largest river on this coast northward of Sekopong. Thus it is necessary to alter the relative situation of the names, because Pires placed *Tulimbavam* south of *Çacampom*. This is confirmed when he says that *Çacampom* 'is in

one side and on the other on Andalas; in the hinterland it is bounded by *Cafre* kings. They say that this one is also a heathen or *Cafre*. This country has pepper; it has gold and the things that Sekampung has; it has lancharas, it has many foodstuffs; it has large rivers in its lands, where its villages are. In these places it is a strong country, because there is only one fathom of water at the entrance of the rivers. They trade in Java and in Sunda, and they do not trade with them in their own country; they take their merchandise there. They have a large quantity of cotton and from here they cross to Java in two days.

Land of the kingdom of Andalas (Amdallor)[1].

The kingdom of Andalas is bounded on one side by the land of Tulang Bawang and on the other by the rich kingdom of Priaman, and in the hinterland by the kings of Menangkabau. In front of it, a day and a night's journey away, it has the land of Sunda, and between Andalas and Sunda is the sea; and the Gujaratees used to come over this to Java and to Grisee (*Agracy*) to take in cargoes of cloves, nutmeg, mace, and white sandalwood, cubeb, etc., because they said that it was all shallows and banks between this Andalas and Sunda and that it was not navigable—that is what they told us—which is not so, because it is deep and easily navigable and it always used to be navigated by the Gujaratees before Malacca collected their merchandise where they all gathered together; and then the Gujaratees ceased making this voyage, although navigation with the monsoon was good, because they came in by Sunda and ran along the coast of Chi Manuk (*Chemano*) and *Pemano*, Cherimon (*Chorobam*), all along the land of Demak (*Demaa*) and Japara, and they turned

sight of Sunda', and that from *Çacampom* they cross to Sunda in one day, and from Tulang Bawang to Java they cross in two days.

[1] *Andallor* must be a transcriber's mistake for *andallos*, or *andalaz*, as rightly written before. According to Pires' account, the coast of *Andalaz* was the northern shore of the Sunda Strait. *Andelis* or *Tanah Andalas* (Land of Andalas) was the name given by several early writers to the south-east part of Sumatra, where there are still two places called Andalas, or even to the whole island. Ferrand, *Malaka*, 1, 455, 456, 483. In the centre of Menangkabau, West Coast Residency, there is a village Andalas (Lat. 0° 55′ S., Long. 100° 54′ E.). On L. Homem's map of 1554, in the southernmost part of Sumatra, there is written *andrelas*, which undoubtedly is a mistake for *andalas* or Pires' *Andalaz*; D. Homem's atlas of 1558 also has *andrelas* and Vaz Dourado's atlases have *amdrelhas*, but farther north.

towards Tuban[1] and from there to Grisee, all of which they did with one wind.

Kingdom of Priaman (Pyramã)[2].

From the kingdom of Andalas I follow round the land, veering to the north-west until I reach the islands of the *Gamispola* group, and where it begins to turn, the land shows us the kingdom of Priaman. Priaman is bounded on one side by Andalas and on the other by Tico, and in the hinterland by Menangkabau. This is a heathen kingdom and the king is a heathen. Three kingdoms join together here on this coast, to wit, Priaman, Tico and *Panfur* or *Panchur* or Baros. All these are rich, and the Gujaratees come here every year with one ship, or two or three, with merchandise. They dispose of it and take away their return [loads] as will be told when we finish speaking of these three kingdoms. The kingdom of Priaman has many horses, which they go and sell continuously in the kingdom of Sunda.

This land of Priaman has plenty of gold, apothecary's lign-aloes, camphor of two kinds, benzoin, silk, wax, honey; it has foodstuffs in plenty for its own land; it does a great trade with the land of Sunda.

Land of the kingdom of Tico (Tiguo)[3].

The kingdom of Tico (*Tiquo*) joins on to Priaman on one side and on the other it joins on to the land and kingdom of *Panchur*;

[1] CHEMANO—The Chi Manuk River that debouches on the north coast of Java. Barros (IV, i, xii), says that this river *Chiamo* or *Chenano* divided Java into two parts, like a channel, from north to south, and it was represented accordingly on Lavanha's map of Java.

PEMANO—Perhaps Pasuruan, on the north coast of Java, Madura Strait, which Lavanha's map represents as *Panian*.

CHORABAM—Cherimon, a place on the north coast of Java, which appears for the first time on the map of *c.* 1540 as *cherbom*.

DEMA and JAPARA—Places on the mid north coast of Java. The map of *c.* 1540 has the two names for the first time, but *dema*, or modern Demak, is wrongly situated east of Japara. *Japara* is found for the first time on Rodrigues' map (fol. 30)—*gepara lugar de pate Nuz*—as well as in one of the Rodrigues' drawings of Java (fol. 108)—*Japara porto de pate Nauz*.

TUBAM—Tuban, a port eastward of Japara. *Tubam* on Rodrigues' maps (fol. 30) and drawings (fol. 103).

[2] Priaman river, harbour and town are situated about the middle of the west coast of Sumatra. *Prim* on L. Homem's map of 1554 and *Priamão* on Berthelot's map of 1635.

[3] The roadstead and town of Tico or Tiku are situated on the west coast of Sumatra (Lat. 0° 25′ N.), where the river of the same name debouches. L. Homem's map of 1554 has *ticos*; *Tico* on Eredia's map, and in the atlas of *c.* 1615–23.

in the hinterland it joins on to the land of Menangkabau. They say that the king is a heathen, and others say that he is a Moor. This [kingdom] has the merchandise we mentioned for Priaman, which *Pansur* also (?) has. This kingdom has many people and does a great trade with the Gujaratees.

Fol. 146r

Kingdom of Baros (Barus)[1].

It now falls to us to speak of the very rich kingdom of Baros, which is also called *Panchur* or *Pansur*. The Gujarat people call it *Panchur*, and so do the Persians, Arabians, Kling, Bengalees, etc. Sumatra calls it Baros (*Baruũs*). It is all one kingdom, not two. It is bounded by Tico on one side and on the other by the land of the kingdom of Singkel; in the interior it has its dealings with the Menangkabaus, and in front of it, in the sea, it has the island of Nias (*Minhac Barras*), about which we will speak.

This kingdom is at the head of the trade in these things in all the island of Sumatra, because this is the port of call through which the gold goes, and the silk, benzoin, camphor in quantities, apothecary's lignaloes, wax, honey, and other things in which this kingdom is more plentiful than any of the others described up to now. Benzoin from Baros, Tico and Priaman is plenteous in the island of Sumatra and very white.

These three kingdoms we have described, to wit, *Panchur*, Tico, and Priaman, are the key to the land of Menangkabau, both because they are all related, and because they possess the sea coast, so that the Gujaratees come there every year and do a great trade; and all the merchandise is gathered together in these kingdoms and they do their trade with the said Gujaratees. One, two or three ships come every year; they sell all their clothing, and take in a great deal of gold and silk, much benzoin, much lignaloes, camphor of two kinds—a great deal of the edible kind—much wax, much honey. The Gujaratees dispose of all this merchandise because it is made up of goods consumed

[1] The once famous port of Barus or Baros, on the north-west coast of Sumatra, is today an unimportant place, though healthy and the permanent residence of a government representative. L. Homem's map of 1554 has *bairos* and D. Homem's atlas of 1558 has *baros*, the latter form occurring on other later maps. It appears as *Fansur* in the *Mohit*. G. Schlegel says that '*Fansur* or *Pantsur* represents the Malay name *Pantjur*, water gushing out of a *pantjuran*, a gutter or aqueduct'. '*Fansur* is the Arab pronunciation of the Malay *pantjur*'. *Op. cit.*, pp. 9 and 79.

in the country, and the people are many, and it goes from there to Sunda and to the Maldive (*Díua*) Islands,—because the Maldive Islands reach to opposite Sunda, and go on along the whole of Sumatra on the western side up to *Gamispola* and up to Cannanore, and from these parts they go to the Maldive Islands in five days, according to the statements of the merchants who sail from the Maldives (?)

So having done their trade the Gujaratees return wealthy, and they sell and trade as they will. The pilots say that the route from Baros to Sunda is not very clean, and that up to Baros it is clean all along close to the land. I went behind this island a matter of fifteen leagues, and close to the land we found twenty-five fathoms.

Island which is called Nias (Maruz Minhac)[1].

In front of the kingdom of Baros is this island which is called Nias. It has many people; it has fish oil and a great deal of dried fish and rice. They say that opposite to Priaman there is an island [*blank*][2] where there are only women and they have no men, and that they are got with child by others who go there to trade and who go away again at once and that others are made pregnant by the wind. This opinion is held by the people of these parts, in the same way as the enchanted queen in the hill of Malacca called Gunong Ledang (*Gulom Leydam*).[3] The

[1] In front of Baros lies Nias, the largest of the islands off the west coast of Sumatra. Marsden says that 'on the western side of Nias, and very near it, is a cluster of small islands, called P^{0}. Nako-nako [Naku Archipelago], whose inhabitants are of a race termed Maros'. *History of Sumatra*, p. 478. The native name for the island of Nias is *Tano-niha* (land of the people). It seems as if *Maros* and *Tano-niha* are combined in Pires' *Maruz Mjnhac* or *Mjnhac Maruz*. The *Mohit* (p. 71) refers to the many islands named *Mîcâmârôs*, lying off the north-west coast of Sumatra, which clearly correspond to Pires' *Mjnhac Maruz*. One of Eredia's maps (fol. 24v.) has *Pulomâs*, though south of the equator, and Berthelot's map has *P.miaes*.

[2] This must be Siberut, the largest and northernmost of the Mentawei Islands. Pigafetta tells a similar story: 'Our oldest pilot told us that in an island called Ocoloro, which lies below Java Major, there are found no persons but women, and that they become pregnant from the wind.' Robertson's edition, II, 169–71. Marsden says that in south-eastern Sumatra 'they believed the inhabitants of the island *Engano* to be all females, who were impregnated by the wind'. *The History of Sumatra*, p. 297. Yule refers to this very old fable and suggests that Pigafetta's *Ocoloro* and *Engano* are perhaps the same. *Marco Polo*, II, 406.

[3] *Gulom leydam* corresponds to Eredia's *monte de Gunoledam*, 'a lofty mountain, about half a league (9022 feet) high, a little more than a league around the base, and quite isolated', where, 'according to the Malay fable,

people believe in this, as others believe in the Amazons and the Sybil of Rome.

Kingdom of Singkel (Quinchell)[1].

The kingdom of Singkel is bounded on one side by the kingdom of Baros[2] and on the other by the kingdom of Melabah (*Mancopa*) or *Daya*, and in the interior by strong, savage, bestial people who eat men. This king is a heathen. This [kingdom] has benzoin, silk, some pepper, a little gold; it has small lancharas; it has rivers; it is not a very rich affair. They say that throughout this kingdom they eat men who are enemies. They trade here from Pase and in the kingdoms of Baros, Tico, Priaman.

Fol. 146v.

Kingdom of Melabah (Mancopa).

The kingdom of *Mancopa* or *Daya*[3] (it has both these names) is bounded on one side by Singkel and on the other side it goes almost as far as the islands hard by the land of *Lambri*. This king is a heathen. In the interior it is bounded by [land inhabited by] strong brutal people of the mountains range that goes above Pase and Pedir. This king's country is large. Inside the country he is a powerful warrior king. The enemies they capture they eat. They trade there from Pase and Pedir. They do not eat [all] men, only those with whom they are at war. This [kingdom] has silk, benzoin and things from that part. Those who go there go in small *parãos*. They bring cloths from Cambay of the coarse [kind].

Kingdoms of Menangkabau (Menancabo).

And since the account of the whole of the island of Sumatra all around is now done in accordance with the promise [in the account of its] first country, it would not look well now to leave

that Queen *Putry*, companion of *Permicuri*, who founded Malacca, withdrew into retirement, and there by magic art remained immortal to the present day' (fol. 32). *Putri* means a princess. Two of Eredia's maps (fols. 11 and 13) have *Gunoledam Monte*, correctly situated. This is Mount Ophir (Gunong Ledang = the huge mountain), 4187 feet high, just north-east of Malacca.

[1] *Quinchell*, or *chinquele* as written before—The Singkel River debouches on the north-west coast of Sumatra, near Singkel roadstead and Singkel point. Berthelot's map has *Senquil*.

[2] Although in the MS it is written *Pão*, this is obviously a transcriber's mistake.

[3] *Mancopa* corresponds to Melabah, a port and point on the north-west coast of Sumatra (Lat. 2° 46′ N.). Barros says that when Diogo Pacheco went to discover the *Ilhas do Ouro*, he sailed around the north of Sumatra towards *Baros*, and arrived in front of the 'Kingdom of *Daya*, which would be some twenty leagues from that of *Achem*, which is towards the west on the point of the Island' (III, iii, 3).

the kings of Menangkabau without speaking of them, because they are favoured with gold, the metal which God chose.

The kings of Menangkabau are three. The chief one is called *Raja Çunci Teras*, which is the place where he resides; the second is called *Raja Bandar*, brother of the king already mentioned; the third is called *Raja Bonço* or *Buũs*[1]. These are the kings of Menangkabau. The first they say has been a Mohammedan for a short time—almost fifteen years; the [other] two they say are still heathens. These often quarrel, and there is war between them most of the time.

Neighbouring ports of Menangkabau and what land is called Menangkabau.

On the Malacca side, beginning at the land of Arcat up to Jambi, the land is called Menangkabau, although it is more properly the hinterland, and on the other side of the island of Sumatra, towards the south, are Priaman, Tico and *Panchur*. All the gold in the land of Menangkabau goes out through these ports, and without doubt the most important part of the whole island is here, where the gold is found, whether there is little or much in the whole island (?). From Arcat to Jambi and from Priaman to Baros or *Panchur*, with the three kings of Menangkabau, is more properly called the land of Menangkabau.

Places and gold mines in the land of Menangkabau.

The chief mine from which the most gold is obtained, and the largest, is the country through which the river called *Çuencynjgujs* flows; and the second, where it is found more in powder, is called *Marapãlaguj*.[2] They say that all the three abovementioned kings can collect from one mine and the other, which

[1] The two chief mines mentioned by Pires below were situated in a region where the gold mines of Sumatra are in greater number to-day. This corresponds better to Pires' location of Menangkabau (between Arcat, Jambi, Priaman and Baros). It seems that the three places connected by Pires with the names of the kings of Menangkabau may be: Sungidaras (0° 12′ S.—100° 20′ E.), Bandarpitiak (0° 25′ N.—100° 30′ E.) and Banjol (0° 3′ S.—100° 13′ E.).

[2] ÇUENCYNJGUJS—Besides the volcano Soenggirik (Lat. 1° S.), there is, well in the hinterland of Menangkabau, a small river, the Si Njnje, a tributary of the Kampar, which might suggest Pires' *Çuençynjgujs*.

MARAPÃLAGUJ—The names of many places in Menangkabau begin with the word *Muara* or *Mora*, which means confluence or mouth of a river. Combined with other words it designates some place situated at the mouth of a river, or even the name of a district or region. There is a Muara (Lat. 1° 1′ S., Long. 100° 56′ E.) at the confluence of a small stream with the river Palanghi, a tributary of the Indragiri, in the mountainous hinterland of Menangkabau, westward of the volcano Soenggirik.

is a law of the land, and that no Moor may go to the mines. Only the heathen lords have the mines and they have the gold and from there it is distributed to the kings of Menangkabau, and from the three kings it is distributed to others, and [as for] the amount of gold which is obtained from the said mines every year, they say that they get two bahars of gold, and more according to the Moors.

Sea in the land of Menangkabau.

Those who have already been in the land of Menangkabau say that there is a sea of fresh water, which must be six leagues round and two leagues across, and that there are many villages round it and that they sail on the said sea, and that this sea is formed of water that comes from a large mountain range, and that there is good fishing in it and that the fish goes bad a short time after they have caught it, and that this lake is under the jurisdiction of all three kings.

Fol. 147r.

Measure around the island of Sumatra.

According to what they say, it appears correct that the island of Sumatra is seven hundred leagues round, beginning from the islands of *Gamispola* until you get back to them, going round as we have said, and there is no doubt that it has the said seven hundred leagues and more[1].

There are many heathen kings in the island of Sumatra and many lords in the hinterland, but, as they are not trading people and known, no mention is made of them. From here onwards we will speak of the island of Java and Sunda and we will proceed with the account of them in this order.

It must not be forgotten that this island of Sumatra has so many inhabitants that large quantities of clothes from the Kling and Gujaratees are used there, and when things were in the order they used to be, they all came to Malacca mostly to bring the merchandise from the whole island and to take the cloth and other merchandise to their own countries according to the custom of each.

[1] Barbosa (II, 181) and Castanheda (II, cxi) say that 'Çamatra is 700 leagues in circuit as reckoned by the Moors who sail round it on both sides'. No doubt Pires' information is from a similar Arab or Malay source. Seven hundred leagues, i.e. 2,240 miles or 4,144 kilometres, is a surprisingly accurate reckoning for that time. The circuit of the island is estimated at 2300 miles. Marco Polo had said already that 'it has a compass of two thousand miles or more'.

[JAVA]

Description and account of the prosperous and proud and rich and chivalrous island of Java and Sunda—what can be known of them.

The account will begin with the kingdom of Sunda and from there we will end at Blambangan (*Bulambuam*), which is the end of the known lands which have *pates*, and after we have spoken about the lords who live on the sea coast, we will then speak of the great heathen king within the hinterland of Java and of his chief captain *Guste Pate*, and we will start by telling what is known of the kingdom of Sunda.

These are the lands of Java which have *pates*, lords and governors, and now as for Sunda.

[*Sunda*] First the king of *Çumda* with his great city of *Dayo*, the town and lands and port of Bantam, the port of Pontang (*Pomdam*), the port of *Cheguide*, the port of *Tamgaram*, the port of *Calapa*, the port of Chi Manuk (*Chemano*); this is Sunda, because the river of Chi Manuk is the limit of both kingdoms.

Now comes Java and we must speak of the king within the hinterland.

The land of Cherimon (*Cheroboam*), the land of *Japura*, the land of Losari (*Locarj*), the land of Tegal (*Teteguall*), the land of Samarang (*Camaram*), the land of Demak (*Demaa*), Tidunan (*Tidumar*), the land of Japara, the land of Rembang (*Ramee*), the land of Tuban (*Tobam*), the land of Sidayu (*Cedayo*), the land of Grisee (*Agacij*), the land of Surabaya (*Curubaya*), the land of *Gamda*, the land of Blambangan, the land of Pajarakan (*Pajarucam*), the land of *Camtã*, the land of Panarukan (*Panaruncã*), the land of *Chamdy*, and when this is ended we will speak of the great island of Madura[1].

Measurement of the land of Sunda. Some people affirm that the kingdom of Sunda take up half of the whole island of Java; others, to whom more authority is attributed, say that the kingdom of Sunda must be a third part of the island and an eighth more. They say that the island of Sunda is three hundred leagues round. It ends at the river Chi

[1] Pires does not keep his promise, because he only speaks of Madura much later, at the end of the account of all the islands of the Eastern Archipelago.

Manuk. They say that from the earliest times God divided the island of Java from that of Sunda and that of Sunda from that of Java by the said river, which has trees from one end to the other, and they say the trees on each side lean over to each country with the branches on the ground, large trees and beautifully tall.

The king of Sunda is a heathen and [so are] all the lords of his kingdom. Sunda is [land of] chivalrous, seafaring warriors—they say more so than the Javanese, taking them all in all. They are men of goodly figure, swarthy, robust men. The king's son inherits the kingdom, and when there is no legitimate son it is by election of the great ones of the kingdom. It is the custom in Sunda for the king's wives and nobles to burn themselves when he dies; and so when anyone of lower rank dies in his house the same thing is done, that is, if they wish to do so, not because the women are persuaded by words to die, only those who want to do it of their own accord. And those who do not are Beguines[1] leading a life apart and people do not marry them. Others marry three or four times. These few are outcasts in the land.

Fol. 147v.

King and people of Sunda.

The land of Sunda has as much as four thousand horses which come there from Priaman and other islands to be sold. It has up to forty elephants; these are for the king's array. The kingdom of Sunda is justly governed; they are true men. The people of the sea coast get on well with the merchants in the land. They are accustomed to trade. These people of Sunda very often come to Malacca to trade. They bring cargo lancharas, ships of a hundred and fifty tons. Sunda has up to six junks and many lancharas of the Sunda kind, with masts like a crane (?), and steps between each so that they are easy to navigate.

After the king of Sunda, who is called *Samg Briamg*, and his viceroy, who is called *Cocunam*, and after his Bendahara, who is called *Mãcobumj*, in the country, there come the lords captains of cities and places and ports. As in Java the lords are called

[1] *Beguinas*, which may be translated as Beguines, does not necessarily mean women belonging to some religious order or community. In Pires' time the word also meant women living in poverty and penance. However, Barros says: 'As to the married (Javanese) women, when their husbands die, they must die with them, as a point of honour; and if they fear to die, then they must retire as nuns in their convents (the kind that existed in Java).' IV, i, 12. See Pires' description of the '*Tapas* of Java', p. 177.

pates; in the language of Sunda they are called *paybou*: for instance, so-and-so *paybou* of such and such a place, because the language of Sunda is not that of Java, nor that of Java of Sunda, although it is only one island which is divided by the river Chi Manuk. [It is] very narrow in places, but the land is joined and all one island, and it has the said division which cuts it and runs through it so that it is in two, but anyone who was in the country would see this, because in places the branches of the outermost trees touch each other.

City where the king is.

The city where the king is most of the year is the great city of *Dayo*[1]. The city has well-built houses of palm leaf and wood. They say that the king's house has three hundred and thirty wooden pillars as thick as a wine cask, and five fathoms high, and beautiful timberwork on the top of the pillars, and a very well-built house. This city is two days' journey from the chief port, which is called *Calapa*. The king is a great sportsman and hunter. His country contains stags without number, pigs, bullocks. They do this most of the time. The king has two chief wives from his own kingdom and up to a thousand concubines. The people of Sunda are said to be truthful.

Merchandise of the kingdom of Sunda.

It has a certain amount of better pepper than that from Cochin—up to a thousand bahars a year; it has a great deal of long pepper; it has enough tamarinds to load a thousand ships;

[1] Barros says that 'The principal town of this kingdom (Sunda) is called *Daio*, situated a little in the interior' (IV, i, 12), and it is represented in this position on Lavanha's map of Java. L. Homem's map of 1554 and D. Homem's atlas of 1558 have *chodaio* next after it, and eastward of *Sunda calapa* (Batavia); Dourado's atlases have *odaio* similarly situated. Crawfurd says: 'What place Daio was, if such place existed at all, it is impossible to conjecture, as no place resembling it occurs in Javanese topography.' *Dictionary, s.v.* Sunda. But according to Pires' account, *Daio* or *Dayo* was situated somewhere about the place where Buitenzorg stands today, twelve miles westward of which there is a hill called Dahoe (939 metres). Veth asserts 'We undoubtedly recognize in (Barros') *Daio* the Sundanese word for city, i.e. *dajuh*. By it no other city can be meant than Padjadjaran'. *Java*, I, 278–9. However, the second map at the end of this volume of Veth's work has *Dajuh* on the very spot where the modern Buitenzorg is situated—twenty-eight miles due south of Batavia. According to Crawfurd, 'Pajajaran is the name of an ancient kingdom of Java, the capital of which was situated in the Sunda district of Bogor, about forty miles east of Jacatra or Batavia. The site is indicated by the foundations of a palace, and by a monumental stone'. *Dictionary, s.v.* Pajajaran.

it trades chiefly in male and female slaves who are natives of the country | as well as others they bring from the Maldive islands, because they can get from Sunda to the Maldive islands in six or seven days. Their chief merchandise is rice. Sunda also has gold of eight *mates*[1] proof. It has a great many coarse cloths of its own kind, which also come to Malacca. *Fol. 148r*

There is rice that Sunda can sell, up to ten junkloads a year, unlimited vegetables, countless meats, pigs, goats, sheep, cows in large quantities; it has wines; it has fruits; it is as plentiful as Java; and they often come from Sunda to Java to sell rice and foodstuffs, and two or three junks come from Malacca to Sunda every year for slaves, rice, and pepper, and *pangajavas* come from Sunda to Malacca every year with the said merchandise, and take the following back to Sunda: *Food-stuffs.*

They buy white sinabaffs, both large and small, *synhavas*, *pachauelezẽs*, *balachos*, *atobalachos* (these are white cloths). They buy Kling cloths, *enrolados* of large and small *ladrilho* which are then marketable, and they buy much. They buy pachak, catechu and seeds from Cambay. They buy *bretangis* and clothes from Cambay, *turias*, *tiricandies*, *caydes*[2] in quantities. A great deal is *Merchandise of value in the kingdom of Sunda.*

[1] *Mate*—A touch or test of gold used in the East.

[2] BALACHOS and ATOBALACHOS—In his description of Negapatam, Pedro Barreto de Resende says that there were in the country 'Many cloths, printed as well as white, and of every kind, and cheap; the white ones are called *enrrollados*, which are thin like *bofetas*; *ballachos*, *cotonias* of two threads; and the printed ones, many sorts of *tafessiras* of cotton thread, *sarasas* and many other sorts of them'. *Livro do Estado da India*, fol. 321r. See Dalgado, *s.v.* Bofetá, Cotonias, Tafecira, Saraça. *Cotonias* were 'some kind of piece goods, apparently either of silk or mixed silk and cotton' (*Hobson-Jobson*, *s.v.* Cuttanee), among which were the *balachos* and *atobalachos*. Weaving is still one of the chief industries of Choromandel.

LADRILHO is a Portuguese word meaning 'tile', or 'little square' or 'squares'. *Enrolados de ladrilho* must mean chequered *enrolados*, or chequered woollen cloths. See note p. 93. Dalgado records the word *Ludrilho*, meaning perhaps a 'raw or coarse cloth', mentioned in a document of 1601 referring to Mozambique. *Ludrilho* may be a simple corruption of *Ladrilho*.

BRETANGIS—Cotton cloths (blue, black or red) formerly exported from Cambay. Dalgado, *s.v.* Bertangi.

TURIAS, TIRICANDIES, CAYDES—'*Turundam*, said by the weavers to mean "a kind of cloth for the body", the name being derived from the Arabic word *turuk* "a kind", and the Persian one *undam* "the body", is a muslin which was formerly imported, under the name of *terendam*, into this country'. J. A. Taylor, *A Descriptive and Historical Account of the Cotton Manufacture of*

used there and bought for gold. Areca, rosewater and things like that are bought in Sunda.

Coinage of Sunda. For small money, cash from China. They are pierced through the middle like *ceitis*, so that they can be threaded in hundreds. Every thousand is worth five Malacca *calais*; for large money native gold of eight *mates* proof is current, which is worth three hundred *calais* (which are nine cruzados) the *tumdaya*[1] (which is fifteen drams well weighed).

Ports of Sunda. Bantam[2]. The kingdom of Sunda has its ports. The first is the port of Bantam. Junks anchor in this port. It is [a] trading [port]. There is a good city on the river. The city has a captain, a very important person. This port trades with the Maldive islands and with the island of Sumatra on the *Panchur* side. This port is almost the most important of all; a river empties there by the sea. It has a great deal of rice and foodstuffs and pepper.

The port of Pontang (Pomdãg)[3]. The second port in the said kingdom of Sunda, going towards Japara, is Pontang, which is already a lesser port than Bantam. It has a great town. The people who trade with the ports mentioned above trade in this port. This port is on a river on the sea. They say that junks anchor there and that it is a trading port. It has rice, foodstuffs and pepper.

Dacca, in Bengal, p. 46. London, 1851. Apud Yule, *Hobson-Jobson, s.v.* Piece-goods (Terindams). *Tiricamdis* may correspond to the '*tucamdya nylora*, which are green and red cloths ornamented with painted birds', and *Caydes* may correspond to the '*candya azares*, which are thick cloths from Khorasans (*Coraçones*)', of the *Lembrança de Cousas da India em 1525*, p. 49.

[1] When referring to the currency minted by order of Albuquerque in Malacca, the *Comentários* say: 'the opinion which found favour with everyone was that the gold coin should weigh a quarter of a *tundia*, which is worth among us a thousand *reis*'. (III, xxxii). As at that time the *cruzado* was worth 400 *reis*, the value of 9 *cruzados*, or 3,600 *reis*, mentioned by Pires' is not far from the 4,000 *reis* of the *Comentários*. Farther on, Pires refers to 'The Java *tundaia* or tael'.

[2] Barros mentions *Bantam*, and Lavanha, editor of the first edition of the Fourth *Decada*, gives some particulars in a marginal note about this port and town which he calls both *Bantã* and *Banta*. (IV, 8, xii). In *Livro de Marinharia*, p. 251, it is called *Sumdabãta* and *Sumdabamta*. It appears distinctly for the first time as *banta* on L. Homem's map of 1554.

[3] The eastern extremity of Bantam bay is formed by the delta of the Pontang River, and a few miles inland there is the village of Pontang. Though well known to the Portuguese and mentioned by Barros as *Pondang* (IV, i, 12), it appears for the first time on Lavanha's map, as *Pondang*, and on Berthelot's map as *Pontan*.

The third, going in the direction mentioned, is the port of *Chegujde*. This port also has a town and a good one. Those we have mentioned trade there, and Priaman, Andalas, Tulang Bawang, Sekampung and other places. Junks anchor there. It has an important captain. It has rice, vegetables, pepper, many foodstuffs.

The port of Chegujde[1].

The fourth port is that of *Tamgara*. It is a port like the above. It has a goodly town and trade. It has a captain. It is a trading place like all the above mentioned. It has the things the other have.

The port of Tamgara[2].

[1] In his enumeration of the Sunda ports Barros places *Cheguide* between *Tangaram* and *Pondang*. IV, i, 12. Crawfurd says that Barros' *Cheguide* is 'probably meant for Chitarum, "indigo or blue river".' *Dictionary*, p. 422. But the Chitarum River debouches at the eastern end of Batavia Bay, and according to Pires' enumeration *Cheguide* was situated much more to the west, before *Calapa* (Batavia), as it also appears on Lavanha's map. The old Portuguese rutter from Malacca to Sunda says, very accurately, that 'sailing from *Pomta de Charnão* (Tanjong Pontang) eight leagues (twenty-five and a half miles) due east you will find an island (Middelberg), and I will not mention the many more, farther out to sea;... two or three leagues east-south-east you will see other islands, and proceeding towards the land you will see a point (Tanjong Pasir or Untung Java) made by the land of Java, and on it a very long bank, and you will continue along it. At this point a river comes out into the sea, and there Francisco de Sá erected a *padrão* (see note on *Calapa*, below) for the king of Portugal on 30 June 1527, and he gave to this river, where he put this *padrão*, the name of *rio de Sã Jorge*, and the negroes call it *Çidigy*'. Then, three leagues beyond a small island, is the port of *Sunda-calapa*. *Livro de Marinharia*, pp. 251–2. This river *Çidigy*, or the Chi Sadane —'the only river (between Tanjong Kait and Tanjong Pasir) of any importance, which enters the sea by five months', according to the Admiralty *Pilot* —must be Pires' *Cheguide*. One of the main branches of the Chi Sadane, the Muli River, debouches by two mouths exactly where the bank lies which is referred to in the rutter.

[2] There are two places between Pontang and Batavia that may correspond to Pires' *Tamgaram* or *Tamgara*: the village Tangora, on the coast, six miles eastward of Pontang, and Tanara, a place situated one mile inland, on the Chi Durian, a couple of miles further eastwards. The best anchorage is off Tanara, in from two to four fathoms. If one of these places corresponds to Pires' *Tamgaram*, it should have been mentioned before *Cheguide*. Or *Tamgaram* may correspond to Tangerang, an important place eastward of Batavia, eight miles inland on the Chi Sadane, and connected with it by a branch of the Chi Angké, which debouches between *Cheguide* and *Calapa*. To complicate the problem still more, there is a village called Muara Tangerang, one mile inland from the mouths of the Muli River, the branch of the Chi Sadane at the mouth of which was *Cheguide*.

Fol. 148v.

The port of Calapa[1].

The port of *Calapa* is a magnificent port. It is the most important and best of all. This is where the trade is greatest and whither they all sail from Sumatra, and Palembang, *Laue*, *Tamjompura*, Malacca, Macassar, Java and Madura and many other places. These nations trade also in the other ports. This

[1] *Calapa* corresponds to modern Batavia. The map of *c.* 1540 has the following names on the north-west of Java, reading from east to west: *aguada dalaim, Calupu, aguada do padrã, Cumda*; L. Homem's map of 1554 has *aguada de sigide, chodaio, Sunda calapa*; similarly in Diogo Homem's and Vaz Dourado's atlases. On Berthelot's map of 1635 the place is already called *Batavia*. When he enumerates 'the six most remarkable ports of Java', Barros does not mention *Calapa*; in its place he puts '*Xacatara*, also called *Caravam*'. IV, i, 12. *Xacatara* is Jacatra or Jakatra, once the main city of the Hindu-Javanese Empire of Pajajaram; *Caravam* is by Crawfurd identified as 'Krawang, a different place', namely the *carnão* mentioned in *Livro de Marinharia*, p. 252. But Barros in the next chapter refers twice to *Calapa*, without again mentioning *Xacatara* or *Caravam*. In the old rutter, reference is made to 'a port called *Sumdacalapa* and it has a river', the situation of which corresponds to Batavia. *Loc. cit.* In *A brief Description of a Voyage performed by certain Hollanders to & from the East-Indies, with their Adventures and Success (1595–7)*, there is the following statement: 'The chief haven in the island (Java Major) is called Sunda Calapa', and farther on '. . . *Icatra*, a town about 10 leagues from Bantam', '. . .*Icatra* (Jacatra), which is only remarkable for its river, and the country about it very fertile in fruits and provisions. In time past it was called *Sunda Calapa*, which had been a rich town of merchandise, but upon some occasions, and by reason of this hard usage, the merchants had withdrawn themselves from thence; therefore at this present there is little or nothing to do'. *A Collection of Voyages and Travels*, II, 404–13, London 1745. According to Crawfurd (*Dictionary*, p. 44) the site of the old town is that of the old native capital, Sund-Kalapa, or 'Sunda of the coco-palms', called in the polite language, from the Sanskrit, Joyakarta, popularly Jacatra, meaning 'work of victory'. The *Encyclopædie van Nederlandsch-Indië* says that 'the conservative Chinese always mention Batavia as Kalapa, thus keeping the tradition of their forerunners who settled there in the sixteenth century or earlier', *s.v.* Soenda Kalapa. In 1522 the Captain of Malacca, Jorge de Albuquerque, sent a ship under the command of Henrique Leme to a port of Sunda, with a present for the local king and offers of friendship; a treaty was signed on August 21st, and the Portuguese were authorized to build a fortress there, and a *padrão* or pillar was set up on the site chosen for the fortress building. From here certainly comes the *aguada do padrã* (watering-place of the *padrão*) on the *c.* 1540 map; the fact that it is inscribed between the words *Cumda* and *Calupu* shows simply a confusion on the part of the c. 1540 or an earlier cartographer, who may have used more than one different original, giving three place-names to what is in fact one and the same place—*Calapa*. The *agoada de Joham lopes dalluim*, on Rodrigues' map (fol. 30), is the *aguada dalaim* of the *c.* 1540 map and *aguada de sigide* of the other maps, corresponding to Tanjong Sentigi. See Appendix II. *Chodaio*, next to *Sunda calapa*, is perhaps a mispelling for *Ho Daio* (The Daio).

port is two days' journey from the city of *Dayo* where the king is always in residence, so that this is the one to be considered the most important. It is almost joined to the land of Java, except that Chi Manuk is between them, and from Chi Manuk here takes a day and a night with a favourable wind. The merchandise from the whole kingdom comes here to this port. This port is well governed; it has judges, justices, clerks. They say that [it is] already [laid down] in writing [that] whoever does so and so will get so and so by the law of the kingdom. Many junks anchor in this port.

The port of Chi Manuk (Chemano).

The port of Chi Manuk is the sixth port. This is not a port in which junks can anchor, but only at the harbour bar, so they say; others say 'yes'. Many Moors live here. The captain is a heathen. It belongs to the king of Sunda. The end of the kingdom is here. Chi Manuk has good trade. Java also trades with it. It has a good large town.

These lords captains of these ports are very important people. Each of them is much feared and greatly reverenced by the dwellers in the said places. They are great hunters. They spend most of their time in pleasure. They have well caparisoned horses. They vie greatly with the Javanese, and the Javanese with them. They say that the people of Sunda are more valiant than those of Java. These are good men and true, and the Javanese are diabolic, and daring in treacheries and they are proud of the boast of being Javanese.

The people of Sunda and Java are neither friends nor enemies. They keep themselves to themselves. They trade with one another, and also if they meet on the sea as pirates, whoever is better prepared attacks, and so they use here, however great the friendship or relationship between them.

The kingdom of Sunda does not allow Moors in it, except for a few, because it is feared that with their cunning they may do there what has been done in Java; because the Moors are cunning and they make themselves masters of countries by cunning, because apparently they have no power. The kingdom of Sunda is ended. Now we will enter into the kingdom of Java and what I have observed of it will be told.

[*Java.*]

Island of Java all round, beginning at Cherimon (*Choroboam*) up to Blambangan (*Bulambaum*); and first we will speak of the heathen king of the interior and of his chief captain *Guste Pate*, and afterwards of the Moorish *pates* of the sea-coast in order.

They say that the island of Java used to rule as far as the Moluccas (*Maluco*) on the eastern side and [over] a great part of the west; and that it had almost all the island of Sumatra under its dominion and all the islands known to the Javanese, and that it had all this for a long time past until about a hundred years ago, when its power began to diminish until it came to its present state, as will be described below.

It is because of this power and great worth that Java had, and because it navigated to many places and very far away—for they affirm that it navigated to Aden and that its chief trade was in *Bonuaquelim*, Bengal and Pase—that it had the whole | of the trade *Fol. 149r.* at that time. All the navigators were heathens, so that it thus gathered together such great merchants with so much trade along its sea coasts, that nowhere else so large and so rich was known. Some of them were Chinese, some Arabs, Parsees, Gujaratees, Belgalees and of many other nationalities, and they flourished so greatly that Mohammed and his followers determined to introduce their doctrines in the sea-coasts of Java [together] with merchandise.

Land of Java.

The island of Java is a large country, four hundred leagues round, beginning at Chi Manuk and going along the Blambangan side and turning along the other side to the other end. We will not speak of the sea-coast now, but only of the hinterland. It is well shaded country, not marshy but of the same type as Portugal, and very healthy.

The king of Java is a heathen; he is called *Batara Vojyaya*[1]. These kings of Java have a fantastic idea: they say that their nobility has no equal. The Javanese heathen lords are tall and handsome; they are lavishly adorned about their person, and have richly caparisoned horses. They use krises, swords, and lances of many kinds, all inlaid with gold. They are great hunters

[1] *Batara Vojyaya*, or *Batara Vigiaja* as spelt farther on, corresponds to Batara Browijaya. *Browijaya* was one of the titles assumed by the sovereigns of Majapahit, the last Hindu kingdom of Java before the advent of Mohammedanism in the island. At the end of the thirteenth century the Browijaya assumed also the title of Batara, from the Sanskrit *Avatara*, the incarnation. Raffles, *The History of Java*, I, 299, II, 148, 151; Campbell, *Java*, p. 63.

and horsemen—stirrups all inlaid with gold, inlaid saddles, such as are not to be found anywhere else in the world. The Javanese lords are so noble and exalted that there is certainly no nation to compare with them over a wide area in these parts. They have their head shorn—half tonsured—as a mark of beauty, and they always run their hands over their hair from the forehead upwards and not as we do, and they are very proud of this.

The lords of Java are revered like gods, with great respect and deep reverence. The land of Java is thickly peopled in the interior, with many cities, and very large ones, including the great city of *Dayo* where the king is in residence and where his court is. They say that the people who frequent the court are without number. The kings do not show themselves to the people except once or twice in the year. They stay in their palace, like the kings of Cochin in the cave (?), and there they are with all the pleasures and with feasts, with great quantities of wives and concubines. They say that the king of Java has a thousand eunuchs to wait on these women, and these eunuchs are dressed like women and wear their hair dressed in the form of diadems.

And because the Javanese, trusting in themselves and given to this life, have lost a great part of their lands, the kings do not command, nor are they taken into account, but only the viceroy and chief captain, which each of them has; and the one who is ruling now in Java is *Guste Pate*[1], his viceroy and his chief captain. This man is known and honoured like the [real] king. All the lords of Java obey him. Him they honour. This governor commands in every thing; he holds the king of Java in his hands; he orders him to be given food. The king has no voice in any thing, nor is he of any importance. Do not make a gesture towards a Javanese from the navel upwards, nor make as if to touch its head; they kill for this.

The viceroy of Java, and its chief captain, is called *Guste Pate*. He was formerly called *Pate Amdura*[2]. It is he and no one else Guste Pate.

[1] *Guste* was an honorary title given to a high personage, such as a regent or prince of the blood.

[2] This is the more likely translation, but it might equally be: 'The former one was called Pate Andura'. Dames thought that 'probably Pate Udora (or Pateudra) is identical with Pate Unur.' II, 191. But Pires' account shows that *Pate Andura*, *Udra*, or *Udura* and *Pate Unus* are different persons.

who rules all Java in the places and lands of the heathens. *Guste Pate* is the father-in-law of the king of Java. This *Guste Pate* is a knightly man; he is always fighting in wars. He is always at war with the Moors on the sea-coast, especially with the lord of Demak. When he goes to war they say he will take two hundred thousand fighting men, two thousand of whom will be horsemen and four thousand musketeers. The king of Tuban told me this, and as they are great friends and the king of Tuban is his vassal, he may exaggerate his power. The Javanese are hunters; they have many fine hounds with collars and rings of gold and silver.

Fol. 149v. The Javanese are men who, if they write once and do not get a reply, do not write again, although it may be of great importance to them, and this in embassies and things like that. The Javanese are daring men and determined to die. They are gamblers and play for high stakes in their way, and so much that sometimes they stake their children.

Amocos. There are among the nations no men who are *amocos* like those in the Javanese nation. *Amocos* means men who are determined to die (to run amuck). Some of them do it when they are drunk, and these are the common people; but the noblemen are much in the habit of challenging each other to duels, and they kill each other over their quarrels; and this is the custom of the country. Some of them kill themselves on horseback, and some of them on foot, according to what they have decided.

Javanese death custom. It is a custom of Java, and of the countries which we shall describe later, that when the king dies, many of his chief wives and concubines burn themselves alive, and some of the king's people; and this is also done when the lords die, and any other important man. This is among the heathens and not among the Javanese who are Moors. And the women who do not burn themselves, drown themselves of their own free will with music and feasting. And when their husbands die, the most important women and men, when they are nobles, die by the kris, and so do the noblemen who want to die with the king. The common people drown themselves in the sea, or burn themselves.

Tapas means observants, like Beguines. There are about fifty thousand of these in Java. There are three or four orders of them. Some of them do not eat rice nor drink wine; they are all virgins, they do not know women. They wear a certain head-dress which is a full yard long and the end of which turns over like a crosier, and where it fits on to the head it has five white stars; and this contrivance is like the material of a black horse-hair sieve. And these men are also worshipped by the Moors, and they believe in them greatly; they give them alms; they rejoice when such men come to their houses. They do not eat in anyone's house, but out of doors. They go two and two by law, and in threes, and they do not go about alone. People do not touch these mitres of theirs; they say they are sacred. I have sometimes seen ten or twelve of these in Java. *Tapas of Java.*

Many Javanese women do not marry and [remain] virgins. They have houses in the mountains and there they end their lives. Others become Beguines after they have lost their first husband—those who do not want to burn themselves. And they say that there are a large number of these in Java, that there must be more than a hundred thousand women; and afterwards they live in chastity, and they die in this, and they have houses in places for such retreat; and so the women, like the men, ask for food for the love of God. *Custom of those of the observance of Javanese women*

The land of Java is [a land] of mummers and masks of various kinds, and both men and women do thus. They have entertainments of dancing and stories; they mime; they wear mummers' dresses and all their clothes. They are certainly graceful; they have music of bells—the sound of all of them playing together is like an organ. These mummers show a thousand graces like these by day and night. At night they make shadows of various shapes, like *beneditos*[1] in Portugal. *Javanese mummers.*

The Javanese have state oxen as sleek as genets, with carved horns and hoofs; and they have two of these in a cart and on top of the cart are beautifully constructed cabins of ivory and other woods, and there they drive when they want to. The oxen are *Oxen in Java*

[1] This word is perhaps related to the *sambenito* or sanbenito (*saccus benedictus*), formerly worn by penitents. It is possible that the *tápih*, or petticoat, worn by the graceful Javanese dancers, suggested the comparison to Pires.

trained exactly like horses, and they go along with their horns facing the *teatro*[1] and the carts go backwards (?); and this is a fair fashion and it looks very graceful, and it is a stately thing. And all the merchandise is carried all over the island of Java in ox carts.

Fol. 150r.

Javanese eunuchs.

They have a great many eunuchs in Java. They go about dressed in women's clothes; they wear their hair on top of the middle of their heads like a diadem. They serve as guards for the women, because the Javanese are very jealous men, and no one sees their women, except among the common people. But every nobleman, knight and rich man is careful that his women shall be seen by no one, and they are more ready to die about this than about anything else. The land is so much accustomed to this that they do not fail in any point of this custom and they keep it entirely.

Custom of the king of Java when he goes out with his women to amuse himself.

When the king is to go out, a proclamation is made in the city that the king is going merrymaking or hunting. No noblemen, of whatsoever estate and condition, leaves his home, nor any important man. The king goes out with two or three thousand men with lances in sockets of gold and silver. These go in front; then his concubines in carts, and very wantonly displayed (?) and very well dressed; and then his wives on elephants ornamented as with vairs, and each of the concubines and wives is followed by thirty women on foot, each according to her rank. And behind comes the king wandering along with his *Guste Pate*, and they take hounds and greyhounds, and other [men] bearing three-pronged hunting spears beautifully inlaid. Any one found in a street through which the king goes or is to go, dies for it whoever he may be, unless it be a woman or a boy under ten years of age.

The lords of Java—those who are lords in their own lands—go out in the same way, [the people being] under pain of death. The day he goes hunting he is no less respected in his land than the king in his; so they kill as if they were kings. This is the custom in Java. I heard of this in exactly the same way in Tuban, not only of the lord of Tuban, but this state is also kept up by

[1] Though the use of the word *teatro* in this case is not easy to explain, it is possible that Pires meant by it the decorated body of the cart.

his son-in-law who will inherit Tuban on his death; and I saw this also in Sidayu.

Law of Java concerning the inhabitants.

Every man in Java, whether he is rich or poor, must have a kris in his house, and a lance, and a shield—they are not all round wooden shields. And no man between the ages of twelve and eighty may go out of doors without a kris in his belt. They carry them at the back, as daggers used to be in Portugal, because arms are cheap in Java, and this is the custom of the country.

Courtesies in Java.

The *pates* are bowed to by their countrymen as in worship with hands above the head. And they put their right hands on each other's chests, and when they speak they cross their hands; and this [this is done by] the common people with the lords, and they speak at a distance about four or five paces and more often through a third person; because this is the polite custom to speak to lords through a third person when they are accompanied. I did not see the courtesies in the interior of the island of Java at the king's court. I saw them on the sea coast in the Moors' country. These Moorish *pates*, as will be told later, are great lords, and when they speak of courtesy and civility they say that there is every thing at court, and riches. And they speak of *Guste Pate's* affairs with great respect.

They say that the Javanese used to have affinity with the Chinese, and one king of China sent one of his daughters to Java to marry *Batara Raja Çuda*, and that he sent her to Java with many people of China, and that he then sent money in the cash which are now currency, and they say that there was a junkload of them, and that that king was a vassal, not a tributary, of the king of China and that the Javanese killed all the Chinese in Java by treachery. Others say that it was not so, but that one king was never related to or knew the other, and that the Java cash were brought to Java for merchandise, because the Chinese used to trade in Java long before Malacca existed. But now they have not been there for the last hundred years. *Fol. 150v.*

Ports subject to the king of Java and his Guste.

The ports subject to the said king are three: one belongs to the Moors and the other to the heathens, and the third to a son of *Guste Pate*, viz., Tuban which belongs to *Daria Timã de Raja*, a moor who is a vassal of the said king; and another is Blambangan which belongs to *Pate Pimtor*; and the other is *Gamda* which belongs to *Guste Pate's* son.

Merchandise of Java, and food-stuffs.

The land of Java has only heathen [merchandise]: infinite quantities of rice of four or five kinds, and very white, better than that anywhere else; it has oxen, cows, sheep, goats, buffaloes without number, pigs certainly—the whole island is full [of them]. It has many deer of great size, many fruits, much fish along the sea coast. It is a land with beautiful air, it has very good water; it has high mountain ranges, great plains, valleys—a country like ours. The people are very sleek and splendid, without blemish, with strong bodies, such as the said country demands. They are not black men, but rather white than black; and just as we stroke hair downwards they do it in the opposite way for elegance—this is not very appropriate for this chapter. Java also has delicious wines of its own kind, and many oils; it has no butter nor cheese; they do not know how to make it.

Java has a goodly quantity of gold, eight and eight and a half *mates* proof; it has many topazes; it has cubeb, up to thirty bahars a year, and there is none anywhere else; it has long pepper; it has tamarinds, [enough] to load a thousand ships. There is very good cassia fistola in the jungles; there is cardamon, not much, rice, which is the chief merchandise, vegetables, slaves. For merchandise they have countless Javanese cloths, which they take to Malacca to sell. There is also a topaz mine in Java. They have enough copper and *fruseleira* bells for the needs of these parts. It is a great merchandise.

Merchandise which is of value in Java and which goes from Malacca.

All Cambay cloth and whatsoever merchandise comes from there to Malacca, all are of value in Java; Kling *enrolados* of large and small *ladrilho*, *taforio*, *topitis*[1], and other kinds of cloths from Bengal, sinabaffs of all kinds, bleached and unbleached and of all other kinds; so that note should be taken of the large number used by so great a people, and all these are supplied from Malacca, and they get some few by way of *Pamchur*—some, but really it is nothing. And there is a good market for

[1] TAFORIO—No such word appears to exist in Portuguese. It may stand for *tafecira*, an old term for several oriental cloths like chintz, either of silk or cotton.

TOPITIS—A coarse cotton cloth from Ceylon. From the Cingalese *tupatti*. Spelt *topetījs*, or *topetins*, further on.

the tails of white oxen and cows that come from Bengal and Gujarat.

Coins and weights of Java.

The coins of Java are cash[1] from China; a thousand is worth twenty-five *calais*—of those at a hundred for three cruzados. A thousand are called a *puon*, and for a thousand they give you thirty less, for that is the custom of the country. They take these thirty as dues for the lord of the place; and all the trade is done with these [coins]. Java has no coinage of gold or silver. They like our money very much, particularly the Portuguese money; they say that the country where such money is made must be like Java.

The Java *tumdaya* or tael is a quarter part more than that of Malacca. A *tundaya* of gold of eight *mates* proof is worth twelve thousand cash, which are worth nine *cruzados* at the rate of one thousand three hundred and thirty three and a third per *cruzado*. When the gold is taken from Java to Malacca there is a gain of one in every five.

Every hundred and forty cash weighs one of our *arráteis* of sixteen ounces. A *cate* contains two hundred and forty Java cash, because the Java bahar contains two hundred catties and weighs forty-eight thousand cash; but I bought only by the one I took with me.

The Java *ganta* of rice and vegetables is smaller than that of Malacca—twenty-five Java *gantas* make twenty in Malacca[2]; and these weights and measures in all the different places will be dealt with generally in another book. There is hardly any profit on the merchandise that goes from Malacca to Java; but there is a good profit on the return.

The chief dues customarily paid in Java on the merchandise *Fol. 151r.*

[1] Nunes refers to the '*caixas* that come from Java, which are of copper, larger than *ceitis*, pierced through the middle'. *Lyvro dos Pesos*, p. 41. Pires said above, when dealing with the 'Coinage of Sunda': 'For small money, cash from China. They are pierced through the middle like ceitis'. Farther on, dealing with the Malacca coinage, he says that 'every hundred *cashes* make one *calaim* and weigh barely 33 ounces', the *calaim* being worth 12 *reis*.

[2] According to Nunes the Malacca *ganta* was equal to 5 Portuguese *quartilhos* (1.75 litres), and the Moluccas *ganta* was bigger, equal to $5\frac{1}{3}$ *quartilhos* (1.86 litres). *Lyvro dos Pesos*, pp. 40, 58. He does not mention the Java *ganta*, but following Pires' information it was equal to 4 *quartilhos* or a *canada* (1.4 litres). See note p. 101.

Dues that are paid all over Java for voyages, and presents from those who go there with merchandise.

that goes there by sea are the anchorage dues; and for these a present is made, and they pay four hundred cash out of every ten thousand on the merchandise which is sold in the country.

I have already spoken of the lords of the island. Now I will begin to tell of the Mohammedan *pates* who are on the sea coast, who are powerful in Java and have all the trade because they are lords of the junks and people.

How the Javanese lords on the sea coast became Mohammedans.

At the time when there were heathens along the sea coast of Java, many merchants used to come, Parsees, Arabs, Gujaratees, Bengalees, Malays and other nationalities, there being many Moors among them. They began to trade in the country and to grow rich. They succeeded in way of making mosques, and mollahs came from outside, so that they came in such growing numbers that the sons of these said Moors were already Javanese and rich, for they had been in these parts for about seventy years. In some places the heathen Javanese lords themselves turned Mohammedan, and these mollahs and the merchant Moors took possession of these places. Others had a way of fortifying the places where they lived, and they took people of their own who sailed in their junks, and they killed the Javanese lords and made themselves lords; and in this way they made themselves masters of the sea coast and took over trade and power in Java.

These lord *pates* are not Javanese of long standing in the country, but they are descended from Chinese, from Parsees and Kling, and from the nations we have already mentioned. However, brought up among the bragging Javanese, and still more on account of the riches they have inherited from their antecessors, these men made themselves more important in Javanese nobility and state than those of the hinterland; and each of them is reverenced in his land as though he were something much greater. We will now begin to tell of each and of his land. Their lands extend as far as the mountains, which must be seven or eight leagues.

Because our account carried us straight along the coast of Sunda through the lands of Java up to Chi Manuk, as we have said, we will now turn to Cherimon and we will end at Blambangan, telling who is the Mohammedan in each and what junks and people it has; and first we will speak of Cherimon.

The land of Cherimon is next to Sunda; its lord is called *Lebe Uça*. He is a vassal of *Pate Rodim*, lord of Demak. This Cherimon has a good port and there must be three or four junks there. It has a great deal of rice and many foodstuffs; it must have as many as ten small lancharas—they say that it has not so many now. This place Cherimon must have up to a thousand inhabitants. *Pate Quedir*—the one who revolted in Upeh[1]—lives in this place Cherimon. There must be five or six merchants in Cherimon as great as *Pate Quedir*, but they all and the lord of Cherimon do honour to *Pate Quedir*, because they hold him to be a bold merchant and a knight. About forty years ago this place Cherimon was heathen, and the lord of Demak at that time had a slave from Grisee, and he made the said slave a captain against Cherimon, and the lord of Demak gave him the title of *pate* of Cherimon, and this his slave from Grisee who was lord of Cherimon is grandfather of this *Pate Rodim* who is lord of Demak today[2]. *Cherimon* (Choroboam).

This place Cherimon is about three leagues up the river; junks can go in there, they say. It is not a strong affair. This place has better wood for making junks than anywhere else in Java, although there is not much wood in the whole of Java.

The land of *Japura* is bounded on one side by Cherimon and on the other by the land of Losari (*Locary*)[3]. It is a country with two thousand inhabitants in villages. It belongs to *Pate Rodim*. The *pate* of Losari is called *Pate Codia*. This place has up to five lancharas; it has two junks. This place has a great deal of rice and wax, honey, foodstuffs. The people of *Japura* work on the land. The *pate* of this place is a knight, and a first cousin of *Pate* *Fol. 151v.* *Land of* Japura.

[1] *Pate quedir*, or Patih Katir, fought against the Portuguese in Malacca in 1512. He had been appointed by Albuquerque, in succession to Timuta Raja, as chief of *Upe*, or Upeh, a Javanese suburb on the bank of the Malacca River, opposite the town of Malacca.

[2] If Crawfurd is right, this may agree with his opinion that *Pate Rodim's* mother was not a princess of Champa, but 'more probably the Creole descendant of a man of that nation'. See note, p. 185.

[3] *Japura* may correspond to the Chi Sangarung, which debouches at Tanjong Losari. Three miles inland there is a place called Losari, in a small district of the same name.

Rodim. He obeys the said *Pate Rodim*, lord of Demak; he is almost like a captain of his in the said place. This *Pate Rodim's* father took this place *Japura* by cunning, and it has remained in his hands until today. It has a port, and you go up the river to the town.

Land of Tegal (Teteguall). The land of Tegal is bounded on one side by *Japura* and on the other by Samarang (*Camaram*). This place has more rice than any other place in Java, here along the coast. The *pate* of this place is an uncle of *Pate Unus*; he obeys the lord of Demak. It has a port and a river, where they load quantities of rice and other foodstuffs. This place has one junk, and sometimes it has nothing. It has small lancharas. They say that the land of Tegal is a land with four thousand inhabitants. They live in villages, not many together. The place Tegal must have about one thousand five hundred inhabitants; this place has as many as seven or eight merchants.

Land of Samarang. Samarang is joined to Tegal at one end, and at the other to the land of Demak. The pate of Samarang is called *Pate Mamet*. He is father-in-law of *Pate Rodim*, lord of Demak, and is obedient to Demak. It has a port, not a very good one. I has rice and foodstuffs. This place has three junks, and four or five lancharas. It has about three thousand inhabitants. Now it has not a single junk; it is a country with no means of sailing, because those it had were burned in Malacca and it is unable to make others, according to what everyone says.

Land of Demak (Demaa). The land of Demak is bounded on one side by Samarang and on the other by the land of Tidunan (*Tidanã*). The land of Demak is larger than those we have described from Cherimon up to Demak. Its city has about eight or ten thousand houses, according to what they say. *Pate Rodim* is lord of this country. He is the chief *pate* in Java. They make him out to be head of all the lords of Java who are his friends. *Pate Rodim's* father was a knight, a person of great judgement, and *Pate Rodim's* grandfather was a man from Grisee. Some say that he was a slave of the lord of Demak in whose time he happened to go to Demak; others say that he was a merchant. He is given with more authority as a slave.

This *Pate Rodim* is closely related to the lords of Java because his father and grandfather have many daughters and they were all married to the chief *pates*. He is so powerful that he subjugated all the land of Palembang and of Jambi and the islands of *Monomby* and many other islands over against *Tamjompura* and made them all obedient to him. He is greatly respected, this *Pate Rodim*. Rice and other foodstuffs come from his lands to Malacca. His father was a man who could collect together forty junks from his lands; now he could not collect ten, because this *Pate Rodim* was very young, and he must be about thirty now, and he gave himself over to concubines and his country has greatly fallen away from what it was before[1].

And moreover, all that remained to him was destroyed in Malacca when *Pate Onus*, his brother-in-law, came to fight in the year fifteen hundred and twelve. He has many fighting men; he must have thirty thousand men in Java, and he must have ten

[1] *Pate Rodim*, or Ráden Patáh, is supposed by some to be a grandchild of Angka Wijáya, Batara Browijaya of Majapáhit. His father was Aria Dámar, Prince of Palembang on Sumatra, an illegitimate son of Angka Wijáya. Aria Dámar married a Chinese Princess of Champa, formerly married to his father, who gave her to him when she was pregnant. Aria Dámar and the Princess of Champa had two sons, Ráden Patáh, the eldest, and Ráden Húsen. They were sent later on by their father to the court of their grandfather the Batara, in Majapáhit. But Ráden Patáh, when he grew up, refused to live at Majapáhit, and later on founded Demak, and declared war on his grandfather. The latter sent an army against him under the command of Ráden Húsen, but Ráden Patáh, after being defeated, finished by beating the army of the Batara, and Majapáhit, 'the great and magnificent capital of Java, fell in 1475 to become a wilderness', and the Batara fled. 'Ráden Patáh Adipáti Jimbum' was the first Mohammedan sovereign of Demak, and reigned from 1477 to 1519, when he died at a great age. Raffles, *History of Java*, II, 125 *seqq.*; Campbell, *Java*, 78 *seqq.* Crawfurd, however, dismisses 'the story of the princess of *Champa*, and of the birth of *Raden Patah*'. He calls her 'a Chinese, or more probably the Creole descendant of a man of that nation . . . some humble female, clandestinely withdrawn from *Champa*, and *procured* for the king of Java's harem'. 'This woman was repudiated by the Javanese monarch, when pregnant of *Raden Patah*, and made over to *Arya Damar*, chief of the Javanese colony of *Palembang*, in Sumatra, said to have been Browijoyo's own son. *Raden Husen* was a real son of *Arya Damar*, by the same mother.' *History of the Indian Archipelago*, II, 310–13; Campbell, *op. cit.*, p. 129. Much of what Pires says about *Pate Rodim* conflicts somewhat with several writings on Javanese history. He says, for instance, that in his time *Pate Rodim* was thirty years old, though it seems that he was much older. Pires wrote according to what he heard, and in spite of possible inaccuracies his information is none the less valuable on many points.

thousand in Palembang. He is constantly at war with *Guste Pate* and with the lord of Tuban. He has lost many people in war, and he is poor, and he has only five or six *pangajavas* in Demak and not a single junk, and if he did not beg Malacca in its mercy to make him its vassal and protect him, and to give him an outlet for his merchandise, he would be utterly lost, because as he has
Fol. 152r. not done any trade for three or four years | he is greatly exhausted, so that he must of necessity be a tributary to Malacca for his own salvation, and the people are already leaving his land for other places because there is no trade in merchandise.

He used to get rid of all the crops from his lands in Malacca; thus he used to send [them] in his junks and *pangajavas*, while merchants from Malacca went to his country in junks, from which trade he used to have large quantities of merchandise in his lands, and made a large profit. And because he does not do it now, he is ruined, and they say that he and *Pate Unus* spent more than a hundred thousand *cruzados* on the armada that came against Malacca. There is no doubt that he is at the end of his resources, because that is what they say. He could not live if he did not rely on Malacca. Large quantities of merchandise are consumed in his country, from the Gujaratis as well as from the Kling and from China and Bengal, of which the country is now in want for the reasons we have mentioned. Demak has a rich river. Junks cannot enter it except at full tide.

Land of Tidunan (Tidanã)[1]. The land of Tidunan is bounded on one side by Demak and on the other by Japara. This *pate* is called *Pate Orob*. He is an uncle of *Pate Onus*—brother to his father. They say that he does not obey anyone. He is a man of good judgement, by what they say. He has no junks now; he has two or three *pangajavas*. He has a good river; junks cannot get into it. This country has a great deal of rice and many foodstuffs. The land of Tidunan must have two or three thousand men, and this [*pate*] often fights with the people of the hinterland, and helps *Pate Rodim's* people, because *Guste Pate* often attacks Demak, Tidunan (*Tidonam*) and Japara, and inflicts losses on the people of the

[1] *Tidanã* or *Tidonam*. A few miles up the river Serang, which discharges into the sea seventeen miles north-north-east of Samarang, there is the village of Tidunan. *Tidumar*, as spelt above (p. 166), must be a transcriber's mistake.

country. They say that [*Pate Orob*] with his advice governs *Pate Unus* and *Pate Rodim*, and they obey him like a parent; but each of them is more powerful than the said *Pate Orob*.

Land of Japara.

We are now in the land of *Pate Onus*, the knight of whom the Javanese speak, because they say that he is a great warrior in Java and very prudent; and this *Pate Unus* had a great deal of land in his possession. His grandfather was a working man in the islands of *Laue* and he went to Malacca with very little nobility and less wealth; and he married in Malacca and had the son who was father to *Pate Unus*. And in Malacca he went on making money and traded in Java, and about forty or forty-five years ago he cunningly killed the *pate* [of] Japara, which was weak and nothing much [of a place] with ninety or a hundred inhabitants; and he also took the land of Tidunan. Afterwards, and through his cunning, it became such that he peopled it and it was united (?). He was the most famous lord of Java for his strength and for his good fellowship among his own people.

The port of Japara is at the foot of a great and very high mountain called [Muria][1]. The land of Japara is bounded on one side by Tidunan and on the other by the land of Rembang (*Rame*). Japara has a bay with a beautiful port. In front of the port are three islands like those of Upeh[2], and large ships can enter into it. Those who sail past Japara can see the whole town. This is the best port we have described up to now, and in the best situation. Everyone who wants to go to Java and to the Moluccas calls there in the land of Japara. It is a land well shaded. He was such a daring man that he took the island of

[1] This mountain, the name of which was left blank in the MS, corresponds to the Muria mountains, about twelve miles from the coast. Their highest and most conspicuous peak is Sutorengo, 5233 feet (1595 m).

[2] About two and a half miles west of the mouth of the Malacca River lies the islet Upeh, northward of which there are some rocks that emerge at low tide. One of Eredia's maps (fol. 11v), showing the country around Malacca, has this *Pulo Vpe* and one of the rocks. There are not three islands in front of the port of Japara. There is the Panjang island, lying by the southern entrance to Japara road, nearly two miles from the mouth of the Japara River, which might resemble Pulo Upeh; but there are no other islands. Perhaps Pires refers to some part of the reef that extends from Kelor far to the northward; the peninsula of Kelor (projecting from the main shore opposite Panjang) was formerly an island. Island and reef might have reminded him of Upeh and the neighbouring rocks.

Banka under his jurisdiction, and that of *Tamjompura*, and *Laue* and other islands, and made his country great. Japara used to have many junks, and he was nearly as great a lord as the lord of Demak, though Japara is under Demak, which has more people and more land. And the son, *Pate Unus*, wanted to put together what remained of his father's wealth and what wealth *Pate Rodim* had, and decided to take Malacca from the then king of Malacca, because he had taken offence because they had not done honour in Malacca to the captain of a junk of his as he had hoped. And in the meantime Malacca was captured by the Governor of India, Afonso de Albuquerque; and when they heard this, the mollahs and chief people there were said what enterprise could be more just than to take the city from the
Fol. 152v. Portuguese. And [having made] this decision | they completed their armada in the space of five years with the help of Palembang and came down on Malacca, about a hundred sail, and the smallest of the hundred cannot have been less than two hundred tons burden, and they were received in front of the port of Malacca, where they did not remain at anchor for more than about six hours. They anchored at night fall, and at midnight they went away with the land breeze, and about seven or eight reached home; the others were burnt and sunk and captured. About a thousand men were killed, and as many more captured.

And even in his own port of Japara the *Pate Unus* was not safe, and said that the Portuguese had treated him gently. And now he goes hunting. *Pate Unus* is twenty-five years old. He is greater than all the Javanese in nobility and presumption. He is waiting for them to propose peace, certain that they must propose it as it fits them. Japara now has three junks and two or three *pangajavas*. His country has a great deal of rice. In his country they use what we have already enumerated for Java. He is married to a sister of *Pate Rodim*, and he asked the late king of Malacca for one of his daughters in marriage and sent ambassadors about it.

The port of Japara is at the foot of a very high mountain. And in this mountain there is a plain three or four leagues in extent, and Japara is on the edge of a plain on flat ground, not marshy but very good and well shaded. They say it has beautiful meat and much fish. Japara certainly appears to be the key of all Java, because it lies on the point and is in the middle of all Java, and it is the same distance from there to Cherimon as to Grisee. It is a great trading place because it is a port, and they say that from there the merchants used to scatter to other places, not to mention Grisee.

Land of Rembang (Ramee).

The land of Rembang is joined at one end to Japara and at the other to the land of *Cajongam*[1]; and because *Cajongam* was destroyed by *Guste Pate* it had no more inhabitants; Rembang took some of it and so did Tuban, so that we can say that at the other side it [Rembang] joins the land of Tuban. The *pate* of Rembang is called *Pate Morob*. He is an uncle of *Pate Unus*, and *Pate Unus* is his sister's son. This country has a great deal of rice and it has wood for junks and they used to be made there of old. They say that he has none now, and has about two *pangajavas* because he supported *Pate Unus* in his plan against Malacca and each of them lost what he put in the armada.

He is at war with the people of the hinterland. They say he is a man who must have about four thousand men in his country. They work the land and live on their crops. His country has large bays; it is well shaded. *Pate Rodim* has a large slice of the land of *Cajongã* in his country. *Pate Rodim* is a nephew of his also. Some of this land is jungle and is not cultivated, because Tuban came down on it and destroyed it, and others do likewise. I saw a large piece of this land with great palm groves and other trees and without inhabitants, because they also fear the Bugis; they fled when the land of *Cajongã* was destroyed. The merchants who have money come and make junks in this land of Rembang.

Tuban (Tubam).

The land of Tuban touches the land of *Cajongam* and Rembang on one side, as we have said above, and on the other side it touches Sidayu (*Çedayo*) and along the coast it is supported by *Guste Pate*. The *pate* of Tuban is called *Pate Vira*. As a mark of honour *Guste Pate* has now given him the name of *Anatimao de Raja*, which is a very honoured name. The town of Tuban has a series of palissades [within] a crossbow [shot] of the sea; it is

[1] Possibly Saranjawa, a village at the mouth of a small river, half-way between Rembang and Tuban.

surrounded by a brick wall, partly of burned and partly of sun-dried bricks; this must be two spans thick and fifteen high. Around the walls on the outside there are lakes of water, and on the land side are large *carapeteiros*[1] and brambles against the wall, which is pierced with large and small loopholes, and has high wooden platforms along the wall inside. Tuban is on a plain
Fol. 153r. and | Tuban must have about a thousand inhabitants inside its walls. Every important person has his bricked enclosure, with well-made doors, and with his people's houses inside, according to what he has. At one large bombard shot from the land you can anchor in two fathoms and three and four, and at one *berço*[2] shot it is about a fathom and a half; and at low tide there are breakers, and when the tide ebbs it goes back two or three crossbow shots, and there is fresh water at low tide, and quite sweet water in springs, and if you put your feet down without noticing the holes you get stuck in the mud up to your middle. So this land of Tuban is subject to *Guste Pate*, and this is the nearest port to the city of Daha (*Daya*)[3] where *Guste Pate* has his residence; and they have made an agreement that *Guste Pate* will help him with ten or twenty thousand men when enemies come upon Tuban, because all the Moorish *pates* of Java hate him because he is friendly with the *Cafre*. The men of Tuban are knights—more than any of the other Javanese. No lord of Java

[1] *Carapeteiro* is the name given in Portugal to a small thorny tree, the subspecies *Piraster* of *Pirus communis* Linn. Pires was obviously referring to some native thorny plant which reminded him of the *carapeteiro*.

[2] An ancient short cannon, much smaller than the bombard.

[3] *Daya*, or *Daha*, as spelt farther on. Though the *Encyclopædia van Nederlandsch-Indië, s.v.*, says that Daha, capital of the Hindu Empire of the same name in Java, was 'somewhere between Panorogo and Madioen', which corresponds to the western side of the Willis mountains, Crawfurd (*Dictionary, s.v.* Dāa) asserts that this ancient kingdom of Java corresponds 'with the modern province of Kadir', which is on the eastern side of those mountains. Campbell is quite positive in identifying Dáha with Kediri. (*Java*, pp. 60–3), and a map dated December 31st 1889, published by Verbeck, has *Djaha*, a place where there are ruins and stone inscriptions, eight miles north-west of the town of Kediri. Tuban is indeed the nearest port, on the northern coast of Java, to Kediri, which lies fifty-five miles due south through almost flat country. Tuban is distant forty-nine miles from *Djaha*. This agrees also with what Pires says below, that Daha is distant two days of good going from Tuban, in a land of waggons and roads. Lavanha's map has *DAIA* written near the coast, between *Agaci* and *Passaruam*.

is friendly with him. Because his town is strong and difficult to land at, and [because] he is allied with *Guste Pate*, he fears no one and he gets the better of them all.

Because he is a kinsman and friend of *Guste Pate* he has richly inlaid things in his lands; he has krises, lances of many kinds; he has three-pronged hunting spears; he has caparisoned (?) genets; he has three elephants; he has a thousand hounds and others [which are] bloodhounds; he has two hundred concubines; he has rich and well-built houses, where he lives. He rides every morning in waggons with a great deal of wood-work done in a very beautiful way. He does not come out into the countryside, as he shuts himself up, except sometimes very late he rides on elephants and sometimes on horses. He spends three days in the town and as many more out hunting. The country is well shaded, with a great deal of rice which come from inland; it has many kinds of wood, much wine and much fish and good water.

It has many tamarinds, much long pepper; and cubebs is sent there; [it has] beef, pork and kid and goat flesh, venison, chickens and countless fruits; the land is plenteous in all these, and [he] shows himself a great servant of the king our lord. His people speaks to him from afar, but he embraces us and hopes that through his truth and good [faith] he will come to be chief person in Java. He is a man of between fifty-five and sixty. He is Javanese by birth; his grandfather was a heathen and afterwards became Mohammedan. This man does not seem to me to be a very firm believer in Mohammed.

The man who will inherit the land on his death is the son of one of his sisters and married to one of his duaghters. This man did not make such a good impression on me as the old lord of Tuban. You will reach the city of *Daha* in two days of good going. [This is a] land of waggons, good [country], well shaded like our own, not marshy, with roads going through populated country. There are heathens in the town; they live in a quarter by themselves. The land is well populated, with important houses. There are many knights in Tuban. I saw a heathen in Tuban who came there from the court to see us. They said he was a nobleman. He had three handsomely caparisoned genets, with stirrups all inlaid, with cloths all adorned with richly worked gold, with beautiful caparisons; he brought with him about ten men with rich lances. He was robust, tall, freckled, with his hair curly on the top and frizzy; and they all did him obeisance. And he only came to see what sort of men we were, and he lodged outside the town and did not go out except once during the day, towards afternoon; and I talked to him many times. The lord of Tuban often professes that he was the first to accept and maintain friendship with the Portuguese; and he says that he does not want his sons to remember him for anything else. He is a good man and his friendship is faithful, and he is certainly always deserving of favour. If the whole country is added together, there must be six or seven thousand fighting men in Tuban; it has no junks nor cargo *pangajavas* of its own.

Land of Sidayu (Cedayo)[1]. The land of Sidayu is joined on one side to the land of Tuban and on the other to the land of Grisee. The lord of Sidayu is called *Pate Amiza*; he is a nephew of *Pate Morob*, the lord of Rembang, and he is first cousin to *Pate Unus* and second cousin to *Pate Rodim*. He is a youth of twenty years old. He is married to the daughter of the lord of Grisee. He has with him a brother of his father's who is called *Pate Bagũs*. I talked to these people many times in Sidayu. This *Pate Bagũs* governs the country; the youth goes hunting with his concubines.

Fol. 153v. Sidayu is not a trading country. It is smaller than Tuban. The town there is surrounded by a wall, like Tuban. It is a poor affair, with few inhabitants. There are important men who live on their crops. He must be a man with two thousand vassals; they defend his country. The coast is bad for landing, all stones. It has rice and foodstuffs; it has no junk nor *pangajavas*. They say that the land is good inland. The people of Sidayu are more rustic than any of those described up to now and the country is largely heathen. This [lord] is friendly with the lord of Tuban.

Land of Grisee (Agãcij)[2]. We have reached Grisee (*Agracij*), the great trading port, the best in all Java, whither the Gujaratees, and [people of] Calicut, Bengalees, Siamese, Chinese, and [people of] Liu-Kiu (*Lequeos*),

[1] *Çidaio* on one of the maps (fol. 30) and *Rio de çidaio* in one of the drawings (fol. 99) of Rodrigues.

[2] *Agãci* or *Agraci* corresponds to Grisee or Geresik. *Agraçi* on Rodrigues' map (fol. 37) and drawing (fol. 96).

used to sail of old. This is the jewel of Java in trading ports. This is the royal port where the ships at anchor are safe from winds, with their bowsprits touching the houses. It is called the merchants' port; among the Javanese it is called the rich people's port. Grisee is bounded by Sidayu, and on the other side by Surabaya (*Curubaya*), and it has the large island of Madura facing it, within sight.

The sea beats against Grisee (*Agraci*), and it has two towns which are separated by a little river, which is almost dry at low tide. *Pate Cuçuf* is lord of the larger of the towns with the greater number of inhabitants; and *Zeynall* of the other port. These two are constantly at war; and they do not go from one part to the other or from the other to the other on pain of death; and sometimes they make truces—at the time of their harvest, or when junks come to the port; and afterwards they go back to their enmity. This has been going on for a long time. *Zeynall* sets himself up as a knight; the other has more men. Each defends himself against the other, and they live like this with sentinels. *Pate Cuçuf* is Malayan by birth. *Pate Cuçuf's* grandfather is called [*blank*] and his son (the father of *Pate Cuçuf*) is called *Pate Adem*. This *Pate Adem* came and settled in Malacca; he had his houses in Malacca and traded in merchandise. In Malacca he married a Malayan woman, by whom he had *Pate Cuçuf*, and the said *Pate Cuçuf* lived in Malacca for a long time. On the death of the grandfather, *Pate Adem* went to Grisee to take possession of his land, and a long time afterwards he sent from there to Malacca to summon his son, who went there with all his household. On the death of the father, who was called *Pate Adem*, the said *Pate Cuçuf* stayed in Grisee. This man used to have the trade with the Moluccas and Banda (*Bandam*) as long as he had junks. This *Pate Cuçuf's* grandmother was a sister of Sri Nara Diraja (*Cerina de Raja*), the father of the Bendahara whom the king ordered to be beheaded here; and the late king of Malacca was also a grandson of this Bendahara, father of the one they killed, so that *Pate Cuçuf* is a second cousin german to the late king of Malacca[1].

[1] The history of Malacca before the arrival of the Portuguese is a complicated affair. As far as I was able to ascertain, a sister of the Bendahara Tuan

This *Pate Cuçuf* is a merchant and much given to trading in merchandise. He has many merchants in his country. He is a man of good judgement. He must be about fifty years old. There used to be many junks and many cargo *pangajavas* in his port; now there are none. He has many *calaluzes* and *naviotes*[1] for raids, as have the other *pates* of Java, all of whom have a large number of *calaluzes*, but they are not fit to go out of the shelter of the land. They are carved in a thousand and one ways, with figures of serpents, and gilt; they are ornamental. Each of them has many of these, and they are very much painted, and they certainly look well and are made in a very elegant way, and they are for kings to amuse themselves in, away from the common people. They are rowed with paddles. They ought to be used in Portugal, in state. The land of Grisee contains about six or seven thousand men.

Many cloths of all kinds are disposed of in Grisee, and in large quantities. They are sold to most of Java and to many other islands. And because he used to own the shipping to the Moluccas and Banda, he and his merchants used to buy large quantities, and great trade was done in Grisee. And through the destruction of Malacca they do not navigate, nor do they trade,

Ali Sri Nara Diraja was mother of Raja Kasim, who was the fifth king of Malacca, with the title Muzaffar Shah. Tuan Ali Sri Nara Diraja made an arrangement with his nephew Muzaffar Shah, and married one of the latter's wives, Tuan Kundu, who was divorced for the purpose. From this marriage two children were born—Tuan Senaja, afterwards wife of Alauddin (son of Mansur Shah, the sixth king, who was son of Muzaffar), the seventh king of Malacca, and Tuan Mutahir, the Bendahara slain in 1510 by his nephew the Sultan Mahmud (eighth king of Malacca, and son of Tuan Senaja). Cf. Winstedt, *A History of Malay*, pp. 44 *seqq*. But perhaps the grandmother of *Pate Cuçuf* was another sister of Sri Nara Diraja, not Muzaffar Shah's mother; otherwise Pires would probably mention it, and the relationship would be much more complicated. In any case, *Pate Cuçuf*, being a grand-son of a sister of Tuan Ali Sri Nara Diraja, was second cousin german of the king Mahmud of Malacca. The *Malay Annals* refer to the visits of this 'Javanese noble Pateh Adam' to Malacca, and his adventurous marriage to Tuna Manda, an adopted daughter of the Dato Sri Nara Diraja, who was a brother of Tuan Mutahir. Wilkinson, *The Malacca Sultanate*, pp. 60 and 50. So Pires is right once more, though the mother of *Pate Cuçuf* was only the adopted daughter of Dato Sri Nara Diraja.

[1] CALALUZ—A kind of swift rowing vessel used in the Indian Archipelago.

NAVIOTE—This word, unknown in Portuguese today, must be the same as *naveta*, an antiquated word meaning a small ship or craft.

nor have they any junks, because most of the Javanese junks come from Pegu, where the Javanese—and other people who bought in Malacca—used to send for them to be made; because the Pegu people bring the merchandise and the junks all as merchandise, and having sold | the merchandise they used to *Fol. 154r.* sell the junks. And because it is already five years since this stopped, and the Governor of India burned and defeated all the enemy junks, they were all left without any, and they have no junks.

And so Java is alone and without junks in the way that has been described, and the lords who used to have junks before their defeat have none now, and those they were able to muster were taken by *Pate Unus*, and when he was routed he only brought three back, so that the whole of Java and Palembang has not as many as ten junks and ten cargo *pangajavas*, which are like ships. Java is more for *calaluzes* and small *pangajavas* than for large junks, because Pegu used to supply them all with junks—Pedir, Pase, Pahang and Java and Palembang. Most of them are from Pegu. Some are made in Java, but they are few, and most of these purchases were made in Malacca. The Javanese are not capable of making ten junks in ten years.

I have already talked about *Pate Cuçuf*, the lord of the chief town of Grisee. There now remains [to tell of] *Pate Zeinall*; and because his land lives for the most part on its own crops [and has no trade], and they fight in the interior of the island with his enemies, there is nothing worth spending time on, because he has nothing on the sea; on land he defends himself against his neighbours. The Javanese say that this *Pate Zeinall* is a knight and the oldest of all the *pates* in Java. He has many relations: he is an uncle of *Pate Amiza* of Sidayu, and of *Pate Unus*, and the brother-in-arms of the old *Pate Rodim*, and now he is the same thing to *Pate Rodim* the son. He is full of fancies, and poor. He says that should the Captain-Major [Afonso de Albuquerque] make peace with the lord of Demak, the lords of Java would almost be forced to make it also, saying that the lord of Demak stood for the whole of Java.

Land of Surabaya (Çurubaia)[1].

The land of Surabaya is bounded on one side by the lands of Grisee and on the other by the lands of *Ganda*. The lord of Surabaya is called *Pate Bubat*, and *Guste Pate* has now given him the name of *Jurupã Galacam Jmteram*, which means 'the excellent captain'. He is a knight and a person of great authority, more honoured in affairs of arms than any of those who are now living along the sea-coast, whether Javanese or Moorish; and all the Javanese rely on him, on his personality and counsel. He has a great deal of land and he is often at war with *Guste Pate*, and sometimes they are friends. He has many war *calaluzes* at sea. He is a brother-in-arms of the lord of Grisee. They say that his grandfather was a heathen slave of *Guste Pate's* grandfather. Others say that his grandfather was from Sunda. In any case he is greatly esteemed. He must have about six or seven thousand fighting men in his country.

He is constantly at war, and he is not given to any other exercise. All his Javanese neighbours receive counsel and help from him. He is closely related to the Moorish *pates*. He is very much at war with the *pate* of Blambangan, who is a heathen enemy of his. The Javanese also send him help when the other attacks him, because the *pates* of Blambangan and of *Gamda* are more powerful. This [*Pate Bubat*] is greatly esteemed because he is always at war. His land has foodstuffs like the other Javanese lands, because all the land of Java has them. The merchandise goes out from Grisee. He very much wants there to be friendship with Malacca, and they say that he is working hard for it. He has already written to this fortress, and they have written him twice. This *pate* is poor. His land has neither junks nor *pangajavas*. They live on their crops, as others do in Java. Sometimes his captains go plundering on the sea.

Land of Gamda[2].

The land of *Gamda* is large. It is joined on one side to Surabaya and on the other to lands of *Canjtam*, Panarukan (*Pana-*

[1] It appears as *ssurubaia* on Rodrigues' map (fol. 37) and as *Surubaia* in the drawing (fol. 96).

[2] As the port of Surabaya is at the mouth of the Kali Mas, the northernmost branch of the river of Surabaya delta, it may possibly be that Pires' *Gamda* was situated at the mouth of the Kali Brantas, the southernmost branch of the same delta, some twenty miles from the former. Near the mouth of the Kali Brantas there is a village called Djangan.

rucam), Pajarakan (*Pajurucam*). The *pate* of *Gamda* is called *Pate Sepetat*. He is a heathen, son of the great *Guste Pate* of Java. The Moors have reached as far as here and were thrown out by *Guste Pate*, who gave these lands to one of his sons. From here onwards there are no Moors except in the Moluccas, and those of Banda. His country is very plenteous, with many warriors, and he is always fighting with Surabaya. They say that this son of *Guste Pate* is a knight and important person on account of his father, and greatly esteemed. He is married to the daughter of *Pate Pijntor*, lord of Blambangan, and he is also | married to the daughter of the great lord of Madura. He has *Fol. 154v.* many horsemen, and many lords of Java are with him. He has *calaluzes* on the sea.

And with the help of his father-in-law he has prevented the Moors from passing beyond Surabaya for a long time. His land has many foodstuffs; it is not a trading country. They all live in plenty on their crops, and they all have plenty of delights and pleasures. There must be ten thousand men in the land of *Gamda*.

Lands of Canjtam, *Panarukan, Pajarakan*[1].

These three lands individually used to have *pate* lords, and very important lords of great authority. It must be about eight years since they had them, and another five since they were destroyed. *Canjtam* is joined to *Ganda*, and *Canjtam* to Panarukan, and Panarukan to Pajarakan and Pajarakan to Blambangan. These *pates* made *Pate Pular*, lord of *Canjtam*, their chief; and they say that, because they worked to allow the lord of Surabaya to enter in, these three *pates* were killed and their lands taken by the lord of Blambangan. And now they have no

[1] CANJTAM, or *Camtã* and *Canjtão*, as spelt before. There is a place and a river Kraton, a few miles south-east of Kali Brantas, near Pasuruan, which might suggest *Canjtam* or *Camtã*. As Pires says, all these places were situated at the mouths of rivers.

PANARUCAM or *Panurucã* is Panarukan. It appears for the first time as *panaruca* on the map of *c.* 1540.

PAJARUCAM or *Pajarucã* corresponds to Pajarakan, a small place today, which the *Eastern Archipelago Pilot*—II refers to as Tanjong Pajarakan, seventeen miles east of Probolonggo and thirty-four miles west of Panarukan. However, Pires erroneously placed *Pajarucam* after *Panarucam*. *Padjarakan* is the only place shown between *Pasoeroean* and *Panaroekan*, rightly situated on the eastern side of the bay, on a seventeenth century *Schetskaart van Oost-Java en Madoera*, contained in Mac Leod's *Atlas behoorende bij de Oost-Indische Compagnie*, N° V. *Pageruca* on the map of *c.* 1540.

pates and are under the jurisdiction of Blambangan; and they say that each of these three countries is almost as important as each one of those that have been described. As with Sidayu, the rivers are on the sea-coast. They are countries with many foodstuffs and they used to have a large population.

Land of Blambangan (Bulambuam).

The land of Blambangan is bounded on one side by the above countries of *Canjtam*, Panarukan, Pajarakan, and on the other side by *Chamda*[1] in the interior, and from there onwards it is all mountainous country until it reaches the land of the king of Java, which should in truth more properly be called [the lands] of *Guste Pate*. The *pate* of Blambangan is called *Pate Pimtor*. He is a great gentile lord, a fearsome knight, and greatly respected in Java, especially by the heathen lords. He held all the Moors so that they could not proceed farther. His country has many inhabitants, and he also has a large number of small craft on the sea. There are no more *pates* after this one. The people are rustic, like [people] of the mountains, and they obey *Guste Pate*.

This lord of Blambangan is so exalted, because he has both the lands of *Canjtam* and Panarukan, Pajarakan and the lands of *Chande*, that they all fear him greatly. He is the son of a sister of *Guste Pate*. This is a man who lives well on his crops. He has many horses in his lands; he alone has more than all the lords of Java, including Moors. The people of Blambangan are warlike. The land is rich. It is not necessary to speak of *Chande* because it is inland, and he has taken it.

Many male and female slaves come from his lands to be sold in all Java. He has a multitude of them in his country. When their lords die they take their wives to the fire; thus they lose their bodies in this life and their souls burn in the next. And thus in *Gamda*, when a lord dies his wives kill themselves, or burn or drown in the sea, as I have already told.

[1] BULAMBUAM corresponds to Blambangan, the south-easternmost point of Java. *Balambuão* or *ballambuaõ* in Dourado's atlases.

CHAMDA, *Chandy* or *Chande*, must correspond to Jamber or Djember, a town and district in Besuki province, the easternmost part of Java. This is perhaps what Couto called the 'Kingdom of *O Valle*' (IV, iii, 1), and Lavanha inscribed on his map as *O VALE*. It probably refers to the great valley between the two mountains Hiyang, 10132 feet (3088 m) and Raung, 10932 feet (3332 m), twenty-nine miles to the east.

The great island of Java is finished, as well as I have been able to examine and investigate it, verifying my facts with many people; and whenever they seemed to me to agree thoroughly, I have written that down, and they certainly are not out of the right order ; and there is no doubt that there are more things in Java, and more important things, than are related, and thus up to now I had not heard tell how nobility, pride, determination and daring are in truth found in these parts; the Malays are haughty indeed, but their haughtiness was learned from the Javanese. Comparisons ought not to be made, because the Javanese are haughty and proud by nature, and the others by accident or art. And if this account is to speak honestly of the Javanese matrons, it is not a lie that they are so preposterous that they kill themselves with a kris if anything displeases them, and they sometimes kill their husbands; and it is a custom in Java for a woman to be searched before she goes to her husband, because they carry secret krises. This is the custom among the nobles.

And that it may be known there is no greater pride than in Java, *Fol. 155r.*
there are two languages, one for the nobles and the other for the people. They do not differ as the language at court does with us; but the nobles have one name for things and the people another; this must certainly be the same for everything.

Where but in Java is it customary for the women of good birth to have their pomp, their clothes, their golden crowns and diadems like the Javanese? When they go out they go in state looking like angels. There is no doubt that in the world there are [no more] presumptuous women, and for this reason many die virgins in their houses when they cannot gratify themselves by marrying great people. For where does this pride spring from, if it is not natural to the country? For when the women are so presumptuous, what will be the case with the Javanese men, [so] prosperous and proud that neither a father nor a mother dare put a hand on their son's head in a caress, nor a husband on his wife's. A wife can count her husband as the king of the earth.

And those of the *pates* who are along the sea-coast of Java and who do not yet feel so noble as those inland—because they were slaves and merchants a couple of days ago—are so proud that all of them are respected as if they were lords of the world. Each of them goes out hunting or pleasure-seeking in such exalted style. They spend all their time in pleasures, with retinues with so many lances in holders of gold and silver, as we should use iron, so richly inlaid, with so many harriers, greyhounds and other dogs; and they have so many pictures painted with images and hunting scenes. Their cloths are adorned with gold, their krises, swords, knives, cutlasses are all inlaid with gold; [they have] numbers of concubines, genets, elephants, oxen to draw the wagons of gilt and painted woodwork. They go out in triumphal cars, and if they go by sea [they go] in painted *calaluzes*, so clean and ornamental, with so many canopies that the rowers are not seen by the lord; [there are] beautiful apartments for his women, other places for the nobles who accompany him, all certainly in accordance with his whim, [as] men who cherish their own importance greatly.

[SOUTH-EASTERN ISLANDS]

So that our account may proceed in order and without any interruptions, we will run on to Banda (*Bamdam*); and because it is our intention to speak of Banda as it is the [most important] place among the islands between, their account will not be extensive but brief, as they are not so profitable, to wit, right next to Java are the islands of Bali (*Baly*) and of Lombok (*Bombo*), the island of Sumbawa (*Cimbava*), the island of *Byma*, the island of Sangeang (*Foguo*), and the islands of Solor (*Soloro*), Alor (*Malua*), Kambing (*Lucucamby*), *Citor*, *Batojmbey*, and many others that are in this chain[1].

[1] At the beginning of the sixteenth century there was some information about Sumatra, Java, the 'Spice Islands', and some other far-eastern places, through the relations of Marco Polo, who called at Sumatra at the end of the thirteenth century, Friar Odorico, who visited Sumatra, Java, and perhaps Borneo, a few years later, and some Arab travellers. But this information was scanty and vague; and still vaguer, if any at all, was that about the chain of islands which lie eastward of Java. Pires is the first to give definite news about these islands beyond Java; to some extent it is completed by Rodrigues' maps and drawings. Barbosa, though writing a little later, is much less well-informed than Pires. After them come Pedro Reinel's maps of *c.* 1517 and *c.* 1518, Jorge Reinel's world map of 1519, Lopo Homem's atlas of 1519, and

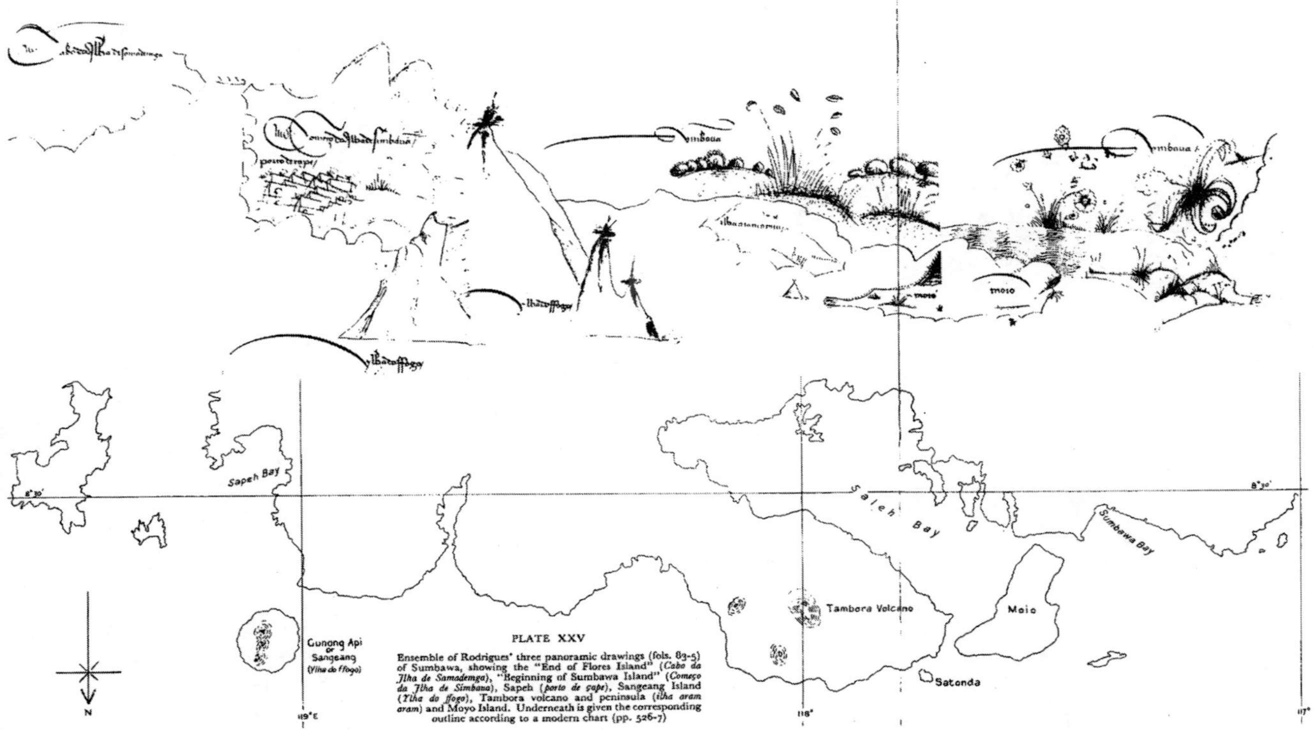

PLATE XXV

Ensemble of Rodrigues' three panoramic drawings (fols. 83-5) of Sumbawa, showing the "End of Flores Island" (*Cabo da Jlha de Samademga*), "Beginning of Sumbawa Island" (*Começo da Jlha de Simbaua*), Sapeh (*porto de çape*), Sangeang Island (*Ylha do ffogo*), Tambora volcano and peninsula (*ilha aram aram*) and Moyo Island. Underneath is given the corresponding outline according to a modern chart (pp. 526-7)

The islands of Bali, and Lombok, and Sumbawa. The first island next to Java is Bali, and the other is Lombok and the

Reinel's map of *c.* 1524. Pigafetta's *Primo viaggio intorno al mondo* has several drawings or maps of islands visited by Magellan's expedition and other islands of which he obtained information. Almost all these drawings refer to the voyage after the expedition reached the Philippines until it left Timor, through the Eastern Archipelago, which gives the drawings special interest for us. Pigafetta's original manuscript, written perhaps in 1524, is lost, but there are four copies extant dating from the first half of the sixteenth century: one in Italian, in the Ambrosiana, Milan; two in French, in the Bibliothèque Nationale, Paris, nos. 5650 and 24224; one in French, belonging to the Phillips Collection, Cheltenham. Then there is a gap in the sources of information, which again become available with the map of *c.* 1540, and later ones. But the disposition of these numerous islands, sometimes with very irregular coastlines, like that of north Sumbawa, and the imperfect knowledge that writers and cartographers had of them, all contributed to the great confusion in their description and mapping, so that several of them sometimes appear as a single one, one appears as two or more. To add to the confusion it happened that contemporary writers and cartographers used different names for the same place, according to their source of information, or spelt them differently; and transcribers of original writings, and cartographers reproducing earlier prototypes, often distorted the spelling given to native names, with the result that some of them became unrecognizable, or their origin extremely difficult to trace. This happened, for instance, with Pires and Rodrigues.

BALY, which is recorded on Rodrigues' map (fol. 36) as *Bllaram*, appears as *bancha* on Reinel's map of *c.* 1524, and later as *bale* on L. Homem's map of 1554, and *Balle* in Dourado's atlases. The *Livro de Marinharia* has *Bamcha* and *Vamcha*, corresponding to Bali (p. 264). On the representation of all these islands in Rodrigues' drawings, see Appendix II.

BOMBO corresponds to Lombok. It is likely that Pires wrote 'lombo' where the transcriber read *bombo*. Rodrigues has *Lomboquo* on his map, but no other early map records it. In the drawings he calls it *amJane*; Galvão has *Anjano*; the rutter refers to it as *Amjane*. Reinel's map of *c.* 1524 has *amgeane*. This name must correspond to the lofty Mount Rinjani (12350 feet or 3764 m.) which is the largest volcano in the whole archipelago, right in the middle of the northern part of the island.

CIMBAVA, BYMA and ILHA DO FOGO—Pires refers to the island of Sumbawa as if it was two islands: *Cimbava* and *Byma*. It takes its name from the village of Sumbava, on the north coast of the western part of the island. Bima, on Bima Bay, is situate on the north coast of the eastern part. Rodrigues' map has *ssimbaua*; Barbosa calls it *Jaua menor* (Java the Less) and *Çindoaba* (see Dames, II, 194); L. Homem's atlas of 1519 has also *IAVA MINOR INSULA*, which Denucé had already identified as Sumbawa (*Les Origines*, pp. 120, 134); on one of Eredia's maps (fol. 28r.) the whole island is called *bima*. Among Rodrigues' drawings there are three of the north coast of the island, all named *Simbaua* or *Symbaua*. Reinel's map of *c.* 1524 has *bima*, *moio*, and *amajam*; L. Homem's map of 1554 also has *aram*; *aramarã* in D. Homem's atlas of 1558; *araö araö* in Dourado's atlases. These last have also *bima*.

other Sumbawa. All these have kings. Each of them has many ports and many waters, many foodstuffs, many slaves, male and female. They are robbers; they have lancharas; they go plundering; they are all heathen. They bring foodstuffs and cloths of their kind for merchandise, and many slaves and many horses which they take to Java to sell.

P. Reinel's maps of *c.* 1517 and *c.* 1518, and J. Reinel's map of 1519 have *ilha do fogo*; the map of *c.* 1540 has *ganuape*; L. Homem's map of 1554 and D. Homem's atlas of 1558 have *guluape*; in the rutter this island is called *Gunapim*, and it is accurately situated 'more or less 12 leagues from *Arrã arrã*'.

SOLORO—Pires' *Soloro* does not mean only the small island of today, or even the small group of Solor Islands, but the large island of Flores as well. The next of Rodrigues' maps (fol. 37) shows part of a large island which is also called *Solor*, having at its eastern end *Cabo das frolles*. But fourteen of his drawings are named either *Sollote* or *Solloro*. The island that is depicted next to Sumbawa, on P. Reinel's maps of *c.* 1517 and 1518, has *cabo da frroresta*, an obvious corruption of *cabo de frolles*; L. Homem's atlas of 1519 has *CANDIN INS.*, the old *Sandji* of El Edrisi (Denucé, *op. cit.*, p. 120), corresponding to Flores; Reinel's map of *c.* 1524 has *c. do ferro*, *Solor*, and *a entrada de solor* (the strait); the map of *c.* 1540 has *c. das fl.*, and eastwards *J. de solor*; L. Homem's map of 1554 has *lucarãge* (Nusa Raja) and *c. do feros*(?) in the middle of the island; Dourado's atlases have *dos ferros*, *llusartaia* (Nusa Raja), *llusatãrete* (Rusa Linguette), *c: das froles*, all on Flores island, and south-eastwards, fairly accurately placed, *osolor*. All this shows once more how the cartographers, copying from map to map names they did not know, could disfigure them until they became almost unrecognizable and even meaningless.

MALUA corresponds to Alor or Ombai island. The name still survives in 'Malua passage', between Alor and Timor. It appears for the first time on Torreño's map of 1522, as *malua*, and then on the anonymous map of *c.* 1523 (in Turin), on Mercator's globe of 1541, and on two maps of the *Islario* of Alonso de Santa Cruz (14 and 101, ed. Real Sociedad Geográfica, Madrid, 1926), as a result of the information brought by the ship *Vitoria* of the Magellan expedition, which arrived in Spain in September 1522. Galvão called it *Mauluoa*.

LUCUCAMBY corresponds to Kambing island, northward of Timor, between Alor and Wetta. It appears as *Nossocamba* (Ambrosian MS) or *Nossocãbu* (Paris MS 5650) on Pigafetta's drawing of Timor, and as *lucacambiu* on one of Eredia's maps (fol. 48v.).

ÇITOR—I was unable to discover, from this unrecognisable name, anything that might suggest what Pires meant for, or the transcriber disfigured as, *çitor*.

BATOJMBEY may correspond to Wetta, Wetar or Wetter island, which on the map of *c.* 1540 appears as *batubor*, and as *Batuombor* (Ambrosian MS) or *Batuambar* (Paris MS 5650) on Pigafetta's drawings. On other early maps it is inscribed as *terra alta* (*terra lata* on Reinel's map of *c.* 1524). *Batu* means rock or stone in Java-Malay.

The island of Bima, beyond these, is a large island belonging to a heathen king. It has many *paraos*, and many foodstuffs in great plenty; it has meat, fish; it has many tamarinds; it has a great deal of brazil, which they take to Malacca to sell, and they go there from Malacca for it because it sells well in China, and the Bima brazil is very thin. It is worth less in China than that from Siam, because that from Siam is thicker and better. Bima also has a large number of slaves and many horses which they take to Java. This island has trade. They are swarthy people with straight hair. This island has a number of villages, and also many people and many woods. People who are going to Banda and the Moluccas call here, and they buy many cloths here, which sell well in Banda and the Moluccas. This island has some gold. Javanese cashes are current there. *The island of Bima* (Byma).

Next to this island is the large island of Sangeang, very mountainous and peopled with many inhabitants. These people go about plundering. It has many ports and many foodstuffs and many slaves to sell. This island has a fair for robbers, who come here to sell what they have stolen from the other islands. It has a heathen king and they all all heathens. It is at the beginning of the road to Timor which will be dealt with after Solor. *Fol. 155v.* *The island of Sangeang* (Foguo).

The island of Solor is very large. It has a heathen king. It has many ports and many foodstuffs in great plenty. It has countless tamarinds; it has a great deal of sulphur, and it is better known for this product than for any other. They take a large quantity of foodstuffs from this island to Malacca, and they take tamarinds and sulphur. There is so much of this sulphur that they take it as merchandise from Malacca to Cochin China, because it is the chief merchandise that goes there from Malacca. Between this island of Solor and that of Bima is the channel of the Timor islands, where the sandalwoods are, which will be described next. The same merchandise is of value in the said islands as in Java. *The island of Solor.*

Between the islands of Bima and Solor there is a wide channel along which they go to the sandalwood islands. All the islands *Islands of Timor*[1] *where the white sandal-wood comes from.*

[1] By 'Islands of Timor' is meant the great Timor Island, and Sumba or Sandalwood Island, as it is still called. Rodrigues' map (fol. 37) has *A Jlha de timor homde naçe o ssamdollo* (The Island of Timor where the sandalwood grows).

from Java onwards are called Timor, for *timor* means 'east' in the language of the country, as if they were saying the islands of the east. As they are the most important, these two from which the sandalwood comes are called the islands of Timor. The islands of Timor have heathen kings. There is a great deal of white sandalwood in these two. It is very cheap because there is no other wood in the forests. The Malay merchants say that God made Timor for sandalwood and Banda for mace and the Moluccas for cloves, and that this merchandise is not known anywhere else in the world except in these places; and I asked and enquired very diligently whether they had this merchandise anywhere else and everyone said not.

With a good wind you can sail from this channel to the islands of the Moluccas in six or seven days. These islands are unhealthy; the people are not very truthful. They go to these island[s] every year from Malacca and from Java, and the sandalwood comes to Malacca. It sells well in Malacca, because it is used in all the nations here, more especially among the heathen.

Merchandise that is of value in Timor.

They take sinabaffs there, *panchavilezes*, *sinhauas*, *balachos*, *cotobalachos*, which are white cloths, coarse Cambay cloth, and [in return] for a little merchandise they load their junks with sandalwood. The voyage to Timor is remunerative, and unhealthy. They leave Malacca in the monsoon and on their way to Banda; they say that on this route there are reefs between the lands of Bima and Solor and that the junks are lost unless they go through the channel, and there is this risk for about half a league, and that it is good to enter by day.

Batu Tara (Batutara)[1].

Opposite the islands of Solor is the island which is called Batu Tara. It is a heathen island with many foodstuffs. From it the route is straight ahead for Banda and for Amboina; and

[1] *Batutara*—Batu Tara or Komba island (Lat. 7° 47′ S., Long. 123° 36′ E.) lies some twenty-five miles northward of Lomblen, the largest island of the Solor group. Rodrigues' map has *Batutara*. Ships going from Malacca to the Spice Islands followed the course Java—Batu Tara—Buru; thence either to Banda or to the Moluccas. So the course is described in the rutter in the *Livro de Marinharia* (p. 267). This is how Rodrigues came to record *Batutara* on his map, because he passed by there when he went to Banda with Antonio de Abreu in 1512. Hamy (*op. cit.*, p. 175) identifies Rodrigues' *Batutara* with Wetter or Wetta island, a mistake due perhaps to the fact that Galvão refers to *Vitara*, probably meaning Wetta, after Malua.

because the other islands along by Solor are not much good for trade because they are out of reach, I do not deal with them. They are all lands of heathen robbers; they have foodstuffs, much rice, sago. I will now speak only of Banda, as we are so fond of the fruits of its soil.

[BANDA, CERAM, AMBOINA]

The islands of Banda are six; five produce mace and one has fire [a volcano]. The chief one is called Pulo Banda. This one has four ports: Celammon (*Calamom*), *Olutatam*, Lontar (*Bomtar*), Komber (*Comber*). In comparison with the others this *Islands of Banda* (Bamdam)[1].

[1] Rodrigues' map (fol. 37) has a group of seven or eight small islands of different sizes with the inscription—*Jlhas de bamda Homde Naçem as maçes* (Islands of Banda where the maces grow). P. Reinel's maps of *c.* 1517 and *c.* 1518 have 'Islands of *babãy*; here are the maces', *babãy* being a miswriting for *bãda*; L. Homem's map of 1512 has *y: de bamda*; Torreño's map of 1522 has *Y*ᵃ*s de bandam*; Reinel's map of *c.* 1524 has *banda*; most of the later maps have either *Banda* or *Bandam*.

The island DE FOGUO (fire, referring to the volcano) is Gunong Api.

PULLO BAMDAM is Lontar or Great Banda Island. Of this island's four ports mentioned by Pires, *Calamom* corresponds to Selamo or Celammon, which lies on the west side of the island's north point; it may be Pigafetta's *Zoroboa*, the name he gave to the largest island in his drawing of *Bandan* archipelago. *Olutatam*, which Barros calls *Lutatam* (III, v, 6) giving it as the main port, may correspond to a place called Ortata or Gt. Waling, on the north side of the island, opposite Neira. *Bomtar* (perhaps a transcriber's mistake, in which he mistook the *l* for *b*, as in the case of *bombo* or Lombok), corresponds to Lontar, which gives its name to the island and lies on the north side, opposite Gunong Api. *Comber* is Komber, between Ortata and Selano.

PULO AEE is Ai or Aij Island, which lies westward of Lontar. It is called *Pulae* by Pigafetta and *Ay* by Barros.

PULO RUD is Run, the westernmost island of the group. It is called *Pulurun* by Pigafetta and *Rom* by Barros, and it appears as *P. rond* on Berthelot's map of 1635. This map is the first to give a fairly complete representation of the Banda group. Besides *Banda* and *P. rond*, it shows *P. caPas*, or Kapal Island, which lies north-westward of the north point of Lontar, and *P. Soangin*, or Suangi Island, thirteen miles north-west of Gunong Api. Ai, Gunong Api and Rozengain (this last too near to Lontar) are also represented, but without names.

PULO BOMCAGY, possibly a transcriber's mistake, must correspond to Rozengain, which Pigafetta calls *Rosoghin*, and Galvão and Barros call *Rosolanguim*; it lies five miles east-south-east of Lontar.

LANACAQE must correspond to Nailaka islet, which lies close to the north coast of Run Island. Pigafetta calls it *Lailaca*.

island has a greater quantity of mace. These [islands] have villages; they have no king; they are ruled by *cabilas* and by the
Fol. 156r. elders. | Those along the sea-coast are Moorish merchants. It is thirty years since they began to be Moors in the Banda islands. There are a few heathen inside the country. In all there must be between two thousand five hundred and three thousand persons in these islands. The mace is a fruit like peaches or apricots, and when it is ripe it opens and the outer pulp falls, and that in the inside turns red, and this is the mace on the nutmeg, and they gather them and put them to dry. This fruit is ripe all through the year; it is gathered every month. About five hundred bahars of mace must be produced every year in the islands as a whole, or even six hundred; and there must be six or seven thousand bahars of nutmeg, and that every year, sometimes more, sometimes less. It is not always of one kind, and they say that these islands used to produce a thousand bahars of mace. This island alone which is called Banda is larger than all the others put together. Another island is called Neira. This is a port where the Javanese anchor; it is called Port Neira. It produces mace. And the other three islands, to wit, Pulo Ai (*Aee*) and Pulo Run (*Rud*) and Pulo *Bomcagy*, are three small islands which produce mace. They have no ports in which you can anchor. They bring their mace to the island of Banda. All are in sight of and near to one another. I do not speak of the island [of *Fogo*][1] because it does not trade, nor of another small island called Nailaka (*Lanacaqe*) which produces sago.

The people of these islands have straight black hair. They are richer now than they used to be, because now they sell their mace better and for better prices. Formerly the Javanese and Malays used to sail to these islands every year bringing a little cloth, calling at Java. They sold there the most and best of their cloths for cashes and for other low-class things, and went from there to Sumbawa and to Bima, and they sold the merchandise they brought from Java in these two islands. They used to make a profit both on what they sold in Java and on what they took from Java to the said islands of Bima and Sumbawa; and in the

[1] This island is Gunong Api; the word *fogo* is obviously omitted in the MS.

islands they used to buy cloth that sold well in Banda, and in exchange for it and for Java cashes they used to buy mace; and as soon as the junk reached Banda they used to take command of the country, and bought as they wished as long as they stayed there; and when the people of Banda had good cloth in their hands it was a great novelty to them, and they used to fix a price for the people of the country, and the captains of the junk were adored by the people.

Now, since these islands of Banda have been visited by the ships and have come under the jurisdiction of the King our lord, it is not done like this, but the people of Banda can obtain the rich cloth in great quantities and at small prices, always receiving favours and gifts and good companionship from the Portuguese, who go there to buy for gold and rich things that which the Moors buy for straw, and they are still discontented with our companies.

Merchandise we take to Banda.

Sinabaffs of all kinds and every other kind of fine white cloth from Bengal; all the cloths from *Bonuaquelim*, to wit, *enrolados* of large, medium and small *ladrilho*, *topetins* and cloth of all kinds from Gujarat, so that the people of Banda must be called fortunate, and it is not without cause that the kings of the Moluccas, who know about the things of Banda, sigh for us, as will be told when the noble islands are described. And the merchants who used to sail there used to buy for old pots and trinkets and beads from Cambay and other things like that, so that there is no doubt that Banda is wealthier now. Banda also has cloves which come in loads from the Moluccas to Amboina and from Amboina to Banda, this in twelve or fifteen days with the monsoon. A bahar of cloves is worth the same as a bahar of mace, and one of mace the same as seven of nutmeg, and they will not sell you mace and nutmeg except together, that is, if you want a bahar of mace you have to buy seven bahars of nutmeg, because otherwise the merchandise could not stand it, because the nutmeg would be lost if they did not sell it in this way. | The *Fol. 156v.* chief merchandise for Banda is the Gujarat cloth, to wit, red and black *bretangis*, *caçutos*, white and black *maindis*, *coraçones* cloth, *patolas*, and after these [there is] cloth from Bengal and after Bengal from *Bonuaquelin*, from Gujarat, *lamedares*, many *sabones*[1]. When the account is made up, each bahar of mace costs three *cruzados* or three and a half, according to the goods for which you buy, and there are some for which it costs four; as for cloth, the finer it is the more you have to pay, because their idea is [to have] coarse clothing for the people, and because people come to Banda from a great many outside islands to buy Banda cloth, from Gillolo (*Bato Ymbo*)[2] to *Papua*[3], from Papua to the Moluccas, and many other islands. They buy in Banda according to the weight of the Malacca bahar; whoever goes there takes the scales and weighs freely in Banda. Banda has ivory tusks and gold, which are brought from other islands to be sold.

The islands of Banda have hardly any foodstuffs. The surrounding islands bring foodstuffs to sell there, and the junks that go there take rice from Bima and things to eat. Sago is used for money in the country. Sago is bread, the same shape as a brick; it is made of the pith of a tree and baked very hard. They

[1] MAINDIS and PANOS DE CORAÇONES. It is not clear whether 'white and black *maindis*' (the meaning of which I cannot find) are the same as *panos de coraçones*, or whether they are two different kinds of cloth. Again, *panos de coraçones* may mean 'cloths from Khorasan' or 'cloths with hearts' (painted or embroidered). PATOLA was a silk cloth, sometimes embroidered or mixed with cotton. When referring to the 'Isles of Bandam', Barbosa mentions '*Patolas* (that is to say Cambaya cloths)'. II, 198. SABONES may mean soaps. Or is it perhaps the name of some other cloth? The whole sentence is very confused indeed.

[2] *Bato Ymbo* may correspond to *Batochina*, the old Portuguese name for the southern peninsula or the whole of Gillolo Island or Halmaheira. One of the highest mountains in Gillolo is Mount Ibu (4528 feet or 1260 m), whence flows the Ibu River. *Batu* means rock or stone in Malay.

[3] Rodrigues' map has to the north of Ceram a large island, the situation of which suggests Gillolo, with the inscription—*Jlha de papoia e a Jente della sam cafres* (Island of Papua and its people are *Cafres*). The map of *c.* 1540 has *as jlhas papuas* to the east of Gillolo; Dourado's atlases have the north coast of a large land denominated *Costa dos papuas* (*c.* 1573), or simply *OS PAPVAS* (1580), close to the coast of Gillolo, which corresponds to the north-east coast of New Guinea; in Luís' atlas of 1563, prior to Dourado, the same coast is already called *noua guinea*. The Malay word *papuwah* stands for 'frizzle-haired', i.e. the *cafres* mentioned by Rodrigues. It is likely that Pires, as well as Rodrigues, refers to the north-west part of New Guinea, though the information they had of the islands westward of Banda and the Moluccas was incomplete and rather confused. Later on, in his description of the island of *Batochina* (Gillolo), Pires refers to 'the island of Papua, which is about eighty leagues from Banda'.

PLATE XXVI

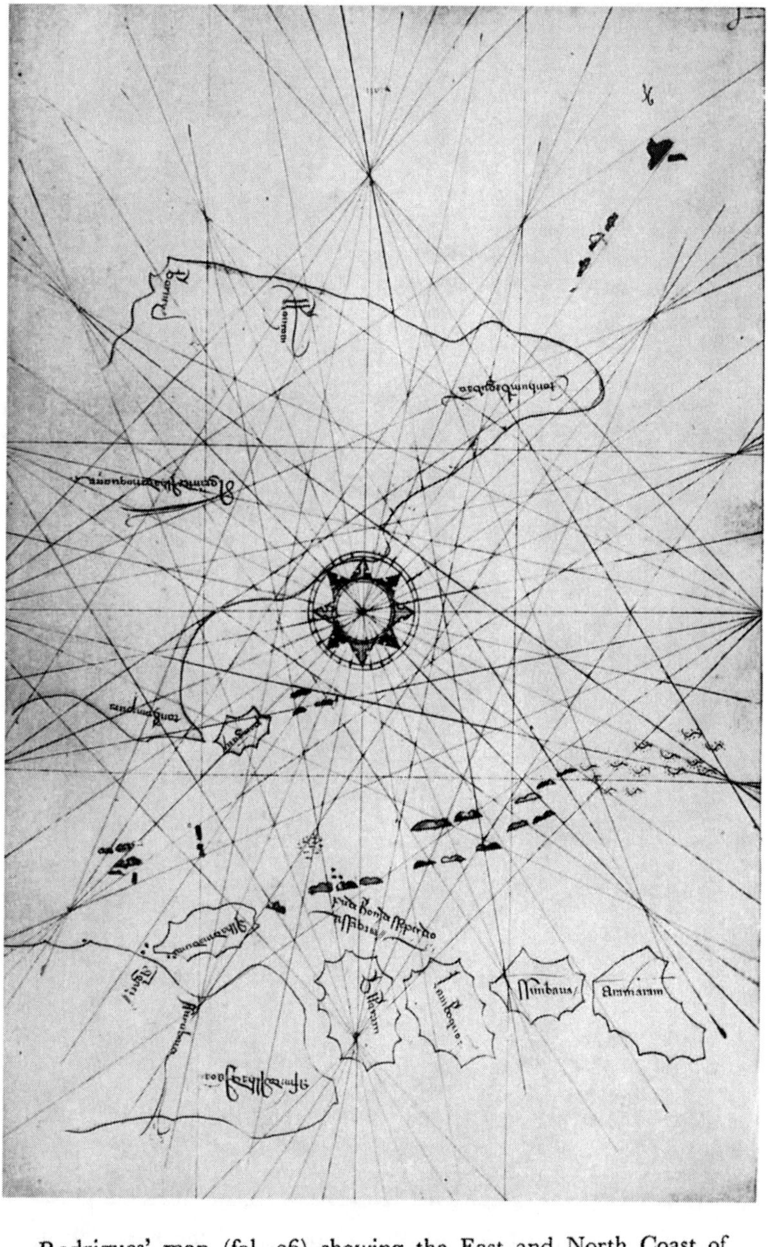

Rodrigues' map (fol. 36) showing the East and North Coast of Borneo, eastern end of Java, Madura, Bali, Lombok and Sumbawa (pp. 522-3)

PLATE XXVII

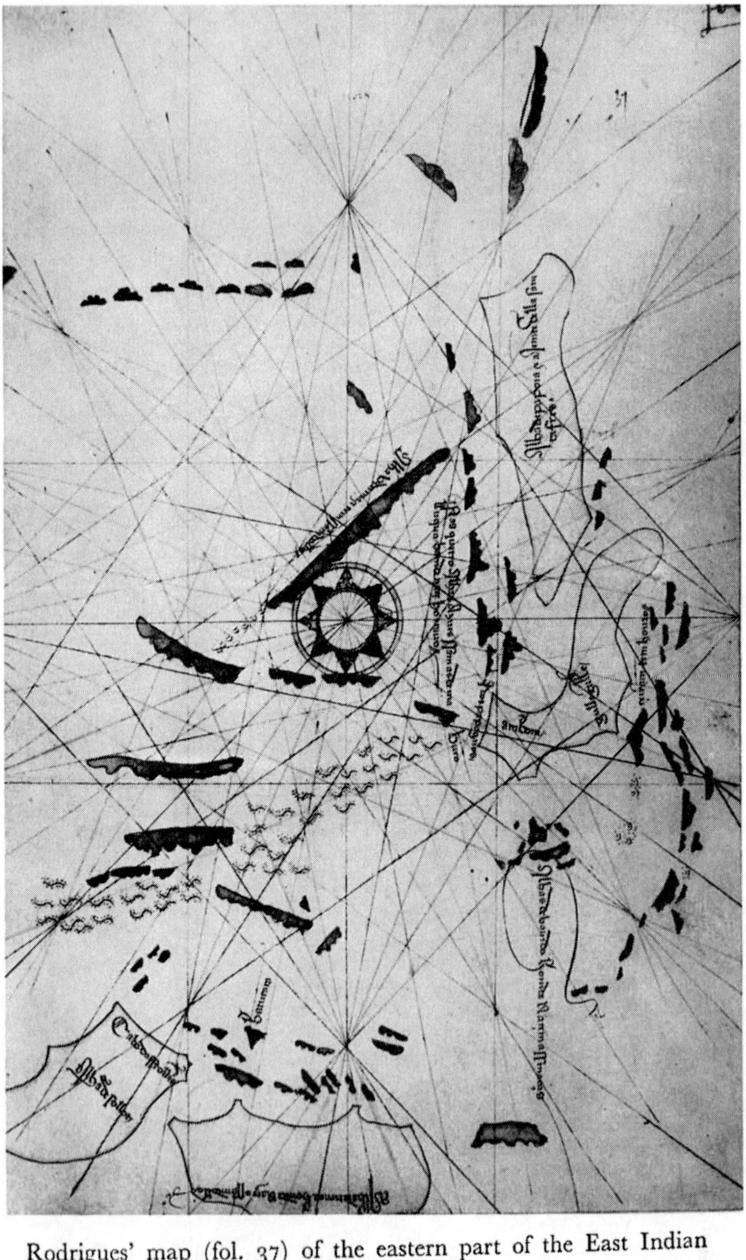

Rodrigues' map (fol. 37) of the eastern part of the East Indian Archipelago (p. 523)

bring a great deal from the islands near to the islands of Banda, and it is used for money—so much sago for such and such a thing, in the same way as pepper in Pase. Banda has some large islands two or three days' journey away, from which they obtain supplies. They belong to heathens, all of them agricultural people.

Three islands are near Banda. The *nore*[1] parrots come from the island of Papua. Those which are prized more than any others come from the islands called Aru (*Daru*)[2], birds which they bring over dead, called birds of paradise (*passaros de Deus*), and they say they come from heaven, and that they do not know how they are bred; and the Turks and Persians use them for making panaches—they are very suitable for this purpose. The Bengalees buy them. They are good merchandise, and only a few come.

Two days' sail away, or less, is the end of the large island of [*Ceram*] Ceram (*Ceirã*)[3]; this is leaving out Amboina (*Ambom*), because Amboina is almost up against the islands of Ceram. The islands of Ceram begin at the island of Goram (*Guram*)[4] and almost touch the Moluccas; and the island is narrow and can be navigated on the inside along by Amboina as well as on the outside, and so it has ports on both sides, and villages inland. The ports of Gule Gule, *Bemuaor*, *Cejlam*, and others are on the way to

[1] *Nore* or *lory*, from the Malay *nūri*, 'a name given to various brilliant-coloured varieties of parrots which are found in the Moluccas and other islands of the Archipelago'. *Hobson-Jobson*, *s.v.* Lory; Dalgado, *s.v.* Nore. Rodrigues' map has written *I dos papagaios* (Island of the Parrots) between *Buro* and *Ambom*.

[2] Pires' *ilhas Daru* corresponds to *ilhas de Aru*, the islands of Aru. The map of *c.* 1540 is the first to record *aru*; it appears again in Dourado's atlases.

[3] Ceram or Serang. Rodrigues shows on his map a large island on which are written the names *ambom* and *gullegulle*; between this island and certain small islands to the east is written *çeiram tem houro* (Ceram has gold). No doubt this last inscription refers to Ceram, because Gule Gule is situated there. L. Homem's atlas of 1519 has a more correctly shaped *SEILAM. INSULA*. Reinel's map of *c.* 1524 has *ceilam*, indicating a small island east-north-east of Ceram; the map of *c.* 1540 has *J. de cajlom*. But in D. Homem's atlas of 1568 the island has written across it *batachina de ambo*.

[4] Goram or Gorong lies south-east of Ceram. It actually gives its name to a group of three small islands—Goram, Panjang and Manawoka.

Banda, and behind are *Tana Muar*, Uli (*Olu*), *Varam*[1]; and they say that the navigation behind is very safe. To sum up, the Amboina islands are these: Amboina, Hitu, Haruku (*Ytaqoay*), Honimoa, Nusa Laut (*Vulmiçalao*). If in what I say of these islands, together with Banda, I disagree with the pilots, it is not my fault, because in this I am relying on people who have been

[1] GULE GULE—After Rodrigues' map had recorded *gullegulle*, the port that he visited with Abreu in 1512, almost every Portuguese map up to the seventeenth century shows that name, properly situated at the south-east end of Ceram. There still exists a place Gule Gule, or Goele Goele, on the south side of the south-eastern extremity of Ceram. Gule Gule lies at the south-west corner of a lagoon which separates the south-east point of Ceram from the mainland. Hamy situates Gule Gule at Piru bay, on the south-west coast of Ceram, 'au fond de la baie de Tarouno, où la rivière Kolli-Kolli porte encore le nom que le commandant portugais attribue à son mouillage (Guli-Guli)'. *Op. cit.*, p. 167. Though there is a small stream called Kole Kole on the east side of Piru bay, the name Gule Gule still survives where all the early Portuguese maps rightly placed it—at the south-eastern extremity of the island.

BEMUAOR—It seems as if Pires' description is following the south coast of Ceram, from east to west. *Bemuaor* may correspond to Bemu, an anchorage near the mouth of a river—Wai Bobot—at the eastern side of the large Teluti bay, about the middle of the south coast of Ceram. The last part of the word *muaor* may be related to *muar*, which means 'mouth of a river' in Malay.

CEJLAM—At the end of Elpaputi bay, on the south coast of Ceram, one of the principal places is Paulohi or Poeleh; on some Dutch maps of Ceram it is also called *Sahoelaoe* or *Sahoelaoe Lama*, the pronunciation of which is not far from the Portuguese *Cejlam*. It is curious to note that the whole island of Ceram is called *Seilam* in L. Homem's atlas of 1519, and *I. de cajlom* on the map of *c.* 1540. Reinel's map of *c.* 1524 has a small island called *ceilam* off the north-east end of Ceram; Dourado's atlases have the same small island under the names of *cailam*, *cailaö* or *caillaö*.

TANA—There is a good anchorage in front of Tanah Gojang village, in Piru bay. However, there is also Tanjong Tanduru or Tananurong, the north-west corner of the island, which might suggest Pires' *Tana* or even *Tana Muar*.

MUAR—Galvão says that after Buru and Amboina the ships of Abreu 'coasted along that [island] which is called *Muar Damboino*, and anchored in a haven called *Guli Guli*'. I was unable to establish any connexion between Pires' *Muar* and Galvão's *Muar Damboino*, which seems to refer to Ceram, though some connexion certainly exists between the two.

OLU—There is a village, river and cape called Uli on the north coast of Ceram.

VARAM—This may correspond to a place called Wairama, at Hatiling bay, close to the port of Wahai, the most important on the north coast of Ceram. It is possible that the word was originally written *Uaram*, the *v* of *Varam* standing for a *u*.

there; I have learnt this from Moors, from their charts, which I have seen many times, and if their charts are not to be trusted, let it be clear that this should be for reading and not for navigation.

The people of Banda are cunning enough to have a village in the mountains where they foregather when they feel they are in any danger in the villages along the sea coast, and they collect everything up there in the mountains; and Banda is something so small and weak that it is at the mercy of any junk that goes there, whether it be Javanese of Malayan. And after that there is nothing more to be said of Banda. I have decided to pass on to the Moluccas, where our aims are paramount, by way of Amboina.

Islands of Amboina (Ambon).

Amboina is one island and next to it are Hitu (*Yta*), Haruku (*Cuaij*), Honimoa (*Vull*), Nusa Laut (*Nucalao*)[1], and they are

[1] AMBON, or Amboina, is represented together with Ceram as a single island on Rodrigues' map. Albuquerque says in his letter of 20 Aug. 1512 that the ships of Abreu's expedition might go 'to be overhauled (*espalmar*) at a cape called *ambam*, on a large island which lies four days' sail from the Clove Islands' (*Cartas*, I, 68); in the *Comentários* (III, xxxvii) *Amboino* is substituted for *ambam*. L. Homem's atlas of 1519 has *ambonyo*, well separated from Ceram, though south-westward of *buyo* or Buru (also called *Buyo*, in *Livro de Marinharia*, some old written forms of *r* being easily mistaken for a *y*); Torreño's map of 1522 has *ambuon* south-west of *gelolo*, between *buiro* and *Ya S de bandam*; Reinel's map of *c.* 1524 has *anboina*(?) on the western part of Ceram; the map of *c.* 1540 has an island close to the south-west of Ceram, corresponding to the Amboina group, but *J. danobueno* is written over Ceram; later maps usually have *amboino*. The Dutch still call the Amboina island Ambon.

YTA—Although, above, this word was coupled with the next, so as to form *Ytaqoay*, the two words are here distinctly separated as *Yta* and *cuaij*. *Yta* must correspond to *Ito* or Hitu, perhaps reported to Pires as a distinct island from Amboina, which consists practically of two islands of unequal size lying parallel to each other, united at one point by a low sandy isthmus less than a mile in width. The northern, and larger, peninsula is called Hitu. Amboina road is in the southern peninsula, which forms with the southern coast of the northern peninsula, west of the isthmus, the large and deep Amboina bay. Guerreiro (1601) refers to the port, town and island of *Ito*, as distinct from *Ambóino*, where the Portuguese had the main settlement and fort. The other islands of the group, which he mentions, are *Oma*, (Haruku) *Oliacer* (Saparua or Honimoa), and *Rossalau* (Nussa Laut). *Relação Anual*, II, 2, xvi, xvii. Berthelot's map of 1635 has *hito*, written on the north coast of *Amboena*. According to Crawfurd (*Dictionary*) the natives call the island Hitu, the usual name being derived from that of its chief town—'Ambun'.

all nearly up against the coast of Ceram. The people of the island are woolly-haired, bestial; they have no merchandise and they have not a very good port; they have no trade. It is a place of
Fol. 157r. dangerous people. Those who want to pass on | to the Moluccas stay there, as is known. They could pass if they wanted to, but because the Moors have no metal anchors and are not seamen, but leave everything at the slightest danger and go swimming away, they do not do their navigation as they should. It always took two or three years from Malacca to Banda and the Moluccas, and many junks are lost; and it is not surprising, because the Moors from these parts know nothing at all [of seamanship], and the mariners are slaves, and it is all the same to them whether they are in Java or the Moluccas, so they have no need to hurry, and consequently make their journeys long. I now pass on to the Moluccas to which Amboina is subject.

MOLUCCAS

We have reached the Molucca (*Maluqo*) islands,[1] because it is not our intention to go farther on from here, as there is no need

CUAIJ—This may correspond to Oma or Haruku island, the next to the east of Amboina, from which it is separated by Haruku strait. On the western part of the south coast of Haruku there is the village of Oma, eastward of which is another place and cape called Waisoi or Wasai.

VULL—As in the case of *Ytaqoay*, the transcriber had previously written *vullmjçalao* as one word; but here the two words are well separated. *Vull* must be *Oliacer*, Saparua or Honimoa island, the third of the large islands in the Amboina group, lying eastward of Haruku and very close to it. This corresponds perhaps to the *nucilloell* which appears in Dourado's atlases, south-east of *amboino*, and is mentioned by Castanheda as *Nunciuèl* (VIII, cc). It is possible that this is meant for 'Nusa Uel'.

NUCALAO—Nusa Laut, the easternmost island of the Amboina group, lying south-east of Saparua and very close to it. It may be the *allaö* or *allam* seen in Dourado's atlases, next to *nucilloell*. So the relative positions of Amboina, Haruku, Saparua and Nusa Laut follow the order in which Pires mentions the four names.

[1] Francisco Serrão, the captain of one of the ships in Abreu's expedition to the Spice Islands, was the first European to visit the Moluccas, where he arrived in 1512, living there probably until the beginning of 1521, when he died. Abreu's fleet arrived back in Malacca in December 1512, and Rodrigues left for India at the beginning of January 1513, before he could know of the first information sent by Serrão from Ternate, which reached Malacca in the middle of 1513. This is why the Moluccas on Rodrigues' map (fol. 37)

for this, but just the clove islands, and from there I will turn back home.

The Molucca islands which produce cloves are five, to wit, the chief one is called Ternate and another Tidore and another Motir (*Motes*) and another Makyan (*Maqujem*) and another Bachian (*Pacham*). And there is also a great deal of wild cloves in the port of Gillolo (*Jeilolo*) in the land of the island of Gillolo (*Batochina*). According to what they say, Mohammedanism in the Molucca islands began fifty years ago. The kings of the islands are Mohammedans, but not very deeply involved in the sect. Many are Mohammedans without being circumcised, and there are not many Mohammedans. The heathen are three parts and more out of four. The people of these islands are dark-skinned; they have sleek hair. They are at war with one another most of the time. They are almost all related.

These five islands must produce about six thousand bahars of cloves a year—sometimes a thousand more, or a thousand less. It is true that merchandise bought in Malacca for five hundred *reis* will buy a bahar of cloves in the Moluccas. The bahar is by Malacca weight, because they weigh it in accordance with that, and the merchants take the scales, as it is sometimes worth more, sometimes less, just a little. There are six crops of

have only the inscription—*estas quatro Jlhas Azues ssam as de malluquo homde naçe ho crauo* (these four islands [painted in] blue are those of *Maluco*, where the clove grows). P. Reinel's map of *c.* 1517 and that of *c.* 1518 have 'islands of Maluco where there is the clove'; L. Homem's atlas of 1519 has *MALVC⁹. INSVLE*; J. Reinel's map of *c.* 1519 has 'islands of Maluco from where the clove comes'. Torreño's map of 1522, and the planisphere of *c.* 1523 (Turin), both drawn in Spain after the arrival of the *Vitoria*, the only surviving ship of Magellan's expedition, which had passed through the Moluccas in 1521, are the first to record the individual names of the islands. Torreño's map has *terranati, tidorj, maqujan, bachiã*, and *INSVLA DE GELOLO*; the planisphere has *tarenate, tedore aqui cargarõ* (Tidore, here they loaded), *motil, maq . . ., gilolo*; Pigafetta's manuscript has *Tarenate, Tadore, Mutir, Machiam* or *Machian, Bachiam* or *Bachian*, and *Giailonlo, Giailolo, Giaiallo* or *Iaialolo*. The first known Portuguese map to give the names of the islands is that of *c.* 1540, which has *ternate, montell, maquiam, bacham*. Varthema describes the voyage he says he made to 'the island of *Monoch* where the cloves grow', and refers to 'many other neighbouring islands . . . uninhabitated'; but the famous Bolognese was never there. Barbosa mentions *Pachel* (*Pachan* or *Bachiam*), *Moteu, Machiam, Tidor* and *Tanarte*. Pires is, however, the first to give a proper description of the Moluccas, and Rodrigues the first to represent them on a map, though neither was ever actually there.

cloves every year. Eight junks used at one time to go from Malacca to Banda and the Moluccas, and three or four [of them were] from Grisee, and as many more from Malacca. The ones from Malacca belonged to *Curia Deva*[1], a Chetti merchant, and those from Grisee to *Pate Cuçuf* who had the trade there; and there were other merchants as well, both Javanese and Malay, but these two were the chief merchants; each of them has made a large sum of gold in this trade. Cloves were always worth nine or ten *cruzados* a bahar in Malacca when they were plentiful, and twelve cruzados a bahar when they were scarce.

The island of Ternate, our friend. The chief island of all the five is the island of Ternate. The king is a Mohammedan. He is called Sultan *Bem Acorala*[2]. They say he is a good man. His island produces at least a hundred and fifty bahars of cloves every year. Two or three ships can anchor in the port of this island; this is a good village. This king has some foreign merchants in his country. They say that the island must contain up to two thousand men, and up to two hundred will be Mohammedans. This king is powerful among his neighbours. His country is abundant in foodstuffs from the land, although many foodstuffs come to the Molucca kings from other islands, as will be told later. Only the king of Ternate is called Sultan; the others are called Raja. He is at war with his father-in-law, *Raja Almançor*[3], king of the island of Tidore. He has as many as a hundred *paraos*. The island must be six leagues round. There is a mountain in the middle of this island, which yields a great deal of sulphur, which burns in great quantities[4]. This king has half the island of Motir (*Motei*) for his own,

[1] According to Barros (II, ix, 4) this *Curia Deva* was an enemy of the Portuguese and helped and incited *Pate Quedir* and *Pate Unus* against them.

[2] Barbosa calls him *Soltam Binaracola*, and Pigafetta *raya Abuleis*. However, Barros says that 'the name of this king of Ternate (who helped Serrão) was *Cachil Boleise*, a man of great age and much prudence, whom the Moors held almost for a prophet in what he said'. (III, v, 6).

[3] Barros (III, viii, 9–10) refers extensively to *Almançor*, king of Tidore, and his quarrels with the Portuguese. Pigafetta calls him *raia sultan Manzor*.

[4] Actually Ternate island, eight miles long from north to south, and six miles broad, is composed almost exclusively of a conical volcano, 5184 feet (1580 m) in height, which has been in a state of constant activity for more than 300 years.

whence he gets many foodstuffs. [The people of] Ternate are more tractable than those in any of the other [islands], although another has a better port, and more trade because of it. They say that this king dispenses justice. He keeps his people obedient. He says he would be glad to see Christian priests, because if our faith seemed to him good he would forsake his sect and turn Christian.

This king of Ternate, being a man of good judgement, when he heard that Francisco Serrão was in Amboina, sent for him and for other Portuguese who were wrecked in the voyage of António de Abreu, and received them in his country and did them honour; and the said king wrote letters to Malacca saying how he and his lands were the slaves of the King our lord, as will be seen at greater length in his letters, which were brought by António de Miranda who went to Banda and sent to Amboina whither the letters had arrived, having been brought by Francisco Serrão, who returned to Ternate, because that was the arrangement[1]. *Fol. 157v.*

The people of Ternate are knights among those of the Moluccas. They are men who drink wines of their kind. Ternate has good water. It is a healthy country with good air. The king of Ternate has four hundred women within his doors, all daughters of men of standing; he has many daughters by them. When the king goes to war he rallies forth with a crown of gold, and his sons wear them also as a mark of dignity. These crowns are of moderate value.

Merchandise there is in Ternate.

The country produces cloves. A great deal of iron comes from

[1] Barros says that in 1513 'António de Miranda went with a fleet to the Islands of the Moluccas and Banda'. (III, v, 6). Patalim, who was then Captain of Malacca, also says in his evidence in the so-called 'Process of the Moluccas' of 1524, that he sent 'Miranda with three ships, which went to Banda, and from there to the Moluccas, where they found Serrão'. *Cartas*, IV, 167. Amboina was then considered part of the southern Moluccas, which may explain the rather confusing information given by Barros and Patalim. However Pires, who was writing in Malacca shortly after the return of Miranda, is more precise. His information is confirmed by the very detailed and accurate evidence given in the same 'Process of the Moluccas' by Brandão, who declares that Miranda had not gone farther than Banda. *Ibidem*, p. 170. Next year, 1514, Miranda went again to Banda, but only in 1515 did two junks under the command of Álvaro Coelho reach Ternate, returning to Malacca laden with cloves.

outside, from the islands of Banggai (*Bemgaia*)[1], iron axes, choppers, swords, knives. Gold comes from other islands. It has some little ivory; it has coarse native cloth. A great many parrots come from the islands of Morotai (*Mor*)[2], and the white parrots come from Ceram.

Merchandise of value in Ternate. Coarse cloth from Cambay is of value in the Moluccas; and for the finer sort, all the *enrolado* cloth from *Bonuaquelim*, with large, medium or small *ladrilho*, *patolas*, all the coarse and white cloth, as for instance, *synhauas*, *balachos*, *panchavelizes*, *cotobalachos*; but the principal merchandise is cloth from Cambay and the tails of white oxen and cows which they bring from Bengal.

How cloves grow. Cloves have six crops a year; others say that there are cloves all the year round, but that at six periods in the year there are more. After flowering it turns green and then it turns red; then they gather it, some by hand and some beaten down with a pole, and red as it is they spread it out on mats to dry, and it turns black. They are small trees. Cloves grow like myrtle berries, a great many heads grow together. All this fruit is in the hands of the natives, and it all comes through their hands to the seacoast.

Although this island of Ternate is the most distant of all from Amboina, and the next in order ought to be the nearest to Amboina, which is Bachian (*Pachão*), yet as Ternate is the best, it has been described first, and also because the king is a vassal of the King our lord; and now I will go towards Amboina, describing the islands.

[1] Banggai Island is one of the more important in the Banggai archipelago, which lies 300 miles south-west of Ternate, off Banggai peninsula, on the east coast of central Celebes. Barbosa says: 'Not very far off from these islands (the Moluccas), to the west-south-west, at thirty leagues away, there is another inhabited . . . island called Tendaya (or Bangaya, in the Spanish version). Much iron is found there which is taken to divers countries'. Dames thought that 'it is undoubtedly the island of Banggi which lies off the northernmost point of Borneo'. (II, 205). On Berthelot's map of 1635, Banggai island is correctly situated but called *Pangara*.

[2] Morotai or Morti island lies thirteen miles east of the north-eastern point of Gillolo, with the small Rau island and some islets close by. When later describing the island of *Batochina*, or Gillolo, Pires asserts that the 'islands of Mor' limit Gillolo on the north. Berthelot's map has *morotay* correctly situated.

After leaving Ternate for Amboina [and] sailing three leagues, you see the island of Tidore. It is an island which is about ten leagues round. The king of this island is a Mohammedan, an enemy of the king of Ternate and his father-in-law. This king has about two thousand men in his country, about two hundred of whom are Mohammedans and the others are heathens. The king is called *Raja Almançor*. He has many wives and children. His country produces about one thousand four hundred bahars of cloves a year. There is no port in this island where ships can anchor. He is as powerful a king as the king of Ternate. He is always at war. These two are the most important in the Moluccas, and they compute that this king must have eighty *paraos* in his country. This king has the king of Makyan (*Maqiem*) for his vassal. *Island of Tidore* (Tidora).

Half the island of Motir is also subject to this king. His country produces many foodstuffs: rice, meat, fish. They say he is a man of good judgement. This king is very desirous of trading with us, because the Moluccas Islands are going to ruin, and for the last three years they have only gathered a few cloves, because of the drop in navigation since the capture of Malacca.

Six leagues sail from this island of Tidore is the island of Motir. This island is about four or five leagues round. It has a mountain in the middle. Half the island obeys the king of Ternate and the other half the king of Tidore; each of them has stationed his captain in his own land. This island is entirely heathen; it has about six hundred men. This island produces about one thousand two hundred bahars of cloves a year; each captain will have four or five small lancharas. This island produces many foodstuffs, and each part supports its own lord. The captains of these islands are heathens, knightly men, important people, and they are friends. *Fol. 158r.* *Island of Motir* (Motei).

Both the king of Tidore and this island of Motir bring their cloves in *paraos* to the island of Makyan to be sold, because the port where the junks come and anchor is there.

Five leagues away from the island of Motir, the island of Makyan appears. This island of Makyan is eight or nine leagues round; it has about three thousand men; it has a hundred and thirty *paraos*. It produces about one thousand five hundred *Island of Makyan* (Maquiem).

bahars of cloves a year. The king is called *Raja Ucem*. He is a Mohammedan, and [so are] about three hundred men in his country. This island of Makyan has a very good port. This is the island where the junks load, and they bring the cloves to be sold here from all the islands, with the exception of Ternate, whither [some people] also go because of the port where they can anchor. The king has almost as many foodstuffs as the others, and he has more people and *paraos* than Tidore.

The *Raja Ucem*, king of this island of Makyan, is a first cousin of the *Raja Almançor*, king of Tidore, and this king is to some extent subject to the said king of Tidore. There are a few foreigners in this port, and they greatly long for peace with us. They say that he is a good man, and this is a land with more trade than the others, and thus the junks come and anchor here. The port is safe and good. Almost all the people are heathens. They come to this island with merchandise from many islands. They have an abundance of foodstuffs and good water, and they say that the people on the sea-coast are tractable.

Islands of Bachian (Pacham)[1].

From this island of Makyan which I have described, it is almost fourteen leagues to the islands of Bachian. These islands of Bachian are ten or twelve. The island called Bachian produces cloves, the others do not. The king of this island is called *Raja Cuçuf*. He has more land and more people than any of the kings of the Moluccas, and more *paraos*. This king is a half-brother of the king of Ternate; they are great friends. Almost all the people are heathens. They have good ports. Those who have to load cargoes in the Moluccas come here to sight this land, and they go from here to other islands. Bachian is a chain of islands which goes up to Ceram opposite Amboina. This island produces about five hundred bahars of cloves every year. It produces a great deal of pitch; it does not produce many foodstuffs, but they

[1] Bachian Island is the largest and southernmost of the five true Moluccas. There are many islands near Bachian, the largest of which are Great Tawali or Kasiruta, and Mandioli near the western part; about fifteen miles northwards lie the Ombi islands, eighty miles north of the north-western part of Ceram. It seems that Bachian was first known to the Portuguese as *Pacham*. Besides Pires' reference, there is at least another contemporary document—the evidence of Bartolomeu Gonçalves in the 'Process of the Moluccas'—where the island is several times called *Pacham*. *Cartas*, IV, 163–4. Barbosa's *Pachel* is certainly related to *Pacham*.

bring plenty of them from the other islands. They do a great deal of trade in their land. This island has parrots, mats and other things which people come there to buy.

According to information I obtained, it is a very short time since the cloves in this island were wild—in the same way as wild plums become cultivated plums and wild olives become cultivated olives—and they say that originally these cloves were not made use of, because the trees were covered up in wild places, and that during the last ten years the cloves have been made as good as any of the others, and that the cloves in this island are increasing greatly. It is forty leagues from this island to the island of Amboina. All the cloves from these five islands are of equal goodness if they are gathered when they are perfectly ripe.

In this island they also dry the branches of the trees with many leaves on. This is merchandise, because in our part of Europe the said leaves are used instead of betel, and since dried betel has no flavour | they put the leaves in its place. It is a merchandise *Fol. 158v.*
which they used to take to Venice by way of Alexandria, and it must be quite twenty years that I have been using the said leaves in Portugal instead of the said *folio Indio* which is betel[1].

That ends the account of the five Molucca islands, coming from Ternate to Amboina; and if that is not in order, go back in the account from Amboina to Ternate, beginning with Bachian. Do not say that the navigation from Malacca to the Moluccas is dangerous, for it is a good route and convenient for our ships, and with monsoon winds you can sail to Banda or Amboina in a month, and from there to the Moluccas in a day

[1] We have seen already (p. 54) that Pires was wrong in identifying *folio indio* with betel. But it seems that the leaves of the clove tree (*Caryophyllus aromaticus* Linn.) were used as a substitute for the *folium indum*, though Orta (*Coll.* XXIII) dismisses the idea. Linschoten says that 'the leaves called Folium Indum . . . have a sweet smell, almost like Cloves'. Hak. Soc. ed., II, 130–1. Though he had not been in the Moluccas, Pires certainly knew the clove leaves well, and his statement is certainly most interesting. In his letter of 8 Jan. 1515 to the King of Portugal, Jorge de Albuquerque, then Captain of Malacca, writes that António de Miranda had arrived from Banda, whence he went to Amboina to meet Serrão, and he was sending a branch with leaves and a stem of the clove tree; then he adds that Tomé Pires would explain all these things. *Cartas*, III, 136–7.

or two. Our well-equipped ships will not linger in Amboina; they must go on to the Moluccas, especially anyone who has been able to learn and investigate how to come from Portugal to the Moluccas in such a short time; anyone will be able, as is known, when his turn comes and if he works—anyone who is jealous that things should be accomplished in the service of the King our lord—to make the journey of the Moluccas not by way of the coast of Java, but by Singapore, and from Singapore to Borneo and from Borneo to the island of Buton (*Butum*)[1] and then to the Moluccas. Anyone who has sailed to the Moluccas has always found this a very good way, in a monsoon, and quick. The Java way to the Moluccas was officially established in this manner: the route from Borneo to the Moluccas suits us well, and the Java way suits the merchants of Malacca; the Borneo one suits us because we do not put in to ports from country to country, selling here, selling there, making money in each place in such a way that the time draws out; and as they have little capital and the sailors are slaves they make their journeys long and profitable, because from Malacca they take merchandise to sell in Java, and from Java merchandise to sell in Bima and Sumbawa, and from these islands they take cloth for Banda and the Moluccas, and that which they have kept in reserve from Malacca. The people of Banda and the Moluccas adore them. And so they do their trade, which they could not do along the way by Borneo and Buton and Macassar.

We do not seize the opportunity of adding to our profits in their crude way, nor are we as leisurely as they, because we take paid people only. We take on liberal supplies and good cloth and set out on our journey. We do our trade like Portuguese who are not accustomed to it, and the petty cloths of the royal merchants are carefully kept because they regret [they cannot take the richer?] merchandise; and thus we make our way quickly. Therefore the Borneo route suits us better, because we already know (God be praised!) that it is good and fairly profitable.

After the Moluccas I have spoken of five islands; now I should

[1] Buton island appears like a prolongation of the south-eastern peninsula of Celebes. Banda lies due east of the north part of Buton. *Buton* on Berthelot's map.

also like to speak of the island of Gillolo on account of the port of Gillolo, which has a great deal of cloves, and is near to our friend Ternate.

The island of Gillolo is a long arm of land. One end of it is opposite to Amboina and Ceram and on the other side it extends towards the north to the islands of Morotai. It is very large. It is entirely heathen. It has many foodstuffs and many people and many *paraos*. Some of them go pillaging; some of them go trading—like all other nations. It is six leagues from Ternate to this island. This is the port which is called Gillolo (*Jeilolo*). This is the only port in the island of Gillolo. It has a Mohammedan king. His port has many foodstuffs. He is an enemy of the king of Ternate, and they raid and rob one another. Like the island of Bachian, this land of Gillolo (*Jeilolo*) has a great deal of wild cloves; they say that they are working to make it good. This island has a good port, and the people are somewhat whiter than those in the Moluccas.

Island of Gillolo (Bato Chyna)[1].

There are a great many other islands around the Moluccas: towards the north there are the islands of Morotai (*Mõr*) and *Chiaoa*, Tolo, Banggai (*Bemgaya*), and Sulu (*Çolor*) to the west of *Celebe*[2], and they produce many foodstuffs. They come and

Fol. 159r.

[1] *Batochina*, or *Batochina do Moro*, was the early name given by the Portuguese to Gillolo island, or Halmaheira, which has a length of about 190 miles from north to south; its width across the centre is about 40 miles. Gillolo bay and roadstead, and Gillolo village, lie about 20 miles north-west of Ternate. 'The island of *Moro*, which they call also *Batochina*, along which lie the Moluccas islands', says Barros. (IV, i, 16). Castanheda refers to the island of *Batachina do moro* (VIII, cxiii). On the map of *c.* 1540 the island is called *Batachj*. In D. Homem's atlases of 1558 and 1568 it is called *abachotina*, though the name is not written on the island, but off its eastern coast; but in the atlas of 1568 Ceram island is called *batachina de ambo* (?).

[2] CHIAOA, coupled with *Mor* or Morotai, as it is, might suggest Tanjong Salawai, the north-eastern point of the north-east peninsula of Gillolo, which lies about thirty-five miles south of Morotai, and might have been taken for an island. Pires' *Chiaoa*, however, must correspond to Siau, a small island north of the north-eastern point of Celebes, which is called *Ciau* by Pigafetta and appears as *chiau* on the map of *c.* 1540, and *Ciao* or *Ciaos* on later maps.

TOLO still survives in 'Gulf of Tolo', formed by the two eastern peninsulas of central Celebes; at the northern end lie the BANGGAI islands. However, the Gulf of Tolo and the Banggai islands lie south-west of the Moluccas.

ÇOLOR corresponds to the Sulu archipelago, which lies north of Celebes, and not west, as stated by Pires. Ribeiro's maps of 1527 and 1529 have *çolo*; *solar* on the anonymous map of *c.* 1540; *osolor* and *osollor* on later maps.

trade in the Moluccas; they bring gold. Some of these islands also have people who are nearly white; but since it is not our intention to write about these islands, because it would mean writing about another hundred thousand, I make neither particular nor general mention of them here, except that they say that in the island of Papua, which is about eighty leagues from Banda, there are men with big ears who cover themselves with them. I never saw anyone who saw anyone else who had seen them. This story should be given no more importance than it deserves.

Having recapitulated the things about the Moluccas in accordance with what is said about them, I will not venture farther; it was only my intention to come as far as here. Whoever is able to write of the great number and infinity of islands there are from the straits of Kampar to Banda and from the straights of Singapore to the islands of Japan (*Jampom*), which are beyond China—and between this island and Banda there must be an area of more than two or three thousand leagues round—whoever is able let him speak of it. And it is certain that many of [the islands] are worth speaking about, because

CELEBE—This is the first time that Celebes is mentioned. The first known cartographic record of the name is to be found on Reinel's map of *c.* 1524, where it is written *çelebes*; the map of *c.* 1540 and D. Homem's atlas of 1558 have *pta dos celebres*; Dourado's atlases have *p: dos selebres*. *Pta. de Celebres* is applied to the north-east point of Celebes, or North Cape. Luís' atlas of 1563 is the first to have *Ilha dos celebres*, though several later Portuguese maps continued to apply *celebres* or *selebres* to the north point only. Rodrigues' map has a long island west of the Moluccas—which very likely corresponds to the north-eastern peninsula of Celebes—with the inscription: *Ilha Vdama ꝛ tem ssamdollo* (*Vdama* island and it has sandalwood). *Vdama* may be a corruption of Menado, an important place at the north-easternmost point of Celebes, which appears as *manado* or *manade* on L. Homem's (1554), D. Homem's and Dourado's maps. Farther on Pires mentions the island *Vdama*, next to *macaçar*, among those that trade with Malacca. Abendanon thinks that the name *Celebe, Celebre* or *Celebres* was first given to the north-eastern point and then extended to the whole island, *Celebe* or *Celebre* corresponding to the Bugi word *sĕllihĕ* (in which the *h* is sometimes pronounced as an *r*) and meaning 'current'; thus *Pta. dos Celebres* would mean Point or Cape of Currents. *Sur la signification du nom de l'île Célèbes*, p. 361 *seqq*. Whatever the origin of the word *Celebe* may be, it was at first used in the singular (it appears also as *Celebe* in the Spanish and Ramusio's versions of the *Book of Duarte Barbosa*. II, 204), and later in the plural, *Celebes*, perhaps because the Portuguese considered it rather as a group of islands than as a single island.

many have gold, but it would be never ending and tedious. I will only speak of the few in this great abundance with which Malacca is in communication now, or was in the past, and I will touch on others in general terms, so that my project may be completed, and if my project does not carry sufficient weight, may I be forgiven.

These are the islands with which Malacca trades, and which trade with Malacca: *Tanjompura*, the island of *Laue*, *Quedondoam*, *Samper*, Billiton (*Bilitam*), *Cate*, *Pamucã*, *Macaçar*, *Vdama*, Madura, in addition to those I have mentioned, as can be seen in detail earlier in this work. I will not speak of *Burney* and the Luzon (*Luções*), because I have already spoken of them in the description of China.

[CENTRAL ISLANDS]

The island of *Tanjompura* is an island which can be reached from Malacca in fifteen days in the monsoon. They go there along the Singapore channel and along the Kampar [channel]; they take their course near Linga, between the islands of Linga and *Monoby*. This island is heathen; it is almost entirely subject

The island of Tanjompura[1].

[1] Pires' 'island' of *Tamjompura* corresponds to Tanjong Puting, on the south coast of Borneo. When Pires wrote his *Suma*, the Portuguese had not yet visited Borneo and Celebes. He was ill-informed, or mistook the information given to him, about these places he mentions as 'islands'; actually most of them were simple ports of Borneo or Celebes. Barros says that Gonçalo Pereira, who had been appointed to the captaincy of the Moluccas, sailed from Malacca in August 1530 via Borneo, where he called at *Tanjapura*, among other ports of that island. He adds that 'near the City of *Tanjapura* there are many diamonds, finer than those of India' (IV, vi, 19). Castanheda repeats exactly the same information (VIII, xxi). Orta mentions an old mine (*roca velha*) of diamonds 'in the Strait of *Tanjampur*, in the regions of Malacca' (*Coll.* 43). Early Portuguese maps enable us to identify the situation of *Tamjompura*. It is shown for the first time on the map of *c.* 1540, as *taJãpura*; then on L. Homem's map of 1554 as *tamJampura*; *taiampur* in D. Homem's atlas; *taiaõpuro* in Dourado's atlases, always on the south coast of Borneo. If these maps left any doubt about the exact situation of *Tanjampura*, Berthelot's map of 1635 is quite explicit: on it *Tanjompura* is already written *Tan Jaõ Pute* and corresponds to Tanjong Puting, exactly in the same latitude (3° 31′ S.). Inland, northward of *Tan Jaõ Pute*, is inscribed: *Aqui he a roca velha dos diamantes* (Here is the old diamond mine). See note on Borneo, p. 132.

to *Pate Unus*, lord of Japara. This island has a *Pate* governor who is lord of the island. It is an island fifty leagues round. It has a great deal of gold, and rice and other foodstuffs; it has many diamonds; it has junks, *pangajavas*; it has many inhabitants. Merchandise comes from Malacca: cloths that are of value in Java, chiefly red and black *bretangis* and cheap white cloth from Bengal. They bring foodstuffs and diamonds and gold. No other place is known where there are diamonds except in the kingdom of Orissa (*Rixia*), near Bengal. These are the best, and then come those from this island of *Tanjompura*, and then those from *Laue*. They are not found anywhere else. The people of this island are traders; they have many slaves which are brought to them from other islands, in addition to their own. They have a great deal of honey and wax.

Island of Laue[1].

This island of *Laue* is four days' journey beyond *Tanjompura*.

[1] Though written *lane*, this is obviously a transcriber's mistake for *laue*, as it appears in early maps and references. In the passages where they refer to *Tanjopura*, Barros also mentions *Lave* and Castanheda *Laue*, as two of the principal seaports in Borneo. When he says that *Laue* is 'beyond *Tanjompura*', Pires seems to mean that it lies eastward of that place. However, all early Portuguese maps which have *Laue*, place it westward of *Tanjompura*. The map of *c.* 1540 has *laue* (or *lane*); *la*(*u*)*e* on L. Homem's map of 1554; *laue onde foi dõ manoel de lima* in D. Homem's atlas of 1568; *llaue döde foi dom manoell de lima* in Dourado's atlases. The chroniclers do not mention this voyage of D. Manuel de Lima to *Laue*, but Castanheda says that in 1537 he was in Malacca (VIII, clxxviii). *Laue* is not to be found on modern maps. Berthelot's map has *Laban*, just north of *Sucadana* (Sukadana), in south-west Borneo, and A. Hamilton's map of 1727 (apud Dames, II, 207) still has *Lava*, south of Sukadana. After the death of Magellan at Sebu, the ships of his expedition went to Palawan and to Brunei in 1521. When describing Brunei (*Burne*) Pigafetta speaks of 'a large city named *Laoe*, which is located at the end of (*in capo de*) this island toward Java Major, which was destroyed and sacked because it refused to obey this king (of *Burne*), but the king of Java Major instead'. This passage has rather baffled Pigafetta's commentators in their attempts to identify *Laoe*. Crawfurd said that *Laoe* was 'probably some place in Banjarmasin', in the south-east of Borneo. *Dictionary, s.v.* Brunai-Town. Mosto, though drawing attention to the *Lao* in Ortelius' *Theatrum orbis terrarum* and to the *Lave* in Mercator's *Atlas*, situated in the south-west of Borneo, concludes: 'Forse corrisponde all'odierno paese di Laut Bumbu con isola annessa, sulla costa sud-est di Borneo verso Iava'. *Pigafetta*, p. 87. This opinion is more or less shared by Robertson, *Magellan's Voyage around the World*, II, 199, by Denucé, *Pigafetta*, p. 164, and by the Viscount de Lagôa, *Fernão de Magalhães*, II, 129. The early Portuguese maps mentioned above, however, leave no doubt of the situation of *Laue* or *Laoe* on the south-west

It is as large as the one above. It has *pates*; it has many inhabitants; they are all heathen. They trade with Java and Malacca, and almost as much with Java as with Malacca. They have diamonds; they have junks; gold in greater quantities than *Tanjompura*; they have merchants. It is a country with many foodstuffs. The people are good. The merchandise mentioned above is of value here; Kling cloth is of value. It is a good trading country. It does not obey anyone. These people are almost like the Javanese, robust, valiant, manly. They have a great deal of wax.

The islands of Quedondoam *and of* Samper *and of Billiton* (Bylitam) *and of* Cate *and* Pamucã *and of* Adema[1].

These six islands written down here surround the two above mentioned, three or four days' journey from one another. They are large islands with many inhabitants; they belong to heathens, to *pates*; they have junks, *pangajavas*. These islands all have gold; they have many | foodstuffs; some of them have cowries, which are good merchandise. There is a great deal of black hellebore and in great quantities; that from these places is the best that is known here. The men of these islands are warlike and great robbers; they plunder in many places; people going with merchandise take precautions. Those in the sea-ports are civilized; the other people are savages. These islands have an infinity of mats of three or four kinds; they have a few rattans; they have dried fish, pitch, foodstuffs, many vegetables; they have wines. These people sail to Java and Malacca.

Fol. 159v.

coast of Borneo. Pigafetta's drawing of the island of *Burne* shows that though he had no idea of the size of the island, he placed *Laoe* on the south-west coast. Mercator's globe of 1541 also has *Lao* on the south-west coast of the island, obviously following Pigafetta's drawing. Pigafetta's spelling of *Laoe* shows that Pires was right when he wrote *Laue* and not 'Lave'. See note on Borneo, p. 132.

[1] QUEDOMDOAM—In the enumeration above, Pires places *Quedomdoam* after *Laue*, and so between the latter and *Tanjompura*. There is a small port called Kandavangan, north of Cape Sambar, which may correspond to Pires' *Quedomdoam*. SAMPER—must correspond to Sampit bay, east of Tanjong Puting. BYLITAM is the island Billiton, east of Banka. CATE—Pulo Laut, an island off the south-eastern part of Borneo, the most important place in which is Kota Baru? Or does it correspond to Kutei, a large region in middle-eastern Borneo, which appears as *CATAY* on Berthelot's map? PAMUCÃ corresponds to Pamukan or Pamkan bay, in the south-east of Borneo. *Pamocan* on Berthelot's map. VDAMA—The transcriber first wrote *Vdama*, but here spelled it *Adema*—one of his many and misleading mistakes. See note p. 222.

The Javanese go and buy junks in these peoples' country, and these people sell the junks when they go to Java. They are great bowmen. They take a great many slaves and gold. The merchandise mentioned in the other islands is of value in these lands; black benzoin from Palembang is of value. Behind these islands is the route to the Moluccas via Macassar and Buton; and they will be described with Borneo (*Burney*) and the Luzon (*Luçoēes*).

The Islands of Macassar (Macaçar)[1].

The islands of Macassar are four or five days' journey beyond the islands we have described, on the way to the Moluccas. The islands are numerous. It is a large country. One side goes up to Buton and Madura and the other extends far up north. They are all heathens. They say that these islands have more than fifty kings. These islands trade with Malacca and with Java and with Borneo and with Siam and with all the places between Pahang and Siam. They are men more like the Siamese than other races. Their language is on its own, different from the others. They are all heathens, robust, great warriors. They have many foodstuffs.

These men in these islands are greater thieves than any in the world, and they are powerful and have many *paraos*. They sail about plundering, from their country up to Pegu, to the Moluccas and Banda, and among all the islands around Java;

[1] Macassar or Mangkasar is the name of the people inhabiting the extreme end of the south-western peninsula of Celebes. The name served at first to indicate the whole island, or the south-western peninsula, but it is now limited to its chief port and capital. On one of his maps (fol. 36) Rodrigues calls Borneo *A gramde Jlha de maquaçer* (The great Island of Macassar), which shows the confused knowledge most early cartographers had of the Archipelago. The map of *c.* 1540 has *os macaçaes*, L. Homem's map of 1554 has *os magasares*, and Dourado's atlases have *os magamsares*, in small script like all the other ordinary names of places, just south of the equator; but the island as a whole has no name. Mercator's globe of 1541, following some Portuguese map now unknown, has a long island running west-east called *Macace*, south of *Burneo* and north of Sumbawa (*Bima*, etc.). Eredia's map (fol. 47v.) has the name *MACAZAR* given to the whole island. In this map the island, fairly correctly situated but without showing the characteristic long peninsulas, is divided into three regions: *CELEBES regiam*, in the north; *BVGVIS regiam*, in the centre; *MACAZAR regiam*, in the south. The atlas of *c.* 1615–23 has the island similarly represented and called *MACASAR*. In Berthelot's map of 1635 the whole island is already named *ÇELEBES*, and only the south-western peninsula is called *macassa*.

and they take women to sea. They have fairs where they dispose of the merchandise they steal and sell the slaves they capture. They run all round the island of Sumatra. They are mainly corsairs. The Javanese call them Bugis (*Bujuũs*), and the Malays call them this and Celates. They take their spoils to *Jumaia* (?) which is near Pahang, where they sell and have a fair continually.

Those who do not carry on this kind of robbery come in their large well-built *pangajavas* with merchandise. They bring many foodstuffs: very white rice; they bring some gold. They take *bretangis* and cloths from Cambay and a little from Bengal and from the Klings; they take black benzoin in large quantities, and incense. These islands have many inhabitants and a great deal of meat, and it is a rich country. They all wear krises. They are well-built men. They go about the world and everyone fears them, because no doubt all the robbers obey these with good reason. They carry a great deal of poison[ed weapons] and shoot with them. They have no power against the junks which can all defend themselves, but every other ship in the country they have in their hands.

The island of Madura.

The island of Madura is a large island, it lies over against Java and in sight of Grisee (*Agacy*). It has many inhabitants and a king. This island of Madura is very extensive; they say that it must be eighty to a hundred leagues in circumference. The *Pate* of Madura is a knight, a very important person. He is a heathen. He is called [*blank*]. He is married to a daughter of the *Guste Pate* of Java. They say that Madura must have fifty thousand fighting men. The best knights come from here and are greatly feared in Java. The people of Madura say they are native Javanese and they are very conceited. They have many heathen priests, very esteemed persons. It is a country with many lancharas. They are well-made men. The country produces many foodstuffs. They have many horses. They use large quantities of cloths in Madura, made in the island itself, and others that come from outside which they wear. They have no other merchandise, except rice and foodstuffs, and many slaves. They have some gold from the trade carried on by the islands already mentioned; and some of these islands border on Madura.

This island is at peace with Grisee. This island of Madura has no Moors and they [the islanders] are our friends.

Fol. 160r.

Account of all the islands.

There is an infinity of other islands. There is no reason to say more, only that all have gold and slaves and trade with one another, and the small ones do this in the larger ones that have been mentioned, and the larger ones trade with Malacca, and Malacca with them, spending and bartering the merchandise. Most of these islands have gold, and they also have corsairs and robbers who live by that alone. The corsairs only sail in light *paraos* and therefore they do not attack junks. And the corsairs who are nearest to Pahang make in Pahang their trading ports, and those near the Moluccas and Banda trade in Bima and Sumbawa and Sapeh (*Capee*)[1], and those near us hold a fair and trade in Aru and in *Arcat*, Rupat. They bring countless slaves, and therefore a large number of slaves are used in Malacca, because they all go there on account of the great trade it has, more than all the kingdoms and ports over here; and so it is called the fortunate river. There are certainly great sailings from here; no trading port as large as Malacca is known, nor any where they deal in such fine and highly-prized merchandise. Goods from all over the east are found here; goods from all over the west are sold here. There is no doubt that the affairs of Malacca are of great importance, and of much profit and great honour. It is a land [that] cannot depreciate, on account of its position, but must always grow. It is at the end of the monsoons, where you find what you want, and sometimes more than you are looking for.

[1] Sapeh is an inhabited place on the east coast of Sumbawa, which gives its name to a bay and the strait between Sumbawa and Komodo islands. Rodrigues' drawing (fol. 83) shows the *porto de çape*, with several houses and trees, at the eastern end of *Simbaua*; the map of *c.* 1540 has *Cape*, though the name is misplaced over the middle of the island. Bima is not a separate island, but just a part of Sumbawa island. See note pp. 201-2.